ACTA UNIVERSITATIS UPSALIENSIS
Uppsala Studies in Social Ethics 15

D1240892

[handwritten dedication:] Jon Gunnemann

with kind regards

from [signature]

Carl-Henric Grenholm

PROTESTANT WORK ETHICS

A Study of Work Ethical Theories in
Contemporary Protestant Theology

Uppsala 1993

Translated and printed with a grant from the Swedish Council for Research in the Humanities and Social Sciences

Abstract

Grenholm, CH, 1993, Protestant Work Ethics. A Study of Work Ethical Theories in Contemporary Protestant Theology. Acta Universitatis Upsaliensis. *Uppsala Studies in Social Ethics* 15. 349 pp. Uppsala. ISBN 91-554-3034-1.

The purpose of this study is (1) to analyse the work ethical theories of six contemporary protestant theologians: Emil Brunner, JH Oldham, Tor Aukrust, Arthus Rich, Günter Brakelmann and John Atherton, and (2) to propose an alternative Christian work ethical theory. The study deals with the kinds of support which can be given for work ethical recommendations, a theory of the meaning of work and a constructive social ethical theory as well as the question of how Christian work ethics relates to humane work ethics.

In the first part of the study, it is argued that the six theologians base their work ethical theories upon different theories of human nature and different parts of a Christian system of belief. They disagree about whether ethics is based upon common human experience.

The second part of the study is devoted to the critical examination of the views of the theologians with reference to certain criteria for a reasonable ethical theory. Thereafter follows a social ethical theory, based upon a realistic view of man, common human experience, and the doctrine of creation and eschatology. This theory in turn provides a basis for a theory of the meaning of work in which the doctrine of vocation is revised and combined with insights from Marxist and psychological theories of work.

Carl-Henric Grenholm, Department of Theology, Uppsala University, Box 1604, S-75146 Uppsala, Sweden

For Annica, Peter, Maria,
Thomas and Micael

Contents

God 161. A Christological humanism 163. A Christian personalism 165. Human beings as active and participating beings 167. Conclusion 168

Preface

How does Christian work ethics relate to work ethical theories which are combined with other philosophies of life? This is a fundamental problem which I deal with in the present study. A work ethical theory contains a theory of the meaning of work and a constructive social ethical theory. These theories are related to convictions which form part of different philosophies of life. However, it may be asked whether Christianity makes some specific contribution to social ethics. It may also be asked whether a Christian theory of work is quite different from views on the purpose and value of work which are related to alternative philosophies of life.

This book is my third investigation concerning work ethics. In *Arbetets mål och värde* (The Purpose and Value of Work) I have analysed the Swedish debate on the organization of work and the computerization of working life. One main purpose was to lay bare the ideological disagreements between the Swedish Trade Union Confederation (LO), the Swedish Central Organization of Salaried Employees (TCO) and the Swedish Employers Confederation (SAF). The result of this study was that LO, TCO and SAF have similar opinions on the purpose and value of work. Their views are not in agreement with classical ideologies such as Marxism and Liberalism, but rather in agreement with theories within modern industrial psychology, mainly a socio-technical theory of work.

In my second book, *Arbetets mening* (The Meaning of Work), I analysed the contents of six different theories on the purpose and value of work. These are a Platonic theory of work, a Lutheran doctrine of vocation, a Marxist theory of work, a Tayloristic theory of work, the theory of work of the human-relation school, and a socio-technical theory of work. In my analysis of these theories I clarified their different views on the purpose of work, the relation between work and human self-realization, and the value of work in relation to other human activities. I also showed how these theories are related to different theories on human nature and different ethical theories.

Against this background, the present study on *Protestant Work Ethics* deals with the question on how Christian work ethics differ from work ethical theories based upon other philosophies of life. The purpose of the study is to analyse the work ethical theories of six contemporary protestant theologians, and to propose an alternative Christian work ethical theory. One main problem concerns the kinds of consideration which form a basis for a theory of the meaning of work and a social ethical theory. The study also deals with the question of whether the protestant doctrine of vocation contains a reasonable view on the purpose and value of work.

During more than twenty years I have had the privilege of being part of the research seminar in ethics at the department of theology in Uppsala. I wish to thank my discussion partners in this seminar for their helpful comments on previous drafts, their encouragement, and their important contributions to my thinking. In particular I am grateful to Ragnar Holte, Göran Lantz, Göran Möller and Mats G Hansson. Special thanks are due to my cooperators within the research project on Ethics of work, Göran Collste, Bertil Strömberg and Algot Gölstam, who have given me many suggestions and impulses also for this investigation.

Craig Graham McKay has skilfully translated my Swedish manuscript into English. I am most grateful to him. I also wish to thank the Swedish Council for Research in the Humanities and Social Sciences for generous economic support to the translation and the publication of the book.

Of utmost importance for my possibility to acclomplish this investigation has been the support and understanding of my family. I am most grateful to my wife Cristina for her love, encouragement and constructive critique. My children, Annica, Peter, Maria, Thomas, and Micael, have given me more friendship, inspiration and hope than I ever thought was possible. I dedicate this book to them.

Uppsala, December 1992

Carl-Henric Grenholm

Introduction

Has Christianity any important contribution to make to the treatment of problems in work ethics? In our secularized society, many would certainly give a negative answer. It is admitted that Christianity contains teachings about forgiveness and divine communion but it gives no guidance about how social and economic institutions are to be shaped. We must treat problems about work ethics from a purely rational standpoint and independently of the philosophy of life we embrace.

At the same time, many would hold that Christianity has profoundly influenced our attitude to work. In our society, this is particularly true of the Protestant work ethic. This involves a doctrine of vocation according to which work has an especially important function in the life of a human being. It is a common contention that this doctrine of vocation has had a crucial influence upon people's attitudes to work in Western capitalist societies. Thereby it has also perhaps influenced the position adopted with regard to problems in work ethics.

In this book, I shall analyse the form such a Protestant work ethic takes today. This will be accomplished by studying different theories in work ethics which are to be found in the writings of a number of Protestant theologians. These theories involve not simply general views about the purpose and value of work but also views about more concrete problems in work ethics concerning employment policies, the organization of work, and the economic system.

What are the grounds for the positions adopted in the contemporary Protestant work ethics? What kinds of arguments are adduced for the various views about employment policy, the organization of work and the economic system? Even theologians may naturally cite common human experiences and considerations as reasons for their ethical views. But to what extent are such standpoints based upon essentially Christian views? This is one of the questions which I shall discuss in the present book.

It may also be asked whether Christianity makes some specific contribution to the treatment of problems in work ethics. How does Christian ethics of work differ from work ethics based upon other philosophies of life? There might be thought to be a large measure of agreement between Christian and humane work ethics. But it is also possible that Christianity leads to the adoption of standpoints in work ethics quite different from those based upon alternative philosophies of life.

Ethics and attitudes to work

This book deals therefore with a number of theories in work ethics. But what in fact is "work ethics "? The answer to this question depends upon what is meant by "ethics". When I speak of "ethics", I mean a scholarly discipline devoted to the study of – and theoretical reflection about – morality. This entails that I distinguish between ethics and morals. By "morals" I understand our views about what is right and wrong, good and bad. "Ethics" on the other hand, means the scholarly study of these views.[1]

This study can take different forms. First it can be a question of "analytical ethics". The task of the latter is to decribe and elucidate human beings' moral views and in addition to clarify the presuppositions on which they are based. Secondly it can be a question of "constructive ethics ", a study which sets out to construct theories indicating what it is that makes a right act, right and a good aspect of character, good. Constructive ethics does not merely analyse the moral views of others but in addition puts forward its own criteria regarding what is right and good. Thirdly, it can be a question of "meta-ethics". Its task is to analyse the semantic function of ethical statements and to deal with the question of how ethical statements can be justified. Meta-ethics raises the following epistemological question: on what grounds can an ethical judgement be said to be valid? As a result, it also requires us to adopt some viewpoint regarding the semantic function of such judgements.

Within constructive ethics, one may distinguish between "social ethics" and "individual ethics". The task of social ethics is to specify the criterion for a right political act. By a "political act" I mean an act which aims to influence how an organized human collective is steered. Such an act can be carried out by individuals as well as by human groups and can affect different types of collective such as a state, a company or a university. The task of individual ethics on the other hand is to specify the criterion for a right private act. By a "private act", I mean an act which is not political. Views differ as to whether the criteria for a right political act are the same as those for a right private act.

A corresponding distinction between social and individual ethics can also be drawn within analytical ethics. Analytical ethics with an emphasis on social ethics is devoted to describing and elucidating views of what constitutes a right political act. This can be accomplished for example by studying those ideologies associated with political parties and labour market organizations. Analytical ethics with an emphasis on individual ethics seeks on the other hand to describe and elucidate views of what constitutes a right private act.

What then is "work ethics"? In this book, it is treated as part of scholarly ethics. It is namely that part of ethics which studies and reflects upon attitudes to work. By "attitudes to work", I mean those views which we entertain regarding what constitutes a right act in working life. These can be views put forward by individuals or organizations about the direction labour market policy should take, about who should regulate technical development or about what constitutes a just wage. By "work ethics", on the other hand, I mean a theoretical reflection about attitudes to work. One of its task is to describe and clarify different views of what is a right act in working life. Another task is to specify the characteristics of a right act in working life.

As a part of scholarly ethics, work ethics can consequently take different forms. First it can be part of analytical ethics where its task is to describe and clarify different views about what is right and wrong in working life. Analytical work ethics also seeks to clarify which arguments can adduced for these views from more fundamental standpoints. Thus it may analyse views about a just wage, about participation in the decision-making process and about the organization of work which occur within the labour market organizations.[2]

Secondly work ethics may belong to the domain of constructive ethics. Its task is to specify the characteristics of a right act in working life. In addition, it has to consider the types of argument which can be put forward for these views. These arguments can in turn be linked to more general constructive ethical theories. It is a constructive work ethics of this kind which is the subject of this book.

Work ethics is often considered as a branch of individual ethics. Inasmuch as it is constructive, it seems that its task should be to provide norms about how individuals should conduct themselves at their place of work. It should indicate what an individual should try to accomplish, how a supervisor should act towards employees and how employees should behave towards their workmates. Analytically, its task is to examine the contents of and grounds for recommendations regarding the acts of the individual.

Work ethics can however also constitute a branch of social ethics. To the extent it is constructive, its task is to specify the characteristics of a right act aimed at influencing the direction of those organized human collectives which play a part in economic life. From this social ethical perspective, work ethics deals not simply with the acts of individuals but also with the acts of human collectives in working life. Inasmuch as it is analytical, it is devoted to elucidating the content of and grounds for differing views about what constitutes a right political act.

We can thus distinguish between four different types of work ethics namely (1) individual ethical and analytical (2) individual ethical and constructive (3) social ethical and analytical and (4) social ethical and constructive. I shall not be concerned with the first two types in this book. I shall exclusively deal with work ethics as a branch of social ethics since work ethics tends to be viewed from this social ethical perspective within contemporary Protestant theology. My own presentation is mainly of the third kind, that is to say work ethics is developed as a branch of social and analytical ethics. The object of my study, however, is work ethics of the fourth kind, namely presentations which are both social ethical and constructive. In the concluding two chapters, I shall also put forward my own proposal for a constructive theory of work ethics.

Work ethical theory

Within constructive ethics, the distinction is sometimes made between "ethical theory" and "applied ethics". The task of ethical theory is to deal with more general ethical problems, such as the problem of determining what characterizes a right act in general. Applied ethics on the other hand deals with those narrowly defined ethical problems which emerge in some particular arena of human activities such as medical research or the relations between the sexes.

Constructive work ethics forms a part of applied ethics in this sense. Among its tasks is that of dealing with the relatively concrete problems about what is right and wrong in working life. Such problems can be called "problems in work ethics". Examples of such problems are (a) what form should employment policy take? (b) what is a just wage? (c) what form should working organizations have and how should technical development be regulated in working life? (d) should employees participate in decision-making? (e) what form should the economic system have for example with regard to the ownership of the means of production?

I shall call the views adopted in work ethics with regard to concrete problems of this type "work ethical recommendations". They are proposals about how to deal with matters arising in working life. Examples of such recommendations are (a) that employment opportunities should be distributed justly by a general reduction in the hours of work (b) that wages should be awarded in accordance with need and not according to performance (c) that work should be organized to provide scope for self-determination, work rotation and job-enlargement (d) that employees ought to participate

14

in decision-making and (e) that the economic system should be able to accomodate both private and public ownership of the means of production.

In this enquiry, I shall deal with three fundamental problems. Firstly what kind of reasons can be adduced for work ethical recommendations? What kinds of argument are acceptable regarding proposals about ways of resolving problems in working life? What kinds of consideration motivate ethical views of this kind? I shall try to exhibit the grounds upon which contemporary Protestant work ethicists base their views. At the same time, I shall put forward my own view about the grounds upon which work ethical recommendations rest.

On the basis of earlier research in this area, some preliminary assumptions can be made about these fundamental considerations. First of all, it can be assumed that work ethical recommendations are based upon statements which are empirically testable. For example they might take the form that certain measures probably have certain consequences. Thus the proposal for employee participation in decision-making may be defended by arguing that this leads both to increased job satisfaction and to increased efficiency. A similar argument can be put forward for organizing work to allow for self-determination and job enlargement. An argument for a policy for full employment is that it is a good way of stimulating economic growth in society.[3]

Such assertions about matters of fact are, however, not sufficient to support work ethical recommendations. They must also be combined with arguments which indicate what is good and right. Thus the proposal about increased self determination and job enlargement can be defended by arguing that job-satisfaction is something which is desirable and good in itself. The proposal about employee participation in decision-making can be defended by arguing that employees constitute one of the groups which have a right to influence since they are affected by company decisions. The advocacy of full employement can be justified on the grounds that all men have a right to work since all men are equal in value independently of race, sex, nationality and capacity.[4]

Secondly there is thus reason to assume that work ethical recommendations rest not simply upon statements of fact but also upon certain "value judgements" i.e. assertions about what is good and upon "norms", that is to say assertions about what is right and obligatory. Such value-judgements and norms can in turn quite often be part of a more embracing constructive social ethical theory. Such a "social ethical theory" contains three types of view. Firstly, it contains one or more fundamental principles regarding what constitutes a right political act. For example an act may be said to be right if it entails the best possible consequences or alternatively it may be said to be right if it respects certain human rights. A social ethical theory also contains certain value judgements about intrinsic value i.e. what is good in itself. A final constituent in such a theory is also a view about the relation between invidual and social ethics.

Thirdly there is reason to suppose that work ethical recommendations are often motivated by different theories of the meaning of work. By a "theory of the meaning of work", I mean a set of logically consistent views about (a) the purpose of work (b) how work is related to human self-realization (c) what value work has in relation to other human activities and (d) what motivates human beings to work hard and efficiently. The view that one should strive for increased job-satisfaction may be a part of such a theory of the purpose and value of work. In contemporary industrial psychology it is frequently maintained that the purpose of work is to satisfy certain fundamental human needs and that work is valuable if it is a means of satisfying for example the human need for self-realization.[5] Analogously, the view that full employment is desirable can be justified in terms of a theory of the meaning of work. It can be maintained that work is one of the activities which enable a human being to attain a truly human life and therefore everyone who wishes to work, ought to have the opportunity to do so.

Thus three different types of fundamental considerations can be assumed to be linked to work ethical recommendations, namely assertions about matters of fact, social ethical theories and theories of the meaning of work. The relationship between these four different components can be illustrated as follows:

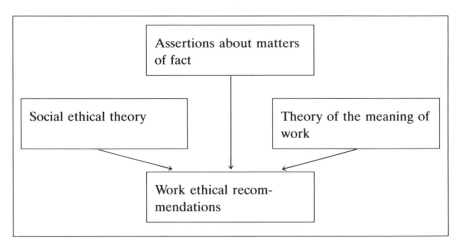

By a "work ethical theory" I mean a set of convictions and assumptions which are logically consistent and which contain at least these four compo-nents. Such a theory therfore contains (a) work ethical recommendations (b)

assertions about matters of fact (c) a constructive social ethical theory and (d) a theory of the meaning of work. In studying work ethical theories, it is an important task to clarify the content of these components. It is also important to show how they fit together.

Ethics and the philosophy of life

Two of the components of a work ethical theory form part of a philosophy of life or an ideology. This is so in the case of the social ethical theory and the theory of the meaning of work. A common feature of both a philosophy of life and an ideology is partly their inclusion of some value system i.e. certain fundamental views as to the good and the right and partly certain general views about human beings, history and the nature of reality.

A philosophy of life can be said to contain three ingredients namely (1) theoretical convictions about human beings and their world, for example a certain view of man, a certain view of history and a view about the origin of the universe (2) a central value system i.e. fundamental views about what is good and right which are of central importance to the person holding them and (3) a basic attitude i.e. a fundamental attitude to life which can either be of the more optimistic or of the more pessimistic kind. These components are interdependent so that if the theoretical convictions change sufficiently then so too will the system of value and/or the basic attitude. The theoretical convictions which enter into a philosophy of life are those which give us an overall picture of reality. In defining "philosophy of life" I shall follow Anders Jeffner: "A philosophy of life consists of the theoretical and value assumptions which constitute or have decisive importance for an overall view of human beings and the world and which forms a central value system and expresses a basic attitude."[6]

An ideology can also be said to embrace these three components. However, an "ideology" characteristically contains views which form the basis for political recommendations and political acts and also views which are common for a relatively large social group. As in the case of a philosophy of life, an ideology contains a central value system and a basic attitude as well as certain theoretical convictions about human beings and the world around them.

A social ethical theory and a theory of the meaning of work are therefore two important constituents of a philosophy of life or of an ideology. They contain fundamental views about what is good and right, thus forming part of the central value system, while at the same time a theory of the meaning of work can also contain certain theoretical convictions. The present investigation is primarily concerned with the role played by these two components of a philosophy of life in work ethical theory.

The second fundamental problem which I shall deal with concerns the type of reasons which can be adduced for these latter components in a work ethical theory. What kind of arguments are acceptable for a constructive social ethical theory? What kinds of consideration can justify a theory of the meaning of work? In my enquiry, I shall try to clarify the views upon which contemporary Protestant work ethicists base their social ethical theories and theories of the meaning of work. At the same time, I shall also put forward my own view about what types of argument can be adduced for theories of this type.

Previous research suggests suitable candidates for the types of consideration upon which such theories are based. Firstly a theory of the meaning of work can be thought to presuppose a constructive social ethical theory. Different views about the value of work may be associated with differing views about intrinsic values and about the nature of a right act. The view that the purpose of work is to produce what is valuable for others is based for example upon the view that the criterion for a right act is that it favours that which is good for all human beings. The view that work has a low value because it does not give the happiness which is achieved through philosophical contemplation is associated with the view that happiness is the highest value in life.[7]

Secondly it is reasonable to suppose that a theory of the meaning of work in general is also associated with a certain view of man. Differing views about how work is related to human self-realization can be linked to differing views about what is common to all human beings and characteristic for human beings as a species as well as to different views about what constitutes a good human life. They can also be linked to different views about human needs.[8] By a "view of man" I mean a collection of general views about what it is that is characteristic of human beings, about what constitutes a good human life and about human beings' possibilities of achieving a good life. Among the constituents of a view of man are views about (a) what is characteristic for human beings as a species (b) what constitutes a good human life (c) what it is, that prevents human individuals from achieving a truly human lives and (d) what capacities do human beings themselves possess to achieve good human lives.

Thirdly it can be assumed that a theory of the meaning of work is also combined with other theoretical convictions which form part of a philosophy of life such as a certain view of history or a certain view of reality. Thus for example a Marxist theory of work is combined with a materialistic theory of history according to which the motive force in historical development is provided by the conflict between the productive power of labour and the forms of production. A Christian theory about the meaning of work can similarly be combined with a Christian view of reality which *inter alia* embraces a doctrine of creation.

What kinds of argument then can be adduced for a constructive social ethical theory? First of all, there is reason to suppose that such a theory is based upon a certain view of man. A view of man embraces a view about the nature of a good human life which can tell us what experiences have an intrinsic value. The views about what is characteristic for human beings as such, which make up a view of man, can also provide a basis for certain fundamental moral principles. Thus for example the principle of the equal and inalienable value of all human beings is motivated by the view that what is characteristic of human beings is their rationality and freedom.

Secondly a social ethical theory is also mutually dependent upon the other theoretical convictions making up a philosophy of life. A certain view of history can be combined with a definite view about what kind of social structure is desirable. The materialistic theory of history encountered in Marxism contains for example not only certain assumptions about future social development but also the view that the classless society is a good society. Certain fundamental moral principles can also be defended on the basis of certain views of reality. Thus there are examples of Christian social ethics where the Divine Will behind the creation is taken to be the criterion of what is right.

Thirdly the fundamental principles and values which make up a social ethical theory can also be assumed to rest upon common human experiences and considerations. By the latter, I mean those experiences and considerations which do not form part of a philosophy of life or which can be common for individuals with different philosophies of life. They do not require to be generally shared by, or to be common for all human beings. On the contrary, individuals who belong to different cultural traditions and social contexts would tend to have relatively different experiences and views. These differences do not however prevent people with differing philosophies of life from sharing certain experiences and considerations.

Many ethicists maintain that the reasons which can be adduced for ethical principles and values, are "common and human" in this sense. They are independent of a philosophy of life inasmuch as they are based upon theoretical convictions which by their nature do not belong to a philosophy of life. According to these thinkers, fundamental judgements about what is good and right are therefore also independent of a philosophy of life in the sense that the reasons which can be put forward for these judgments can be accepted independently of the philosophy of life that is held.

Three types of consideration can thus be assumed to form a basis for social ethical theories and theories of the meaning of work namely theories of human nature, other theoretical convictions within a philosophy of life and finally certain common human experiences and considerations which are independent of a philosophy of life. A social ethical theory may give rise in turn to a theory of the meaning of work. The connection between these five different components can be illustrated as follows:

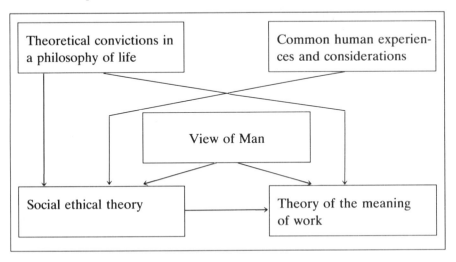

In this way it is probable that social ethical theories and theories of the meaning of work are combined *inter alia* with a view of man and other theoretical convictions in a philosophy of life. It is difficult to specify the exactly relationship between these various components of a philosophy of life. It might be a logical connection of some kind but if so, it is difficult to say which component is logically speaking the primary one. On the other hand these components seem to be mutuallly interdependent in the sense that when the content in one of them is altered, the contents of the others are also altered. I shall hereafter express this interdependence by saying that these components are "based upon" others. By this turn of phrase, I do not rule out the posssibility of these components of a philosophy of life mutually influencing one another.

Christian and humane ethics

The work ethical theories which I shall study in this book are those which are related to a Christian philosophy of life. It can be supposed that the social ethical theories and theories of the meaning of work which have been put forward by contemporary Protestant theologians are based *inter alia* upon a

Christian view of human beings and other theoretical convictions which form part of their Christian philosophy of life. We can call the theoretical convictions which form part of a Christian philosophy of life, a "Christian system of belief". Among such convictions are (a) a doctrine about creation (b) a Christology i.e. a doctrine about Christ and his works and (c) an eschatology i.e. a doctrine about eternal life and the Kingdom of God. This is the usual way of analysing the content of a Christian system of belief and one which is closely related to the three articles which form part of the Christian Creed. In my investigation, I shall try to clarify how contemporary Protestant work ethicists deal with these three parts of a Christian system of belief and to what extent their theoretical convictions form a foundation for the views which form part of their work ethical theories.

The work ethics encountered in Protestant theology is in general combined with a so called doctrine of vocation. Above all it has involved a view about the purpose and value of work. Martin Luther maintains in his doctrine of vocation that the aim of work is to constitute an instrument for God's continuous act of creation and to fulfil the commandment to love one's neighbour. According to Luther, work is able to contribute to human self-realization and thus it enjoys a high value relative to other activities. These views about the meaning of work are combined with an ethical theory which maintains that we carry out the injunction to love one's neighbour by obeying the commandments in the second table of the Decalogue where the fourth commandment has a special status. They are also combined with a certain view of man. According to Luther, we realize ourselves as human beings by following the example of Christ and sacrificing ourselves for others. Finally, they are combined with a doctrine of creation. Luther believes that God's creation is continually in process and that in our own work we participate in this divine work by producing those things which human beings need for the maintenance of life.[9]

An account of Luther's doctrine of vocation will be presented in more detail in Chapter 1. At the same time, I shall touch upon the way in which the doctrine of vocation is presented in Calvinist theology. This has been examined by Max Weber in his book *Die protestantische Ethik und der Geist des Kapitalismus*. Above all, he deals with work ethics put forward by the English 17th century Puritan, Richard Baxter. The latter combines the doctrine of vocation with the doctrine of double predestination so that hard and efficient work is taken as a sign that man has been elected for salvation.[10]

In contemporary Protestant theology, both the Lutheran and Calvinist doctrines of vocation have been much criticized. It is suggested that this doctrine greatly overvalues work and places far too much stress on the obligation to work. In the view of many thinkers, a society with rapid technological development and high unemployment requires an alternative to a more traditional Protestant work ethic.

At the same time, there are many Protestant theologians who believe that it is possible to revise the doctrine of vocation so that it can still today be conceived as a reasonable theory of the meaning of work. They hold that at least some of the views which make up this doctrine can be accepted and that these can be combined with perspectives associated with alternative theories of work. In this way, they put forward a Christian theory of the meaning of work which in conjunction with a social ethical theory forms the basis for more concrete work ethical recommendations.

These are some of the modern formulations of Protestant work ethics which I shall study in the present investigation. My aim is to clarify the work ethical recommendations they give rise to and to indicate how these are related to associated theories of the meaning of work and social ethical theories. In the course of my analysis of these theories of the meaning of work, I shall investigate their attitude towards the doctrine of vocation and in particular I shall indicate whether they require the rejection of that doctrine or whether they believe that it can be adapted to contemporary needs. Another of my aims is to illuminate how both the theories of the meaning of work and the social ethical theories of these theologians are related to a Christian view of man and to other parts of a Christian system of belief.

The third fundamental problem to be addressed in this investigation concerns the relation between a Christian work ethics and other theories of work ethics based on different philosophies of life. Does a Christian philosophy of life make some specific contribution to the treatment of problems in work ethics? By a "Christian work ethics" I mean an work ethical theory which is based upon a Christian philosophy of life. By a "humane work ethics" on the other hand I mean a work ethical theory which is based upon another philosophy of life. It is linked to human experiences and considerations about what is good for human beings. However, it is not combined with a Christian belief in God. The question is therefore whether a Christian work ethics involves social ethical theories and theories of the meaning of work which are in substance completely unlike those to be found in humane work ethics or whether there is at least to some extent an area of common agreement?

The answer to this question depends upon the types of considerations forming the basis of social ethical theories and theories of the meaning of work. Some theologians appear to maintain that a Christian work ethics is wholly or partly based upon common human experiences and considerations i.e. those which do not make up a philosophy of life and which can be common for human beings with different philosophies of life. Given this, they would probably argue that a Christian work ethics partially agrees in content with a humane work ethics. Other theologians maintain that a Christian work ethics is exclusively based upon a Christian view of man and other parts of Christian belief. It is then highly probable that by contrast they emphasize the existence of important divergences between Christian and humane work ethics.

The way in which the relationship between Christian and humane work ethics is understood, depends also upon the parts of Christian belief which are thought to form the basis of a Christian work ethics. Some theologians – e.g. Emil Brunner, Walter Künneth and Helmut Thielicke – believe that ethics is based upon a doctrine of creation. They interpret work as a part of the order of creation whereby human beings constitute an instrument for God's creation. These theologians maintain that there are great contentual similarities between Christian and humane work ethics.[11]

Other theologians maintain that ethics is based upon Christology or escha-tology. Such a Christologically based ethics is to be found in Karl Barth. According to him, Jesus Christ is the measure of what is good and right. Accordingly a Christian work ethics must differ in content from all other work ethics. Work must be carried out in accordance with the Will of God. Moreover the Will of God is something into which we receive insight only through this revelation in Christ. Thus for Barth, we are able to understand the meaning of work in the light of this revelation and by obeying God's command.[12]

Thirdly there are also theologians e.g. Dietrich Bonhoeffer and Ronald H Preston, who maintain that ethics is based both upon the doctrine of creation and upon Christology and eschatology. Bonhoeffer writes about certain "mandates" which come into being with the creation while at the same time adopting the view that God's commandments are understood through the Revelation of Christ. Preston seeks to motivate certain fundamental moral principles on the basis of the doctrine of creation while simultaneously holding that eschatology inspires one to continuous social criticism. These theologians maintain that there are certain fundamental points of agreement between Christian and humane work ethics while at the same time believing that there is a specifically Christian contribution to ethics.[13]

The crucial difference between these theologians arises regarding the significance they attach to Revelation as a source of insight about the content of Christian belief and ethics. Is ethics based upon the Revelation in Christ or is it linked to common human experiences and considerations? There are three possible answers to this question. First, it may be maintained that it is only through the Revelation in Christ that we can gain insight about what is right and good. Secondly it may be argued that ethics is exclusively based upon common human experiences and considerations. Lastly it may be maintained that ethics are based both upon the revelation in Christ and upon common human experiences and considerations.

These three viewpoints are closely related to divergent views about the basis of the content of a Christian system of belief. Some theologians maintain that it is solely through the revelation in Christ that we obtain insight into its content. Others maintain that a Christian system of belief is based both upon Revelation and upon common human experiences and considerations. A conceivable view of the connection between these different components can be illustrated as follows:

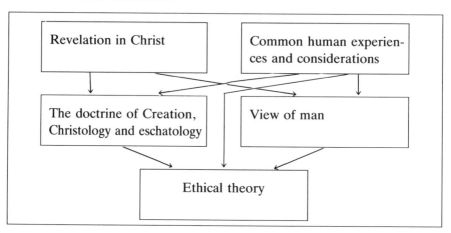

Different theologians however would appear to have very different views about the relationship between these components. Some accord Revelation the decisive role as regards insight into the content of a Christian system of belief and ethics. Others hold that common human considerations form the principal basis of ethics and of at least certain parts of a Christian system of belief. In my investigation, I shall seek to clarify how a number of contemporary Protestant work ethicists view the relations between these components. At the same time I shall put forward my own view of the relation between Christian and humane ethics.

Contemporary Protestant work ethics

Who then are the modern theologians whose work ethics, I intend to analyse? First of all, I shall limit myself in the present investigation to modern Protestant work ethics. There are a number of highly interesting theoretical presentations of work ethics in contemporary Catholic theology. Pope John Paul II 's encyclical, *Laborem exercens* (1981), dealing with human work and the current discussion within Catholic theology which it has given rise

24

to, may be mentioned. In this encyclical, it is maintained on the basis of a personalist view of man that work contributes to human self-realization and that as a factor of production it takes precedence over capital. Bruno Heck's book *Arbeit. Ihr Wert, Ihre Ordnung*, is an example of the discussion stimulated by the encyclical.[14] Earlier discussions of the theology of work such as MD Chenu: *Pour une théologie du travail*, may also be mentioned. In this book, Chenu puts forward the value of work as an activity in which human beings fulfil the task of stewardship which has come to them with the creation. A further example of such a theology of work is Edwin G Kaiser's book *Theology of Work*, in which Kaiser citing Thomistic theology maintains that the purpose of work is to be God's co-worker in the creation, to produce useful goods and services and to realize human potential.[15]

I shall not, however, deal with Catholic work ethics in the present book since otherwise my enquiry would range too widely. It offers a comprehensive and interesting body of material which merits its own investigation. It would also be interesting to compare Catholic and Protestant work ethics but such a task would also take me beyond the boundaries of my enquiry. Such a comparison would demand a relatively detailed treatment of the different theological and philosophical presuppositions of Catholic and Protestant ethics.[16] In choosing between Catholic and Protestant work ethics, I have decided to deal with the latter because it has given rise to a comparatively lively discussion of the Protestant work ethic and its influence upon our attitude to work. It is therefore reasonable to try to discover how this particular type of Christian work ethics is formulated.

Moreover the theologians whose works I deal with, are those who have been active after the First World War. After 1919 and perhaps principally in connection with the Ecumenical Meeting in Stockholm in 1925 there occurred a noticeable break away from social ethics which was infused with the ideas of liberal theology and the social gospel movement. Two of the thinkers I study were among the theologians who in the 1930s laid the foundations of a new movement within Protestant social ethics. As a result, they had a profound influence upon the ecumenical movement. Two other theologians were active in the 1960s and 1970s and have dealt in detail with the problems in work ethics which were then current. Another two are active today and have figured prominently in the discussion of work ethics within German and British theology.

In the present enquiry, I shall restrict myself to studying work ethical theories within contemporary European theology. I shall not deal with any American thinker in social ethics, since problems in work ethics have not been treated so intensively by theologians in the USA in comparison with their European colleagues. An interesting presentation of a theory of the meaning of work is to be found in Robert Lowry Calhoun's book *God and the Day's Work* but it neither contains work ethical recommendations nor a more detailed treatment of social ethical theory.[17] Another American social ethicist I considered dealing with, is J Philip Wogaman, who is a Methodist and Professor of Christian Social Ethics at Wesley Theological Seminary in Washington. He has developed an interesting social ethical theory in his books *A Christian Method of Moral Judgment* (1976) and *Christian Perspectives on Politics* (1988). He also applies this theory in a discussion of employment policy and the structure of the economic system in his books *Christians and the Great Economic Debate* (1977) and *Economics and Ethics* (1986). However, although Wogaman is a leading social ethicist he is not primarily concerned with work ethics. For example, he has not developed a detailed theory of the meaning of work.[18]

I have employed two criteria in selecting contemporary European Protestant work ethicists. First of all I require that the theologians I study, have a well developed and systematic theory of social ethics and work ethics. They must present a work ethical theory which comprises both a theory of the meaning of work and certain work ethical recommendations and at the same time this should be combined with a systematic view of man and a clearly delineated constructive social ethical theory. The second criterion is that they should collectively present a broad spectrum of opinion in questions in social ethics and work ethics. They should have differing opinions about the relationship between Christian and humane ethics, about the criteria for a right political act, about attitudes towards the Lutheran and Calvinist doctrines of vocation, about the meaning of work and about how to relate a Christian theory to other theories of work. They should also belong to different Protestant confessions. Moreover they should belong to different linguistic groups, representing German, British and Scandinavian theology.

On the basis of these two criteria, I have selected six modern Protestant theologians for study. The first is Emil Brunner, a Swiss Reformed theologian (1889–1966) who is one of the most important Protestant theologians of the twentieth century. He was Professor of Systematic Theology at the University of Zürich 1924–1953 and one of the theologians who along with Karl Barth played a fundamental role in coming to terms with European liberal theology. Brunner has written several major works dealing both with Christian system of belief and with ethics. His most important books in this sphere are *Das Gebot und die Ordnungen* (1932) and *Gerechtigkeit* (1943).

The second thinker is the British missionary and theologian JH Oldham (1874–1969). He was one of the foremost pioneers within the ecumenical movement and played a leading role already during the first World Missionary Conference, which took place in Edinburgh in 1910. From 1921 to

1938, Oldham was Secretary of the International Missionary Council. Oldham was one of the leaders in Life and Work and chairman of their study department from 1934 to 1938. In this capacity he was one of those responsible for organizing and preparing the conference in Oxford in 1937. As a social ethicist, he played an important part in the preparations for the first Assembly of the World Council of Churches in Amsterdam in 1948. His most important work in this connection is *The Function of the Church in Society* (1937) which formed part of the preparatory material for the 1937 Oxford conference, together with *Work in Modern Society* (1950) which Oldham wrote as part of a World Council of Churches research project into the meaning of work, which was carried out between the assemblies in Amsterdam (1948) and in Evanston (1954).

The third thinker is Tor Aukrust, a Norwegian and Lutheran theologian who was born in 1921. He has written several important works dealing with Christianity, culture and world-view. His most important work in this field is *Mennesket i samfunnet. En sosialetikk* in two volumes (1967–68). This is one of the most ambitious works in social ethics and work ethics which has been produced by a Scandinavian theologian in recent years.

The fourth theologian is Arthur Rich (1910–1992), a Swiss thinker dealing with social ethics and work ethics. He succeeded Emil Brunner in 1954 as Professor of Systematic Theology in Zürich, where he also created an Institute for Social Ethics in 1964. He was a Reformed theologian and has written dissertations on Zwingli's theology and Pascal's anthropology. Rich's most important books in the field are *Glaube in politischer Entscheidung* (1962), *Christliche Existenz in der industriellen Welt* (1964), *Mitbestimmung in der Industrie* (1973) and *Wirtschaftsethik*, vol I and II (1984 and 1990).[19]

The fifth thinker is the German Lutheran theologian, Günter Brakelmann, who was born in 1931. He is Professor of Christian social theory in the Faculty of evangelical theology, at the University of Bochum. He is also the head of SWI (Sozialwissenschaftlichen Institut der Evangelischen Kirche in Deutschland) in Bochum. Brakelmann's most important relevant publications are *Abschied von Unverbindlichen* (1976) where he seeks to construct a Christian social ethics which provides him with a perspective for looking at democratic socialism and *Zur Arbeit geboren? Beiträge zu einer christlichen Arbeitsethik* (1988).[20]

My sixth candidate for study is John Atherton, an Anglican theologian who was born in 1939. He is Canon Theologian of Manchester Cathedral and has been a director of the William Temple Foundation in Manchester, a clerical institute dealing with the questions of working life. He has been an Industrial Chaplain and has written his doctoral thesis on R H Tawney as a Christian social ethical thinker. Of special interest in this field is Atherton's book *Faith in the Nation, A Christian Vision for Britain* (1988).

Interesting work ethical theories have been put forward by other Protestant theologians whom I have not considered here. One of these is Karl Barth who devotes sections III/1 and III/4 of *Kirchliche Dogmatik* to a relatively detailed treatment of problems in work ethics. I have however chosen to devote my attention instead to Oldham because his social ethical theory is more developed than that of Barth. Another thinker is Helmut Thielicke who in section II/I of *Theologische Ethik* writes in detail about the meaning of work and current questions of working life. However among those who have developed a contemporary Lutheran doctrine of vocation, I have chosen to deal with Tor Aukrust since I wish to have a representative of Scandinavian theology. An alternative to Aukrust is NH Søe, who also writes about the doctrine of vocation in *Kristelig etik* but Barthian ethics are already sufficiently well represented. I have also considered devoting some attention to the Swedish thinkers, Karl-Manfred Olsson and Ludvig Jönsson, who have interesting discussions of problems in work ethics in their respective books *Kristendom – demokrati – arbete* and *Människan, mödan och arbetsglädjen*. However, Tor Aukrust supplies a more systematic work ethical theory and deals in a more thorough fashion with fundamental theological and social ethical issues.

Finally over and above John Atherton, there are a number of interesting representatives of British social ethics. One of them is Ronald H Preston who was Professor in Social and Pastoral Theology at Manchester University from 1972 until 1981. In his books *Religion and the Persistence of Capitalism* (1979), *Explorations in Theology* (1981), *Church and Society in the Late Twentieth Century* (1983) and *The Future of Christian Ethics* (1983) he has developed a detailed and interesting social ethical theory which is subsequently applied in a discussion about the structure of the economic system. Preston is not however primarily concerned with work ethics and has for example no detailed theory of the meaning of work.[21] I have therefore chosen instead to focus attention on one of the British theologians who has provided more detailed arguments for work-sharing as a way of combatting unemployment and for an alternative to the traditional Protestant work ethic. One of these is Roger Clarke, who belongs to the Church of Scotland and is Assistant Director at William Temple Foundation in Manchester. He puts forward a detailed critique of "traditional work ethic" in his book *Work in Crisis* (1981) which aroused great attention. His social ethical theory is however fragmentary and his theological reflections are less penetrating than those of Atherton. Another writer who deserves mention is David Bleakley who has criticised the Protestant work ethic in his books *In Place of Work: The Sufficient Society* (1981) and *Work: The Shadow and the Substance* (1983).

However these books also lack a detailed social ethical theory and a work ethical theory. For that reason, I have decided to focus my attention on John Atherton along with Brunner, Oldham, Aukrust, Rich and Brakelmann.[22]

Analysis of work ethical theories

The initial aim of the present enquiry is to analyse the work ethical theories which are to be found in the writings of contemporary Protestant theologians. This entails clarifying the meaning of their work ethical recommendations, their theories of the meaning of work and their social ethical theories. It also implies clarifying the various reasons they adduce for their ethical positions. I am above all interested in the way in which they interpret the relation between their work ethical theories and their view of man and the other theoretical views which form part of a Christian philosophy of life. I thereby seek also to elucidate their view of the relationship between Christian and humane ethics.

My analysis of the work ethical theories to be found in the writings of contemporary Protestant theologians will proceed in six steps. First of all, in Chapter 2, I try to clarify their work ethical recommendations. Here I focus attention upon their views about (a) the aims and implementation of employment policy (b) the meaning of a just wage (c) the organization of work (d) the desirability of worker participation in decision-making and (e) the structure of the economic system. I shall also investigate what arguments they consider can be adduced for their recommendations in work ethics. To what extent are these based upon theories of the meaning of work or upon social ethical theories or upon common human experiences and considerations?

Secondly in Chapter 3, I shall endeavour to elucidate their theories of the meaning of work. Here four analytical questions are raised (1) What is the purpose of work? (2) How does work relate to human self realization? (3) What value should be placed upon work as an activity? (4) What motivates us to work hard and efficiently? When modern Protestant theologians answer questions of this kind they in general discuss the doctrine of vocation as it has been presented in earlier Lutheran and Calvinist theology. Another of my aims is therefore to clarify their attitude to this doctrine and to examine any revision of it they may propose.

In clarifying the theories of the meaning of work which are encountered in the writings of contemporary Protestant theologians, I shall also relate these theories to a number of other theories of the meaning of work. I call these a Platonic theory of work, a Marxist theory of work, a Tayloristic theory of work, a human-relations school theory of work and a socio-technical theory of work.[23] At the same time, I shall also try to make clear the arguments put forward by these theologians on behalf of their theories of the meaning of work. To what extent are these theories based upon social ethical theories, theories of human nature or upon other types of consideration?

Thirdly in my analysis, I shall clarify what social ethical theories are combined with the theologians' work ethical recommendations and theories of the meaning of work. This will be accomplished in Chapter 4. Three analytical questions are raised (1) what are the criteria for a right political act? (2) what possesses an intrinsic value, that is to say, has a value in itself? and (3) what is the relationship between individual and social ethics? In the same chapter, I shall also examine the arguments put forward by the theologians on behalf of their differing social ethical theories.

Theories of the meaning of work and social ethical theories are frequently related to a certain view of man. Therefore fourthly, I shall clarify the view of man encountered in the writings of these theologians. This forms the subject of Chapter 5. Here four analytical questions are raised (1) what is it that uniquely defines human beings as a species? (2) what constitutes a good human life? (3) what is it that prevents human beings from attaining such a life? (4) to what extent are human beings able by their own efforts to attain a good human life? Once again, I shall also look at the types of consideration which form the basis for the theological answers to these questions.

Fifthly I shall investigate to what extent these theological work ethical theories are related to other theoretical components in a Christian philosophy of life. Theories of the meaning of work and social ethical theories are often combined with other, non-anthropological parts of a Christian system of belief. Sometimes a certain version of the Christian doctrine of creation forms the basis of such theories. Sometimes Protestant theologians base their social ethical theories upon Christology. In other cases, eschatology has great influence in shaping a Christian social ethics and work ethics. In Chapter 6, I try to indicate how these different components of a Christian system of belief are employed and developed by the theologians I deal with. In particular, I am interested in the influence of these three parts of a Christian system of belief upon the theologians' view of man, their social ethical theories and upon their theories of the meaning of work.

After this analysis, I am then in a position in Chapter 7 to clarify how the theologians see the relationship between Christian and humane ethics. I deal with the question of whether Christian belief makes some specific contribution to work ethics or whether the work ethics associated with a Christian philosophy of life is identical in content with a humane work ethics. The answer to this question depends in turn upon the answer given to the question regarding the type of reasons which can be adduced for the criteria employed in a social ethical theory. One possible view is that ethics is based upon common human experiences and considerations so that Christian social ethics is indistinguishable from humane ethics. An alternative viewpoint is that ethics is based upon the Revelation in Christ and that therefore a Christian social ethics has a character entirely different from humane ethics. A third possible view is that both both common human considerations and arguments from Revelation can be put forward on behalf of different parts of Christian social ethics, thus explaining the partial – but only partial – agreement between Christian and humane ethics.

Construction of a work ethical theory

The second aim of this investigation is to propose and develop my own Christian work ethical theory. In particular, I am interested in the two components of a philosophy of life which make up such a theory. At the same time, I shall discuss the work ethical recommendations which can be combined with my proposal for a social ethical theory and a theory of the meaning of work. In order to formulate such recommendations, a relatively detailed sociological analysis of the facts of working life and of the probable consequences of various policies is required. Carrying out such an analysis would take me beyond the bounds of the present enquiry. I shall therefore be able only to hint at some of the recommendations which might form part of a work ethical theory. My main concern is to discuss how a social ethical theory and a theory of the meaning of work can be developed.

This discussion is based on my critical analysis in Chapter 8 of the six theories of work ethics studied. By way of introduction, I formulate a number of criteria for a reasonable Christian work ethics. These consist of a number of formal criteria which specify what kind of reflection can serve as a foundation for such a theory and how the components making up the theory are related to one another. On the basis of these criteria, I then critically examine the theories proposed by the theologians, testing the arguments which they adduce for their standpoints and raising objections to various views they put forward. This then supplies me with a basis for my own construction of a work ethical theory.

Thereafter my aim is to develop my own proposals for a constructive social ethical theory. This is done in Chapter 9 where I discuss the criterion for a right political act by considering various differing philosophical ethical theories. In this chapter, I also put forward my own views about what types of reasons can be put forward for a social ethical theory. I have devoted particular attention to the relationship between a social ethical theory and the theoretical views which form part of a Christian philosophy of life.

Finally it is my intention to try and develop my own theory of the meaning of work. This is accomplished in Chapter 10. I discuss how far it is possible to modify the doctrine of vocation in Protestant theology so that it appears reasonable from a contemporary point of view. I shall also discuss the question of how far a Christian theory of work is related to other theories of the meaning of work. Not all the views which make up these differing theories are logically incompatible with one another so that some of them at least could be combined with one another. In an earlier book, I have criticised Tayloristic and Platonic theories while at the same time advocating a combination of a Lutheran doctrine of vocation, a socio – technical theory and a Marxist theory of work. These latter theories contain views which at least to some extent are compatible with one another but at the same time I hold that the doctrine of vocation needs to be revised in certain important respects.[24]

The question which I propose to dicuss is how such a combined theory of the meaning of work could be developed more precisely and whether there are good arguments which can be adduced for such a theory. This requires me to give my own answer to the question of how such a theory is related to a Christian view of man and other theoretical concepts in a Christian philosophy of life. At the same time in this concluding chapter, I shall discuss how such a theory of the meaning of work could be justified on the basis of a Christian social ethical theory.

1. The doctrine of vocation in Protestant theology

What is Christianity's contribution to the treatment of problems in work ethics? In this book, I shall be principally concerned with the analysis of those theories of work ethics which are to found in the writings of a number of contemporary Protestant theologians. Before I pass to this analysis, however, I would like in this chapter to survey earlier contributions to work ethics made by Protestant theology. Above all, I wish to clarify the content of the doctrine of vocation which was developed by Martin Luther because this doctrine is still a subject for lively discussion within contemporary theology. I shall also clarify the doctrine of vocation within Calvinist and Puritan theology and at the same time show how it differs from its Lutheran counterpart.

The doctrine of vocation within Protestant theology must be understood in the light of attitudes to work which were to be found in earlier Christian tradition. I shall therefore also briefly deal with the views of work which are to be found in the Bible and in Thomas Aquinas. In this chapter, I shall also touch upon the attitude of contemporary Protestant theology towards the doctrine of vocation. Above all, I shall devote attention to the criticism of the doctrine of vocation which is to be found in contemporary British theology.[1]

Biblical views of work

In classical Greek philosophy work is accorded an especially low value. In particular, both Plato and Aristotle view manual labour as an activity which is unworthy of a free human being. It is a necessary evil which provides resources for the maintenance of life but it does not bestow happiness and satisfaction. The highest form of goodness is to be attained not through work but through philosophical contemplation.

How then is work viewed in the Scriptures? In the literature on industrial sociology it is often asserted that the Scriptures – like Plato and Aristotle –

accord work a low value. In the Bible, it is claimed, work has no place in Paradise and the Kingdom of Heaven. It is considered as punishment for sin and the ideal embodies a liberation from the toil of labour.[2]

Several exegetists have also held that the Scriptures give expression to a low evaluation of work. They cite the fact that in Genesis it is said not only that God placed man in the Garden of Eden to dress it and to keep it. It is also said that the ground is cursed and that man in sorrow and in the sweat of his face shall eat his bread (Genesis 3:17–19). Work would appear in this context to be conceived as painful evil, God's punishment for sin.

Ivan Engnell is one of the exegetists who takes the view that the Old Testament attitude to work in entirely negative. He holds that according to Genesis, it is not a question of Adam working in the Garden of Eden: it is rather so that he lives there as a more or less divine being with a cultic responsibility but free from work. According to Genesis 3:17 ff, work is the result of an imposed curse and is an activity which becomes necessary after the Fall. Adam's punishment is to toil and sweat over land which is damned and which bears thorns and thistles. According to Engnell, the same low status accorded to work is also to be found in the other books of the Old Testament. Nowhere is there support for the thought that work might be a natural order instituted by God. Work is something which is the lot of slaves ; for the free man it is something evil which is theologically motivated by the story of the Fall.[3]

Several theologians have, however, suggested a completely different interpretation of the statements about work in Genesis. Thus, for example, Alan Richardson maintains that work according to the Bible is a part of God's creation and something which belongs to human nature. Human beings are so formed that they cannot satisfy their material and spiritual needs or fulfil their function as human beings without working. According to Genesis 3, sin brings not work as such but toil: work becomes painful. Such painful work neither belongs to God's creation nor to His intention with human beings.[4]

A similar interpretation of Genesis 3:17–19 has been given by Walther Bienert in his book *Die Arbeit nach der Lehre der Bibel*. He argues that it is the working conditions which alter after the Fall. It is not work itself which is conceived as a curse but the fact that work is now associated with toil and effort. Work's character as toil is a consequence of Sin but work itself is a divine creation which antedated the Fall.[5]

A more profound analysis of views of work in the Old and New Testaments has been presented by Göran Agrell in his dissertation *Work, Toil and Sustenance*. Agrell rejects Engnell's view that the Old Testament view of work is completely negative. He maintains that the view of work taken in

Genesis 2:4b—3:24 is twofold. Firstly, work is conceived as something positive. It is part of God's creation and belongs to human essence as created by God. (Genesis 2:15). By means of work, human beings are able to serve God. They cooperate with God in the activity of Creation. In Paradise, the maintenance of life is a gift of God which human beings obtain independently of their work and there work is free from toil and suffering. Secondly, work is viewed as something negative. With the Fall (Genesis 3:17—19), work becomes hard, the earth becomes cursed and human beings must earn their living by toil. After the Fall, it is necessary for human beings to work for their living and work is harsh and wearing and involves suffering.[6]

This dual view of work is reiterated according to Agrell in the other biblical material. Genesis 2—3 provides a model for the interpretation of other texts in the Old Testament, the Apocrypha and the texts in the New Testament. Even in other parts of the Old Testament work is conceived in its ideal state as a part of God's creation and as something positive which gladdens the heart of the person who carries it out. It is a means of serving God and it can be carried out without toil. But after the Fall, human work involves toil which is necessary if life is to be sustained.[7]

The same dual pespective is to be found in the New Testament. In Matthew 6:25—34, Jesus exhorts his disciples to behold the fowls of the air and the lilies of the field which neither sow, nor reap nor gather into barns, but which nonethelesss obtain life's necessities from God. The point being made in this text, according to Agrell, is that it is God who sustains us and gives us the food and clothing we require, so that we do not need to worry about tomorrow. Jesus also exhorts his disciples to seek first the kingdom of God and his righteousness which implies that the most important thing for man's existence is not work but something else. It does not however constitute an exhortation to human beings to imitate the birds and lilies and not work. This text, according to Agrell, also presupposes that human beings normally work to maintain themselves. However, it is at the same time stressed that even if we – unlike animals and plants – work, we have to be conscious that our maintenance is in the final analysis a gift of God. In this and other synoptic texts, Agrell maintains, there is also an eschatological perspective. At the present period of time, which comes after the Fall and before Christ's Second Coming, work involves toil. However this element of toil will cease in the future fullness of God's Kingdom.[8]

This eschatological ideal is also evident in 1 Thessalonians 4:9—12 where Paul exhorts the Thessalonians to work with their hands. This text, says Agrell, should not be interpreted as a criticism of the low value accorded to manual labour which was to be found in Greek philosophy. A more reasonable interpretation is that Paul's polemic is directed against a view to be found in certain Christian circles that there was no longer any need to work since Christ's Second Coming was imminent. Paul means that the last days have begun but are still to be completed and therefore it is still necessary to work to sustain oneself. In the period we live in, work is also physically wearing and the suffering it involves can be interpreted as a participation in the suffering of Christ. The eschatological ideal, however, sees work as devoid of toil: man receives his sustenance from God independently of his labour.[9]

According to Agrell, the same ideal is presupposed in 2 Thessalonians 3:6 – 15 where it is said that those who do not work, will not eat. The aim of work is also here identified with obtaining the necessities of life and this is accomplished only through work. If a human being does not work, then a burden is placed upon others. This injunction to work presupposes the eschatological view that Christ's Second Coming is not immediately imminent. The ideal is that human beings are able to maintain themselves without pain. At the present moment in time, however, it is necessary to labour and sweat to do so.[10]

Agrell thus holds that the double view of work which is to be found in the Old Testament provides an interpretative model which is applicable to the texts in the synoptic tradition, Paul's epistles and the deuteropauline tradition. In these texts, there are divergent views about the imminence of Christ's Second Coming and the extent to which the fullness of God's Kingdom has been brought about. However, common to all the texts is the assumption that in the present age – that is to say after the Fall and before the Second Coming – work is necessary if we are to maintain ourselves and involves toil. In the ideal state of Paradise and the Kingdom of Heaven, work can be carried out without toil. We are sustained by God independently of our labour and one important purpose of work is service to others.[11]

In Agrell's view, the aim of work according to the New Testament is obtain means to maintain ourselves. He therefore criticizes Walther Bienert's view that there is strong Biblical support for the Protestant doctrine of vocation. According to Bienert, the twofold commandment to love is at the centre of Christ's work ethics as it it presented in the Gospels. Applied to work, this commandment means that human beings by their work must love their neighbours as themselves. The purpose of work is to serve others. Negatively, the commandment requires that we must not be a burden to others while positively it requires that human beings should work for the benefit of others. The reason for working is not simply to maintain ourselves but also to contribute to the maintenance of our neighbour.[12]

In Göran Agrell's opinion, Bienert gives the commandment to love a greater role than the texts allow. It is held not only in the Old Testament but also in the synoptic tradition and Paul's Epistles, that the purpose of work is our own maintenance. On the one hand, maintenance is in the last analysis a gift of God which man, ideally conceived, receives independently of his labour. On the other hand, after the Fall, work is said to be necessary for our survival. It is certainly said, for example in Ephesians 4:28, that the purpose of work is to obtain resources for actively serving others. We must work to have something "to give to him that needeth". The idea, however, is not as in the Lutheran doctrine of vocation to produce something which is useful to others but rather by working to obtain resources which in turn can then be used to providing charity to the needy.[13]

I do not find Agrell's objection to Bienert convincing. Even if there is no text in the New Testament in which work is directly related to the commandment of loving our neighbour, this does not need to mean that there is no Biblical support for the view that work should also be a service to others. The twofold commandment to love is said in the Gospels to be a summary of the law and thereby a fundamental norm in Christian ethics. In order for this commandment to be relevant, it ought therefore to be applied in the human activity of work. If one does not restrict oneself to an analysis of isolated pronouncements about work, it seems reasonable to suppose that this fundamental norm applies to all human activity including work.

Thomas Aquinas on manual labour

Thus in the Scriptures, we do not find a uniformly low evaluation of work. Although the toil which is associated with work is the result of the Fall, release from work is not taken as an ideal. However, when the Christian Church during its first centuries encountered the Hellenistic world, its thought was influenced by ideas to be found in Greek philosophy. This is also to some extent true with respect to the attitude to work. The low evaluation of work and in particular manual work, present in Greek philosophy influenced a number of Christian thinkers.

At the same time, several Church Fathers hold that work is a meaningful activity. Clement of Alexandria maintains that work has a value not simply as a means of maintaining life. Origen writes that work is given with the creation and is therefore a valuable activity.[14] Tertullian too, does not assign work a low status even if he holds that work is less valuable if it produces something which is evil.[15] In Augustine, we encounter a relatively high valuation of work. He holds that work belongs to the order of creation. Thus through work, man becomes God's co-worker in his continuous act of creation. Augustine maintains that work itself is not a consequence of sin. Sin causes work to be a matter of sweat and tears but in eternity, work will be released from this toil.[16] Augustine also maintains that even those who wish to serve God, have a duty to work. He sharply challenges those who have maintained that the servants of God should devote themselves entirely to spiritual exercises and avoid manual labour. If we do not work, we become parasitical on others.[17]

It was later argued within the monastic system that it was also necessary for the members of the order to engage in work. Thus Basil's rule from the 370s specifies that prayers and psalms must not be used as a pretext for neglecting work. On the contrary it is necessary to work for three reasons. First work provides us with the necessities of life. Secondly work allows us to provide also for the wants of the needy. With reference to Ephesians 4:28, it is maintained that the purpose of work consists in serving our neighbour. Thirdly a life engaged in work is also good for the mortification of the flesh. For these reasons, the aim of piety is not flight from work. Work is just as important as prayer and psalm singing and we should devote ourselves especially to tilling the soil since it is necessary for our maintenance.[18]

A lower evaluation of work is however to be found in the writings of the leading theologian of the Catholic Church, Thomas Aquinas. His view of the purpose of work and its value is clearly influenced by Aristotle whose philosophy he in general often cites. Thomas distinguishes between the contemplative and active life. The contemplative life is dedicated to the love of God and belongs together with that which is characteristic for human beings, namely the intellect. The active life is dedicated to loving our neighbour and also makes use of inferior parts of the human soul. Work belongs to the active life while stillness belongs to the contemplative life.

In close agreement with Aristotle, Thomas maintains that the contemplative life takes priority over the active life. In his main argument for this thesis, Thomas cites Luke 10:24 where Jesus says that Mary, who symbolizes the contemplative life has chosen the good part. He also puts forward a further eight arguments on behalf of this thesis. The contemplative life involves the best element in human beings, namely the intellect, whereas it is a lower form of human reason which is involved in action. The contemplative life engages that which is characteristic for human beings in contrast to animals, namely intellect. The contemplative life is also more constant and enduring, it provides greater pleasure and gives human beings more satisfaction than the active life. It consists in a certain stillness and peace and it is loved for its own sake whereas the active life is devoted to something else. The contemplative life involves the divine whereas the active life involves what is human. Thomas admits that if one suffers from a shortage of material welfare, the active life can be better than the contemplative, but where this is not the case, the contemplative life is to be preferred.[19]

38

In this argumentation, Thomas draws upon the Aristotelian view of man as a rational animal. Human beings are animals but what distinguishes them from other species, is their intellect. Human beings are created in the image of God and God is the highest intellect. Therefore the intellect is the foremost part of the human soul. Like Aristotle, Thomas distinguishes between speculative reason which is focussed upon God and practical reason which is focussed upon our fellow human beings ; it is the former which is to be esteemed more highly. In accordance with this, the contemplative life which is devoted to the love of God, takes precedence over the active life which is devoted to love of our neighbour. This thesis also expresses Thomas' view that the commandment to love God and the first part of the decalogue must take precedence before the commandment to love our neighbour. Thomas embraces a teleological ethics according to which the criterion of a right act is that it leads to good consequences. He holds that there are two types of good – the general good (commune bonum) which is the object of duties towards human beings and the universal good (universale bonum) which is the object of duties towards God. Of these the universal good has priority and consequently the commandment to love God and the contemplative life must also be more greatly esteemed than the commandment to love our neighbour and the active life respectively.

The performance of duties qualifies one according to Thomas for blessedness (beatitudo). By carrying out the law, human beings win merit in the eyes of God. Another of his theses is that the contemplative life wins greater merit than the active life. Thomas does not deny that the merits of the active life are great but he maintains that those of the contemplative life are even greater. The basis of these merits are love of God and love of one's neighbour but it is more meritorious to love God than it is to love our neighbour. Contemplative life is, therefore, more meritorious than the active life. One of the objections to this thesis which Thomas cites, is that the active life brings with it greater merit since one speaks of profit when it is a question of wage and wages are associated with work. But against this argument, Thomas maintains that the external toil increases the wage which is of a transitory character while love of God increases the merit which is related to the important wage, namely eternal blessedness.[20]

Thomas does not dispute that the active life, including work, has a certain value. The circumstance that the contemplative life is superior to the active life and entails greater merit in the eyes of God does not prevent Thomas from believing that the active life is also important.[21] On the contrary, he holds that the active life is useful and necessary as a service to one's neighbour. On the other hand, it is evident that Thomas like Aristotle, gives a relatively low value to manual labour. He shares the view that human happiness is obtained not by working but by philosophising. In contrast to Augustine, he therefore maintains that members of a monastic order are not obliged to carry out manual labour.

By "manual labour", Thomas understands "all human activities by means of which a human being can earn his living in a justified way, whether it is carried out with the hand, the feet or the tongue". Both members of an order and the laity, he holds, are obliged to carry out manual labour according to 1 Thessalonians 4:11. The duty of manual labour is a part of natural law and both members of an order and the laity are bound by that law. However, says Thomas, the requirement of manual labour has been placed on human beings collectively. Each individual cannot however carry out all the work which is necessary and is not obliged to perform manual labour. There must be a division of labour so that for example certain individuals are respectively tradesmen and farmers whereas others are judges and teachers. Therefore not all those who fail to undertake manual labour, are guilty of sin. The members of an order are no more obliged to undertake manual labour than are the laity. Thomas holds that his view does not differ from the standpoint of Augustine. Augustine opposes those who maintain that members of an order are not permitted to undertake manual labour. But it does not thereby follow that the members of an order are under an obligation to undertake manual labour.

In close agreement with Basil's monastic rule, Thomas holds that manual labour has four aims. First it provides for one's maintenance. As such, manual labour is subsumed under the commandment of practical necessity, that is to say, it is necessary to the same extent that its goal, subsistence, cannot be attained without manual labour. A person who is unable to obtain a living by any other means, is obliged to undertake manual labour but if one can gain a living in another way, one is not obliged to undertake manual labour. It follows that the members of an order are not always obliged to earn their living by manual labour.

Secondly, the purpose of manual labour is to remove idleness which according Thomas gives rise to many evil things. Thirdly it aims to restrain desires by the mortification of the flesh. In these two respects, manual labour is not subsumed under the commandment of practical necessity since it is possible to mortify the flesh or remove idleness in many ways other than by manual labour. This is also a reason why members of an order are not obliged to undertake manual labour.

Fourthly the aim of work is to obtain the means to allow one to give alms. Neither in this respect does manual labour come under the commandment of practical necessity. However if there is a need and we are obliged to give alms then according to Thomas we are obliged to undertake manual labour if we have no other assets with which to support the poor. Members of an order are also required to give alms i.e. to share what they have with the poor. But they are not always required to undertake manual labour for this purpose. They are obliged to undertake manual labour only if they cannot obtain the resources for alms by any other means.

One of the objections to this thesis which Thomas discusses, is that the possession of spiritual duties is not a reason for avoiding manual labour. He refers to Augustine according to whom even those who are engaged in manual labour, can pray, sing hymns and read the Scriptures. Thomas counters this argument by maintaining that one can devote oneself to spiritual activities in two distinct ways. We can privately devote ourselves to spiritual activities and in this case we are not prevented from engaging in manual labour. But we can also serve the public good by devoting ourselves to spiritual activities and in this case we are released from manual labour. In the latter case, it is necessary to devote ourselves completely to these activities and therefore it is reasonable that we receive material support from those who derive benefit from this spiritual work.[22]

Thomas thus holds that it is not obligatory for members of an order and for every specific individual to undertake manual labour. At the same time, he holds that there is a natural law which requires human beings collectively considered to undertake manual labour. In comparison to other activities, however, he assigns this work a relatively low value. Thomas shares the Aristotelian view that we cannot by such an activity achieve what is specifically human and thus attain blessedness. Because human beings are rational, the contemplative life is more valuable than the active one.

Luther's doctrine of vocation

Martin Luther ascribes a considerably higher value to manual labour. His doctrine of vocation was partly developed in direct opposition to the monastic system. Luther maintains that we serve God and our neighbour not by hiding ourselves away in a monastery but by carrying on our daily work in society. Good deeds consist not in some specifically religious acts but in serving our fellow human beings by carrying out our usual everyday activities at home and at work. In these activities each and every person is "called" to live according to the injunctions embodied in the Ten Commandments.[23]

Martin Luther lived and preached in a feudal society where political and economic structures were characterized by a hierarchy of superiors and subordinates. It was a markedly agricultural society where people devoted themselves above all to farm work of various kinds. There was no sharp division between work and leisure since it was customary to work at or near home. When Luther writes of "work" he means the occupations which were carried on in this feudal society. He employs the concept "work" in a broad sense to denote an occupation which can be carried out both in the home and outside it. It is not merely an activity which is paid in money.

The concept of "vocation" (vocatio) is used by Luther in several different ways. It denotes (1) the exhortation contained in the preaching of the Gospel, to be converted to the Kingdom of God and (2) the exhortation which is given to certain people to become a priest. It also however denotes (3) an exhortation to discharge one's duties in society – whether in the form of an external occupation or position – in a proper fashion. When Luther speaks of "vocation" in this sense, he uses the word "Beruf". In this sense, the concept denotes two different types of occupation and position, namely (a) a person's position in the home and in the family as father or mother, husband or wife, son or daughter and (b) the occupation from which persons derive their basic income e.g. farmer, tradesman, prince or soldier. The fact that the vocation is exercised not only at work but also in the home, entails that a person can have several vocations at the same time.[24]

Luther's doctrine of vocation can be understood on the basis of his doctrine of good deeds. He holds that we have to do such deeds precisely in our worldly vocations. Luther writes that good deeds should not be done to obtain righteousness in the eyes of God but to promote what is best for others. Good deeds are not specifically religious ones but are rather deeds of ordinary life whether at work or in the family. We perform such deeds not by going into a monastery and devoting ourselves to prayer, fasting and the giving of alms but by serving our fellow human beings in the earthly state to which we have been assigned.[25]

Good deeds according to Luther are those which agree with God's commandments. These are summed up in the Decalogue, which in turn is summarized in the twofold commandment of Love. Luther therefore in *Von den guten werken* devotes himself to interpreting the commandments which make up the Decalogue. His interpretation of these commandments allows one to say which apects of human character are good. He claims that of the commandments which make up the second table of the Decalogue, it is the fourth Commandment which has the highest priority. This implies that obedience is the highest virtue of the good qualities which are commanded in the second table and that disobedience is a greater sin than, for example, licentiousness and covetousness.[26]

In *Deutsch Catechismus* the Decalogue is interpreted in a teleological way so that every commandment is given in order to protect certain values. Luther writes that all of the commandments in the second part encourage us (a) not to cause our fellow human beings any suffering or harm and (b) to do well by other human beings i.e. to promote what is good for them. An act would seem to be right according to Luther if it promotes what is good for other human beings and if it does not cause other human beings any harm.[27]

Luther's ethics are humanely based in the sense that he assumes that every human being can know what deeds are good with the help of their practical reason and independently of revelation. He embraces a doctrine of natural law according to which law comes into being with the Creation, with life itself. At the same time, Luther maintains that Christian ethics has a content which in part differs from the content of humane ethics. In the imitation of Christ, the Christian must be prepared in certain situations to relinquish their own rights and to sacrifice their own best interests for the sake of others. The Christian must be ready for suffering in the imitation of Christ and sometimes to bear His cross.[28]

Luther's doctrine of vocation can also be understood on the basis of his doctrine of the two kingdoms. Luther holds that God wages the battle against the presence of evil in two ways. First of all, it is waged in the spiritual kingdom. Here God operates through the Word and announces the gifts which belong to a human being's salvation. The preaching of the gospel belongs to this spiritual kingdom. Secondly the battle is waged in the temporal kingdom. In this kingdom, God operates by the sword and through superiors and the temporal order and thus maintains the external order in society. Temporal law operates in this kingdom. God is active in both these kingdoms and thus struggles against evil.[29]

Luther believes that the two kingdoms promote two different kinds of righteousness. In the temporal kingdom, God wishes to bring about civil righteousness and the means He employs is the sword. In the spiritual kingdom on the other hand, He wish to achieve spiritual righteousness or Christian righteousness and the means He employs to achieve this goal, is the Word. God subjects one and the same person to both kingdoms. For this person, according to Luther, deeds belong to the temporal kingdom. In this kingdom, human beings have a vocation to serve their neighbour in the family and at work. They are subject to temporal law and must endeavour to do good deeds in order to promote civil righteousness. In the spiritual kingdom on the other hand, vocation and good deeds have no place. In the spiritual kingdom, God demands faith and only faith. Spiritual righteousness is attained only through belief in Christ which God confers by grace alone.[30]

The doctrine of the two kingdoms is combined in Luther with an ethical dualism, according to which a certain normative system is valid for individual ethics while another normative system is valid for social ethics. Luther formulates this by saying that there is a difference between my duties as "person" i.e. in my relation as an individual to other individuals and my duties in my "office", i.e. when I perform a social function which is of importance for the whole of society. As a person, i.e. within individual ethics, I am subject to the norms which have been given in the Sermon on the Mount. It is then my obligation to do good to all my fellow men and for my own part to be ready to suffer injustice. It is wrong to use violence and to extinguish human life. In my office i.e. within social ethics, on the other hand I am subject to another normative system. Here it is a question of a teleological ethics which requires me to carry out that act which leads to the least harmful consequences for my fellow men. In order to protect other human beings, I must in my office stand up to evil and therefore the use of violence can sometimes be right.[31]

According to Luther, the temporal kingdom is focussed upon social life, i.e. political life, family life, working life and cultural life. Vocation, a person's tasks at work and in the family, are part of this. Luther holds that the activities in this kingdom must be directed not according to the gospel but according to the law. This implies that every work should serve one's neighbour and should be a means of permitting their continued existence by for example producing food and clothes. On the other hand, righteousness in the eyes of God cannot be won by vocation. This is to be obtained by faith alone, not by work or by other deeds.[32]

Luther's doctrine of vocation embodies essentially three views. The first is that human beings in their work are co-workers of God in his continuous act of creation. In his interpretation of the doctrine of creation, Luther emphasizes that God's creation is not completed but is still going on. He continues to create at the present time; he goes on uninterruptedly creating the earth anew and providing human beings with all that is necessary for the maintenance of life. According to Luther everything we need for living, is ultimately a gift from God. We need food, clothes and peace and these we receive from our Creator. He gives these things through human beings and their work. God lets human beings work and in this way ensures that we are maintained. The craftsman and farmer, our parents and superiors are the instruments of God by means of which He is able to provide us with the necessities of life. According to Luther, this can be expressed by saying that human beings in their work are God's co-workers in the act of creation: each human being is a "cooperator Dei".[33]

Luther also expresses the fact that human beings are a divine instrument in the act of creation by saying that they are a "larva Dei", that is to say "a mask of God". When God wishes to give human beings various gifts which are necessary for the maintenance of life, he dons a mask, takes on the form of an ordinary human being who attends to his or her business in the home and at work. Thus human beings become God's instruments in serving their

44

neighbour and in supporting the needy in their temporal occupations. God appears on earth as a Creator hidden behind his many "larvae" i.e. superiors, farmers, parents, wives and children. The people in the various offices or ranks to be found in society, are disguises which God wishes us to respect and recognize as created by him for the maintenance of life. Such are the instruments by which God steers the world.[34]

A second component of Luther's doctrine of vocation is the view that the purpose of work is to serve one's neighbour and to promote what is good for other human beings. According to Luther, work is to be employed in producing those things which are of benefit to others. It is in our temporal vocation that we have to fulfil the commandment to love our neighbour. In order to do good deeds, it is not necessary to enter a monastery and carry out specifically religious deeds. Instead one should live among ordinary human beings in the temporal world as ordained by God. There we must do good deeds by following the ten commandments.[35]

Luther holds that work of all types can constitute instruments for serving our neighbour. This is valid not only for intellectual types of employment but also equally for manual labour. It is therefore not the case that the ecclesiastical duties performed by priests and monks are more important than different types of temporal duty. The shoemaker, smith and farmer also have their temporal office and vocation and should thereby benefit and serve other human beings.[36]

To fulfil the commandment to love our neighbour through our work entails, according to Luther, that we fulfil the seven commandments which make up the second table of the Decalogue. This means for example that at work we must obey the seventh commandment which exhorts us not to steal. This is accomplished by not allowing ourselves to be ruled by greed and avarice.[37] Above all it means that we must obey the fourth commandment which exhorts us to honour our father and mother. This commandment takes pride of place in the Decalogue's second table and has priority over the others. According to Luther, it commands obedience towards all our superiors. We are all equal before God but in the temporal kingdom there is no such equality. Instead there are superior and subservient orders which we must, as subordinates in our work, respect by obeying our superiors. At the same time the superiors must care for and protect their subordinates.[38]

Luther's doctrine of vocation is thus combined with the acceptance of the patriarchal superior-subordinate hierarchy which was a feature of feudal society. The purpose of work, he holds, is to fulfil the commandment to love our neighbour and this is accomplished by acting in accordance with the Fourth Commandment. This commandment exhorts us to obey our superiors and to respect the hierarchical social order.

The third view which forms part of Luther's doctrine of vocation is that work is suffering in the imitation of Christ. When we serve our fellow human beings in our vocation, we encounter difficulties and suffering. In his tract *Tractatus de libertate christiana*, Luther maintains that the purpose of work is to serve our neighbour and that Christ in this respect is an ethical ideal. Like Christ we must serve others and only do what is useful for our fellow human beings, without expecting any rewards. Like Christ, we too, must bear our cross i.e. suffer in serving others.[39]

In his polemic against monastic piety, Luther holds that one does not encounter suffering in the imitation of Christ by entering a monastery but by serving others in one's work. In monastic piety, suffering in the form of the mortification of the flesh was designed to simulate the suffering of Christ but this is construed by Luther as an artificial attempt at imitation. Instead he holds that it is in everyday work that human beings encounter the real mortification of the flesh. When in the temporal order, we care for our fellow human beings, we suffer in the imitation of Christ. Unlike the monks, we are not ourselves the cause of our suffering.[40]

Through our work, we should therefore be ready to suffer in the imitation of Christ. On the other hand, Luther does not appear to reckon with the person carrying out the work having any recompense. He might possibly admit that the fact that we serve others in our work can fill us with joy. But the aim of work according to Luther is not to achieve personal happiness in our work. Instead we should be prepared to suffer in the service of others.

Luther does not elaborate any consistent theory of the meaning of work but his doctrine of vocation contains certain views about what is the purpose and value of work. The aim of work, according to Luther, is first of all to serve our neighbour and to care for other people's good. In our work, we have to fulfil the commandment to love our neighbour which implies that we must fulfil the commandments in the second table of the Decalogue. Thereby work has secondly also a deeper pupose, namely to serve as an instrument for God's continuous act of creation. God's creation is not complete but according to Luther goes on all the time and God makes use of human beings as instruments for his continuous act of creation. Thirdly the purpose of work is to bridle our desires by the mortification of the flesh. Luther holds that if one does not work, the body becomes full of lewd desires. In order to suppress these, it is important that men work industriously.[41]

In contrast to Plato and Aristotle, Luther conceives work as a means to human self-realization. He considers that work as part of the divine creation, is one of the fundamental conditions of human existence. A defining feature of a human being, is that they should be a tool for God's continuous act of creation, by serving their neighbour. Luther does not mean that human beings realize themselves as rational beings with a capacity for self awareness and purposive action, through their work. On the other hand, he seems to take the view that work contributes to human self-realization in the sense we thereby can realize ourselves as beings with a capacity for self-sacrificial care for others. Luther writes that we live in the imitation of Christ by serving our fellow human beings in our work. The essence of Christ, the true human being, is that he cares for others and is for this purpose ready to abstain from his own interest. We can realize such a true human life in our work.[42]

Luther in comparison to classical Greek philosophy and Thomas Aquinas, assigns work a considerably higher value. He considers work as an activity whereby several valuable aims can be accomplished. This is the case not only for intellectual work but equally for different types of manual labour. The great value of work derives according to Luther first of all from the fact that it is an instrument for God's continuous act of creation. Through human work God gives human beings what they require to live a tolerable life and this is why it appears valuable. Secondly work is valuable because we thereby achieve what is good for our fellow men. The purpose of work is to serve our neighbour and to the extent that this aim is achieved, work is considered a valuable human activity. Those employments which do not constitute means to serving our neighbour, should be abandoned but work which does serve our neighbour has a high value.

The doctrine of vocation in Calvinist theology

According to Luther, the purpose of work is to realize what is good for other human beings. A person neither profits himself nor justifies himself in the eyes of God through work. Work should be undertaken purely for the sake of others and not for achieving personal salvation.

A somewhat different formulation of the doctrine of vocation is to be found in Calvinist theology. Calvin also stressed the fact that human beings could not contribute to their own salvation by hard work and other good deeds. Like Luther, he held that man is justified before God by grace alone. In later Calvinist theology, the problem arose of whether human beings could know whether they had been elected by God for salvation. It was suggested that a clue to future salvation was to be found in good deeds and success in one's temporal career. Industry was seen not as a way to salvation but on the other hand as a sign that a person was predestined by God for salvation.[43]

The doctrine of vocation in Calvinist theology is combined with the view that human beings must try to the full extent of their powers to magnify the glory of God in the world by carrying out His commandments. Work is therefore interpreted as a God given obligation. Everything we do, should magnify the glory of God and this is also the case with work. In order to magnify God's glory, human beings must work hard in their temporal vocation. At the same time, the doctrine of vocation in Calvinist theology is combined with the doctrine of double predestination. God has already chosen His own and their salvation is an act of grace alone. Human beings are predestined by God either to eternal life and salvation or to eternal death and damnation and cannot influence God's decision by their own deeds.[44]

How is one to know if one belongs to the elect or to the damned? Calvin did not consider this a major problem since he held that it is presumptuous of human beings to try and pierce divine mysteries. We can only obtain knowledge of God's judgement if it pleases Him to communicate it to us. In later Calvinist theology however, the question of the certitude of salvation became a burning issue. It was then maintained that through an intensive temporal activity, we could achieve an inner certitude about belonging to the elect. It is possible to see if God acts in people from their deeds. Good deeds are not a means of justifying ourselves in the eyes of God but they can provide an inner certitude that we belong to those who will attain the bliss of eternal life. This view also stimulates us to industry and asceticism in temporal work. Success in work signifies that we have a good relation to God and belong to the elect.[45]

It is this Calvinist formulation of the doctrine of vocation which Max Weber above all, dwells upon in his well known work, *Die protestantische Ethik und der Geist der Kapitalismus*. Weber's thesis is that the work ethic which was put forward by the Calvinist doctrine of vocation was one of the presuppositions of what he calls the "spirit of capitalism". By this latter phrase, he means a certain attitude towards economic activity which is encountered in Western European and American capitalism, for example in Benjamin Franklin. According to this attitude, characteristics like industry and thrift should be cultivated in order to encourage economic progress. It is the duty of individuals to work hard and to increase their capital, not in order to satisfy their own needs but as an end in itself.[46]

Weber's thesis does not imply that capitalism as an economic system is a product of Calvinist ethics. It is "the spirit of capitalism" which is promoted by the doctrine of vocation: Protestantism has in no way given rise to capitalism. Nor does Weber maintain that the spirit of capitalism could only have arisen as a result of certain influences from Protestantism. The Calvinist doctrine of vocation was not a sufficient condition for the rise of the spirit of capitalism. On the other hand, Weber would seem to hold that this ethic was a necessary condition for this attitude towards the economy. It was one of the factors which contributed to the genesis and wider promulgation of this spirit. Thus Weber seeks to reject a purely materialistic explanation of ideological views while at the same time maintaining the probability that the Protestant ethic was influenced by social and economic conditions.[47]

When Weber writes about "the Protestant ethic" he means primarily the attitude to work which is an integral part of the ascetic Protestantism which developed from Calvinism. In particular he discusses the doctrine of vocation to be found in the writings of the 17th century theologian Richard Baxter, one of the foremost representatives of English Puritanism. The latter holds that hard and continuous manual and intellectual work is important for two reasons. First of all, work is a means to asceticism. It prevents one living a depraved life with unclean habits, particularly sexual obsessions. Secondly work has been enjoined by God as an end in itself. We have a duty to work and unwillingness to work is a symptom of an unsatisfactory relationship to God.[48]

Baxter emphasizes the duty to work in a way totally different from Thomas Aquinas. According to Thomas, the duty to engage in manual labour is one which is placed upon human beings collectively and not upon each individual. Thomas also holds that one purpose of work is to sustain life and that if this can be accomplished in some other way, there is no duty to engage in manual labour. Baxter, on the other hand, allows no exception from the duty to work. Work is God's command to strive actively for his glory which is addressed to every individual, including the rich who could easily maintain themselves in another way. Work also gives the surest confirmation that one belongs to God's elect.[49]

Baxter treats riches as a serious danger and condems the pursuit of money and property. The reason is that with riches comes laxity. The possession of riches is not reprehensible in itself but it can have bad consequences. It can lead to human beings becoming content with what they have acquired and to their enjoyment of riches. This is morally reprehensible because it entails sloth, carnal desires and above all because one is distracted from the desire to live a life of righteousness. Only activity can magnify the glory of God. On earth, human beings must do God's work in order to ensure that they belong to the Elect. Time is therefore infinitely valuable and to waste time is a serious sin which riches can give rise to.[50]

On the other hand, Baxter allows that it is permitted to become rich through work. Riches are only questionable to the extent that they constitute a temptation to sloth but if one achieves wealth by hard work, this is something positive. Material welfare can be considered as a sign that God blesses the elect already in this life and in this way for example a businessman's successful activities can be justified. What one has to reject however, is the notion of wealth as a goal in itself. Puritanism also rejects the spontaneous enjoyment of wealth as well as pleasure, the theatre and secular literature. Our pounds must not be spent in pursuit of our own pleasure but in serving the glory of God. On the other hand, there is nothing against limited consumption and a rational acquisition of goods. Wealth which is acquired as the result of one's profession or trade is considered as a divine blessing. In this fashion, Puritanism releases the profit motive while at the same time limiting consumption. The result is then according to Weber capital accumulation by means of an ascetic obligation to save i.e. just that attitude to life which characterizes "the spirit of capitalism".[51]

The formulation of the doctrine of vocation which is encountered within ascetic Puritanism contributes according to Weber to the emergence of what he calls a specifically bourgeois economic ethics. The bourgeois businessman was convinced that he was covered by God's grace. Given this conviction, he could then look after his own profit interests, arguing that it was his duty to do so as long as he kept himself to what was formally correct, as long as his conduct was irreproachable and as long as he did not employ his wealth in some offensive fashion. At the same time religious asceticism provided him with sober, conscientious and unusually industrious workers who looked upon their work as their life's mission which they had been given by God.[52]

The attitude to work which Puritanism created, had in two respects, according to Weber a very favourable effect on "productivity" in the capitalist sense of the word. First of all asceticism gave human beings a strong motivation for working hard and efficiently. A dedicated piece of work was seen as something pleasing to God, even if it was carried out for a paltry wage. This view was not new but it was given a new depth and emphasis by the Puritanical view of work as the primary means of obtaining certitude about one's state of Grace. Secondly, asceticism made the exploitation of this willingness to work legitimate by also viewing the businessman's profit motive and business activities as a vocation. Industry and thrift lead to wealth and even if riches entail temptations, it is nonetheless regarded as a divine blessing provided it is not used in a offensive fashion.[53]

Contemporary Protestant work ethics

Thus in Calvinist and Puritan theology, the doctrine of vocation is given a somewhat different formulation from that given by Luther. According to Luther's doctrine of vocation, the aim of work is above all to fulfil the commandment to love our neighbour. We cannot in any way influence our relationship to God through our work nor can we justify ourselves before Him. In Calvinist theology on the other hand, the doctrine of vocation is characteristically combined with the doctrine of double predestination. Hard work does not contribute to personal salvation but on the other hand good deeds are an indication that we have been elected by God. According to Luther, we serve our neighbour in our work by fulfilling the ten command-ments. Because he assigns the fourth commandment a high priority, the doctrine of vocation acts as a support for the division of society into a superior-subordinate hierarchy which was a feature of feudal society. The Calvinist doctrine of vocation with its high estimation of duties like industry and thrift instead promotes an attitude to work which is common within capitalist society.

How then is the doctrine of vocation formulated in contemporary Pro-testant work ethics? Several contemporary Protestant social ethical thinkers hold that it is possible to revise the doctrine of vocation so that it also has relevance for problems which arise in working life today. They hold that even if certain of the views which make up this doctrine can no longer be accepted, some at least of its standpoints continue to be valid. It is such revised formulations of the doctrine of vocation which I shall deal with in this book.

According to several contemporary Protestant work ethicists, the doctrine of vocation requires to be revised primarily in two respects. Firstly, many hold that the patriarchal view of society which Luther presupposed can no longer be accepted. Luther formulated his doctrine of vocation in a feudal society, with its superior-subordinate hierarchy. For him, the commandment to love our neighbour in our work is carried out primarily by obeying our superiors. This demand for obedience and subordination is however unac-ceptable in today's society. As a result, Tor Aukrust for example, holds that the doctrine of vocation must be freed from its patriarchal social ideal. According to him, the view that human beings in their work should be co-workers in the divine process of creation means not that they should obey their superiors but that they should seek justice and equality at work.[54]

Secondly, many contemporary theologians believe that the purpose of work is not simply to produce those things which are of value to others. Its aim is also to give some recompense to those who work. Thus for example the American theologian Robert Lowry Calhoun holds that the purpose of work is to contribute to the common good and to satisfy the needs of other persons. In contrast to Luther, however, he holds that it also aims to satisfy fundamental needs of the person engaging in it. For human beings, work should be a means of satisfying needs for food, shelter, security, community and love. Work should also promote individual self-fulfilment and personal development, in the sense that human beings can thereby express and devel-op their individual aptitudes and capacities.[55]

Such a revision of the doctrine of vocation has also been proposed by the Swedish work ethicist, Ludvig Jönsson. The doctrine of vocation, he writes, has often been combined with an ideal of efficiency according to which we should give ourselves to the service of others, almost to the point of totally extinguishing our own self. This has been understood to mean that it is our duty to make a contribution for the welfare of others but to abstain from our own personal reward. In opposing this view, Ludvig Jönsson emphasizes that every human being possesses not only obligations but also certain rights. The commandment to love one's neighbour obliges us to seek both what is best for others but also what is best for ourselves.[56] According to the doctrine of vocation, we must serve our neighbour in our work but this does not entail that it is wrong to obtain some personal reward. The aim of work is both to produce what satisfies the needs of others and to allow the persons carrying out the work to fulfil themselves by developing their individual talents.[57]

The contemporary theologians who seek to revise the formulation of the doctrine of vocation differ, however, in a number of ways. It is these differences which I shall examine in the following six chapters. Already at this point, however, it may be noted that fundamental differences arises from the fact that they have different views about which parts of a Christian system of belief form the basis of work ethics. As a result, they also adopt different views concerning the relationship between a Christian work ethics and other formulations of a work ethical theory.

Some theologians have devised a work ethics which is based on a doctrine of creation. This is a theological entry point which we have already encounted in Martin Luther. His social ethics and theory of work are closely related to the Christian idea of creation. In contemporary theology, Paul Althaus and Walter Künneth for example hold that work is a divine order of creation. In their work, human beings are instruments for God's continuous act of creation. This type of work ethics, based upon a theology of creation is also to be found in the writings of Emil Brunner. He holds that work is a divine order of creation and grounds his social ethics upon the first article with the result that he also holds that there is considerable agreement between Christian and humane work ethics.[58]

One of the theologians who grounds his work ethics upon the doctrine of creation, is Helmut Thielicke. He holds that work belongs to the order of creation and that it is part of the divine intention with human life that human beings should work. At the same time, work after the Fall is always combined with toil and effort.[59] Thielicke writes that the purpose of work is to obtain the necessities of life. It should also aim to serve others. To the extent that this aim is realized, human beings are co-workers of God in his continuous act of creation.[60]

Other theologians have developed a work ethics which is based upon Christology, thus adopting a theological entry point which is completely different from that of Luther. The most influential of these theologians is

Karl Barth. In his writings, there is to be found a Christologically based ethics according to which Jesus Christ is also the measure of what is good and right. Accordingly, he also constructs a Christian work ethics which in his view is entirely different from the content of humane ethics. According to Barth, work is a means of exercising our responsibility before God. It is through work that we must fulfil God's vocation in the present, serving God and our fellow human beings. The work is to be carried out in obedience to God's will and God's will is something into which we obtain insight, only through the Revelation in Christ. To serve others in one's work implies living in the imitation of Christ.[61]

A similar Christological work ethics is also to be found in J H Oldham. He combines a revised version of the doctrine of vocation with the view that it is only through the revelation in Christ that we can decide what characterizes a right act. A similar standpoint is to be found in the writings of the Danish ethicist, N H Søe. According to him, the Lutheran doctrine of vocation maintains that human beings fulfil God's will by working and thereby serving others. According to this doctrine, work is a divine service which is no less valuable than special religious acts.[62] Søe combines this formulation of the doctrine of vocation with a Christological ethics according to which the criterion of a right act is that it is in agreement with the Will of God, which we learn to know through the Revelation in Christ.

Apart from work ethics based upon the theology of creation or upon Christology, there are also other views about which parts of the Christian system of belief form a basis for work ethics. Arthur Rich, for example, holds that social ethics and work ethics are based above all upon eschatology. Günter Brakelmann also relates his social ethical theory both to Christology and eschatology. He criticizes, from an eschatological perspective, the conservatism which has often been combined with a theology of creation of the type embraced by Brunner.

Several contemporary theologians base their ethics both upon the doctrine of creation and upon Christology and eschatology. One of these is Dietrich Bonhoeffer. He writes not about orders of creation but about certain "mandates" which are given with the creation and which form fundamental structures in human life. Work belongs to these mandates, in addition to marriage, the superior order and the Church. At the same time, Bonhoeffer holds that God's commandments and the task of human beings in relation to these mandates, can be understood through the Revelation in Christ. He therefore also reckons with a specifically Christian contribution to ethics.[63]

The American social ethicist J Philip Wogaman also belongs to those who base ethics both upon the doctrine of creation and upon Christology and eschatology. He believes that the principles and values which make up

Christian ethics rest upon certain theological views which in turn build upon Christian tradition and present-day Christian experience. Among these are the following: the doctrine of creation which lends justification to the view that the material world contains that which is good; a Christian view of man according to which human beings have the capacity for both love and selfishness; the doctrine of justification according to which salvation is a gift of God's grace alone; and eschatology according to which a perfect existence is ultimately a work of God. Wogaman holds that ethics is based upon all these different components which make up a Christian system of belief.[64]

The critique of the doctrine of vocation

Several contemporary theologians have thus presented the doctrine of vocation in a revised form. At the same time, however, there are several contemporary work ethicists who have subjected this teaching, especially in its Calvinist formulation, to a more fundamental critical assessment. They hold that the doctrine of vocation assigns work too high a value and lays too much stress upon a human being's obligation to work. In contrast to this doctrine, they maintain that human beings can participate in God's continuous act of creation through other activities than paid work. It is not through work that human beings realize themselves and therefore there are other activities which are equally important.

The social background to this theological criticism of the doctrine of vocation is to be found in the increasing unemployment in several West European countries which has in turn led to increased poverty and social stratification. It is often held that the new computer technology is one of the factors which has contributed to this unemployment and it is therefore impossible to recover full employment. The best way of dealing with this situation is work sharing, with reduced hours of work for everyone and a just distribution of the employment opportunities available. Because work sharing entails increased leisure and more opportunity for unpaid work, it is urgent, so it is claimed, to find an alternative to the Protestant doctrine of vocation. Paid work is given too high a value according to this doctrine. What is needed now, is to emphasize the value of the activities we carry out in our spare time.[65]

The theological critique of the doctrine of vocation is linked in several respects to the parallel discussion of "the Protestant work ethic" in social science. In a study in the history of ideas, which has stimulated discussion, P D Anthony has maintained that the Protestant doctrine of vocation, especially in its Calvinist formulation, is an "ideology of work" in the sense that it has conferred legitimacy upon the prevailing economic system and persuaded the lower social ranks to accept their subservient position. By emphasizing the importance of work and the obligation to work hard, this doctrine has provided capitalist society with ideological legitimacy. Anthony concludes his study by arguing for a reduction in the hours of work and for the view that not all work is valuable.[66]

Several social scientists hold that a work ethic completely unlike the Protestant one is in the process of emerging in today's post-industrial society. Thus for example, James Robertson holds that it is improbable that full employment can be regained. In the future, we shall increasingly be occupied with self-organized work of our own in addition to paid work. When that happens, the "Protestant work ethic" with its high evaluation of paid work will be replaced by a new work ethic. According to Robertson, this new ethics will characteristically accord a higher value to unpaid work such as housework and the care of others.[67]

Other social scientists, however, have questioned the view that "the Pro-testant work ethic" is tending to disappear in the post-industrial society. One of these is Michael Rose. He holds that the attitude to work which finds expresssion in the Calvinist doctrine of vocation, has probably never been widely accepted in Western society. There have also been several other views about the meaning of work. Moreover, he holds that many Western workers continue to regard their work as profoundly important. At the same time, Rose maintains that human views about the purpose and value of work will probably alter gradually as economic conditions in society change.[68]

The theological criticism of the doctrine of vocation has been most sharply formulated by a number of British Anglican theologians. One of these is David Bleakley. He maintains that one reason for high unemployment is rapid technological development. Because all areas of working life are affect-ed by computerization there is a dramatic reduction in the need for labour. Therefore it is also rather improbable that full employment can be achieved again. There is a great risk that we are moving towards a society where a great number of people are permanently unemployed.[69]

Increased unemployment entails increased poverty and difficult social problems. Bleakley therefore holds that massive measures are needed to combat the employment problem. One way is to try and create new jobs. This is possible, for example, within the health and education sectors and in the social services.[70] In addition, Bleakley recommends work sharing. By reducing the hours of work, a just apportioning of the employment opportunities available, would become possible.[71] In a society with work sharing, everyone ought to receive an income from society regardless of whether one has employment or not. It is also important that society creates opportunities for human beings to make use of their increased leisure in a meaningful way.[72]

On the basis of these views, Bleakley criticises what he calls "the Protestant work ethic". This is an attitude to work which originates from the doctrine of vocation in Lutheran and Calvinist theology. According to this view, Bleakley writes, it is a human duty to work and work is conceived as a necessary prerequisite for the dignity of man. Paid work is assigned a high value and is considered as a human being's primary goal in life. According to this view, work is not only an economic means but also a spiritual goal.[73]

Bleakley holds that this "Protestant work ethic" must be replaced by a "life ethic" which does not look upon paid wage earning as a duty. According to this "life ethic", paid work is not more valuable than other activities. Work is not the most important goal in life and is not a necessary prerequisite of human worth. Instead, according to the "life ethic" viewpoint, one should strive to have a better balance between work and leisure. Our leisure activities are assigned a high value and activities other than wage-earning activities are regarded as work.[74]

According to Bleakley, an alternative to the Protestant work ethic is needed because it is unlikely that full employment can be attained in the future. As a result there is a risk that traditional work ethics may wrongly inspire a sense of guilt in people who have been made unemployed. Therefore, says Bleakley, an ethic of work is needed which makes it possible even for the unemployed to be of good heart.[75] A "life ethic" which assigns paid work a lower value would also better agree with the majority working class attitude to work. According to the workers, work is essentially a way of making a living. They look upon work, Bleakley writes, as a means to a goal and not a goal in itself. They achieve happiness in their leisure and do not calculate upon work giving any return other than a monetary one.[76]

A similar criticism of the doctrine of vocation has been put forward by the Anglican theologian Roger Clarke who like John Atherton is a director of the William Temple Institute in Manchester. Clarke too deals with the problems which arise from greatly increased unemployment. This unemployment leads to increased poverty and a growing social and economic gap between those who have work and those who do not.[77] Like Bleakley, Clarke holds that it is unlikely that we can recover full employment. Because of the rapid pace of technological development, there will probably be a continuing shortage of employment oppportunities in the future. Given this situation, the question arises of how existing work should be apportioned. Roger Clarke argues for a just distribution of these work opportunities.[78]

This, he claims, can be accomplished by work sharing. This is a way of organising the existing work so that everyone who wishes to work, has the chance to be at least partly employed. Work sharing can take place either by those having fulltime employment, surrendering a part of it to others so that the employer gets two employees for the price of one or by a general reduction in working hours.[79] A reduction in working hours can be accomplished by dropping the pension age, extending the length of youth education and reducing overtime.[80] At the same time, Clarke holds that measures to stimulate job-creation are needed. In his view, it is possible for example in the public sector to increase the number of job opportunities.[81]

Roger Clarke combines these work ethical recommendations with a criticism of what he calls "the Work Ethic". This is a view which holds that it is our duty to work and that idleness is a sin. According to this view, work is the really important thing in life and of value in itself. It is namely through paid work that we accomplish something of social value and realize ourselves as human beings. Work is therefore an activity which is immensely valuable while those who are unemployed do not live a good life.[82] In Clarke's view, this "Work Ethic" is based on certain standpoints in Protestant theology. The doctrine of vocation in particular as it is formulated in Calvinist and Puritan theology provides a powerful theological argument for the view that it is our duty to work hard and efficiently.[83]

Clarke holds that today we need a new system of values to replace the traditional "Work Ethic" because there is a discrepancy between it and the actual supply of work. In a situation where it is no longer possible to achieve full employment, the "Work Ethic" must be replaced by a new ideology of work.[84] What we need today is a more balanced view which assigns work a less exalted value. According to this alternative view, we make valuable contributions to society also through other activities.[85]

Clarke sees work as a meaningful activity. Its aim is to bring about something which benefits others and thereby to contribute to society. Work is a purposeful activity by which we contribute to the common good. Its aim is also to satisfy the social needs of those who carry it out. Work gives us a social position and allows contact and communion with other human beings.[86] As such, work is a valuable activity. It is valuable as a means in meeting the needs of our fellow individuals and contributing to society. Moreover it has a value as a means of satisfying the worker's own needs.[87]

At the same time, Clarke holds that work does not have the exalted value ascribed to it by the traditional "Work Ethic". There are also activities other than paid work which have great importance in making valuable social contributions. We can also accomplish things which are good for others through our family life and in the company of other individuals in our leisure, while at the same time gratifying our own social needs. As a result, these leisure activities have as high a value as paid work.[88]

Roger Clarke proposes an alternative to the traditional "Work Ethic", which he calls a "Contribution Ethic". Its fundamental thesis is that we realize ourselves as human beings by doing what is good for others. Human beings have two needs, namely the need to belong to society and the need to be allowed to make a contribution to society. Work allows us to do something for others and thereby satisfy both these needs. At the same time, Clarke holds that we can make a contribution to society by means of activities other than paid work. Through family life and in the company of others in our leisure time, we are able to accomplish what is good for others. Therefore these activities also contribute to our fulfilment as human beings.[89]

Roger Clarke and David Bleakley thus are not content merely to propose a revised version of the doctrine of vocation.These British theologians maintain that this doctrine must be replaced by a Christian work ethics of a completely different kind. This is the only way in which the employment problem which has emerged in the post-industrial society can be dealt with. A similar standpoint is to be found in John Atherton. As we shall see, he is a good representative for contemporary Anglican criticism of the doctrine of vocation.

2. Work ethical recommendations

In this chapter, I shall begin my analysis of the work ethical theories which are to be encountered in contemporary Protestant theology. I do this by trying to clarify the content of the work ethical recommendations which are to be found in the writings of the theologians I study. At the same time, I also try to clarify the kind of arguments they adduce for these recommendations. In the material analysed, I shall take up five problems in work ethics.

1. What should should be the aim of employment policy? I shall call this "the employment problem". It is a question initially of whether one ought to underline the importance of full employment. Some hold that a fundamental aim of economic policy should be full employment in the sense that all who wish and are able to work, should be allowed to do so. On the other hand, others maintain that a certain level of unemployment is desirable to promote low inflation and consequently a sound economy. The discussion of employment policy is also concerned with the question of what measures should be taken to reduce unemployment in society. One view is that one should aim at full employment via an active labour market policy, continued technological development and an extension of the public sector. Alternatively it is maintained that that unemployment should be reduced by work sharing and a reduction in working hours. But is it really desirable to share existing work opportunities by a reduction in working hours for everyone?[1]

2. What is a just wage? I shall call this "the wage question". First of all, one has to decide if wage differences in whatever shape or form should be accepted. In the discussion of this question, it is sometimes maintained that a just wage is an equal wage or at least a distribution of income where income differences are minimized. Others hold that wage differentiation is both necessary and desirable. The discussion of wage policy is then concerned with the principles governing such wage differentiation. Some hold that wages should be distributed according to effort and result. Others hold that wages

should be distributed according to need. Still others maintain that wage differentiation should be based upon the relative difficulty of the work.[2]

3. How should work be organized? I call this problem "the organization problem". First of all, there is the question of how the various work tasks are to be divided up among the employees. In the discussion of this question, it is held that a far-reaching division of labour and specialization is necessary in order to increase efficiency. Others maintain that we should try to extend work so that every employee has a number of different tasks. There is also the problem of determining what level of skill is desirable for a given task and whether tasks should be repetitive or varied. The organization problem is also concerned with the question of how much self-determination employees should enjoy in determining their conditions at work and the way in which the tasks are to be carried out. The problem also involves the question of technological development at work. This development has important consequences for the way in which work is organized.[3]

4. Should the employees participate in decision making? I call this problem "the participation question". The issue is who is to make the key decisions within a company. In discussing this question, some hold that those who own the means of production should make the decisions. Others, on the other hand, hold that the employees should also have a say. The question then becomes one of deciding the issues employees should have a say in. Some hold that their influence should be restricted to questions dealing with conditions at workplace level. Others maintain that they also should have a say at the company level about more strategic problems relating to the direction and volume of production. The problem also involves the question of the type of influence the employees ought to obtain. Some propose a system of "consultation" whereby the board solicits the opinion of the employees before making a decision. Others maintain that it should be a genuine "participation in decision-making" which entails that the employees via their representatives actually take part in the actual decision-making itself.[4]

5. What form should the economic system take? I call this "the system question". First of all, there is the question of who should own the means of production in society. In the discussion of this question, some hold that private ownership of the means of production is to be preferred. Others, in contrast, advocate collective ownership of all or at least some of the means of production. There is also the problem of deciding who is to decide what is to be produced and consumed in society. Some propose a market economy where free market forces regulate the allocation of resources without state intervention. Others advocate a planned economy with state intervention and at least some overall central control of the economy.

The aim of this chapter is first of all to clarify the positions adopted by contemporary Protestant work ethicists in regard to these five problems. What work ethical recommendations do these theologians make? What are their views about how the employment problem, the wage problem, the organization problem, the participation question and the system question should be solved? It is also my intention to exhibit the differences between their various work ethical recommendations. Are these theologians agreed about how these five problems should be solved or do they provide different suggestions about how to deal with conditions in working life?

Secondly, the aim of this chapter is to elucidate the types of argument adduced by these six theologians on behalf of their different recommendations. What kind of consideration and theory are their proposals about working life based upon? To what extent do they refer to empirically testable assertions? To what extent are their recommendations in work ethics based upon social ethical theories which specify the criteria for a right action? To what extent are they motivated by different theories of the meaning of work? Are there other types of theory and consideration which back up these recommendations? These are the questions I shall try to answer in the present chapter.

The employment problem

What should be the aims of employment policy in society? What measures should be adopted to reduce unemployment? These questions have been dealt with relatively briefly by three of the theologians being studied. In a book published in the 1930s, Emil Brunner argues that one should draw attention to the importance of full employment. Unemployment, he writes, reveals the curse which hangs over modern economic life. Everyone has the right to work and therefore we should seek to counteract unemployment. In his argumentation, Brunner would seem to suggest that the fact that work belongs to the divine order of creation is an argument for everyone having a right to work. Furthermore the right to work is an argument for adopting a policy of full employment. However no more detailed discussion of the measures needed to reduce unemployment is to be found in Brunner.[5]

Fifty years later, Günter Brakelmann has dicussed the high unemployment which arises in a society undergoing rapid technological development in working life. Brakelmann holds that unemployment has negative consequences for the individual as a person. It entails that the individual loses social contacts and a meaningful existence. It gives individuals the impression that they are not wanted and of being objects controlled by others. Unemployment thus reveals the significance of work for human beings and their experience of life's meaningfulness.[6]

Brakelmann's basic argument for trying to achieve a reduction in unemployment is an argument from rights. According to him, the right to work is a fundamental human right. This right implies that individuals have the possibility of assuming responsibility for themselves and other persons.[7] The right to work is motivated according to Brakelmann by a human being's obligation to work. He holds that work is a "mandate" which human beings have received from God and that it is part of truly human existence to care for the world around one. Human existence consists in fellowship and therefore everyone has an obligation to work and thus to use their capacities for the collective good. It is this obligation which entails that all men have a right to work. If people are to be responsible for others, they must not be refused work. Therefore the state also has a duty to ensure that all citizens have meaningful work so that all can fulfil their task of serving their fellow human beings.[8]

What measures should be taken against unemployment? Brakelmann recommends two types of measure. First of all, economic growth and an economic policy which eliminates trade depressions are required. Secondly Brakelmann also advocates a reduction in working hours and work sharing i.e. a just apportioning of available work. A reduction in the working hours for everyone, he maintains, would allow additional employment opportunities to be created.[9]

Such work sharing has also been proposed by John Atherton, who discusses in his book the economic problems in Great Britain in the 1980s. These problems have arisen in a post-industrial society with a relatively high level of affluence. Permanent unemployment has greatly increased, leading to increased poverty and a growing economic gap between those comfortably off and the poor. In this situation, Atherton recommends a Christian social vision according to which one ought to strive for a "participating and reciprocal society". According to this social ideal, everyone has a right to work. Each and everyone who wishes to work, has a right to work. This is one of the fundamental rights which belongs to every human being in a society which is "reciprocal". Permanent or long-term unemployment contravenes this right.[10]

To remove unemployment, Atherton recommends two measures. First of all, he holds that it is necessary to create new jobs. Secondly he maintains that work sharing and a reduction of working-hours is required. The age limit for the old age pension, says Atherton, can be reduced to 60 and young people should be educated until they are eighteen. Such a reduction in working hours can be combined with an extended notion of the concept of work so that it covers both paid employment and other types of meaningful contribution to society.[11] In addition, Atherton recommends that the unemployed should have a reasonable level of income. There is need for a "basic incomes system" so that everyone can obtain a basic income irrespective of whether they have employment or not.[12]

Atherton advances views about how the employment problem should be solved which are shared by several British theologians. I have already touched upon these views in the previous chapter. As we have seen, Roger Clarke argues for a just distribution of the scarce existing employment opportunities. This can be achieved by work sharing and a reductiuon in working hours. In this way one obtains a better balance between paid and unpaid work and everyone who wishes to engage in paid employment, may do so.[13] At the same time, Roger Clarke also argues on behalf of "job creation" i.e. measures for creating more employment opportunities inter alia within the public sector.[14]

David Bleakley is yet another who argues for a just division of available work by work sharing and a reduction in working hours. At the same time, he also advocates "job creation".[15] It is this package of measures which John Atherton supports. It is probable that he would thereby also reject the type of full employment policy put forward by Emil Brunner. The attempt to provide work for all does not according to Atherton mean that everyone who wishes to work will be able to have paid employment with a 40 hour week up to the age of 65.

The wage question

What is a just wage? Should income be distributed equally or is it just to have wage differentiation and if so what criteria should be used? This question has been discussed by only two of the theologians in whom I am interested, namely Emil Brunner and Tor Aukrust. Their proposed solutions of the wage question differ.

Brunner holds that it is just that the worker receives the wage which he himself and his labour deserve. But what wage does he deserve? According to Brunner, there are two principles competing with one another, namely a principle of needs and a principle of merit. Both these principles, Brunner says, have to be taken into account. On the one hand it is just that the person who achieves superior results is better paid. On the other hand, it is also just that persons who do their best have the possibility of living in a way worthy of human beings even if they do not achieve such good results.[16]

How are these two principles to be weighed in the balance with one another? Brunner's view would seem to be that the merit principle should be accorded greater weight than the needs principle. He writes that each and every one who fulfils their obligation to the community, should have the right to a humanly tolerable existence. This presupposes a levelling out of the differences which now exist. But at the same time according to Brunner it is just that the attainment of results and industry should be rewarded. A just wage is therefore not an equal wage.[17]

In his discussion of the wage question, Brunner proceeds from a certain basic assumption about the meaning of justice. According to this, it is just to divide the good so that each and every one gets their due (suum cuique). This principle of justice implies that one should reduce existing inequalities. It does not however imply that one should strive for equality and equal distribution. The differences which exist between different individuals in different social roles must be taken into account.[18]

Tor Aukrust adopts a different standpoint. He gives three criteria for a just wage. First of all it is a wage which is in reasonable proportion to the work effort involved. Secondly, a just wage gives the employee a just portion of the material wealth in society. A just distribution of the good, according to Aukrust, implies that each and every one is entitled to their due (suum cuique). In contrast to Brunner, he holds, however, that this implies that we must take into account the needs of each and every one. Thirdly Aukrust maintains that a just wage confirms the human worth of employees and their intrinsically equal value in relation to others. It is not the effort put into the work which is rewarded but the person behind the work-effort.[19]

How are these three principles to be weighed in the balance with one another? Aukrust's answer to this question differs from Brunner's. He holds that the first principle provides justification for wage differentiation. The second and the third principle on the other hand favour instead an equal wage principle. When one weighs up these criteria, Aukrust maintains that the equal wage principle should be implemented as far as possible while the wage differentiation principle should be accepted only insofar as it is necessary to do so. A certain weight should be attached in wage differentiation to work-effort, responsibility, training and personal qualifications. At the same time Aukrust holds that minimal wages should be raised so that differences between wages do not become too dramatic.[20]

Aukrust's view would seem to be that the equality and needs principles ought to be assigned greater weight than the merit principle. Wage differentiation which takes account of the work effort involved may be necessary if society is to function but the aim should be an income distribution based upon needs and upon the equal value of all. Aukrust cannot therefore accept Brunner's view that it is the merit principle which has the greater weight.

Tor Aukrust also discusses the piecework system which makes income directly proportional to work-effort. He raises three objections to such a wage system. First of all, workers are continually compelled to think of their wage since everything they do is valued in money. Secondly the system is based on a lack of trust in the workers, namely an assumption that they are lazy and work-shy. Thirdly the social prestige and status of the workers are lowered when unlike others they are paid according to this system. For these three reasons, Aukrust holds that workers like employees in general ought to receive payment according to the hours worked, preferably in the form of a monthly salary.[21]

The organization problem

How should work be organized? How should works tasks be divided up among the employees and what level of skill with respect to the tasks is desirable? It is frequently maintained in Western industrial society that increased efficiency demands rapid technological development combined with a hierarchical organization of work. The rationalization movement inspired by the American engineer F W Taylor has been of major significance for this point of view. According to this viewpoint, it is desirable to have a far-reaching division of labour so that every task is broken up into a number of simple, highly limited manual operations. At the same time, the intellectual planning of the work is separated from its manual execution. As a result employees have very little self-determination in their own work.[22]

This view is criticized both by Emil Brunner and J H Oldham. They both reject an organization of work which involves too far-reaching a division of labour. Brunner argues for an organization of work which is so designed that human beings are aware of the purpose of their work and that they are not exchangable. Work can only make human beings happy, he writes, if it promotes the aim of serving one's neighbour. If work does not promote this end, then individuals lose pleasure in their work and it becomes impossible for them to conceive their work as a vocation. The fact that many people have lost pleasure in their work today, does not depend simply on their inability to conceive their work as a God given vocation. A further cause according to Brunner is also to be found in the actual conditions of work. In particular, if work is so organized that the individual becomes merely a replacable cog in a giant machine and where it is difficult to grasp the purpose of the production process as a whole, work risks no longer being seen as a vocation. Brunner writes:

> "Wo der einzelne Arbeiter nur noch auswechselbares Rädchen an einer grossen Maschinerie ist, wo er weder weiss, was aus dem wird, was er tut, noch wem es dient, sondern nur dies weiss, dass daraus andere reich werden, während er selbst arm bleibt, kann er, menschlich gesprochen, nicht mehr seinen Beruf als göttlichen

hinnehmen. Weder erlebt er darin seine Naturüberlegenheit, noch seine Verbundenheit mit den Anderen im gegenseitigen Dienst."[23]

J H Oldham also criticizes an organization of work where the individual becomes interchangeable and is unaware of the purpose of his work effort. He argues against any rationalization and division of labour in industry, which is too far-reaching. Modern industrial society, writes Oldham, is dominated by technological rationality. In the search for lower costs and higher productivity, work is broken up into simpler processes. At the same time, along with this technological rationalization, shift work is introduced which is a further indication that it is the machine which determines the tempo.[24] This development, Oldham maintains, is contrary to a Christian view of man. According to that view, a human being is a person and a social being. Technological and scientific development, however, gives rise to forces which constitute a threat to man as a person and social being. As work becomes separated from both personal and social life, it loses its meaning.

This occurs according to Oldham in two ways. Firstly work loses its personal quality when human beings in their work are forced to be mere operators, anonymous interchangeable entities in a mechanical process, who carry out tasks in which others can replace them. Work then no longer promotes the growth of character: it ceases to be an area for personal and moral activity. In the same way, rationalization leads to depersonalization. Secondly the conditions of modern industrial production have made it more difficult for human beings to feel that in their work they fulfil a useful social function. The employee does not see the end product in use and thus it requires great imagination to look upon work as a contribution to the common good. In this way rationalization is also socially undermining.[25]

What then is the alternative to the hierarchical organization of work associated with the rationalization movement? Brunner and Oldham provide no answers to this question. They put forward no proposals of their own about how work should be alternatively organized. Nor do we encounter any proposals in the writings of Tor Aukrust. He argues at a more general level for an organization of work which gives scope for human qualities. Aukrust appeals for a more humane industrial philosophy where work is organized so as to promote human goals and not simply to increase production.[26]

Aukrust's argument for such a change in the organization of work is that it helps to counteract human beings' alienation. He holds that the goal should be to make work an activity worthy of human beings. It is a question of overcoming human alienation in relation to work and to oneself. This demands a change in the personal life style of human beings but it also presupposes a change in working conditions. Lack of pleasure in work can partially be compensated by richer and more meaningful leisure activities. But this does not make work itself more worthy of human beings. In order to put an end to human alienation, certain social changes are needed, among them a just wage system, industrial democracy and also a humane organization of work.[27]

Arthur Rich and Günter Brakelmann both provide more detailed proposals for alternative ways of organizing work. They both link their own proposals to the changes in the organization of work which have been put forward by Fred E Emery, Einar Thorsrud and other representatives of the so-called socio-technical school. Arthur Rich argues for employees participation in decision making at work place level, i.e. being able to influence how their own work is to be carried out. He agrees with Einar Thorsrud's proposal for partly self determining shop floor groups.[28] At the same time, he argues also for (a) job enlargement i.e. the employee is given more things to do (b) job-rotation i.e. increased variation in the work carried out and (c) job enrichment i.e. the employee is assigned more tasks demanding greater skill. Such a change in the organization of work leads to both increased production and reduced employee alienation.[29]

Rich puts forward two main arguments for an alternative organization of work along these lines. First of all, it encourages employee participation and partnership between the different contracting parties at the work place. Secondly it contributes to the solution of what Rich calls "the social question" by counteracting the dehumanization of human beings. The rationalizations inspired by Taylorism have resulted in work becoming inhuman and repetitive. What is needed now according to Rich is instead to reduce the monotony of work by increased variation in work which can be achieved *inter alia* by job enlargement. Thereby a humanization of the production process is brought about. By giving employees more duties they acquire increased responsibility in their work. The status of the employee is changed as a result and the employee becomes more of a subject and co-responsible member. Thus a humanization of the worker is brought about.[30]

A similar view about the organization of work is to be found in the writings of Günter Brakelmann. Like Brunner and Oldham, he criticizes an organization of work which involves repetitive tasks, far-reaching specialization and a low level of self-determination. He holds that such an organization of work is basically inhuman. Repetitive work of the kind advocated by F W Taylor leads to alienation, social isolation and a reduction of the employee's responsibility and personal creativity. Brakelmann also criticises Elton Mayo and the so-called human relations school. The latter are right about the significance they ascribe to the working group for the employee's motivation to work but like Taylorism they have been too uniformly concerned with the aim of increasing productivity.[31]

In criticising Taylorism and the human-relations school, Brakelmann argues for what he calls a "humanization of working life". Like the socio-technical school, he holds that this can be achieved through a system where the technological and social organization achieve an optimal unity. Brakelmann, like Rich, advocates an organization of work which has four basic characteristics. It is an organization with (a) job rotation which means that the employee alternates according to plan between different workplaces and tasks (b) job enlargement by which the employee becomes responsible for several tasks through by bringing together structurally similar elements of the production process (c) job enrichment which involves bringing together structurally dissimilar elements such as planning and production into larger units and (d) partly self-determining work groups which allow the employees greater say in how the work is carried out.[32]

Brakelmann's argument for such a socio-technical organization of work is based upon rights. He holds that all human beings have a right to humane conditions at work. Human beings do not simply have a right to work but also a right to meaningful work. This argument in turn is combined with a Christian based theory about the meaning of work. According to this theory, one should strive for humane work conditions and work which is worthy of human beings. Work conditions should be organized so that they show respect for the value of human beings.[33]

Günter Brakelmann also discusses the question of how one can control technological development given the rapid computerization of working life. He maintains that technology must not become an end in itself. Instead it should be seen as a means to achieve humane ends.[34] In itself, Brakelmann holds, technology is neither good nor evil. The key question concerns instead the goals it promotes. Technology should be organized so as to provide an optimal solution for the aims of human beings. In order for this to be the case, the employees must be given an opportunity to influence technological development.[35]

The participation question

Should the employees participate in decision-making? Should they have influence not simply at the shop-floor level but also at the company level in more strategic matters? Two answers have been proposed to this question by the thinkers I have chosen to study. One view is that adopted by Emil Brunner. He holds that this kind of participation in decision-making is contrary to a just division of economic power. Brunner criticizes attempts to bring about economic democracy and maintains that the majority are not always aware of what is in their best interest. Economic democracy, he writes, can destroy the economic order. The elimination of competent leadership in economic life is even more disastrous than it is in the sphere of politics.[36]

Brunner holds that a hierarchical order with genuine undelegated authority is required in economic life. It is just to have a hierarchical-patriarchal structure in economic life. At the same time, Brunner maintains that although the economic leader is not responsible to his workers, he is nonetheless responsible for them. He alone must make the key decisions but at the same time he must treat the workers as full members of the working community. Therefore they must be accorded a certain co-responsibility.[37]

Hitherto the capitalist as the owner of the means of production has alone had the right to determine working conditions. The worker has had no say in the matter. This, according to Brunner, is demeaning for the worker. He is deprived of his dignity as a human being.[38] To rectify this unjust situation, Brunner urges that the employer should be aware that as a master he is a servant. Competent leaders are needed but so also is a functioning work community. Employers must therefore "listen" to the workers and as far as possible give them responsibility.[39] While Brunner rejects employee participation in decision-making, he appears to advocate consultation that is to say, the board of the company should listen to the views of the employees before making a decision.

A completely different standpoint is adopted by Tor Aukrust. He advocates a general right of participation in decision-making i.e. industrial democracy through legislation. This participation can be exercised partly directly by the employees having influence over their own work situation and partly indirectly by the employees having their representatives on the board. The aim of such industrial democracy is according to Aukrust to increase the influence and responsibility of the employees, to promote cooperation between employees and management and to increase production efficiency by giving the employees greater responsibility and improving cooperation.[40]

Aukrust puts forward three arguments for the right to participate in decision-making. First of all, labour as well as capital gives a right to influence. Basic to the right to participate is an investment, that is to say, one has contributed something "of one's own" to the company. According to Aukrust, this does not need to be capital. We can also invest our time, our labour, our skill and our human worth. This form of investment which the employees also make, is according to Aukrust just as important as capital. Therefore labour also gives a right to participation in decision-making.[41]

Secondly, participation promotes cooperation and solidarity within the company. Aukrust refers to what he calls "the solidarity principle". A naturally given social group in which human beings depend upon one another, constitutes, he writes, a genuine community of interest. An important task is then to eliminate potential sources of conflict within the group and to try to achieve a real sense of community. This solidarity presupposes a fundamental notion of equality and therefore the employees should participate in decision-making.[42]

Thirdly the employees have a right to participation because they both have the capacity and willingness to shoulder responsibility. According to Aukrust, there is an inner connection between right and duty i.e. between the right to participate in decision-making on the one hand and ability and willingness for responsibility on the other. Individuals do not have a right to participate in decisions where they lack competence. Similarly participation requires a willingness to answer for the consequences of a decision. Participation is therefore identical with co-responsibility. Because both competence and willingness to shoulder responsibility is to be found among the employees, they have a right to influence.[43]

An even more penetrating argument for participation in decision-making is put forward by Arthur Rich. Unlike Brunner, he holds that it is not enough merely to consult the workers so that they can present their point of view before the management make their decision. Instead Rich believes that one should strive for participation which allows the workers via their representatives to play an active role in the decision process.[44] We should aim at such participation at three levels. First of all, employees should participate at company level which is possible only indirectly through the appointment of representatives to the board of the company. Rich recommends that the employees should have as many board representatives as the stockholders.[45] Secondly they should participate at departmental level so as to achieve participation and cooperation instead of confrontation and class struggle.[46] Thirdly the employees should participate at shop-floor level which can be achieved through partly self determining groups.[47] By means of such participation at all levels of the company, labour is given the same recognition as the other factors of production.[48]

Rich puts forward three arguments for participation in the decision-making process. The first is that participation in general is promoted. Rich holds that we should aim for cooperation between the factors of production – capital, labour and management. The aim should not be "confrontational cooperation" with – as in Marxism – an eye to the class struggle. Instead we should work towards "participatory cooperation" which implies participation and cooperation between the different factors of production. Participation in the decision-making process is, according to Rich, a means of achieving this kind of participatory cooperation. It is a way of involving the production

70

factor of labour in a participatory cooperation with the other factors of production. Its core feature is the cooperation and participation of the employees in the decision-making process.[49] According to Rich, such a division of power also brings about solidarity and "partnership" between those representing the different factors of production.[50]

Secondly the workers are said to have a right to participation in the decision-making process. This is an argument from rights of the kind already encountered in Aukrust. It is not simply capital but also labour which confers a right to influence. Rich holds that labour's right to participation in the decision-making process does not imply an end to the capital owners' right to have influence but rather its limitation and relativization. Such a limitation is entirely justified since the production factor labour also has a right to influence.[51]

Arthur Rich's third argument is that participation in decision-making is the best way of solving the social question. For him, "the social question" is concerned with how the industrial worker is to have a human status in modern working life.[52] In capitalist society where the workers do not own the means of production, there is a great risk for the worker being treated as a commodity. Human beings are dehumanized by being treated merely as "labour inputs" and not as responsible persons. The employee is degraded to the status of an impersonal object and is not treated as a subject with personal responsibility.[53] This dehumanization is brought about not least by the division of labour in industrial society which entails the atomization of work into parts and a division between the intellectual planning and manual production aspects of work.[54]

According to Rich, the solution of the social question lies in countering the treatment of human beings as commodities and their dehumanization. Rich discusses different attempts to solve the social question. One of them supposes that the problem can be solved through an increased standard of living but this is to overlook the fact that the problem is not simply a question of the level of material welfare. Another proposal is to compensate bad working conditions by increased and improved leisure facilities. This overlooks the fact that work is something which makes a human being a real human being. A third proposed solution suggests in the manner of Elton Mayo and the human relations movement, humanizing working conditions by consultation between the employers and the employees. This however, according to Rich, fails to achieve real partnership.[55] Consequently none of these suggestions is sufficient. The solution of the social question requires instead a change in the fundamental structures of working life.[56]

What kind of structural change is then required? One way of solving the social question is that proposed by Marxism, namely the collective ownership of the means of production. Rich criticizes this standpoint. Another approach is a humanization of the production process by job enlargement and job rotation. But according to Rich this is not sufficient. In addition there has to be a humanization of the conditions of production. This entails designing them so that not only those who represent capital but also the workers become co-responsible subjects. It is this which can be accomplished through participation in the decision-making process.[57]

Employee participation in decision-making is thus the best way to solve the social question. Once the workers are able to participate in the decision-making process, their subsidiary status in industry will be overcome. Their individual and collective status is altered so that they become co-responsible human beings. In this way the dehumanization of the employees and their reduction to the status of commodities can be successfully counteracted and the social problem thereby solved. Such a solution does not presuppose a socialization of the means of production. It is sufficient with employee participation and the cooperation between labour and capital which this participation makes possible.[58]

Günter Brakelmann adopts a position which in several respects is akin to Rich's. He argues for participation in decision-making in working life and defends the 1976 West German legislation regarding this. The employees have a right to participate in the decision-making process at all levels of working life, Brakelmann holds, and employees and employers ought to have equal representation on the decision-making bodies.[59] This does not presuppose a nationalization of the means of production nor does it imply a restriction in the right to private ownership. Instead Brakelmann advocates what he calls "participatory socialism" with the private ownership of the means of production and equal participation in the decision-making process for both stockholders and the employees. This allows for cooperation between people who are free and equal.[60]

Brakelmann's argument for participation in the decision-making process is above all an argument from rights. Both ownership and labour, he holds, give a right to influence. Ownership and labour are two "institutes of rights" which are equally necessary. Therefore one can equally speak of the right of ownership and the right of labour. Not only ownership but labour as well gives a fundamental right to participation in the decision-making process. The workers' right to participation is based on the fact that they contribute their physical and intellectual labour. The right to participation is founded on the very fact that human beings work and are expected to work. Brakelmann writes that it is a "Recht aus Arbeit".[61]

Participation in the decision-making process therefore does not conflict with liberty and fundamental rights as several employers have maintained.

72

Workers as well as capital owners have certain rights.[62] Nor does participation entail any restriction in the right of ownership. Both work and ownership give rights and both these rights are equally important. Just like the capital owners, workers have a right to participation in the decision-making process given that they contribute their labour.[63]

Brakelmann holds not merely that the right of labour is just as important as the right of the capital owner. He also writes that society should be organized so that labour has priority over capital. The reason for this is that work is intrinsic to human beings, a "proprium". Work has a fundamental significance for human beings and for their own view of themselves as human beings whereas property is not the same kind of intrinsic constituent of human existence.[64] For this reason Brakelmann holds that there should be a "partnership" between the factors of production, capital and labour. Such a partnership based on equal rights corresponds to parity in participation in the decision-making process, which entails that the employees have as great a say as the capital owners. Labour must not be subservient to capital and the capital owner has no right to the final say about decision-making.[65]

The system question

How should the economic system be organized? Who should own the means of production in a society and who is to decide what is to be produced and consumed? This question is dealt with in three different ways by the six theologians considered in this study. The first view is that to be found in J H Oldham and Tor Aukrust. They leave unanswered the question whether one should aim at a capitalist or socialist system. Instead they are content to specify more general guidelines about the organization of the economic system.

J H Oldham argues for production based on needs. The purpose of work, he writes, is to serve our neighbour and this implies that the main task of the economic order is to produce goods which are useful to the consumer. The aim of production is to maintain human life and this would seem according to Oldham to imply that we should try to achieve as high productivity as possible. At the same time, he maintains that we have to take account of the people employed in the production process. We also ought to strive for the greatest possible job satisfaction for the employees. Like the human relations school, Oldham however holds that increased job-satisfaction is a means to attaining the chief aim, namely higher productivity.[66]

The doctrine of vocation, however, does not only justify demands for increased productivity. Oldham also stresses that production should be organized so as to satisfy the needs of the whole man. The majority of trades and professions are important instruments in serving one's neighbour. Priests, teachers, health care personnel, social workers, artists, scientists and scholars, lawyers, farmers, industrial workers and craftsmen have all equally important tasks in ministering to the needs of their fellows.[67] But at the same time, Oldham maintains that there are types of activity in modern society which do more harm than good. The production of luxury goods of doubtful value or the production of weapons which can kill, can hardly be said to minister to the fundamental needs of human beings.[68]

The corollaries which Oldham derives from this observation, are primarily concerned with individual ethics. If some type of work does not answer to human needs then the Christian may wish to do something else. The doctrine of vocation is thus of primary importance in an individual's choice of career. It becomes a question of selecting a vocation which gives us the possibility of serving God and satisfying the needs of our fellow human beings. But Oldham also hints at certain social ethic consequences, certain recommendations for a change in the direction of production. The whole industrial structure should be organized so that production caters to important human needs and serves necessary social purposes. Moreover, writes Oldham, it is important that the conditions under which work is carried out are such that it is possible for human beings to feel that they are serving God and their fellows in their work. Changing these basic conditions of work often requires political activity. The Christian's task is to try to ensure that every job promotes the satisfaction of genuine human needs and that it does not prevent human self-realization.[69]

Oldham adopts no hard and fast position regarding the choice between a capitalist or socialist system. The same is true of Tor Aukrust. He does not wish to argue for a specific economic system. On the contrary, he emphasizes that there is no specifically Christian economic system and there is no social order which can be said to be uniquely Christian. Christian social ethics allows room for different viewpoints about how society should be organized.[70]

The important difference between different economic systems arises, according to Aukrust, when one balances the desire to achieve efficiency against the desire to achieve justice.[71] The advantage of the capitalist system with its market economy and the private ownership of the means of production, is that it promotes efficiency. On the other hand, this system gives less scope for justice and humane working conditions.[72] The advantage of the communist system with its planned economy and the collective ownership of the means of production is that it embodies a desire to do away with human alienation so that human beings can realize their intrinsic nature as human beings, while at the same time pursuing justice.[73] A third alternative is social democracy with social planning of the economy but the private ownership of the means of production. In this system, importance is also placed on striving after a just society where there is respect for the human value of the workers.[74] Aukrust however does not indicate which of these three alternatives he himself prefers.

The second way of dealing with the system question is to be found in the writings of Emil Brunner and Arthur Rich. Both advocate a capitalist system while recommending certain fundamental changes in it. Brunner holds that the economic system is part of the divine order of creation. Without this order, human beings cannot exist. In itself, Brunner writes, the economic system is ethically indifferent but it becomes ethically important as a means to attaining certain goals.[75] This implies that the economic order does not constitute an end in itself as economists have sometimes maintained. Instead it is a means for achieving other goals.[76]

What goals then should the economic order promote? Brunner's answer to this question is that it should constitute a means of serving our neighbour. Like Oldham, he holds that production should be aimed at satisfying needs. The goods and services produced should be those which satisfy fundmental human needs. According to Brunner, this is a fundamental thesis in the doctrine of vocation. This doctrine specifies that we must serve our neighbour in the economic order. There is no Christian economic programme, Brunner writes, but God's commandments and Will give guidelines for the economic system. The doctrine of vocation maintains that the primary purpose of the economic system is to satisfy human needs and maintain human life.[77]

How then is the economic system to be organized? Brunner criticizes capitalism, that is to say a system with private ownership of the means of production. This system entails that labour and thereby the worker are degraded to the status of a commodity. As a result work loses its value and the worker is treated as a means to an end.[78] According to Brunner, capitalism is too individualistic a system: it does not give sufficient scope for the individual's responsibility for the common good. From a Christian perspective, private property is not some absolute but exists within the limits set by the common good and common responsibilities. Human beings have a right to private ownership but this private ownership must promote the good of all the people. Therefore pure capitalism must be rejected.[79]

At the same time, Brunner also criticizes socialistic communism i.e. a system with the collective ownership of the means of production. He seems to hold that this system is far too collectivist. Without the private ownership of the means of production, there is no individual responsibility. Every individual is subject to the will of the collective. There is a danger in a socialist society that the state will have so much power that there is no room for individual liberty.[80] Brunner holds that according to the Christian view human beings are created by God to enjoy both freedom and community. Human beings are both individual and social beings. Capitalism emphasises freedom to the exclusion of community. Socialism does the reverse and emphasises community so much that the liberty of the individual is curtailed.[81]

As a result Brunner does not recommend the socialization of the means of production. He does not advocate a transfer of private property to collective ownership. Instead he proposes a limitation of the capitalist's right of disposition. He advocates a system of private ownership where the owners are responsible for the common good. Capitalism must also change so that the owners treat the workers not as objects serving their own interests but as subjects.[82] Moreover Brunner wishes to make room for both the free market and economic planning on the part of society. He proposes a market economy while simultaneously holding that state intervention is required. Left to itself, the market does not promote the common good. Economic planning is needed to promote both freedom and the common good.[83]

Like Brunner, Arthur Rich also accepts capitalism, while arguing for fundamental changes in this economic system. Rich discusses in some detail the question of how one is to judge socialism from the standpoint of Christian social ethics. Socialism seeks to solve the social question, i.e. the question of how the reduction of human beings to the status of commodities and their dehumanization can be countered. It holds that this can be achieved by the transfer of the means of production from private to public ownership. In this way, it is maintained, human alienation can be overcome and the worker transformed into a subject in working life.[84] In Rich's view, this however, has shown itself to be Utopian. The socialization of the means of production does not mean that the workers will achieve liberation. In socialist countries, the workers have not overcome their reduction to the status of objects but instead have been completely dominated by the party bureaucracy.[85]

Rich holds that socialism rightly draws attention to structural evils i.e. that social structures give rise to a dehumanization of human beings. But socialism in his view has a far too optimistic view of man. It believes that human beings can attain a decisive liberation by their own efforts for social change. This is however impossible, Rich claims. According to Christian belief, human beings can attain this liberation only in the Kingdom of God. There are in other words limits to what human beings can achieve here on earth. Socialism is a form of secular messianism which must be rejected.[86]

Rich criticizes a socialistic planned economy and argues for a market economy. He does not accept a completely free and unregulated market. The market has to be regulated in order to protect the environment and to promote international justice and a new economic world order. However, this does not require a planned economy.[87]

Nor according to Rich, does the solution of the social question require the collective ownership of the means of production. Instead he recommends participation in the decision-making process and changes in the organization of work. The social question is to be solved not through socialism but through participation i.e. a cooperation between labour and capital with the retention of the private ownership of the means of production.[88]

Rich criticizes institutions of ownership where the majority are excluded from joint ownership and joint control of the productive property. A concentration of property in relatively few hands leads to an exclusive position of power and is inconsistent with striving for human fellowship. He holds that instead one should aim for partnership which can be achieved by the employees becoming joint owners of the means of production through the acquisition of shares, and by participation in decision-making i.e. representation on the board.[89] The decisive point however is not who owns the means of production but how decisions are reached i.e. how power is distributed within the company. As in the case of the question of participation in the decision-making process, the question of ownership must be judged on the basis of the social ethical criterion of "participation" so that the employees obtain influence.[90]

A third approach to the system question is to be found in the writings of Günter Brakelmann and John Atherton. Both favour democratic socialism. Brakelmann has a detailed discussion of the question of whether such a democratic socialism is compatible with the kind of social ethics associated with Christian belief. He maintains that a Christian can be a socialist although Christian ethics and the socialist viewpoint are not identical. Personally Brakelmann believes that democratic socialism is the best system and has many important similarities with Christian social ethics.[91]

One argument for democratic socialism is that it promotes such values as freedom and justice. It is wrong, Brakelmann asserts, to maintain that socialism entails lack of freedom. On the contrary, social democracy has been the major force in the struggle for freedom and justice. It has defended democratic society while at the same time it has worked for social justice.[92]

Another argument in favour of democratic socialism, according to Brakelmann, is that it has a reformist view of society. It regards its aims as relative and works for permanent reforms. A socialist society is not conceived as static and perfect but rather as a society where values like freedom, justice and solidarity can be realized to a great extent. This view is very similar to the view of society which is associated with Christian ethics, according to which it is necessary to be continually changing human social institutions.[93]

A third reason in favour of democratic socialism, according to Brakelmann, is that it is humanistic and personalistic, in the sense that its goal is the individual as a person. Its aim is for man to be treated as a subject and not as an object. It therefore strives for the participation of all men in decision-making. This implies not simply a formal right to influence but substantial and equivalent participation for all those involved in politics, economics and education. The goal is a democratization of all areas of life and not only of political life.[94]

A fourth reason in favour of democratic socialism is that it draws attention to the importance of the equal value of all human beings. It sees human beings as equal partners with equal rights. As a result, it constitutes the most consistent political attack upon a non-egalitarian society. In this, there is an affinity with Christian belief which professes the equal value of all men and therefore fights against social inequality.[95]

Brakelmann maintains that neither private ownership nor collective ownership of the means of production constitute some final goal. It is important to have a certain critical distance to both these forms of ownership. The important thing however is that ownership does not lead to abuse of power and that the economic system is designed to promote the general good.[96]

According to Brakelmann, society should be designed so that work is given a central place. It is not ownership but working together which constitutes the basis of society. Work has therefore a high value and takes priority over property. For this reason, one ought to pay more attention to the rights associated with work.[97] Such a work based society according to Brakelmann also promotes justice. Differences in income and wealth are now too great so that economic levelling is required. Brakelmann seems to take the view that democratic socialism more than other systems promotes justice and accords work a central place.[98]

John Atherton also recommends democratic socialism. He presents detailed arguments against *laissez-faire* capitalism where the free market is a law unto itself and the state's activities are restricted to a minimum. *Laissez-faire*'s minimalistic view of the state is inadequate because human beings as stewards, have a responsibility for their fellow men and the environment.[99] The market economy certainly promotes the freedom of the individual but it cannot deal with environmental destruction and resource limitation. Nor does it provide for the needs of medical care and education. It appears to lead to poverty, income differences and the economic concentration of power. *Laissez-faire* capitalism is also combined with an inadequate moral viewpoint which lays too great an emphasis upon self-interest. It thereby neglects

78

the fact that the goal of the economic system is to promote the common good.[100]

Atherton also criticises Marxist state socialism where production and the allocation of resources is looked after not by the market but by the state according to a centralized plan. He holds that this kind of socialism takes too rosy a view of the state. Centralization leads to inefficiency and lack of freedom of choice for the citizens.[101] A centrally planned economy can lead to increased growth and reduced unemployment but it lacks an efficient price system and fails to pay sufficient attention to consumers. Nor is the accompanying Marxist moral viewpoint a good one since it neglects human rights. Moreover, in believing that human beings can become good in the classless society, it adopts too positive a view of man.[102]

According to Atherton, one should aim for a society which is democratic and which provides scope for several political alternatives. He also recommends a market economy since the market is a excellent device for the production and allocation of resources.[103] He therefore prefers what he calls "democratic capitalism" to laissez-faire capitalism and state socialism. It is a society with political democracy and a mixed economy with great scope for private ownership. Great emphasis is placed on the market although the state is assigned a certain role in promoting justice.[104]

An even better alternative, according to Atherton, is however democratic socialism. It is a democratic society with a market economy where one also relies upon state planning to promote justice and equality. The state has a responsibility to promote the common good with the result that the market is not accorded as much freedom as under democratic capitalism. In such a society, there is democracy in both political and economic life. Democratic socialism, according to Atherton, aims for both equality and freedom. It seeks to iron out income differences, it advocates cooperation rather than individualism and competition and at the same time it rejects state bureaucracy and large scale public ownership.[105]

Conclusion

What work ethical recommendations are to found in the writings of present day Protestant theologians? What are their views about the solution of the employment problem, the wage question, the organization problem, the participation question and the system question? In this chapter we have seen that the six theologians whom I deal with give to some extent different solutions to these problems in work ethics.

We have encountered two differing views about how the employment problem is to be solved. One we may call "the full employment line". It holds that society should give prominence to full employment. This standpoint can be found in Emil Brunner who however does not provide more detailed suggestions about possible measures to reduce unemployment. The other view is what we can call "the work sharing line". It suggests that unemployment can be reduced by a reduction in working hours and work sharing. Through a reduction in working hours, more employment opportunities are created and a more just division of the work available is brought about. This viewpoint is put forward by Günter Brakelmann and John Atherton. Both hold that everyone has a right to work and that society ought to take also other measures to create new jobs.

There are also two views regarding the wage question. One can be called "the merit line". It holds that the principle of merit is the most important critieria for a just wage. According to this principle, it is entirely just that someone whose results are superior receives more money. This is the view of Emil Brunner who assigns the merit principle precedence over a principle of need according to which each and every one who does their best, ought to have a chance to have a humanly tolerable life. The second view can be called "the equal wages line". It maintains that the principle of equal pay which respects each and every one's needs and the equal value of all human beings, should be fulfilled as far as possible. This is the view of Tor Aukrust who simultaneously believes that one must allow room, where necessary, for wage differences which take into account the difference in effort put into their work by different human beings.

There are two different answers given to the organization problem in the material studied. There is first of all "the human relations line". It holds that one should avoid organizing work in such a way that there is too far reaching a division of labour and rationalisation and where individuals become replaceable and cannot see the purpose of their work. This view is to be found in Emil Brunner, J H Oldham and Tor Aukrust. They do not however offer any proposals for how an alternative organization of work should be set up. The second view is one we can call "the socio-technical line". It maintains that work should be organized to give more scope for job enlargement, job rotation and job enrichment and partly self determining work groups. This view is held by Arthur Rich and Günter Brakelmann who like the socio-technical school argue for an organization of work where the technological and social organization achieve an optimal unity.

Also in the case of the participation question, there are two distinct views to be found in contemporary Protestant work ethics. There is what can be called "the consultation line". It holds that key decisions are the exclusive responsibility of the company board but at the same time before making a decision the board should listen to the views of the employees. This is the approach adopted by Emil Brunner. He holds that participation in decision-making is contrary to a just division of economic power. The second viewpoint can be called "the participation line". It holds that employees should participate in decision-making not only at factory-floor level, as regards their own work and its conditions, but also at the company level as regards more strategic matters. This view is to be found in the writings of Tor Aukrust, Arthur Rich and Günter Brakelmann who believes that the employees should have as many representatives on company decision bodies as the employers.

The system question is dealt with in three different ways by the theologians I study. There is first of all "the indifference line". According to this position, no fixed line is adopted about whether one should aim for a capitalist or socialist system. It is sufficient to have general guidelines for the economic system. This is the line put forward by J H Oldham and Tor Aukrust. Secondly there is "the reform line". The capitalist system, subject to certain proposed fundamental changes, is recommended. This is the position of Emil Brunner who holds that private ownership should be combined with a restriction on the rights of disposal of the owners of capital, and with social economic planning aimed at the common good. This view is shared by Arthur Rich, who holds that the private ownership of the means of production ought to be combined with participation in the decision-making process and a socio-technical organization of work. The third view can be called "the socialization line". It proposes democratic socialism as a goal. This is a society which embodies both political and economic democracy. It has a market economy but also state economic planning in order to reduce economic differences in society. This viewpoint is adopted by Günter Brakelmann and John Atherton.

What types of consideration form the basis for these different work ethical recommendations? What are the arguments adduced by these six theologians for their proposals regarding working life? There are four different types of theory and considerations which form the basis of these recommendations.

First of all, these work ethical recommendations are combined with different theories of the meaning of work. Brunner adopts a version of a Protestant doctrine of vocation. He holds that work is part of the divine order of creation and that human beings through their work become God's co-workers in the creation. One purpose of work according to Brunner is to serve our fellow human beings. We are called in our work to serve one another. This theory forms the basis of Brunner's argument for what I have called the full employment line and the human relations line. It also forms the basis of his view that the economic order ought to be designed to become a means for serving our neighbour.

81

Oldham also holds that the purpose of work is to serve our fellow human beings and to bring about those things which satisfy the needs of human beings. For this reason, he holds that the economic system should be designed to promote high productivity and to cater for needs. Oldham also maintains that human beings at work are creative individuals – God's co-workers in his continuous act of creation. Work should therefore be organized so that it provides, as far as possible, scope for creative professional skills.

The view that work must contribute to human beings' self-realization is to be found in the theory of the meaning of work espoused by Aukrust. As a result he holds that anything which contributes to the self-alienation of human beings must be opposed. One should try to organize work in such a way that it is worthy of human beings. For this reason, Aukrust believes that one should aim both for a change in the organization of work and for participation in decision-making. The latter helps in ensuring that work is an activity worthy of human beings.

Rich's arguments are also based upon certain views about the purpose and value of work. He holds that the essential humanity of human beings should emerge in work, in the sense that they do not simply function as objects but as responsible persons. This presupposes that employees also are able to participate in the decision-making process in working life.

Günter Brakelmann holds that work is a mandate received by human beings from God at the creation. This implies that it is a constituent of a truly human existence. For this reason, all human beings have a duty to work. This duty is the basis for man's right to work which is the fundamental reason for seeking to reduce unemployment. The basis of what I have called the socio-technical line is according to Brakelmann that human beings also have a right to a meaningful and humane work. Since work is a constituent of human existence, the worker also has a right to participation in the decision-making process.

In Atherton's exposition, the work sharing line is combined with certain views about the purpose and value of work. He holds that all human beings have a right to work since work is meaningful and is assigned a high value. At the same time, he holds that other activities besides paid employment are valuable as a means of contributing to society.

Secondly the work ethical recommendations encountered in the writings of contemporary Protestant theologians are combined with differing social ethical theories. Emil Brunner holds that a right political action must agree with God's intentions with the divine orders of creation. Work and the economic order constitute one such order. Fundamental to Brunner's social ethical theory is a principle for just distribution according to which the good should be so distributed that each and every one receives their due (suum cuique). This implies that we must take into account both similarities and dissimilarities between human beings. In Brunner, this principle of justice is combined both with the merit line and the the consultation line.

The social ethical theory which is held by Aukrust includes several moral principles. One of these is a principle of the equal value of all human beings. Aukrust's views about the wage question and the organization problem is based upon this principle. His theory also includes a principle of just distribution, which is the basis for what I have called the equal wages line.

Arthur Rich sets forth a social ethical theory which includes several social ethical criteria. These form the basis of his arguments for the participation line. One of Rich's fundamental principles is that one should aim for participation and partnership, that is to say cooperation bettween human beings in institutions. It is such cooperation between the different factors of production where everyone participates that can be achieved through participation in the decision-making process. Another basic principle is that one should oppose the dehumanization of human beings and their reduction to the status of things. Participation in the decision-making process is a means of solving the social question by promoting the humanization of human beings.

The social ethical theory espoused by Brakelmann includes the view that one should stand up for certain fundamental human rights. All men have a right to work and therefore one should seek to reduce unemployment by work sharing. Everyone has a right to meaningful work and therefore one should strive for a humane organization of work. Work establishes a right to participation in the decision-making process and therefore the employees in a company should have as great an influence as the capital owners. In his argument for the socialization line, Brakelmann also cites the principle of the equal value of all human beings as well as such basic values as freedom and justice.

The socialization line in Atherton is also combined with a social ethical theory. It involves the views that one should seek the common good and not only one's own interest, that one should try to achieve a just distribution of the good, that one should stress both the importance of freedom and equality and that one should respect certain basic human rights.

Thirdly these theologians' work ethical recommendations are combined with certain assertions about matters of fact which are empirically testable. In general it is a question of claims that certain measures have certain probable consequences. These can be said to constitute a kind of common human consideration in the sense that they are independent of the philosophy of life which is held. They are based upon theoretical convictions which have nothing to do with a philosophy of life.

Aukrust's work ethical recommendations are based upon such assertions about factual circumstances. The formulation of such recommendations, he holds, requires a situational analysis i.e. a description of society and the situation of human beings. In Aukrust, the participation line is also combined with certain assertions about the probable consequences of acts. Thus for example he holds that participation in decision-making promotes solidarity and cooperation and thereby also lead to more efficient production.

The recommendations about work ethics put forward by Rich and Brakelmann also are based upon such assertions about matters of fact. In his arguments Rich cites the probable consequences of different types of decision-making and different ways of organizing work. He is primarily interested in their consequences for employee participation and for the humanization of human beings. Brakelmann holds that a society based on democratic socialism will probably achieve goals such as freedom and justice.

Atherton's social analysis is of great importance for his treatment of the system question and the employment problem. He analyses the possibilities which different economic systems have to actually promote efficient production and the allocation of scarce resources. On the basis of this analysis, he recommends a market economy. Atherton also makes an assessment of the probability of once again achieving full employment. Since he holds that this probability is low, he recommends work sharing so that all those who wish to do so can share in the available employment opportunities.

Fourthly the work ethical recommendations which are encountered in the writings of contemporary Protestant theologians are also combined with differing theories of human nature. This is clearest in the case of J H Oldham. He holds that human beings are persons, whose lives constitute a conversation with God and are also social beings which stand in relation to other human beings. This view of man forms the basis of his view that work should be organized so that it does not involve too far-reaching rationalization and division of labour. When human beings in their work are forced to become mere operators, anonymous replaceable parts in a mechanical process, work loses its personal quality. It no longer promotes personal development but on the contrary constitutes a threat to human beings as persons. Rationalization and the division of labour also make it more difficult for human beings to feel that they are social beings who in their work fulfil a useful social function. The employee does not see the finished product and has therefore difficulty in perceiving their own efforts as a contribution to the good of the community.

The treatment of the system question in Brunner, Rich and Atherton is also combined with a view of man. Brunner holds that human beings are created both for freedom and community. He therefore criticizes capitalism because it forgets community and socialism because it restricts freedom. Rich holds that human beings can attain final liberation only in the Kingdom of God. In the here and now, their possibilities are limited. He therefore holds that socialism has too optimistic a view of man when it holds that human beings can attain final liberation by social change. A similar criticism of socialism's over optimistic view of man is to be found in Atherton.

We have therefore discovered that there are four different types of consideration which form the basis of the work ethical recommendations put forward within contemporary Protestant theology. They are theories of the meaning of work, social ethical theories, assertions about matters of fact and theories of human nature. Assertions about matters of fact constitute a kind of common human consideration i.e. they are theoretical considerations which are independent of the philosophy of life held. The connections between these different components can be illustrated as follows:

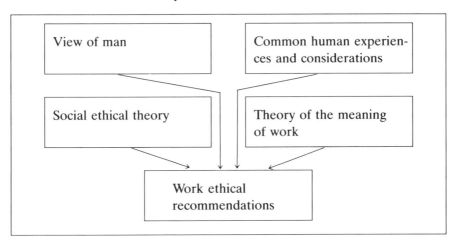

The illustrated connections are valid in the cases of Arthur Rich and John Atherton. There are no explicit references to common human considerations in Emil Brunner and J H Oldham. Nor does Oldham refer to his social ethical theory when he sets forth his recommendations concerning work ethics. Tor Aukrust and Günter Brakelmann make no explicit reference to their view of man when they make proposals about how working conditions should be changed.

3. Theories of the meaning of work

In the previous chapter, we have seen that the differing work ethical recommendations to be found within the contemporary Protestant work ethics, are motivated *inter alia* by differing theories of the meaning of work. These are theories which contain views about the purpose of work, about how work is related to human self-realization, about what value should be placed on work as an activity and about what drives human beings to work hard and efficiently. The theories of the meaning of work put forward by contemporary Protestant theologians are in general revised versions of the doctrine of vocation. They are often, however, also related to theories within other philosophies of life and ideologies.

The aim of the present chapter is first of all to clarify the content of the differing theories of the meaning of work which are put forward by contemporary Protestant work ethicists. This will be done by raising four analytical questions with reference to the material studied. (1) What is the purpose of work? This question deals with the end or ends, for the sake of which the activity of work is carried out. (2) How is work related to human self-realization? This question is concerned with whether work is a means of attaining self-realization in some sense or whether we realize ourselves through other activities. (3) What value should be assigned to work? That is to say, what value does work have in comparison with other human activities and what are the underlying grounds for these judgements? (4) What drives human beings to work? That is to say, what is it that can serve as a motivation for employees to work harder and more efficiently than they do at present?[1]

In order to elucidate the authors' views about the purpose and value of work, I try to indicate how they judge and revise the doctrine of vocation as presented in earlier Lutheran and Calvinist theology. As we have seen in Chapter 1, Martin Luther asserted in his doctrine of vocation that the purpose of work was first of all to constitute an instrument for God's continuous act of creation. Secondly the purpose of work is to fulfil the commandment to serve our neighbour by caring for what is good for others. Above all, in our work we must obey the fourth commandment which enjoins us to obey our superiors. Luther also holds that work is suffering in the imitation of Christ. When we serve others in our vocation, we meet with difficulties and reverses and in so doing, we sacrifice ourselves for the sake of other human beings. According to the Lutheran doctrine of vocation, work has a relatively high value as an instrument for God's continuous act of creation and as a means of bringing about what is good for others.

In Calvinist theology, as we have seen, the doctrine of vocation is given a somewhat different formulation. When Max Weber writes about "the Protestant ethic" he deals with the idea of vocation which is to be found in English Puritanism and primarily in Richard Baxter. The latter holds that it is our duty to work hard because work is an ascetic means which prevents a depraved life. At the same time he maintains that work is an end-in-itself ordained by God. Baxter's doctrine of vocation is combined with a doctrine of double predestination. God has already chosen His own but by working hard and carrying out good deeds one can attain certainty that one belongs to the elect.

I wish to enquire how contemporary Protestant work ethicists judge these differing forms of the doctrine of vocation. Do they hold that it is possible to revise the doctrine so that it can be put forward today as a reasonable theory of the meaning of work? What content do they then ascribe to this doctrine? Or do they hold that they doctrine must today be surrendered for some other theory of the purpose and value of work? In this case what are their objections to this doctrine?

In order to clarify the views of these theologians I shall also try to indicate how they stand in relation to five other theories of the meaning of work. The first of these theories I call "a Platonic theory of work". It cultivates views about the purpose and value of work which are to be found in Plato and Aristotle. According to this theory, work has a relatively low value. Human beings cannot realize themselves through work, in the sense of fulfilling that aspect of themselves which is specific for human beings as such. What is specifically human, is that human beings are rational so that self-realization is attained through philosophical contemplation and not through work. The purpose of work is in part to obtain those resources which are necessary for the maintenance of life and in part to produce those things which are useful to other human beings. On the other hand, work is not an activity which allows the worker to achieve happiness and contentment. Consequently manual work in particular has a lower value than other human activities.[2]

The second theory I shall call "a Marxist theory of work". It puts forward certain views to be found in Karl Marx, both in his theory of alienation and in his theory of surplus value. This theory views work as a necessary precondition of self-realization. The aim of work is in part to give the worker resources for his maintenance and in part to produce those things which satisfy the needs of other men. In addition, the purpose of work is also to allow human beings to realize themselves as a self-conscious being. What distinguishes human beings as a species from animals according to this theory is the fact that they are conscious and as conscious beings they are able to realize themselves through purposeful and creative work. According to Marxist theory, work is valuable because it is a means of creating products which satisfy human needs, because it can provide the worker with happiness and freedom and because it can be a means to human self-realization. In capitalist society, work is alienated but in the classless society is emerges as an activity of great value.[3]

The third theory may be called "a Taylorist theory of work". It is based on certain views about the purpose and value of work which are to be found in Frederick Winslow Taylor's theory of "scientific management". A Taylorist theory maintains that human beings' primary motive in working efficiently is the desire for economic gain for themselves. The purpose of work is in part to provide employees with the economic resources needed for increasing their material affluence and in part to produce the goods and services needed by others, thus increasing the welfare in society. On the other hand, work according to this theory is not a vehicle for human self-realization. Thus work has a relatively low value. It has a certain value as a means to the maintenance of life and increased welfare in society but it has a lower value than those leisure activities which satisfy our needs.[4]

The fourth theory to be considered is "the human relations school theory of work" which is based on ideas about the meaning of work shared by the industrial psychologists Elton Mayo and JAC Brown. According to this theory, individual attitudes to work are largely determined by the informal work group to which the individual belongs. This group influences employee attitudes by creating norms about the efforts that are expected of the employee. In this sense the main driving forces behind work are social ones. The theory maintains that certain social needs should be satisfied through work. The purpose of work is not simply to produce goods and services which increase social welfare and provide the employee with economic resources to satisfy needs outside of work. Its aim is also to satisfy the employee's need of social status, approval, emotional security and social intercourse. When these aims are achieved, work has a relatively high value.[5]

The fifth theory to be considered may be called "a socio-technical theory of work". It develops views which are to be found in a number of contemporary industrial psychologists and sociologists such as Fred E Emery, Einar Thorsrud, Robert Blauner, Bertil Gardell and Paul Blumberg. According to this theory, the primary human driving force behind working efficiently is the desire to satisfy certain higher psychological needs. The purpose of work is both to produce what is useful for others and to satisfy the employee's need for freedom, meaning, social integration and self-fulfilment. According to a socio-technical theory, work can and should be a means to self-fulfilment. This does not imply that employees are able to realize through their work what is specific for human beings considered as a species but that they are thereby able to develop their individual talents. To the extent that work constitutes a means of satisfying the higher psychological needs of the employee, it has a higher value compared with other human activities.[6]

My query is now how those present day Protestant writers about work ethics whom I have chosen to study, judge the content of these five theories of the meaning of work. These theologians often explicitly express opinions about the views which form part of these theories. They often discuss the relation between the doctrine of vocation and a Platonic or Marxist theory of work. They often relate their own views to different theories in modern industrial psychology. By clarifying their assessment of these theories, I shall be able to make their own views about the purpose and value of work clearer.

The aim of this chapter is however not merely to elucidate the content of these theologians' theories of the meaning of work. A secondary aim is to clarify the type of arguments they put forward for their differing theories. What kind of considerations and theories form the basis of their views regarding the purpose and value of work? Are they motivated by certain constructive social ethical theories which contain views about the characteristics of a right action? Are they combined with certain theories of human nature i.e. about what it is that is sets human beings apart as a species and what are the needs of human beings? Are they combined with other theoretical views which are part of their philosophy of life? Or is it possible to argue for these theories by referring to considerations and experiences of a common human character? I also hope to provide answers to these questions in the present chapter.

Work as an order of creation

One of Emil Brunner's fundamental theses is that work belongs to the Divine order of creation. One of the orders of creation which Brunner writes about is "die Arbeitsgemeinschaft". According to this, we are required to work because it is God's will and it is also part of man's nature to do so. Brunner therefore criticizes a Platonic theory which holds that work, especially manual work, should be avoided because man is intended for other more important activities. He also criticizes what he holds to be the view of Medieval Catholic theology, namely that the ideal life is "vita contemplativa", that human beings did not work in Paradise and that work is something which came into existence first with the Fall. According to Brunner, work is an activity which accords with God's will in the Creation. It is an activity which belongs to the fundamental conditions for human existence.[7]

Brunner also maintains that human beings in their work are God's co-workers in His continuous act of creation. The primary purpose of work is to be an instrument for the divine work of creation. Through their work, human beings are to reign over nature and be its stewards. This does not imply that human beings have a right to tyrannize and destroy nature. Like modern environmental thinkers, Brunner speaks of nature having an intrinsic value which must be respected. But at the same time, he emphasizes that human beings are created in the image of God and as such are placed over nature. Human beings have a right to rule over nature and to reshape it. This is accomplished through their work.[8]

A second purpose of work, in Brunner's view, is to serve one's neighbour. The Creator gives us what we need for our maintenance on condition that we as human beings in our work serve one another. Thus in our work, we function as "larvae Dei", the masks of God, instruments for the Divine care of our fellow human beings. Work is a means of obtaining what we need for our own survival and for creating a humane civilisation. But the primary purpose of work is to serve our fellow human beings. Through this service of others, Brunner writes, we glorify our Creator and obey His will. It is a "vocation" which is given by God. This vocation applies to different types of work, both intellectual and manual. Even manual labour can constitute "spiritual work" in the sense that it accords with God's Will and serves the human community.[9]

Is work a means for attaining human self-realization in some sense? Emil Brunner does not deal with this question explicitly. His view that work belongs to the fundamental conditions of human existence and is an intrinsic part of human nature, could, however, be considered as an answer to this question. Brunner would seem to hold that work is one of the activities by means of which human beings are able to achieve a truly human life.

What value has work in comparison with other human activities? We have seen that work according to Brunner belongs to the divine order of creation and is a means for His continuous act of creation. As such it is something valuable and an important activity in human life. It does not generally have a lower value than other activities. Nor is it the case that manual labour has a lower value than intellectual work. What makes work valuable is above all its being a means of serving one's neighbour. Brunner writes that the service of our neighbour forms a criterion of a good work. It is our duty to do that work which best serves human life. That work serves our neighbour is the criterion that it is morally valuable. A work which is not in harmony with the ideal of serving our fellow men, lacks value. This is how, according to Brunner, the purpose of work determines how human beings are to work and the type of work that they must do.[10]

At the same time, Brunner also emphasizes that work does not have an intrinsic value. The Sabbath commandment which obliges us to rest, he writes, is an indication that work is not an end in itself. This assertion can be interpreted to mean that there are other things in life which are just as important as work. Work must not dominate life and we ought also to rest. Work and rest are together part of life's rhythm where there is a balance between different activities. We have right to enjoy ourselves and to be glad. Rest, weariness and joy are important parts of life. At the same time, Brunner wishes to underline the fact that work is not an end in itself but should be directed towards the service of others and thereby dedicated to the glory of God.[11]

According to Brunner, work can also be a curse. It can be abused and thus become a curse instead of a blessing. This occurs when human beings abuse their task of ruling over nature. This task must be carried out in accordance with God's Will and His purpose with the creation. Sin and pride, *hubris*, can however lead us to ignore the Will of God, with the result that our civilizing activities become a curse.[12] It can also lead to the individual losing the meaning and joy of work. Human beings begin to worship things instead of God and communion between men is dissolved. Man loves not human beings but only things. Work loses its dignity and becomes a form of slavery and civilization degenerates. Brunner holds that this happens in the materialistic civilisation of today. Human beings become bound to things, money dominates the world and the value of work becomes lost.[13]

Brunner's theory of the meaning of work has great similarities to the doctrine of vocation as it is formulated by Martin Luther. Like Luther, Brunner holds that human beings by their work are God's co-workers in creation. Work belongs to the order of creation and its purpose is to constitute an instrument for God's continuous act of creation. Like Luther, Brunner also maintains that the purpose of work is to serve our fellow human beings. It is precisely in this sense that work can be understood as a "vocation" which is given by God. The criterion that work is valuable, is also that it is a means of serving our neighbour. Such service of our neighbour can be performed both in manual and intellectual work.

In these respects there are evident similarities between Brunner's work ethics and Luther's doctrine of vocation. Unlike Luther, however, Brunner does not maintain that work is a cross, a suffering in the imitation of Christ. Instead he seems to mean that work should also give joy and contentment to those who do it. At the same time, Brunner maintains that work is not an end in itself. It is only a means to achieving other ends and there are other things in life which are just as important as work.

What then is Brunner's opinion of those theories of work which are to be found in other philosophies of life? As we have seen, he criticizes the negative view of work, especially of manual labour, taken by a Platonic theory. Work is not a necessary evil which ought to be avoided and to give way for other more important activities. For work, Brunner holds, belongs to God's order of creation and therefore it is the Will of God that we have to work, including engaging in manual occupations. It is not the case that we should try to evade work in order to devote ourselves instead to the more valuable theoretical life.[14]

Brunner's theory exhibits on the other hand certain similarities to some ideas which are to found in a Marxist theory of work. Civilization, he writes, is the result of work. Civilization is the process through which nature is placed at the disposal of human beings for their own ends. This occurs with the help of human rational activity. This line of reasoning has affinities with a Marxist theory of work. Brunner writes that human beings work primarily to obtain resources for survival. But there is an important difference between the work of human beings and animal activity to maintain life. Animals do not work; they merely obey their instincts. Human work by contrast has a conscious purpose. It is a conscious, purposeful – not an instinctive – activity. Like Marx, Brunner also emphasizes that humans are social beings. They are necessarily members of a society and carry out their work in cooperation with others.[15]

Work as service to one's fellow human beings

What is the meaning of work according to J H Oldham? In his book, *Work in Modern Society* his aim is above all to formulate a Christian doctrine about the meaning of work which can be applied in accordance with the conditions of modern society.[16] But what has the Christian view of life to say about the meaning of work? In his answer to this question, Oldham refers to the doctrine of vocation in Protestant theology. According to the Christian view of man, human beings are called to live in the world and to serve God in their earthly lives. This, writes Oldham, is a fundamental point in the Protestant doctrine of vocation. According to this doctrine, the Christian does not first and foremost serve God by retiring from the world and entering a monastery but by their everyday occupation. The monastic order is not the supreme expression of a Christian life: rather we are called to carry out ordinary work and to live in the world. All work, Oldham writes, is considered as service to God.[17]

Like Brunner, Oldham writes that work is laid down by God. Work as such belongs to the divine order of creation. Without work, human beings cannot survive. It is essential as a means of maintaining humanity's existence. As such, work also is part of God's purpose with human beings. It is an important expression of the essential nature of humans as beings created in the image of God. The task of human beings is to rule over all living things and to cooperate with God in his continuous act of creation. This is accomplished by work. In all work, there is also an element of toil and monotony. This, according to Oldham, is the result of the Fall. But work as such predates the Fall. It is ordained by God as part of the order of creation.[18]

What then is the purpose of work? Oldham writes that the purpose of work is first of all to serve one's fellow human beings. The purpose of both manual and intellectual work is that it should serve our neighbour and the community to which we belong. According to Oldham, the notion that work must serve our neighbour is an integral part of the Christian view of man. According to this view, human beings are both persons and social beings. Since they are not isolated individuals but social beings, their work becomes meaningful only inasmuch as it serves society. Oldham writes:

>"Work in the Christian view is inseparable from service to our fellow-men. The understanding of work in this sense is inherent in the conception of man as existing not in individual isolation but in community and in responsibility for his 'neighbour'. Work has a Christian meaning only if the occupation is one by which society is truly served."[19]

The purpose of work, according to Oldham, is secondly to take part in God's act of creation. He writes that human beings in their work are God's co-workers in the process of creation. Work is shared creation. In this view of human beings as reshapers of the world, there emerges a profound difference between Christian attitude to work and that associated with classical Greek philosophy. Human beings are commanded in Genesis to rule over the earth and in Oldham's view this is tantamount to saying that work has to be creative and human beings co-workers in the divine act of creation. This also means that it is desirable that work is transformed into a creative activity in the sense that one makes use of the skills of human beings and that tasks at work as far as possible provide scope for almost artistic creation. This is not possible in all types of work. Within modern industry there are, for example, many types of work which must be carried out irrespectively of whether they provide an opportunity for creative skill or not. But, Oldham says, one should try as far as possible to accomplish this end.[20]

How is work related to human self-realization? Oldham answers this question somewhat differently from Brunner. He emphasizes that it is not simply through work that human beings attain a truly human life. In his view, work constitutes only part of a human being's life. Leisure is also required. The combination of work and leisure, Oldham holds, is important and human beings must devote themselves both to work and the contemplative life. Together they contribute to a rounded development of personality.[21] Work has its limits, Oldham writes, and must not be seen as an end in itself. Human beings attain their supreme definition not in their work but in communion and worship.[22] These assertions of Oldham suggests that he rejects Marx's view that human beings realize themselves as a species by devoting themselves to work, i.e. vita activa. Oldham's view seems to be that the vita contemplativa, worship and rest are a fundamental means for human self-realization.

What value has work in relation to other human activities? Oldham holds that work is valuable as a means of serving one's fellow human beings and of producing those things answering to the needs of others. It is also valuable as an activity whereby human beings participate in God's continuous act of creation. Oldham also rejects the view that spiritual and cultural work is more valuable than manual work of various kinds. Both manual and intellectual work are valuable as a means of serving our fellow human beings. At the same time, Oldham stresses that work is neither an end in itself nor the most important element in life. As we have seen, it is not in work but in communion and joy that human beings attain their supreme definition. For this reason, work is not the most valuable human activity.[23]

Oldham writes that work in our society is often viewed as the real content of life, the highest value in life and as a thing of value in itself. Frequently it has been regarded as an end in itself and as an activity whereby human beings can attain ultimate liberation. In both liberalism and socialism, the importance of work has been stressed with the aim of inspiring people to maximum industry and productivity.[24] Oldham however rejects such an attitude to work. Work is not an end in itself nor is it life's sole fulfilment. Oldham writes:

> "In the Christian view work is not only an obligation; it also has its limits. Work is not an end in itself, nor the sole fulfilment of man's existence. His life is made up of activity and rest, work and worship, in rhythmical succession."[25]

What then are the forces which drive human beings to work hard and efficiently? Like the human relations school, Oldham holds that these forces are above all social ones. In order to understand human motives for working one must note the significance of the work group. As Elton Mayo has shown in the so called Hawthorne investigations, it is this work group, Oldham writes, which shapes the individual's norms and experiences of work. The management are not linked to individuals but to work groups within which there are strong social bonds. Employees seek also to satisfy their social needs in their work.[26]

There are several factors, Oldham writes, which motivate human beings to work. Contrary to what F W Taylor maintained, people do not work merely to obtain financial recompense for themselves. Nor do they work only for the good of society and for the good of other people. Oldham holds that both these theories are far too simple. Human beings have several motives for working hard and efficiently. Some people simply like their work. For others, different driving forces are operative. However a primary driving force for the majority, Oldham holds, is a natural feeling of responsibility and obligation. This feeling is socially conditioned. It depends, Oldham writes, upon other peoples' expections of one and upon the supportive influence derived from someone else's approbation. Like the human relations school, Oldham thus holds that attitudes to work are largely determined by the value which other people place upon the efforts involved.[27]

Oldham's theory of the meaning of work as we have seen, exhibits great similarities with Luther's doctrine of vocation. First of all, Oldham holds that work belongs to the divine order of creation. It has been commanded by God and belongs to the fundamental conditions of human existence. Secondly Oldham, like Luther, holds that human beings in their work are God's co-workers in his continuous act of creation; they are responsible partners in creation. Thirdly he believes that the purpose of work is to serve our fellow human beings thus fulfilling the commandment to love our neighbour. Unlike Luther, however, Oldham does not speak of work as a cross and suffering in the imitation of Christ. He also emphasizes that work is not an end in itself and that human beings do not fulfil themselves merely by work but also through a contemplative life.

What then is Oldham's opinion of those theories of the meaning of work which are to be found in other philosophies of life? Like Brunner, he criticizes a Platonic theory of work. This theory involves far too low an assessment of the value of work, in particular manual labour. In contrast to this, he emphasizes that both manual and intellectual labour are valuable as a means of serving our fellow human beings. It is not the case that manual labour is demeaning for human beings and they should devote themselves solely to spiritual and cultural work. An additional factor contributing to the value of work is that it is a creative activity. Oldham writes that in Christianity, as opposed to a Platonic theory, human beings are viewed as world-shapers who in their work, are co-workers of God in his continuous act of creation.[28]

Unlike Brunner, Oldham also criticizes a Marxist theory of work. This theory in his view assigns too high a value to work. It namely maintains that work is the activity through which human beings attain self-realization as human beings. By contrast, Oldham holds that human self-realization is attained not merely through work but also through contemplative activity. It follows that work is not the most valuable activity in life.

On the other hand, Oldham appears to be drawn to the human relations school theory of work. Like it, he holds that it is the work group which moulds employee norms and attitudes to work. The feeling of obligation which most persons have towards their work, is socially conditioned. Those who belong to the work group accord individual efforts a high value and this motivates the employee to work hard and efficiently. Thus we find in Oldham a combination of the Protestant doctrine of vocation and the human relations school theory of work.

A revision of the doctrine of vocation

As we have seen, both Brunner and Oldham agree with certain of the fundamental views making up a Protestant doctrine of vocation. In the writings of Tor Aukrust, we find a more detailed criticism of the Lutheran doctrine of vocation. He maintains that this doctrine entails three views. First of all, human work is a means for God's continuous act of creation. Working life represents acts of creation which God Himself carries out with human hands. Work is therefore a part of the divine order of creation.[29] Secondly, the doctrine of vocation maintains that the meaning of work is to "create". This does not mean to develop and realize oneself in the modern, individualistic sense. Instead, to create means to serve our neighbour and to devote ourselves to the unselfish care of others.[30] Thirdly, the meaning of work for the person carrying it out, does not lie in realizing certain innate talents. Instead work is a cross, something which disciplines human beings and breaks down the self. It is the true form of Christian asceticism.[31]

Can these views be accepted today? Aukrust holds that Luther's doctrine of vocation presupposes a patriarchal view of society which cannot be accepted today. As a result, a new interpretation of the doctrine of vocation is needed so that it is released from this social standpoint.[32] This new interpretation entails a revision of the doctrine in three respects. First Luther's doctrine is combined with a demand for obedience which presupposes a patriarchal relationship between the superior and the subordinate. One must be obedient towards one's superior and accept one's situation at work even if it is unjust. Aukrust counters this by arguing that it is work itself and not the relationship between superior and subordinate which constitutes a divine order of creation. In contrast to Luther, the demand for justice must be given much greater stress.[33]

Secondly, Luther on the basis of his patriarchal view of society, rejects the career motive in a profession or trade. Each and every one has to keep to the social position to which they have been assigned. It is necessary to defend the necessary stability in patriarchal society.[34] Aukrust however holds that today people have to be prepared to embark upon a career where the choice of profession depends on personal qualifications, so that different human talents can be put to use.[35] In order for people today to be co-workers in the continuous Divine act of creation, it is essential that they have a career and thus place themselves at the disposal of their neighbour and of their society.[36]

Thirdly, the doctrine of vocation is combined with a belief in Divine Providence. God's work of creation can be accomplished through work and this takes place with the help of Divine Providence.[37] In Luther this belief in Providence is closely bound up with his patriarchal view of society. Human beings' strong ties to their social rank bears witness to God's Providence. In contrast to this, Aukrust maintains that human beings in today's society are not placed once and for all in a profession or trade.[38] The belief in Providence which is associated with the doctrine of vocation is thereby given another content which emphasizes that man's relation to God is more important than their work. This gives the working person both strength and courage.[39]

What then is the purpose and value of work according to the revised doctrine of vocation recommended by Aukrust? Aukrust begins by maintaining that the question of the meaning of work is closely connected with the question of life's meaning. Modern work is not exclusively an economic and sociological problem. It has also a religious dimension. If human beings find a meaning to life, they can also accommodate work within a wider context of meaning.[40]

The purpose of work, according to Aukrust, is first of all to be a co-worker in God's continuous act of creation. The fundamental idea embodied in the doctrine of vocation is that work is a sharing in the continuing process of divine creation.[41] The foundation of this doctrine is the belief in creation and not the patriarchal view of society. In Aukrust's view it is therefore possible to apply it to modern work by freeing it from Luther's social view.[42] The doctrine then holds that God creates through the work of human beings. Work is a divine order of creation, a tool for divine creation in the present.[43]

The purpose of work according to Aukrust is secondly to serve our fellow human beings. This is also a fundamental view embodied in the doctrine of vocation which can be accepted today. Work entails carrying out a definite divine task. Its purpose is to serve other human beings and thus to fulfil the commandment to love our neighbour. It is by promoting what is good for others that work is an activity by which human beings become instruments of God's work of creation.[44]

How then is work related to human self-realization? Aukrust holds that in contrast to Luther, a reinterpretation of the doctrine of vocation ought to give greater scope to human self-realization. Work's significance for the individual, he writes, is not only in being a "cross" or a "discipline". By means of their work, human beings can actualize their potentialities and talents. According to the Christian view of creation, it is important for human beings to realize themselves in the sense of using their native talents since these are a gift from God. This according to Aukrust, can take place through work.[45]

Aukrust thus holds that work can contribute to human self realization in the sense that human beings can thereby develop their intrinsic potential. He also writes that a fundamental aim in a Christian work ethics is that work should be an activity worthy of human beings in the sense that it allows for human self-realization. There are social conditions and factors in working life which prevent this and which lead to human self-alienation. An important task is therefore to change these conditions thus allowing work to regain its human dignity.[46]

At the same time, Aukrust maintains that both work and leisure contribute to the general personal development of human beings. This is not something which is achieved merely through leisure as a Platonic theory insists. Nor is it something which is only attained through work, as a Marxist theory maintains. Human self-realization is promoted both by work and leisure activities.[47] Aukrust also maintains that striving for self-realization through work must be limited by the commandment to love one's neighbour. It is also important to realize that there will always be negative factors in work, serving to discipline human beings.[48]

What value has work in comparison with other activities? Aukrust holds that work is a valuable activity. The foundations of its value are to be found in the fact that work is a means for God's continued work of creation, that it is a means for serving our fellow human beings and that it allows us to realize ourselves as regards the development of our personal talents. Aukrust assigns work a higher value than is the case in a Platonic theory of work. The reason for this is that work and not merely leisure activities are means to self-realization and happiness. But Aukrust also assigns work a lower value than does a Marxist theory because leisure activities as well as work contribute to the service of others and to personal self-fulfilment.[49]

Aukrust claims to try to achieve a balance between the respective values of work and leisure. Work is valuable in part as a means to humanity and communion with others and in part as a means to the development of personality and self-realization. But leisure activities are also important. Leisure too can be time devoted to one's fellow human beings and to the love of one's neighbour. Leisure activities can also promote personal development and self-realization. It follows that both work and leisure activities are valuable.[50]

We have seen that Aukrust proposes a fundamental revision of the Lutheran doctrine of vocation. What is his opinion of the theories of the meaning of work which are to be encountered in other philosophies of life? Like Brunner and Oldham, he criticizes a Platonic theory of work. This theory, he believes, assigns work far too low a value. Plato and Aristotle consider work, and above all manual work, more or less as a necessary evil. It is not possible for human beings to attain a perfect life through such an activity. The highest goal of life is happiness and this cannot be attained through manual labour but only through intellectual activity. In opposition to this view, Aukrust maintains that work too can contribute to human personal fulfilment. He therefore assigns work a higher value than it receives in a Platonic theory.[51]

Like Oldham, Aukrust simultaneously criticizes a Marxist theory of work. In his view, this theory assigns work far too high a value. The value of work is emphasized so much that it is "deified". Work is considered as the defining feature of human beings in the sense that it is the activity through which human beings are able to realize their potential. Work becomes so central that it usurps God's place. Thus, according to Aukrust, there is an "apotheosis of work".[52] According to a Marxist theory, human beings make themselves and realize their own true selves through work. Without work, human beings cease to be true and perfect human beings. Against this view, Aukrust maintains that leisure activities can also contribute to human self-realization. For this reason, work has a lower value than that ascribed to it by a Marxist theory. Christianity also maintains that work is important but without this leading to the apotheosis of work.[53]

Like a Marxist theory, Aukrust holds that we ought to strive for working conditions where work contributes to human self-realization. In agreement with this theory, he also holds that there are certain external social conditions such as lack of participation in the decision-making process which lead to human beings being alienated from themselves. However unlike a Marxist theory, Aukrust maintains that alienation is caused not merely by external social conditions and administrative rules in the workplace but also by the personal attitude to life displayed by the individual. To remove alienation, it is not enough merely to change society as Marx held. It is certainly the case that a just system of wages, a humane organization of work and participation in the decision-making process contribute to the reduction of human alienation. But according to Aukrust, a change in the individual's personal attitude to life is also required.[54]

Finally Aukrust criticizes a Taylorist theory of work. He rejects the theory of "homo oeconomicus" and the theory of motivation which is associated with it. Wages according to Aukrust are not the prime motivation for human work. There are also other forces which drive human beings to work efficiently. Among them is the worker's desire for significance and his desire to have his worth as a human being confirmed in his work.[55]

Work as human fellowship and self-realization

Arthur Rich does not formulate a particularly detailed theory of the meaning of work. When one considers the detailed discussion he otherwise devotes to problems in work ethics, his discussion of the Protestant doctrine of vocation and his treatment of the question of work's purpose and value, is surprisingly short. His work ethical recommendations are based more upon a social ethical theory than upon a theory of the meaning of work. However there are also certain views about the purpose of work and its relation to human self-realization to be found in Rich's writings.

The purpose of work according to Rich is both to gain some personal recompense and to serve one's fellow human beings. Human beings must work both to ensure the maintenance themselves and to fulfil the commandment to love one's neighbour by serving others.[56] The most elementary basis of work according to Rich is the necessity of obtaining one's daily bread i.e. food, drink, clothes, accommodation and money. To strive for these things is not contrary to the Christian ideal of love. It is part and parcel of the social ethical criterion of "human fellowship".[57] At the same time "human fellowship" implies that one cares not simply for oneself but also for other human beings: one lives in the company of other human beings and for them. We should also in this sense live in fellowship at work. Work allows us to do something good for others: we are able to perform a service for our fellow human beings. For this reason, Rich writes, work has also the character of an obligation. It is our duty to care for others.[58]

Rich holds that work is one of the activities which contributes to human self-realization. It is not the case that human beings only become really human through leisure activities. Work also plays its part. Rich writes that work is part of a human being's "humanum" i.e. that which defines their essence. Animals have no awareness of work in the human sense. It is a specifically human characteristic to devote oneself to creative activity leading

100

to the transformation of nature and the production of those things which nature cannot create. Work was already given with the creation, before the Fall. According to Rich, Gen 3 implies that toil and suffering are a consequence of sin, not work by itself.[59]

Rich writes that human beings make their humanity concrete in work. The humanity of human beings must be embodied in work in the sense that human beings must function not merely as objects but as responsible and active subjects. In other words, human beings must not be reduced to the status of things in work. Instead, they must have personal responsibility so that they function as responsible subjects.[60]

What is the value of work in comparison with other activities? Rich holds that work is a valuable activity. Christian belief does not take the negative view of work exemplified in classical Greek and Roman culture. Work is connected with the very being of human individuals, something which belongs, so to speak, to their very characterization.[61] The value of work is also based on the fact that it is an activity by which we bring about some good for others: it is a service to our fellow human beings. Work is good because it is a way of living in human fellowship.[62]

Rich holds that because work, as a means of caring for others, is a duty, it follows that every human being has a right to work. Human beings can only be obliged to work if they also actually have work. For this reason, all human beings have a right to work. All human beings have to work and no one is to be unemployed.[63]

We have seen that Tor Aukrust recommended a fundamental revision of the Lutheran doctrine of vocation. What is Arthur Rich's view of this doctrine? He appears to hold that the doctrine of vocation is still relevant for a Christian work ethics. In medieval theology, work was undervalued by conceiving "vocation" as a call to leave working life and enter a monastery. Luther countered this view, Rich writes, by rightly maintaining that vocation applies in ordinary everyday work. Human beings are called in their work to serve their fellow human beings and to fulfil the commandment of loving their neighbour.[64] Rich maintains that the doctrine of vocation in Calvinist theology received a somewhat different formulation from that in Luther in that it was combined with the doctrine of double predestination. Hard work and caring for others is conceived as a sign that one has been elected by God and this helps to inspire efficient efforts at work.[65]

Secularization has led, Rich writes, to a change in our views of work. The word "vocation" today has a meaning different from that in Protestant theology and simply means a skilled job to which one devotes one's life. However the view still prevails that one should work as hard as possible to increase the general welfare. This leads to what Rich calls an "economization" of work. This is associated with far-reaching division of labour where the individual does not see the result of his own limited efforts. Production is capital intensive and the majority do not own the means of production but merely function as labour inputs.[66]

Rich holds that in such society it is difficult to use the concept of "vocation". In a capitalist society with far-reaching division of labour, human beings are reduced to the status of things. They are dehumanised and lose pleasure in their work. When this happens, human beings no longer look upon their work as a "vocation". They give up this notion and treat their work not as a "call" or "vocation" but as a "job". This job is necessary for their maintenance but real life is something which goes on outside of it. In this sense, the concept of "vocation" is no longer adequate for modern working life.[67]

The doctrine of vocation has however still relevance, Rich holds, in the sense that it indicates that human work is associated with an assignment. The assignment is to transform work into what it ought to be, namely human beings serving their fellow human beings. By means of this service, human beings should create the spiritual and material values which allow everyone to live a life that is worthy of human beings. According to Rich, the assignment is to transform the conditions of work so that work in this sense becomes possible. The aim is to oppose the economization of work so that it becomes a humane and social activity in which human beings can be subjects. This can be brought about by a change in the organization of work and through participation in the decision-making process. In this way, Rich believes, the notion of vocation can even have relevance in our society as a social ethical aim.[68]

What view does Rich take of other theories of the meaning of work? First of all he criticizes the Tayloristic theory. According to this theory, the purpose of work is primarily to provide economic resources for the maintenance of life. Work is not conceived as a means for human self-realization. As a result, Taylorism can recommend far-reaching division of labour, where work is atomized into a sequence of simple operations and there is a differentiation between the intellectual planning and the manual production aspects of work. According to Rich, this lead to personal dehumanization, a reduction of human beings to the status of things. The worker is reduced to an object and deprived of personal responsibility. As a result Taylorism is contrary to Rich's view that work should be a means to self-realization.[69]

In contrast to Oldham, Rich also criticizes the human relations school. It is true that like this school he holds that one should strive for conditions at work which give evidence of human fellowship and which enable the worker to function as a responsible person. However according to Rich, the type of cooperation between employees and employers recommended by the human relations school, creates more of a feeling of partnership than a genuine participation in the decision-making process. Real partnership requires work to be organized in a different way from that recommended by the human relations school.[70]

Finally Arthur Rich also criticizes a Marxist theory of work. Like this theory, he seems to hold that work is a means to human self-realization. He also holds that work as a creative activity is something specific to human beings. On the other hand, he holds that socialism does not give a satisfactory solution to the social question. It seeks to remove human alienation by transferring the means of production from private to collective ownership. This however has been shown to be Utopian. Socialization neither means the liberation of the workers nor their triumph over their reduction to the status of objects.[71] A Marxist theory also takes too postive a view of human beings according to Rich. It believes that human beings can liberate themselves unaided and create a perfect society. But this is not possible. In the light of the Kingdom of God, every society is imperfect.[72]

Work as mandate and right

What is the meaning of work according to Günter Brakelmann? He writes that work is a fundamental fact of human existence which theologically can be understood in relation to God's covenant with human beings. God has created the world and has given human beings the responsibility for reigning over the world around them. According to Brakelmann this can be expressed by saying that work is a "mandate" bestowed upon human beings by the Creator. With the act of the creation, God has given human beings this activity which allows them to obtain their means of subsistence from nature. At the same time, this mandate gives human beings a specific responsibility. By working, human beings ought to rule over the earth i.e. take responsibility for the world around them. In their work, human beings are God's co-workers in his act of creation. In this respect, work is anthropologically speaking a "basic datum". It is a part of what is human. something which characterizes human beings as being made in the image of God.[73]

One purpose of work, according to Brakelmann, is thus to participate in God's continued creation. By working, human beings should assume responsibility for their surroundings and shape them, thereby becoming a God's co-worker in his creation. By being co-workers, Brakelmann writes, the lives of human beings are given meaning. If their work is devoid of meaning, so also are their lives.[74]

A second purpose of work, according to Brakelmann, is to serve our neighbour. Work is a social activity which allows human beings to do something for others. By means of work, human beings can live a life of human fellowship and make an active contribution to the life of the community. They do not simply produce what is needed for their own lives but they also show a concern for the world around them and thus demonstrate their sense of human fellowship. Brakelmann even writes that it is the duty of human beings to work and thereby to accomplish something for other people. This duty arises from the fact that work is a mandate which God has given to human beings at the creation. To refuse to work is to refuse to be a human being among human beings.[75]

This duty to work according to Brakelmann entails a right to work. If human beings are denied work they are then prevented from caring for the world around them. It is therefore the responsibility of the state to ensure that all its citizens have an opportunity to work. The duty to serve our fellow human beings through work is matched by a corresponding right to work.[76]

According to Brakelmann, human beings not only have the right to work: they also have a right to humane working conditions. He holds that along with the right to work there are rights based upon the fact that human beings have been given the assigment to work. One such right is the right to work that is worthy of human beings. Since work is a mandate and a duty, the worker has right to working conditions which are worthy of human beings.[77] Brakelmann agrees with the papal encyclical *Laborem exercens* in holding that human beings are to be treated as persons in their work and that working conditions should be so designed that their value as persons is respected.[78]

An important task is therefore to humanize work and to create working conditions which respect the value of human beings. This implies placing human beings at the centre and not treating workers purely as objects of economic interest. It also entails providing scope for personal responsibility and organizing work along non-hierarchical lines. A humanization of working conditions, Brakelmann holds, therefore involves both participation in the decision-making process and self-determination. In this way human beings can be given greater responsibility in their work so that their value is respected.[79]

Brakelmann also maintains that in our work we are equals who have to cooperate with each other without a hierarchical division into superiors and subordinates. As he expresses it, even if we have different functions in the work process, we are equally entitled "partners" at work. Human beings at work are disposed to cooperate with other human beings. They are part of a socially organized work process and carry out their work in conjunction with others. It is therefore a perversion of society when we allow working life to be dominated by an élite. If the owners of the means of production are exclusively responsible for making all the decisions, cooperation between those who are involved in the work process is threatened. Brakelmann therefore holds that all ought to be partners on an equal footing in working life. One reason for this view is that all human beings are equal before God and all share in the responsibility of being God's co-workers in His continuous act of creation.[80]

What about the relationship between work and human self-realization? Brakelmann writes that human beings through their work can realize themselves as free and creative beings. Work allows them to perfect themselves as autonomous human beings who are responsible for God's continuous act of creation. In this way work contributes to human self-realization. At the same time, however, Brakelmann emphasizes that human beings cannot be true human beings through work and their own exertions. Brakelmann thus criticizes both the humanistic and Marxist "self-realization theories" which believe that human beings can liberate themselves through work. Although work is fundamental for human beings, they nonetheless realize themselves as persons only through their relationship to God. It is when human beings are subject to the Will of God that their essential humanity comes into being.[81]

Brakelmann also maintains that although we should strive for a humanization of work, we have to be aware that human work is always combined with toil and effort. We can seek to reduce toil and to promote self-realization through work but we have to retain a realistic attitude towards this goal. After the Fall, work can never be completely released from toil. Nor can alienation in work be completely removed. New efforts will always be needed in humanizing conditions at work.[82]

Brakelmann criticizes on the basis of a Lutheran doctrine of justification those "self-realization theories" which maintain that human beings can attain salvation through their own efforts. Human efforts are needed to achieve more humanity, freedom and justice both in political life and at work. According to a Lutheran doctrine of justification, however, one cannot achieve a truly human life through one's own efforts. To be a true human being is a gift.[83] Human beings must exert themselves, but not to be saved. Instead they should do it to serve other people and for the sake of others. A true human life, however, is to be won in faith, independently of all exertions.[84]

What value has work when compared to other activities? Brakelmann holds that work has a high value because of God's assignment to human beings to take responsibility for the continuous act of creation through their work. It is also valuable as a means of maintaining life, as a means to social contacts and integration in society and as an activity whereby others are served and human beings take responsibility for the world around them.[85] At the same time, Brakelmann holds that human beings cannot realize a true human existence through work. They become true human beings not by working but through their relationship to God. Work is not therefore the supreme value in life.

Like Aukrust, Brakelmann thus rejects both too low and too high an estimation of work. On the one hand, work is valuable as a means of incorporating human beings in society and as an instrument for serving others. On the other hand, he holds that work must not be made into something divine or glorified. Work is not the ultimate goal of life and it is not that which give human beings their value. It is not through work that human beings achieve a truly human existence and therefore there are other activities which are valuable.[86]

Brakelmann's theory of the meaning of work is highly similar to a Lutheran doctrine of vocation. Like this, he holds that work is given with the creation and that its purpose is to participate in God's continuous act of creation. Also like this, he holds that another purpose of work is to serve our neighbour. Citing the Lutheran doctrine of justification, Brakelmann maintains that human beings cannot realize a truly human life and attain salvation through their work.

At the same time, Brakelmann emphasizes his critical distance to what he calls the "Protestant work ethic" i.e. the attitude towards work which he holds that Protestantism has helped to foster. According to this moral viewpoint, paid work has a high value and it is the duty of the employee to work hard and efficiently. According to Brakelmann, such an attitude to work develops under specific social conditions. A fundamental transformation of working life is now taking place and and as a result our values, including our attitudes to work, are also changing. A new understanding of life's meaning is in the process of emerging, Brakelmann hold, in which unpaid work is accorded much more scope. He calls this a "communicative work morality" which stresses creativity, responsibility and the ability to cooperate and which has an increased importance alongside the Protestant work ethic.[87]

How then does Brakelmann judge other theories of the meaning of work? We have seen that he criticizes a Marxist theory. He seems to hold that this theory estimates work too highly. The "apotheosis" of work rests upon the assumption that human beings can attain a true human existence through work. Contrary to such "self-realization theories", Brakelmann maintains that human beings become true human beings not through work but through their relationship to God.

Like Rich, Brakelmann also criticizes a Tayloristic theory of work. This theory, he holds, places too much weight upon human exertions to acquire means for maintaining life. By primarily considering human beings from an economic perspective, it accepts an organization of work which is not worthy of human beings. With the rationalizations recommended by Taylorism, human beings become mere instruments for those owning the means of production.[88]

Like Rich, Brakelmann also criticizes the human relations school theory of work. He holds that this theory adopts a more reasonable view of human nature in the sense that it takes into account human social needs and the importance of the work group for the attitudes of the employee. It thereby recognizes that human drives to work are not merely economic. However Brakelmann holds that this theory is also inadequate because it attaches too much importance to increasing productivity. It contents itself with recommending a "democratic leader style" but fails to recognise the importance of real participation in the decision-making process for the employees.[89]

In the process of criticizing F W Taylor and Elton Mayo, Brakelmann instead supports several of the views of the socio-technical theory of work. He recommends an organization of work and a design of technical systems which satisfy higher human needs. Work conditions should have a form which "humanizes" the existence of human beings. According to Brakelmann, we should also work towards a democratization of working life which embodies real participation in the decision-making process.[90]

A critique of the doctrine of vocation

In Chapter 1 we have seen that a number of contemporary British theologians have criticized what they call "the Protestant Work Ethic". This is a work morality which involves too high an estimation of the value of work and neglects the values attached to other unpaid activities. One of these theologians is Roger Clarke. He criticizes "the traditional work ethic" which treats work as a duty and sloth as a sin. This view assigns work a very high value. According to Clarke, this "work ethic" has its roots in Protestant theology, particularly in Calvinist theology where the doctrine of vocation is combined with the doctrine of predestination.[91]

Clarke holds that this work ethic can no longer be maintained in today's society where it is no longer possible to achieve full employment. Today we need instead what he calls "a contribution ethic". According to this ethic, we realize ourselves as human beings by contributing to the common good in society, but this is brought about not merely by paid work. We can also make valuable contributions to society through other activities such as family life and contacts with others. In consequence these leisure activities have just as high a value as paid work.[92]

A similar viewpoint is to be found in David Bleakley. He also holds that an alternative to "the Protestant work ethic" is needed since it is no longer possible to achieve full employment. Paid work, Bleakley writes, is neither a duty nor the most important human goal in life. There are other activities which are just as valuable. A better balance is therefore needed between work and leisure and between paid and unpaid work.[93]

What views about the meaning of work are to be found in the writings of John Atherton? Like the other British thinkers in the field of work ethics, he adopts a critical attitude towards the doctrine of vocation. He holds certainly that it is worthwhile defending the importance of the core of this doctrine i.e. the view that everyone is responsible for contributing to society *inter alia* through their work. Our vocation is to bring about that which is good for human beings and society. In this sense, Atherton holds, work is a vocation. Moreover paid work has great importance as such a contribution and therefore we do not simply have a right to work but also an obligation to do so.[94]

At the same time, Atherton holds that there are activities other than paid work which contribute to the common good in society. It follows that there also other activities which are just as valuable as paid employment. Atherton also emphasizes that a Christian conception of work must be freed from the misunderstanding which he holds is linked with "the Protestant work ethic". It is not the case that the good things in life including social rights constitute a reward for effort. A Christian work ethics does not entail that certain rights are only obtainable after the display of great exertions at work. Such a view, Atherton holds, has often been ascribed to Calvin but in reality even Calvin recognised that we cannot earn God's love. Rights do not depend on contributions but are presuppositions for contributions.[95]

The purpose of work according to Atherton is first of all to bring about that which is good for other human beings and for society. Work has to make a contribution to society by creating goods and services. Atherton maintains that there are several types of work which do not attain this goal. These are economic activities which do not contribute to the common good. The aim, however, is that work has to contribute to society. Like Roger Clarke, Atherton also maintains that there are activities other than paid work which make such a contribution. It is not simply paid employment that is a meaningful activity. But work is one of the activities which has to promote the good of other human beings.[96]

Secondly Atherton holds that the purpose of work is to contribute to "human fulfilment". He seems to hold that work in this sense is an activity which contributes to human self-realization. It does not imply that work enables human beings to realize that which is characteristic for the human species and therefore to achieve a truly human life. Instead, Atherton's view would seem to imply that work enables individuals to develop their talents and capabilities.[97]

What is the value of work in comparison to other activities? Atherton holds that work as paid employment has great importance and a high value. This value depends in part upon the fact that it contributes to society through the creation of goods and services and in part through its contribution to the individual's development as a human being.[98] Like Clarke, Atherton simultaneously maintains that it is not only paid employment but also other activities which are valuable as a means of contributing to society. There are other activities which benefit human beings and society and which consequently are valued highly. Paid work is not the most valuable activity in life.[99]

Nevertheless work is valuable as a contribution to society. For this reason, Atherton also holds that everyone has a right to work. The right to work belongs to those positive rights which are based on the equal value of all human beings. Longterm unemployment is at variance with this right to employment. There ought to be jobs for every individual who wishes to work. Widescale unemployment cannot be tolerated since it excludes human beings from an activity which allows them to participate in society.[100]

Atherton does not discuss theories about the meaning of work other than those encountered in the Christian tradition. However he briefly touches upon the question of what motivates human beings to work efficiently. He holds that it is not simply a matter of self-interest. There are also other factors such as altruism, sacrifice and the shouldering of responsibility which spur one on to work hard and efficiently. Not the least of these factors, according to Atherton, is the commitment to a good society.[101]

Conclusion

What kinds of theories of the meaning of work are to be found in the writings of contemporary Protestant theologians? What are their views about such questions as the purpose of work, the relationship between work and self-realization, the value of work and the forces driving human beings to work? How do they estimate the Protestant doctrine of vocation and how do they see themselves in relation to other theories of the meaning of work? In this chapter, we have seen that the six theologians which I have selected for study, have partly differing views about the purpose and value of work.

The question about the purpose of work is answered in two different ways by these theologians. The first view is that the purpose of work is partly to be a co-worker in God's continuous act of creation and partly to serve one's fellow human beings. This view may be called the "creation line". It is to be found in Brunner, Oldham, Aukrust and Brakelmann. In Brunner, what we can call an "order of creation theory", is presented. He holds that work belongs to the divine "order of creation" which entails that it is both God's will and belongs to human nature that we have to work. Oldham also speaks of work as such an order of creation while Aukrust writes that work is an activity whereby human beings are instruments for God's continuous act of creation. Brakelmann adopts instead what may be called a "mandate theory". He speaks of work as a "mandate" which human beings have received from God. This implies that it is an activity given with the creation but in contradistinction to an "order of creation", it is not characterized by a given and unchangeable structure. To say that work is a mandate, is to say that human beings have a special responsibility for the world around them. As a result, Brakelmann writes, all men have a duty to work. This duty is also the foundation for the human right to work and also justifies the right to humane work.

The second view is that the purpose of work is to serve our fellow human beings without, however, being an instrument for God's creation. This view which is presented in both Rich and Atherton, may be called the "human fellowship line". Arthur Rich writes that work is an instrument for "human fellowship". In working, human beings ought not simply to care for themselves but they also ought to care for others. It is thus a way of living in fellowship with other human beings. In John Atherton's formulation, human beings make a contribution to the common good in society through their work. At the same time, he stresses that there are activities other than paid work which make such a contribution.

The question of the relation of work to human self-realization is dealt with in three different ways in the material studied. The first view may be called the "activity line". It holds that work is an activity which allows human beings to realize their defining essence – i.e. that which is characteristic of human beings as a species. This is a "species realization theory" in the sense that "self-realization" is taken to mean a realization of that which sets human beings apart as a species and it asserts that work has great significance for this type of self-realization. This seems to be Brunner's view when he maintains that work belongs to the basic conditions of human existence. It is one of the activities by means of which human beings attain a truly human life. Arthur Rich writes that work belongs to those constituents which make human beings what they are. It is specifically human to devote oneself to creative activity which transforms nature. Work allows human beings to realize their humanity as responsible persons.

The second view may be called the "contemplation line". It maintains that human beings realize their essential nature as a species not merely through work but through – and even primarily through – other activities. This is also a species realization theory but unlike the activity line, there is less emphasis placed upon the importance of work as a means of realizing what sets human beings apart as a species. J H Oldham emphasizes that work is only a part of human life and that leisure is also necessary. It is not in work but in communion and worship that human beings attain their supreme definition. In a corrresponding way, Brakelmann also emphasizes that human beings cannot become genuine human beings through their work. A truly human life can be attained only in relation to God. It is therefore something which comes through faith, independently of all one's efforts. Oldham and Brakelmann do not ascribe the same crucial importance to contemplation as a means of human self-realization as does Thomas Aquinas. However like Thomas, they seem to believe that the contemplative life has in this respect greater importance than work.

The third standpoint can be called the "self-actualization line". It maintains that work can allow individuals to develop their individual talents and capabilities. This is not a species realization theory but a "personality development theory" since the "self-realization" involved is not the realization of that which is characteristic of human beings as a species but an actualization of the special talents of the individual. Aukrust writes that individuals through their work can develop their own intrinsic potential while at the same time maintaining that there are also leisure activities which can contribute to this end. In a corresponding way, Atherton also maintains that the individual is able to develop their talents through work.

The question of the value of work is answered differently depending on the different opinions about the purpose of work. The six theologians whom I study are unanimous in holding that one purpose of work is to serve our fellow human beings. They therefore also ascribe to work a relatively high value as a means of achieving this end. Brunner maintains that this is as true of manual labour as it is of intellectual work and that the criterion of whether work is valuable, is that it serves one's neighbour.

According to these theologians, the value of work is also based upon other things. The theologians who adopt the creation line hold that the value of work derives from the fact that it is an instrument for God's continuous act of creation. This is maintained by Brunner, Oldham, Aukrust and Brakelmann. The theologians who adopt the activity line and the self-actualization line hold that work is valuable as an activity which contributes to human self-realization. Aukrust and Atherton hold that work is valuable as a means for the individual to develop their talents while Rich writes that work is valuable as a constituent of human essence and definition.

Several of these theologians at the same time stress that there are also other activities in life which have a high value. This is especially true of those who adopt the contemplation line. Oldham stresses that work is neither an end in itself nor is it the most important thing in life. Brakelmann maintains that human beings achieve a truly human life only in their relationship to God and that therefore work is not the most valuable activity of all. Similar views are also expressed by those adopting the self actualization approach. Aukrust writes that leisure activities are also valuable as means for personal development. Atherton holds that that there are activities other than paid work which contribute to society and which therefore are highly valuable.

Among the theologians considered in this study, we can distinguish three distinct attitudes towards the doctrine of vocation as it has been developed within earlier Protestant theology. The first can be called the "tradition line". According to this standpoint, the views which make up the doctrine of vocation are still acceptable. This view seems to be adopted by Brunner and Oldham. Like Luther's doctrine of vocation, they maintain both that work belongs to the divine order of creation and that the purpose of work is to constitute an instrument for God's continuous act of creation and to serve our fellows. Unlike Luther however, they do not speak of work as a cross and suffering in the imitation of Christ. Brakelmann too holds like the doctrine of vocation that the purpose of work is both to participate in God's creation and to serve one's neighbour.

The second point of view may be called the "revision line". It holds that the doctrine of vocation requires thorough revision before it can be accepted in our society. This viewpoint is adopted by Tor Aukrust. He agrees with Luther that work is important as an activity whereby human beings become instruments of God's act of creation. At the same time, however, he rejects Luther's patriarchal view of society. The doctrine of vocation, in Aukrust's opinion, can neither today be combined with a demand for obedience towards superiors nor with the view that human beings are once and for all assigned to a particular trade or profession.

Rich too can be said to recommend a revision of the doctrine of vocation. He holds that in today's society, it is difficult to conceive of work as a "vocation" since the far-reaching division of labour leads to the dehumanization of human beings and their reduction to the status of things. The idea of vocation can however be understood as an assignment in the sense that the aim should be to give work such a form that it is worthy of the human beings involved in it and that it serves one's fellow human beings.

The third attitude can be called the "alternative line". It holds that the doctrine of vocation needs today to be replaced by an alternative Christian work ethics. This view is put forward by John Atherton. Like the the doctrine of vocation, he holds that human beings have a responsibility to contribute to society *inter alia* through their work. At the same time, he stresses that there are activities other than paid work which benefit the common good in society and which therefore are valued equally highly. In arguing against what he calls "the Protestant Work Ethic" Atherton also asserts that rights do not depend upon contributions. The good things in life, including social rights, do not constitute payment for effort. Günter Brakelmann who otherwise seems to accept the doctrine of vocation, also seems to hold like Atherton that this doctrine attributes too great a value to work.

How then do these theologians judge other theories of the meaning of work? Brunner, Oldham and Aukrust first of all criticize a Platonic theory of work. On the basis of his order of creation theory Brunner asserts that work is not an activity which should be avoided in favour of other more important pursuits. Like Oldham, he holds that a Platonic theory has too low an evaluation of work, especially manual work. This is also Aukrust's standpoint. On the basis of his self-actualization line he maintains that work has a relatively high value as a means towards self-realization.

Oldham, Aukrust and Brakelmann also criticize a Marxist theory of work. Such a theory, they hold, values work too highly. Aukrust writes that a Marxist theory emphasizes the value of work to such an extent that it leads to an "apotheosis" of work and as a result the fact that leisure activities can contribute to human self-realization is overlooked. On the basis of the contemplation line, Oldham and Brakelmann assert that activities other than work are mainly responsible for allowing human beings to realize what is specific for their species. It follows that work does not have as high a value as that which a Marxist theory accords it.

Brunner and Rich display more sympathy for the Marxist theory. Like it, Brunner maintains that the distinguishing feature of human work as opposed to animal instinctive behaviour is that it is conscious and purposeful. Rich holds also like a Marxist theory that work allows human beings to realize that which is characteristic for the human species. At the same time, he also criticizes Marxism's positive view of man and he stresses that human beings cannot create a perfect society through their own efforts.

A Taylorist theory of work is criticized by Aukrust, Rich, Brakelmann and Atherton. They maintain that it is not only desire for personal economic return which motivates human beings to work efficiently. Rich writes also that the purpose of work is not simply to obtain resources for the maintenance of life but also to contribute to human self-realization.

Like the human relations school theory, J H Oldham holds that the main human impulses to work are social. Human attitudes to work are, he holds, largely determined by the attitudes within the work group of which the individual is part. This theory is, however, criticized by Rich and Brakelmann. They maintain that it is not enough with interplay between employers and employees. What is needed, is real participation in the decision-making process. Günter Brakelmann favours instead the views involved in a socio-technical theory of work. Like this theory, he wishes to bring about a humanisation of the organization of work.

What kind of considerations are these different theories of the meaning of work based upon? What sorts of argument do these theologians adduce for their views about the purpose and value of work? There are four different types of theory and consideration which form the basis of these theories.

First of all, these theories of the meaning of work are combined with differing social ethical theories. Brunner combines his order of creation theory with a social ethical theory according to which the criterion for a right action is its agreement with the Will of God as expressed in the divine order of creation. Work is one of these divine orders of creation. God's will is that this order should serve one's neighbour and therefore it is our duty to carry out work which serves human life. In Oldham the creation line is combined with a social ethical theory according to which a fundamental human obligation is to serve God and his fellow men. It is therefore the vocation of human beings in their work to serve the human community of which they are part.

Aukrust's theory of the meaning of work is combined with a social ethical theory based upon the fundamental principle of the commandment to love one's neighbour. This, Aukrust holds, is the only criterion which is unrestrictedly valid. We have therefore to try to fulfil it also in our work by serving our fellow human beings. Rich also analogously justifies his theory of the meaning of work by referring to a social ethical theory. According to him, assertions about the purpose and value of work are to be understood as "maxims" for social decision which are motivated by social ethical "criteria" concerning a truly human life. In Rich's view, a fundamental social ethical criterion is "human fellowship" and therefore the purpose of work is also such human fellowship.

Brakelmann's views are based upon a social ethical theory which lays great stress upon the Christian ideal of love, the principle of the equal value of all human beings, the desire for freedom and justice and certain fundamental human rights. From this theoretical perspective, he holds that the purpose of work is to serve our neighbour and to design working conditions so that they show a respect for the value of human beings. In accordance with this theory, he also places great emphasis upon human beings' right to work and their right to work which is worthy of human beings. John Atherton, on the other hand, combines the human fellowship line with a social ethical theory according to which one should try to bring about what he calls a "reciprocal" society. This is a society where all human beings have in part certain fundamental rights including a right to work and in part a responsibility for contributing to society through *inter alia* their work.

Secondly, these theories of the meaning of work are combined with differing theories of human nature. This is clearest in the case of J H Oldham. He writes that human beings according to the Christian view of man are called to serve God and their fellow human beings in their earthly life and that their assignment is therefore to carry this out by working. Oldham holds that human beings are in part persons who realize themselves as true human beings in relation to God: in part they are also social beings who live in relation to other human beings. Therefore in their work they have to serve society but they attain a truly human life not only through work but primarily through contemplation.

Brunner similarly combines his theory of the meaning of work with a view of man. He maintains partly that human beings are free and responsible and partly that they are not isolated individuals but social beings which belong with others to a community. Aukrust combines the self-actualization line with a view of man according to which the individual has certain innate talents and capabilities which can be developed through work. He also maintains that human beings are responsible for the world around them individually and collectively and that they discharge this responsibility by working.

Arthur Rich's activity line is based upon a view of man which holds that a truly human life is a life in which human beings are not simply objects but are creative and responsible subjects. As responsible persons, they can realize themselves in their work. At the same time Rich maintains that human beings cannot in this world create a perfect society where the true human being is finally realized. Günter Brakelmann on the other hand combines the contemplation line with a view of man according to which human beings realize a truly human existence not through working but through their relation to God. According to his view, a true human life is a gift which we can only receive by faith alone independently of our efforts.

Thirdly, these theories of the meaning of work are combined with other theoretical views which make up a Christian system of belief. This is true of the four theologians who adopt the creation line i.e. Brunner, Oldham, Aukrust and Brakelmann. These combine their theories of work with a doctrine of creation. Emil Brunner, as we have seen, interprets work and the economic order as a divine "order of creation". This is not to be confused with prevailing social orders which also are marred by destructiveness but the norm for these orders is God's Will regarding His Creation. In a corresponding way, Oldham also writes that work belongs to the divine order of creation. At the same time, he maintains that God's act of creation is all the time going on and that human beings through their work, participate in this continuous creation.

According to Tor Aukrust, the belief in creation is the foundation stone of the doctrine of vocation. God carries out his continuous act of creation by calling upon the services of human beings and their work. Aukrust holds that God's act of creation is unfinished but is an ever continuing process in which human beings participate through their work. In a corresponding way, Brakelmann also combines his mandate theory with a creation doctrine. He does not write of work as a divine order of creation. On the other hand, he holds that work is a mandate which implies that it is something which is given by God already in the creation.

Fourthly, these theories of the meaning of work are also combined with certain common human experiences and considerations which have nothing to do with a philosophy of life as such. This seems to be the case for example in the criticism of the doctrine of vocation voiced by both the revision and alternative lines. Aukrust holds that Luther's original doctrine of vocation is associated with a patriarchal social view which can no longer be accepted in our society. Roger Clarke holds that this doctrine cannot be accepted since in today's society it is impossible to achieve full employment. In such a society, the "Protestant Work Ethic" entails that the unemployed have to carry a burden of guilt which is unacceptable. It is probable that Atherton also shares this view while at the same time he stresses that there are also activities other than paid work which promote the common good in society.

Thus we find that there are four different types of consideration which form the basis for theories of the meaning of work within contemporary Protestant theology. These are social ethical theories, theories of human nature, other theoretical convictions which are part of a Christian philosophy of life and common human experiences and considerations which are independent of a philosophy of life. Apart from a view of man, the conviction in a Christian system of belief which is relevant in this connection is a doctrine of the creation. The view of man contains both certain theoretical views and certain views about what is valuable so that it takes up a midway position between the theoretical and ethical components in a philosophy of life. The connection between these different components can be illustrated as follows:

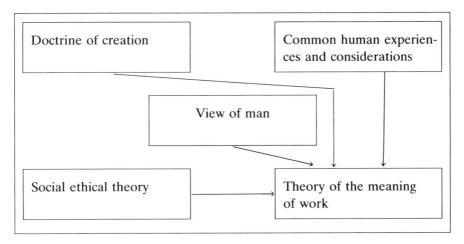

The relationship illustrated above is valid in the case of Tor Aukrust. The theories of Rich and Atherton about the meaning of work are not based upon a doctrine of creation nor does Atherton make any explicit reference to a view of man when he formulates his theory of work. In the case of Brunner, Oldham, Rich and Brakelmann, there are no explicit references to common human experiences and considerations.

4. Social ethical theories

In the two previous chapters we have seen that both the various work ethical recommendations as well as the differing theories of the meaning of work which appear in contemporary Protestant theology are motivated inter alia by different constructive social ethical theories. These are theories which contain views regarding the criteria for a right political act. These theories can contain certain fundamental moral principles, for example a principle for distributive justice and a view about which fundamental human rights ought to be respected. The theories also contain views about what is valuable and what characterizes an intrinsically good human life. Finally they contain a view about the relationship between individual and social ethics.

The aim of the present chapter is first of all to clarify the content of the different social ethical theories which are to be found in the writings of current Protestant work ethicists. To achieve this, I shall raise three questions with regard to the material under discussion. These are: (1) What is the criterion for a right political act? This question is concerned with those properties which are common and specific to all political acts which are right. (2) What has an intrinsic value? This question is concerned with those human experiences and relationships which are good in themselves independently of whether they constitute means of attaining something else which is valuable. (3) What is the relationship between individual and social ethics? This question is concerned with how the criteria for a right private act are related to the criteria for a right political act. The question arises whether these criteria are the same or whether the properties which characterize a right political act are different in character from those which characterize a right private act.

In order to clarify the theologians' answers to the first two analytical questions, I shall relate them to the constructive ethical theories to be found in contemporary moral philosophy. These theories are combined with different views about which ethical problems are fundamental. Some theories deal with the question of what constitutes a right act. We can call these "theories of duty". Other theories deal with the question of the rights of the individual. These can be called "theories of rights". Still others hold that the fundamental ethical problem is concerned with which properties of human character are morally good. We can call these "theories of virtue".

In this connection, I am primarily interested in the various answers to the question concerning the criterion for a right act. An initial answer to this question is that an act is right if and only if there is no alternative with better or less bad consequences. This viewpoint I shall call "consequence ethics" or "teleological ethics". It essentially maintains that a right act has consequences which are at least as good as those of alternative lines of action.

Those who adopt consequence ethics can differ about whose good an act should promote in order for it to be right. One view is that an act is right if and only if it entails the greatest good for the person performing it. I shall call this standpoint "ethical egoism". Another view is that an act is right if and only if it produces the greatest good for all mankind, that is to say both for the person performing it and also for all others. We call such a view "ethical universalism" or "utilitarianism".

Utiliarianism can in turn be formulated in different ways. It can be combined with differing views about what consequences an act should entail if it is to be considered right. One view is that only pleasure is intrinsically good. An act is therefore right if it entails a maximal surplus of pleasure over pain for all mankind. This view can be called "hedonistic utilitarianism" and is associated with the English liberals, Jeremy Bentham and John Stuart Mill. They combine utilitarianism with an "ethical hedonism" i.e. the view that the sole intrinsic good is the experience of pleasure.[1]

In later moral philosophy, we encounter other formulations of utilitarianism which are combined with a critique of ethical hedonism. A second form of utilitarianism is combined with a "pluralistic" theory of values, according to which there is not just one but several intrinsic values. This viewpoint can be called "pluralistic utilitarianism". It has been put forward by the English moral philosopher, G E Moore. He would agree that the criterion for a right act is that it entails consequences which are at least as good as those of every other alternative line of action. On the other hand, he hold that knowledge and love as well as pleasure, are examples of intrinsic values.[2]

A third formulation of utilitarianism is to be found in contemporary moral philosophy. It holds that a right act is one which satisfies the various preferences of as many people as possible. This viewpoint can be called "preference utilitarianism" and is to be found in the writings of the English moral philosopher R M Hare. He holds that it is not certain experiences or mental states such as pleasure or freedom or community to which we assign a certain intrinsic value, which have to be maximized. Instead he holds that a right act is one which satisfies the individual preferences of those persons concerned. Every person makes their own mind up about what is good and we human beings have different interests and wishes.[3]

Such teleological ethical theories are to be distinguished from "deontological theories". The latter maintain that an act can be right even if it does not entail a maximum of good. Deontological theories do not rule out that one of the properties of a right act may be that its consequences are good. On the the other hand, they maintain that the criterion for a right act is not simply that it entails good consequences but that it also has certain other properties.

Deontological theories can also be formulated in various ways. According to so called "rule deontological theories" the criterion for a right act consists in one or more directly obligatory rules which are applicable to a class of acts and these rules are valid whether or not good consequences result from following them. According to "act deontological theories", on the other hand, an act can be right independently of whether it falls under some such general rule. Instead what is crucial, are the properties of the particular act in question.

A classical formulation of a rule deontological theory is to be found in Immanuel Kant. The question of whether an act is right or not is not, according to him, dependent on its real or intended consequences. For an act to be right, it must be carried out in accordance with a general rule of conduct, a "maxim" embraced by the person acting. Such a rule of conduct is valid according to Kant if and only if it satisfies his criterion of "the categorical imperative". This can be formulated as a principle of universalization: "Act only according to the maxim which you can also will to be a general law." The same imperative can also according to Kant be formulated as a principle of human value : "Act so that you treat human nature both in your own person and in every other person always as an end and never simply as a means."[4]

A contemporary formulation of a deontological ethics has been presented by the American philosopher John Rawls. According to him, the criterion for a right political act is not that it maximizes what is good but that it promotes a just distribution of the good. Rawls formulates two principles of justice which specify what such a distribution entails. The first of these asserts that every person must have equal rights to certain fundamental freedoms. Such freedoms as political liberty, freedom of speech, freedom of conscience and those freedoms which are combined with the right to private ownership are to be distributed equally between all citizens. The second principle of justice asserts (a) that income and welfare are to be distributed equally unless an unequal distribution of them is to the advantage of all and (b) that power and responsibility are to be distributed equally but if power is distributed un-equally, it must be linked to positions and offices which are open to all.[5]

Theories of duty are often so formulated that they contain a single funda-mental moral principle which specifies the characteristics of a right act. This is the case with both utilitarianism and Kant's deontological ethics. Such theories could be called "monistic theories of duty". A theory of duty can however also be formulated in such a way that it contains several funda-mental moral principles which together provide a criterion for a right act. We can call such theories "pluralistic theories of duty".

Several theories within contemporary moral philosophy deal with the question of the rights to which individuals are entitled. These theories of rights can be of different kinds. They can be combined with a teleological theory according to which respect for certain fundamental rights entails good consequences for all mankind. In general, however, they are combined with a deontological theory of some kind and thereby with other views about how the rights of the individual are to be justified. It is frequently held that these rights are based upon the principle of the equal value of all men.

These theories of rights can also form the basis for a view about what characterizes a right act. Corresponding to the rights to which particular individuals are entitled there are certain duties imposed on other people. It is therefore possible to maintain that the criterion for a right act is that it must respect certain fundamental rights. There are differing views about what these rights are. It can be a matter of certain "negative rights" such as the right to liberty, the right to property and the right to life. These are negative in the sense that they specify things of which we must not deprive another person. But it can also be a matter of certain "positive rights", such as the right to work and the right to influence. These are positive in the sense that they specify those things which we must promote in others.[6]

The question of which properties of human character are good is often treated in contemporary moral philosophy. Such theories of virtue can also be combined with a view about what characterizes a right act. Both utilitarian and deontological theories assert that the criterion for a right act is solely that the act itself has certain properties. These theories are in this respect "act related". A theory of virtue can however be combined with the view that a right act is also characterized by the fact that it is performed by a person whose character has certain good properties. We shall call a theory of this kind a "subject related theory".

In this chapter, I shall try to clarify the position which the theologians I deal with, adopt towards ethical theories of this kind. Moreover I shall try to clarify their views about the relationship between individual and social ethics. Are the criteria for a right political act the same as those for a right private act or are the criteria applying in social ethics quite different from those in individual ethics? This question can be answered in at least three different ways.

The first view can be called "the dualistic thesis". It holds that the criteria for a right political act in social ethics are quite different from those which pertain in individual ethics regarding a right private act. It is a viewpoint of this kind which is encountered in Martin Luther when in the context of his doctrine of the two kingdoms he sharply distinguishes between "the morality associated with office" and "personal morality". A second viewpoint can be called "the amorality thesis". It holds that only private acts are morally accountable while political acts should not be in general the subject of moral requirements. This view is to be found in Machiavelli and in various theories of the "autonomy" of economics and politics. A third view we may call "the monistic thesis". It holds that the criteria for a right act are the same in social and individual ethics. Both private and political acts ought to be subject to ethical judgement and the same system of norms applies to both private and political acts. This is the view put forward by Jeremy Bentham when he maintains that the principle of utility is valid for both private and political acts.[7]

The aim of this chapter is not, however, merely to clarify the content of the various social ethical theories encountered in the Protestant work ethicists with whom I deal. It is secondly also to clarify the views upon which these theories are based. Are these theories based upon a certain view of man? Are there common human considerations and experiences which form the basis of these constructive ethical theories? Or are they motivated by views which make up a Christian system of belief? I also hope to answer these questions in this chapter.

A theory of justice

Emil Brunner puts forward a "theology of creation" according to which a right political act is one which is in agreement with the divine order of creation. At the same time, he advocates an individual ethics in which a right private act is one which is in agreement with God's Will, which we encounter in a particular situation and get to know only through the Revelation in Christ. Brunner can thus be said to embrace a dualistic thesis regarding the relationship between individual and social ethics. Within social ethics, he formulates a constructive ethics which is completely different from that within individual ethics.

The dualistic thesis is clearly expressed in Brunner's work *Das Gebot und die Ordnungen*. In the first part of this book, he formulates his individual ethics. Its fundamental thesis is that a right act is one which agrees with "das Gebot", that is God's commandment. Brunner writes that everything which agrees with God's Will is good while everything which disagrees with it, is bad.[8] God's Will is something that we can only learn to know through the Revelation in Christ. It is only when God meets us in Christ that we obtain knowledge of what is good and right. In Christ we discover that it is God's Will that we have to love others in the same way that He loves us. We should love God before all else and thereby glorify and honour Him. But we have also to love God by loving our fellow human beings as ourselves.[9]

Brunner's individual ethics would seem to be an act deontological theory. God's commandment, he writes, is particular and concrete. Its content varies depending on the situation. Therefore it cannot be formulated in general rules of action. God requires us to love as Christ loves but the content of this love varies from situation to situation. We are able to discover God's commandment i.e. how we are to love God and our neighbour only in the actual situation. The ethical instructions in the Bible show us what is God's commandment i.e. that we are to love Him before all else but they are not, Brunner writes, to be taken as binding rules.[10]

In the second part of *Das Gebot und die Ordnungen* Brunner deals with social ethics. Here he puts forward a completely different constructive ethical theory. The social ethics advocated by Brunner is based upon a doctrine of natural law. The fundamental thesis is that God's Will is encountered in the divine orders of creation. It is these divine orders of creation "die Ordnungen" which act as a criterion for a right political act. Brunner holds that there are certain orders which are not the work of human beings but are given to human beings by God in the creation and form neccessary preconditions for human life. These divine orders of the creation consist of marriage and the family, work and the economic order, the state and the political order, cultural life and the Church. They are part of the natural law and in them we can discover what is God's Will. A political act is right if and only if it agrees with God's Will concerning these orders.[11] Brunner writes that in existing reality we do not merely see

"besondere Lebenskreise *in* denen, sondern Ordnungen, *gemäß* denen wir zu handeln haben, weil uns in ihnen – wenn auch nur gebrochen und indirekt – Gottes Wille entgegenkommt. Darum nennen wir sie göttliche Ordnungen."[12]

The type of theology of creation encountered in Brunner has often been accompanied by a pronounced conservatism. Brunner emphasizes, however, that the existing social orders are not simply an expression of God's Will concerning the creation but also an expression of the reality of sin. God has planned his creation for a goal which is still not realized because of the evil in existence. As a result, no existing social system can be considered sacred and completely identified with the Divine Will. Brunner rejects a conservatism which maintains that the existing order is God's order. Christians hope for a future Kingdom of God and therefore work for a change of the present conditions.[13]

In spite of this, Brunner's social ethics also has a conservative tendency. He appears to hold that within the orders there should be a hierarchical superiority and inferiority. This is the case for marriage and the family. According to this divine order of creation, there exist certain differences between the nature of the sexes which justifies the differences between man's and woman's social position. The differences which by nature exist between man and woman justify man having different functions from woman and being the head of the family.[14] This is also true of the state and the political order. Brunner certainly rejects every form of pure dictatorship since, given the sinfulness of those holding power, the people must be given the possibility of exercising a certain influence upon the government. But he also dismisses political democracy since the state's task of promoting the welfare of its citizens presupposes an expertise which is not possessed by all citizens.[15]

Brunner justifies this hierarchical order of superiority and inferiority by reference to a certain view of what justice entails. Referring to Aristotle, he holds that it is just that each and every one obtains what is theirs (suum cuique) i.e. each and every one receives their due.[16] What then is each and every one's due? In his book *Gerechtigkeit* Brunner writes that a just distribution of the good ought to take into account human equality i.e. the fact that all human beings have the same value. To be treated justly is to be treated the same as everybody else, in the sense that one receives the same wage for the same work performed and is entitled to the same rights given the same burdens. All human beings have the same value and all those with the same social functions are to have equal rights.[17] But at the same time according to Brunner, justice must take into account the differences between human beings. Human beings in fact differ in kind and function and this difference is also relevant for how the good is to be distributed. Suum cuique does not imply the same for one and all but that one and all must be given their due.[18]

Justice as suum cuique is according to Brunner founded upon God's Will concerning the creation. Behind suum cuique is the Will of the Creator, the divine order which determines what each and every one is entitled to. In the act of creating, God determines what belongs to the created.[19] On the basis of this divine order of creation, justice's connection between equality and inequality can be understood. On the one hand, God has created all men equal. Each and every one is created in the image of God and has therefore a human value which is the same as that of every other human being. On the other hand, every human being is also created with his or her own specificity e.g. as man and woman and this specificity must also be respected.[20]

Brunner's social ethics is deontological in nature. What characterizes a right political act is not that it entails good consequences but that it promotes justice. His social ethics is also a monistic theory of duty. The criterion for a right political act consists of a single moral principle, namely a principle of justice.

In Brunner this ethical theory is combined with a very definite view of man. According to the Christian view of man, he writes, there is on the one hand an important similarity between human beings. All human beings are created in the image of God (imago Dei) which entails that every person has a value as a person which is bestowed equally upon all human beings. As a consequence, one should treat all men equally and all men should have equal rights.[21] On the other hand, Brunner writes, human beings differ in kind and function. God creates individualities and therefore there are actual differences between human beings. These differences are a necessary presupposition for human fellowship.[22]

According to Brunner it is respect for these differences between human beings which entails that justice does not consist in equal distribution. Brunner would almost seem to put forward what we can call "a principle of merit" i.e. the view that a just distribution of the good implies a distribution which is in proportion to certain merits. These differences also provide justification for different human beings having different rights depending upon their different social roles. Man's rights do not coincide with woman's and parents have different rights from their children. Brunner holds that there should be a hierarchical distribution of power and responsibility within the family, the state and the economic order. Such a hierarchical social order is in agreement with God's Will with the orders of creation.[23]

An act deontological theory

In his book on work in modern society, J H Oldham does not propound any social ethical theory. However he does formulate such a theory in an earlier work on *The Function of the Church in Society*. In this book, he argues that the Church has also a prophetic task which entails making its voice heard regarding the ethical questions which are related to social and political problems. The Church can discharge this prophetic task by acting in different ways in the world. It can be accomplished through individual laymen acting in temporal matters or through the guidance of the priesthood or through the recommendations of Church leaders.[24] The individual Christian is involved in social life and as a layman must be engaged with everyday questions. Their task is to try to accomplish God's Will in the world. Theologians and priests can give the laity ethical guidance. At the same time, the Church must also act as one body.[25]

The Church's task according to Oldham is to interpret the ethical implications of the Gospel. This is to be done not simply by specifying certain aims and values but also by providing recommendations about concrete political decisions and acts. In its preaching and teaching the voice of the Church while simultaneously avoiding clerical dominion over political and economic life, must be heard clearly in ethical questions. The Church therefore cannot remain on the fence as regards controversial questions and it has to try to indicate what is and what is not consistent with Christian faith.[26]

What then is the criterion for a right political act? Oldham rejects teleological ethics according to which an act is right if it promotes certain specified goals. What is characteristic of Christian ethics, he writes, is that it is an "ethic of inspiration" and not an "ethic of ends". In contrast to a Thomist moral doctrine or the ethics of the social gospel movement, it does not judge an act to be right or wrong according to whether it can further certain prescribed goals or values. Instead it holds that an act is right if it constitutes an answer to the living and sovereign God who makes His Will known in the present. A right act is performed in obedience to God's Will and in response to his call. Its source is a living communion with God.[27]

Oldham's ethics appears to be deontological theory according to which the criterion for a a right act is not simply that it entails good consequences. Instead what makes an act right, is that it is in agreement with God's Will. In each new situation, we can learn to know God's Will through his Revelation in Christ, in the Bible and in the experience of the Church. As Christians we are called to take part in God's work of creation but this does not imply that there is a programme of action ready to follow. Instead the task is to try to see how God acts, to humbly learn to know his Will and to obey Him. Oldham writes that Christian ethics is more concerned with faith and obedience than with goals and programmes of action.[28]

When Oldham says that he represents an "ethic of inspiration" in contrast to an "ethic of ends" he would seem also to reject a rule ethics and to recommend an act ethics. The criterion for a right act is that it agrees with God's Will and what is God's Will can be decided only in a concrete choice situation. With reference to existentialist thought and Bubers I-Thou philosophy, Oldham holds that a Christian act is characterized not by obedience to certain moral rules but by a living answer to a Person. He writes:

> "The right course for a Christian individual or assembly to take in a particular instance cannot be determined in advance by any abstract rule, but must be an act of obedience to God in face of the concrete situation."[29]

Our duty is to obey God's Will. However according to Oldham it is impossible to specify once and for all by means of a collection of general rules of action what is God's Will. The latter is not an unalterable law which is independent of the situation. Instead we gain insight into the Divine Will in each new specific choice situation. For this reason, we cannot decide what is right with the help of principles which are given in advance but instead solely by responding to God's call in the concrete situation. It is only then that we discover what the particular act is that God wishes us to perform in precisely these cicumstances.[30] According to my interpretation of this standpoint, Oldham can be said to embrace an act deontological ethics.

A fundamental thesis in Oldham's "ethic of inspiration" is thus that an act is right if and only if it constitutes a response to God's commandment in the concrete choice situation. Simultaneously however, Oldham also holds that there are certain general moral principles which provide us with guidance. Individuals do not need to be isolated in currently seeking to do what is God's commandment. They are not isolated but are equipped with earlier experiences which provide guidance about the decisions to be made. A right decision according to Oldham is not a result of the situation in which it is made but the fruit of several previous acts performed in faith and obedience.[31]

Oldham also holds that in the concrete choice situation we can receive guidance from the accumulated experience to be found in the Christian community. We receive it through the Bible, through the teachings of the Church and through communing with other Christians. The Christian decides what is right by responding to God's demands in each new situation while being guided by the teaching of the Church. Insight into God's Will in the present situation is obtained through observing how this Will has already been revealed in Christ, the Bible and the experience of the Church.[32] These assertions of Oldham can be interpreted to mean that Christian ethics gives us certain "provisional rules" which are not binding criteria for the rightness of an act but instead represent analogous experiences which provide us with a certain guidance in every new situation where we are faced with deciding what is right. Oldham can thus be said to embrace an act deontological ethical theory with provisional rules.

J H Oldham's concept of "middle axioms" which has had great importance within ecumenical social ethics, can be interpreted to signify precisely such provisional rules. A right act is one which agrees with God's Will and we discover what is God's Will in each new situation. Oldham holds that it would be tantamount to denying individual moral responsibility to draw up general rules of conduct specifying what is right. But at the same time he writes that the Church must try to specify what political measures are desirable. This can be done by the formulation of "middle axioms" which specify the forms in which the Christian ideal of love is most adequately expressed in a given period and under given circumstances.[33] These middle axioms would seem not to be binding rules but provisional rules which specify what is generally right in a given situation.

Oldham distinguishes between (a) general moral principles ("broad assertions") such as the commandment to love and the duty to strive for social justice and (b) "precise instructions" which specify exactly what is to be done in concrete situations.[34] He holds that (c) the "middle axioms" occupy a level between these general principles and concrete norms. They are rules which are not binding and which are subject to change. Oldham writes:

> "They are not binding for all time, but are provisional definitions of the type of behaviour required of Christians at a given period and in given circumstances.[35]

One of the middle axioms which Oldham mentions is that we ought to strive for what he calls "the responsible society". He clarifies this concept which latterly came to play an important role within ecumenical social ethics in an article in *The Church and the Disorder of Society*, a volume written in preparation for the first Assembly of the World Council of Churches in Amsterdam in 1948. In this article, Oldham holds that human beings according to the Christian view of man, are both responsible and responsive persons. Every human being is responsible before God and their neighbour while at the same time being called to respond to God's call in each new situation. Society ought to be so contituted that it is not inconsistent with this view of man.[36]

For Oldham, the central political question is the conflict between the Western democracies and Soviet communism. Oldham holds that the Church must criticize communism as a totalitarian system. Because human beings under that system become a means for collective aims, it conflicts with the view of man as the image of God and as a responsible being. In communist society, the individual is sacrificed to the collective and the interests of the state.[37] Instead the Churches should try to bring about "a free society" i.e. a society with equal distribution of power, responsibility, freedom of speech and political liberty and a just distribution of material welfare. Oldham calls such a free society where human beings are respected as free and responsible beings, a "responsible society".[38] The view that we should strive for such a responsible society which is not identical with a Western democracy, can be understood as a provisional rule which guides us when we today try to decide which political act constitutes an answer to God's call.[39]

A pluralistic theory of duty

A deontological social ethics is also to be encountered in the writings of Tor Aukrust. He writes that the basis for Christian ethics is the Will of God which is revealed in the gospel about Jesus Christ. What makes an act right is neither that it promotes certain values nor that it is in agreement with certain principles of natural law but that it agrees with God's Will into which we obtain insight through the Revelation.[40] How then can we decide what God requires? Aukrust holds that there are certain given criteria for God's Will and for this reason he rejects an act ethics of the type encountered in Oldham. The New Testament does not place all the responsibility on individuals to decide for themselves what is required of them. Aukrust rejects an existentialist view of man which he considers far too individualistic and holds that it does not conflict with freedom of conscience to provide certain ethical guidance. The individual does not make his ethical choice completely by himself.[41]

According to Aukrust, certain criteria for God's Will are required in deciding what is right in a concrete situation. But in order to apply God's requirements, certain rational considerations are also needed. These involve an analysis of the concrete, historically determined situation. Aukrust therefore proposes a social ethical model which involves three components, namely (1) criteria for the Will of God (2) an analysis of the situation at which God's Will is directed (3) concrete application of the criteria to the actual situation.[42]

What then are the criteria for discovering what is God's Will? Aukrust writes that social ethical criteria help us to distinguish between what is right and wrong. They indicate what values and goals are to guide us in our moral choice.[43] Such criteria are also provided in moral philosophy. In Kantian ethics, the criterion takes the form of the categorical imperative while in utilitarianism it is happiness or welfare. But what criteria are proposed by Christian ethics? Aukrust writes that God Himself through the Biblical Revelation has given certain criteria which allow us to decide what is His Will in new situations.[44] These criteria are of two kinds. There are (a) primary criteria which are specifically Christian and (b) secondary criteria which are humane.[45]

The "primary criteria" are specifically Christian and express what is of central importance in God's Revelation of His Will. They provide a basic frame for ethics without suggesting in more detail how society should be organized. Aukrust mentions two such moral principles. They are (1) an eschatological principle according to which the primary and fundamental aim is to establish the perfect kingdom of God where human beings shall be made perfect. This eschatological goal is God's absolute Will into which we receive insight through the Revelation in Christ.[46] Furthermore there is (2) a principle of human value according to which human beings are ends in themselves and not simply means. This principle of human value is not specifically Christian but according to Aukrust the justification of the individual human being's inviolable worth is specifically Christian. This is based on the the view that all human beings are objects of Divine Love. Human value is not determined by some inherent property in human beings but by God's love in Christ towards human beings.[47]

The "secondary criteria" are not specifically Christian and render the primary fundamental goals concrete. They have a natural law character and are derived from human beings' natural insight into the law of God while at the same time they are also to be found in the Bible.[48] According to Aukrust, these moral principles contain for a start certain "negative criteria" which indicate what is morally wrong. These consist above all of (3) the rules which make up the Decalogue which is a summary of God's ethical demands. The decalogue has arisen in social circumstances different from ours but its commandments tell us what are the fundamental values for our time too.[49]

According to Aukrust the secondary criteria also contain certain "positive criteria" which tell us what we have to do. These are primarily certain principles encountered in the humanistic tradition and different declarations of rights.[50] Among them is to be found (4) a principle of liberty to the effect that we ought to strive for freedom in both the postive and negative sense. This entails that the goal should be freedom in the sense of a realization of human beings' true nature.[51] Also belonging to these criteria is (5) a principle of equality according to which we ought to strive for social equality. This is justified by the fact that all human beings having been made in the image of God and being objects of his love, are equal before God. This equality principle according to Aukrust does not entail a desire for collectivism and conformity. Human beings are created equal but one should also take account of the differences between them as regards ability and personal character.[52]

To the secondary and positive criteria also belongs (6) a principle of justice according to which we should strive for a just distribution of the good. According to Aukrust, justice implies that each and every one is to receive their due (suum cuique). This can be interpreted (a) as a principle of merit according to which each and every one is to receive in accordance with their accomplishment or (b) as a principle of equality according to which the good should be distributed equally.[53] According to Aukrust, Christian ethics interprets justice on the basis of Christianity's primary criteria. This implies that justice is linked to solidarity, care of the poor and respect for the needs of each and every one. In contrast to Brunner, Aukrust seems to reject a principle of merit and recommends instead a principle of need in his interpretation of justice.[54]

Finally the secondary principles also contain (7) the commandment of love according to which we are obliged to care for our fellow human beings. It is on the basis of such an ideal of love that we are able to understand what justice is and what is due to each and every one. All other criteria in Christian social ethics are subsidiary to this principle and are to be interpreted in terms of the commandment of love. Liberty, equality and justice should all express concern for one's neighbour.[55] Aukrust writes that the commandment of love is the only criterion which is unconditionally valid. This presumably implies that this commandment takes pride of place among the secondary criteria. Social ethics is organized hierarchically so that all these secondary criteria are subsidiary to the commandment of love. At the same time, the subsidiary criteria help to give the commandment of love a concrete content.[56]

In contrast to Brunner, Aukrust thus holds that there is not simply one moral principle specifying what it is that characterizes a right political act. He embraces what I have called a "pluralistic theory of duty" according to which there are several moral principles which together define what is to be the criterion for a right act.

In order to apply these social ethical criteria in a concrete situation, Aukrust believes that knowledge about what this particular situation entails is also necessary. A situational analysis is required. Various social sciences can contribute to this situational analysis. Aukrust especially emphasizes the significance of sociology. It provides descriptions of how society is organized which constitute a necessary complement to the social ethical criteria formulated by theology.[57]

The third component of Aukrust's social ethical model is an application of the social ethical criteria to the actual situation. This entails combining the criteria and situational anlysis in an application.[58] This social ethical application has initially a critical function. It manifests itself in a critique of the Church with the aim of specifying its failings as a human institution. Aukrust maintains that it is important that this criticism of the Church is not left merely to the Church's opponents.[59] At the same time, it manifests itself in a ecclesiastical critique of society. Aukrust writes that the eschatological perspective obliges the Church to refrain from underwriting existing social institutions and instead to indulge in a radical criticism of society.[60]

The social ethical application according to Aukrust has also a positive function. Its task is also to specify both what we ought to do and what concretely is God's Will at the actual moment. This must not simply take the form of a banal application which entails the Church setting forth certain long term goals which everyone is agreed about. Nor must it take the form of theological casuistry where the the Church formulates rules to cover every conceivable particular situation.[61] Instead it is a matter of formulating realistic goals which take account both of the fact that in this world we cannot create a perfect society and that it is necessary to have concrete changes so that society can become more worthy of human beings than it is at present. It is an application which takes account of the differences which exist between the Kingdom of God and what can be achieved in the here and now. At the same time it formulates both long term and short term goals for political action.[62]

Aukrust also discusses the relationship between individual ethics and social ethics. He maintains strictly speaking that all ethics is social ethics. One cannot in fact treat the individual as something independent in relation to what is social. But at the same time, Aukrust holds we can speak of "social ethics" in a narrower sense as that part of ethics which deals with such social institutions as the family, working life, cultural life and the political life. These social orders are structures which determine the relations of human beings to one another and social ethics indicates how these institutions should be organized.[63]

What then is the relationship between social and individual ethics? Aukrust criticizes what I have called "the dualistic thesis". This standpoint has often been associated with the doctrine of two kingdoms in Lutheran theology where a distinction has been drawn between a person's morality associated with office and his or her own personal morality.[64] According to these interpretations of the doctrine of two kingdoms, God's absolute demands as represented in the Sermon on the Mount, only apply to the individual's private behaviour while social life is exempt from these absolute requirements. Aukrust rejects this view. He holds that the Sermon on the Mount is valid for both the spiritual and temporal kingdoms. God's absolute demands are relevant to all domains of human life and are therefore important both for individual and social ethics.[65]

Aukrust also criticizes what I have called "the amorality thesis". He writes that there is no human area of behaviour nor sector of society which is ethically neutral and is exempt from God's Will.[66] Sometimes it has been held that economic life is an example of an area which is not subject to ethical judgement. According to Aukrust such a theory of "the autonomy of economics" is contrary to a Christian view of man. Both individually and collectively human beings are responsible for their creation. They are enjoined to rule over the earth and therefore they cannot resign and treat themselves as helpless victims of an insuperable social development. It follows that the criteria of Christian ethics apply to both private and political acts and to the economic order equally as much as to the political.[67]

A subject related theory

A detailed discussion of the relationship between individual and social ethics is also to be found in Arthur Rich. In this discussion, he develops his own terminology which partly differs from the one that I have proposed. Rich holds that ethics deals with human beings and their responsibility for those things they are related to. Human beings are related to their own "selves" i.e. their own inner potentialities, to other human beings as a "thou" and to the ecological world around them as an "it".[68] Three different types of ethics correspond to these relations in human life. "Individual ethics" deals with human beings' responsibility for developing their own potentialities so that they can realize themselves as human beings. "Personal ethics" deals with their responsibility for human beings to whom they are related in an immediate I-Thou relationship. "Environmental ethics" deals with their responsibility for the natural world around them i.e. their ecological partner.[69]

What then is the task of social ethics? Rich writes that man's fundamental relationships are often mediated through certain institutions i.e. orders created by human beings which are historical and mutable. These institutions influence both the I-It relation and the I-Self relation. Most of all they influence the I-Thou relation. Human cohabitation must often be mediated through social institutions of various kinds.[70] "Social ethics" according to Rich, deals with our responsibility for the form these institutions are to take. Personal ethics is concerned with our immediate responsibility for other human beings while the task of social ethics is to specify what form institutions such as the family, the state and economic structures ought to have.[71] According to Rich "economic ethics" is a part of social ethics, dealing with the form economic institutions ought to have.[72]

Sometimes it has been held that ethics consists only of individual and personal ethics and that political and economic behaviour are not to be subject to moral judgement. They follow their own laws. Rich rejects such a theory of the "autonomy" of economics and politics. Christian ethics in his view involves a judgement about how social institutions should be shaped. Like Aukrust, Rich thus rejects what I have called the amorality thesis.[73]

The task of social ethics is thus to indicate the form that social institutions should take. In order to be able to do this, according to Rich, social ethics must be (a) based upon reliable and relevant knowledge ("sachgemäss") which implies that it must be informed about the social reality. Such insights can be obtained from the social sciences. Social ethics therefore includes certain theoretical judgements and factual assumptions. At the same time social ethics must also be (b) humane ("menschengerecht") which entails that it must ask what is right for human beings. Its goal is an organization of society which is right for human beings i.e. the social order ought to be humane. As a result, social ethics also contains certain value judgements and prescriptive assertions.[74]

How then is one to decide what constitutes a "humane" design of social institutions? Rich holds that Christian social ethics has an eschatological entry point. It says what is humane on the basis of a belief in the coming Kingdom of God which has been revealed in Jesus Christ. From this perspective, every social order appears relative. In contrast to both conservatism and revolutionary utopianism Christian social ethics maintains that there is no heaven on earth.[75] But the humanity which achieves its perfect form in Jesus Christ also shows what is good for human beings ("menschengerecht"). It is a humanity involving three basic "existentials" which specify what constitutes a true human existence. These existentials are (1) faith in the form of belief in Christ (2) hope in the form of an expectation of the Kingdom of God and (3) love. They tell us both what defines a Christian existence and what defines humanity in general. Faith, Hope and Love are the pillars of human existence.[76]

The foremost of these existentials is according to Rich, love or agape. Rich writes that this love is a critical court of appeal which examines what is right and wrong but it does not itself constitute a criterion for a right political act. However on the basis of agape certain criteria about what is good for man ("menschengerecht") can be deduced and thereby also about what constitutes a desirable social order. These criteria are not given once and for all time. They are valid for concrete, historical situations.[77] The foremost of these criteria according to Rich is human fellowship ("Mitmenschlichkeit"). This is not only a formal concept like Heidegger's existential "Mitseins" but is a substantial concept which indicates that humanity entails love of one's neighbour and concern for others. But according to Rich there are also several other such social ethical criteria.[78]

On the basis of these criteria for humanity, certain maxims for social decision ("Maximen sozialer Entscheidung") can be derived. These cannot be directly deduced from the criteria but require in addition knowledge of factual social conditions. They take into account both what is "menschengerecht" and what is "sachgemäss". As a result their validity is conditional and relative. They provide concrete recommendations in certain definite situations but they give no final programme for a "Christian social order". An example of such a maxim is that one should strive for an economic order which is neither a pure market economy nor a pure planned economy.[79]

Thus Rich reckons with three distinct levels in social ethical argumentation. At the first level Christian faith provides a basic view about what is humane. A true human existence is characterized by the existentials of Faith, Hope and Love. Foremost among them is agape. At the second level, love provides motivation for certain fundamental criteria about what is good for human beings. One such criterion is human fellowship. At the third level these criteria together with knowledge about social conditions provide a motivation for certain maxims for social decision which specify what is desirable in a concrete situation.[80]

What according to Rich are the social ethical criteria for what is good for human beings? The first of these criteria is "critical distance". The future Kingdom of God which implies a final liberation of mankind and the world, cannot be realized here in time. Therefore eschatology justifies a critical distance to every existing social order in this world.[81] The second criterion is "relativity". It implies that the critical distance should be combined with a relative affirmation of certain social orders here in time. No social order can completely realize the Kingdom of God but there are certain social conditions which ought to be accepted as relative even if they do not have an absolute and perfect character.[82]

The third criterion is "relationality". It specifies a certain attitude towards ethical values. Rich writes that there are no specifically Christian values but that the commandment to love, however, is combined with a special attitude towards values which are commonly accepted. These are affirmed relatively and are interpreted as complementing one another. This is the case, for example, for values like freedom which implies that we dispose over ourselves, and obligingness which implies a preparedness to serve others. These values have a relational character, Rich writes, which implies that considered on their own they are relative and complement one another. True humanity cannot be reduced to either the one or the other of these values.[83]

The fourth criterion is "human fellowship". It specifies that a humane human life is characterized both by the desire for self-realization and concern for other human beings. Contrary both to altruism which sacrifices the "I" and egoism which sacrifices the "Thou" Rich holds that we ought to love both ourselves and our fellow human beings.[84] The fifth criterion is "participation". This specifies what human fellowship implies for the design of social institutions and structures. In such institutions, cooperation is required between different persons and groups so that each and every one treats others as partners. This implies that all those affected have to take part in what has to be done.[85]

A sixth criterion for what is good for human beings is according to Rich "concern for the rest of creation" ("Mitgeschöpflichkeit"). Human beings are related not only to other human beings but also to the rest of creation.

Although as beings created in the image of God they have a special status they also have a responsibility for the natural world around them.[86] A seventh criterion is "participation in the creation" ("Geschöpflichkeit"). It provides a perspective for human existence which belongs with a Christian belief in creation. Human beings, like the world about them, are created beings which implies that there is an ontological difference between God and human beings. At the same time, human beings are free and responsible beings who have a responsibility for the creation.[87]

These criteria for humanity provide a motivation for what Rich calls maxims for social decision. The formulation of such maxims requires partly social ethical criteria and partly knowledge of factual social conditions. The maxims are related to a specific social and historical situation and are therefore not universally valid. They have a relative character, Rich writes, and their validity is conditional and limited to a given situation.[88] The concept of "maxim" does not have the same meaning in Rich as it has in Kant's moral philosophy where it denotes a rule of action which is valid if it satisfies the conditions of the categorical imperative. In Rich, it denotes instead a norm which is determined by the situation and which possesses only a conditional validity. As such it is closely related to J H Oldham's concept of "middle axiom". It denotes a norm which specifies what is right in a specific social situation but not what is right for all time.[89]

Arthur Rich gives several examples of such maxims for social decision. Among them are those work ethical recommendations which I have noted in Chapter 2. One such maxim is that we should strive for job enlargement, job rotation and job enrichment. Another is that we should strive for employee participation in decision making at all levels within a company. Such participation in decision making promotes participation for all the factors of production and Rich also holds that the employees have a right to participate in decision making. A third maxim is that we should strive for an alternative both to a pure market economy and to a pure planned economy. According to Rich, a modified market economy where the State is responsible for certain economic planning and at the same time the employees have a right to participate in decision making, is to be preferred.[90]

How is Rich's social ethical theory related to those constructive ethical theories which are to be found in contemporary moral philosophy? According to Rich the fundamental ethical problem is not what characterizes a right act, but what properties of human character are desirable. A good human being is a responsible person who assumes responsibility for themselves, other human beings and the world about them. Similarly, the fundamental problem in social ethics is not what characterizes a right political act. Rather it is to determine the criterion for the design of human institutions which are good for human beings.

At the same time Rich combines his theory with a critique of the differing views about what is the criterion for a right act. To begin with he rejects both a pure rule ethics as well as a pure act ethics. In contrast to rule ethics, he interprets the maxims for social decision not as general rules but as norms which apply to certain concrete situations. Simultaneously he rejects an act ethics which makes no allowance whatsoever for universal principles or rules.[91]

Rich also distances himself from the "norm or principle ethics" which he holds can be found both in utilitarianism and in different forms of deontological ethics.[92] He does not discuss utilitarianism in detail. On the other hand, he provides a critique of the deontological ethics to be found in John Rawls's theory of justice. Rich holds that Rawls's second principle according to which an unequal distribution can be affirmed only if it benefits those most disadvantaged, is closely related to the criterion of "participation" and therefore can be accepted. On the basis of his understanding of what humanity implies Rich also accepts Rawls's first principle of justice while at the same time criticizing Rawls's priority rule according to which liberty is only to be restricted for the sake of liberty. When Rawls places liberty before solidarity with the economically weak he gives liberty an absolute value which according to Rich is contrary to the criterion of "relationality".[93]

How then is Rich's own theory to be characterized? He himself says in referring to Max Weber that he embraces an "ethics of responsibility" which judges what is right by taking account of what we know and what we can predict about the consequences of acts. He writes that a right political act must have consequences which are acceptable. But he holds that this ethics of responsibility ought to be combined with considerations relating to the acting person's "state of mind". Crucial in deciding whether an act is right is also the state of mind and the inner motivation of the person who carries out the act.[94]

An "ethics of responsibility" of this type differs in several respects from a purely teleological ethics. Certainly it is characteristic of a right act that it should have good consequences. According to Rich it should promote institutions which are good for human beings in the sense that they are imbued by *inter alia* human fellowship and participation. But at the same time, the ethics of responsibility holds that in an imperfect world it is not possible to attain absolute goals. Moreover it maintains that what makes an act right is not only certain properties of the act. The person carrying out the act should also have certain desirable properties. Rich appears to hold that the acting subject should be a responsible person characterized by critical distance, concern for other human beings and for oneself and for the rest of creation.

This entails that Rich can be said to embrace a "subject related theory". The criterion for a right act is not simply certain properties of the act but also certain properties in the acting subject.

A deontological theory of rights

A social ethical theory of a different type is to be found in Günter Brakelmann. In his book *Abschied vom Unverbindlichen*, he asks what the criterion is for a right political act. One of the problems he treats in this work concerns the criteria which Christian belief gives for our political acts. Brakelmann maintains that the Bible does not give any fully fledged political programme and that there is therefore no social order or any political party programme which is identical with Christian belief. He holds that belief nonetheless gives certain criteria for a right political act.[95]

According to Brakelmann the fundamental criterion in Christian ethics is love or agape. The basis for this Christian ideal of love is to be found in God's concern for the human being in Jesus Christ. In Him, God has revealed his love for mankind and in Him we also see how God conceives the true human being. Human beings are called to live in the imitation of Christ, to live in the love which is revealed in Christ. Thus Christ is a measure for both the relationship of human beings to God and to their fellow human beings. A truly human life is a life in love which expresses itself in concrete service to one's neighbour and in concern for one's fellow human beings.[96]

Love expresses itself in part personally in relation to one's neighbour, in a personal account between human beings and in part socially and politically as a concern for human beings through the formation of the social structures in which human beings are involved. Brakelmann writes that these two forms of love form a unity and are not to be separated from one another. The task of love is both concern for the individual and the creation of those social structures which permit a humane life. Brakelmann thus appears to reject what I have called the dualistic thesis. The same ideal of love is to be realized in both private and political action.[97] He also rejects the amorality thesis. Politics is not a law unto itself nor is economic life in any sense "autonomous". Political action is also subject to ethical appraisal on the basis of the same ideal of love which is valid within individual ethics.[98]

According to Brakelmann the Christian ideal of love is combined with a principle asserting the equal value of all human beings. To care for other human beings implies respecting their value and not treating them as objects. In this sense love expresses itself in a striving for humanity. According to the principle of human value there is no difference between human beings and we must treat other human beings as our partners and as our brothers and

138

sisters. According to Brakelmann, this principle can be justified Christolog-ically. Christ's work of atonement implies that all men are equal before God and that all human beings being saved in Christ are brothers and sisters. Brakelmann claims also to embrace a Christian personalism according to which the individual develops as a person first in their encounter with other human beings. He rejects both an individualistic view of man which does not do justice to the social character of human beings and a collectivist view of man which does not do justice to the individual's independence. He writes that a human being is a person whose "I" is formed in relation to others. This personalism also forms the basis for the principle of human value.[99]

The principle of the equal value of all human beings according to Brakel-mann forms the basis for striving for democratic forms of government. Forms of government which involve a superior and subsidiary order are contrary to the equal value of all human beings. In such systems, human beings are treated only as objects or things. Instead according to Brakelmann one should strive for forms of government which respect human value and where a greater number of human beings take part in the exercise of power.[100]

The Christian ideal of love according to Brakelmann also leads us to pursue liberty and justice.[101] Liberty is based upon the freedom which is possible through the belief in Christ. It is a liberty which seeks to bring about the liberty of others and which expresses itself in a concern for their person-ality. Such liberty does not express individualistic self-centredness but instead assumes responsibility for the world and other human beings. It does not separate human beings from one another but expresses itself in service and cooperation.[102]

The goal is however, not only liberty but also justice. Brakelmann is opposed to an individualistic conception of freedom which is not combined with the pursuit of justice while at the same time he rejects the collectivist conception of justice which threatens liberty. Justice according to him is not identical with organized equality while at the same time justice implies that inequality is reduced so that the differences in the conditions of life do not become too great. In order to promote the liberty of the individual, a relative inequality ought to be accepted but at the same time one ought to prevent social inequalities forming the ground for political and economic repres-sion.[103]

Liberty and justice are not conceived by Brakelmann as intrinsic values in a teleological theory. Instead he would appear to hold that we promote liberty and justice by respecting certain fundamental rights. He holds that the principle of the equal value of all human beings is namely combined with certain human rights. As we have seen in Chapter 3, Brakelmann takes the view that every human beings has a right to work. This right is based upon the duty of human beings to work and to make a contribution to others. Brakelmann also means that every human being has a right to work that is meaningful and worthy of human beings. The fact that human beings work forms the basis for this right to humane working conditions. Furthermore Brakelmann holds that all who work have a right to participate in decision making. This right is also based upon the fact that human beings work and have the task of working. Brakelmann does not indicate in what sense he means that these rights are related to the Christian ideal of love and the principle of human value. Clearly however, they form a central component in his social ethical theory which thereby takes on the character of a deontological theory of rights.

A teleological ethics

John Atherton also argues that we ought to respect certain fundamental human rights. This argumentation is, however, combined with a social ethical theory which is teleological in nature. The fundamental components of this theory would seem to be two general principles. The first is that we in our political acts ought to try to bring about a society where there is a community of a similar kind to that of the Christian community which is symbolized by the Body of Christ. Atherton writes that the "Body of Christ" is an image of a Christian community where there exists a mutual interdependence. The parts are mutually dependent on the whole and on each other. All have a contribution to make and all contributions are necessary. The Church as the Body of Christ is according to Atherton a symbol of God's purpose with mankind as a whole. This too must exhibit a corresponding unity and community.[104]

The second principle is that in our political acts we ought to try to bring about what is good for all human beings in society i.e. we ought to seek the common good. This implies that we ought to promote certain values which are held in common by human beings with different philosophies of life. Even if today's society is pluralistic Atherton holds, that there are certain fundamental values about which all are agreed.[105] He goes as far as to say that these values are self-evident and that it is part of human nature to promote them.[106]

Atherton does not state clearly what the values are which ought to be promoted. He maintains however, that there is not only one single value but several basic values which ought to be pursued. Among these are community and solidarity. The aim is a state of togetherness where every person is dependent on every one else. In addition, both liberty and equality belong to these values. All human beings are essentially equal but at the same time one should respect a particular person's liberty as a unique individual.[107]

On the basis of these two principles Atherton puts forward a Christian vision of society which constitutes an image of the common good. We should strive to bring about what he calls a "Participating and Reciprocal Society". It is a vision of society which is valid for both Christians and non-Christians in a pluralistic society. At the same time it is a Christian vision which is motivated by the two images of the Body of Christ and the common good.[108]

What then are the characteristics of such a "Participating and Reciprocal Society"? This desirable society is defined to begin with by the fact that its citizens participate ("A Participating Society"). This implies that it is a society where all participate in the life of the community and in the making of decisions.[109] It is a democratic society which expresses respect for the equal value of all men by recognizing the right of all to participate in the decisions to be made. In this society, democracy is not limited to the political life. It also holds within economic life. According to Atherton, a suitable form for such a democracy is the West German model for co-determination where the employees have influence on the board of the company via elected representatives.[110]

In a "participating society" there also exists according to Atherton a just distribution of the good. What then does justice entail? Atherton appears to align himself with the view of John Rawls that the good ought to be distributed equally unless an unequal distribution benefits those most disadvantaged. He writes that in a participating society no one should be excluded because their living standard is too low.[111]

The society which Atherton recommends is also a "Reciprocal Society". This implies that it is a society where there is a balance between human beings' fundamental rights and their fundamental responsibilities to contribute to society.[112] In this society one respects the view that all men have certain fundamental rights. According to Atherton these are of two kinds. First of all there are "negative rights" which specify what a human being may not be deprived of. This is the right to life, liberty and ownership. The liberties involve political liberties, freedom of speech and association, freedom of conscience and freedom of thought.[113] In addition there are also "positive rights" which specify those things which ought to be encouraged in a human being. To these belong social rights such as the right to medical care, education and housing. The positive rights also include economic rights like the right to work and the right to a basic income for all in society.[114]

In a "reciprocal society", according to Atherton, it is not simply a matter of each and every one having certain rights but that each and every one also has a basic responsibility to make a contribution to society. These contributions are to be understood as a complement to the rights of the individual while at the same time these rights are a precondition for the duties of the individual. However Atherton writes, it is not the case that the rights are a reward for the contribution of the individual so that we earns our rights through our efforts. The contributions which we have to make to society are those activities where we try to bring about what is good for all. We can contribute through our own personal development, through cultural activities and also through our work.[115]

This vision of a "participating and reciprocal society" in Atherton is combined with a definite view of man. The view that everyone should be allowed to participate in society is based upon a Christian view of man according to which human beings realize themselves through an active and participatory life in association with others.[116] Atherton holds that the view that all men have certain basic rights is also based upon a Christian view of man. According to this view every person has a value as an individual forming part of a community which takes precedence over their responsibility to contribute to society. This value arises from the fact that every human being is the object of God's love through his creation and work of atonement. As a result all human beings have an equal value and therefore the rights are universal and independent of the contributions of each person.[117]

Atherton's social vision is also combined with other components in a Christian system of belief. He writes that theology gives us an image of who God is and an understanding of human life from the perspective of a belief in God. These theological reflections give rise to certain "moral presumptions" i.e. certain views about what is right and good.[118] Atherton lays particular emphasis on four such moral presumptions which arise from a Christian system of belief. These are (1) the unique significance of every human being as a being created in the image of God (2) the whole of the human family's fundamental unity in God (3) the equality of every person in the sight of God and (4) God's particular concern for those who are disadvantaged.[119]

Atherton links his reasoning here to the American social ethicist, J Philip Wogaman. In his attempt to develop an alternative to both a pure rule ethics and a pure act ethics the latter proposes certain "moral presumptions" for our decision making. These are certain moral principles which specify what probably is right or good and which can be tested by examining the reasons which speak against them.[120] Among the basic moral presumptions which Wogaman proposes are (1) the goodness of created existence (2) the value of individual human life (3) the human family's unity in God and (4) the equality of all human beings in God.[121]

At the same time that Atherton associates himself with the form of "Christian realism" which is to be found in Wogaman, he criticizes liberation theology. He holds that this runs the risk of developing into a one-sided theology which is not sufficiently balanced. In contrast to liberation theology, Atherton holds that the characteristic of a good society is not only that it promotes that which is good for the poor. There are also other social ethical criteria. Atherton also holds that an unbalanced support on behalf of the poor can create divisions among human beings. In his view liberation theology does not give sufficient weight to the significance of human solidarity.[122]

Atherton's social ethical theory can be characterized as a teleological ethics. Basic to the theory are two general moral principles, namely that we ought to try to bring about a community which is symbolized by the Body of Christ and that we ought to promote the common good. These teleological principles according to Atherton provide a motivation for certain basic human rights. The common good is promoted by the existence of a balance between rights and obligations. But what guidance do such moral principles give to our political acts in concrete choice situations? In his answer to this question, Atherton links his views to that of his teacher Ronald H Preston. The latter holds that Christian belief does not provide justification for detailed political programmes of action but rather for types of norms which in the manner of J H Oldham he calls "middle axioms". These are norms which belong to an intermediate level between general moral principles and detailed political recommendations. They combine insights from Christian faith with an analysis of existing social reality.[123]

Atherton accepts this view while at the same time emphasizing that the term "middle axiom" is an unfortunate one. Instead Atherton speaks of "middle-range moral imperatives". These are not binding for all Christians since Christians have both different theological views and different views about how the social situation is to be analysed. They are provisional and related to a particular situation and they give the lines along which Christian faith can express itself in a given situation.[124] Examples of such middle-range moral imperatives are those work ethical recommendations which we have encountered in Chapter 2. Among them are the recommendations that one should strive for work sharing and a reduction in working hours and that one should try to bring about democratic socialism.

Conclusion

What social ethical theories are encountered in the writings of contemporary Protestant theologians? What are their views about what constitutes a right political act and about what things have intrinsic value? How do they judge the constructive ethical theories encountered in contemporary moral philosophy? How do they see the relation between individual and social ethics? In this chapter we have seen that the theologians I deal with, put forward six distinct social ethical theories.

Several of them can be said to be deontological theories but these are of different kinds. J H Oldham's ethics can be characterized as a "deontological act ethics". He holds that Christian ethics is an "ethic of inspiration" as distinct from a teleological "ethic of ends" according to which the criterion of a right act is that it promotes certain pre-determined goals. This ethic of inspiration is a deontological ethics according to which an act is right if it is in agreement with the Will of God and constitutes an answer to his call. Oldham also rejects a rule ethics and proposes instead an act ethics according to which we can only decide in the actual choice situation what is the Will of God. At the same time he accepts certain "provisional rules" which do not constitute criteria for a right act but give us a certain guidance by reflecting the tradition of the Church and experiences of similar situations. Oldham's term "middle axiom" denotes such provisional rules. They are transitory expressions of the Christian ideal of love which specifies what is right in a given situation. An example of such a middle axiom is that we should try to bring about a "responsible society".

We have encountered a deontological theory of another kind in Günter Brakelmann. His ethics can be characterized as a "deontological theory of rights". A fundamental criterion in his social ethical theory is the Christian ideal of love which obliges us to care for other human beings. This ideal is combined with a principle of equal value of all human beings which obliges us not to treat other human beings merely as objects. The ideal of love encourages us to pursue both liberty and justice which however, are not to be conceived as intrinsic values in a teleological theory. Rather we promote liberty and justice by respecting certain basic rights. According to Brakelmann the principle of the equal value of all human beings is combined with such rights. Among them are the right of all human beings to work, the right to a meaningful and humane work and the right to participate in decision making for all those who work.

A third type of deontological theory is to be found in Emil Brunner. It can be characterized as a "monistic theory of duty". Brunner holds that there is only one moral principle which specifies what characterizes a right political act, namely a principle of justice. Within individual ethics Brunner advocates an act deontological theory of the same type as Oldham. There the criterion for a right act is that it is in agreement with the Will of God the content of which we discover only in the concrete choice situation. Within social ethics, however, a natural law ethics is valid according to which a right act is one which agrees with the divine order of creation. According to Brunner there are certain orders which are given by God in the creation, namely marriage and the family, work and the economic order, the state and the political order, cultural life and the Church. The criterion of a right political act is that it is in agreement with God's Will regarding these orders. This implies according to Brunner that there should exist a hierarchical order of superiority and inferiority. It is just that each and every one receives their due (suum cuique). This means that justice should take account of the equality of all human beings i.e. the fact that all men have the same value. But at the same time, justice should also take account of the fact that human beings differ in kind and function. God's Will regarding the orders of creation is therefore closely related to a "principle of merit" according to which it is just that the good is distributed in proportion to certain merits.

A fourth kind of deontological theory has been put forward by Tor Aukrust. It can be characterized as a "pluralistic theory of duty". In contrast to Brunner, Aukrust holds that there are several basic moral principles which together provide a criterion for a right act. Like Oldham, Aukrust holds that an act is right if it is in agreement with the Will of God but at the same time he rejects an act ethics of the type encountered in Oldham since he hold that there are certain criteria for God's Will. Aukrust formulates these as general moral principles. Two of these are "primary criteria" i.e. those which are specifically Christian. They are (1) an eschatological principle according to which the fundamental goal is to establish the Kingdom of God and (2) a principle of human value according to which human beings are goals in themselves and not simply means. The other five are "secondary criteria" i.e. those which are common. They are (3) the rules which make up the Decalogue (4) a principle of liberty according to which we ought to try and achieve both negative and positive freedom (5) a principle of equality according to which we ought to try to bring about social equality (6) a principle of justice according to which we ought to try to bring about a just distribution of the good and (7) the commandment of love according to which we are obliged to care for our fellow human beings. Of these criteria the love commandment comes first and is the only one which is unconditionally valid. According to Aukrust in order to apply these principles in a concrete situation one also requires knowledge about the content of the situation which can be obtained through a sociological analysis.

A completely different kind of social ethics is to be found in Arthur Rich. He embraces a "subject related theory" according to which the criterion for a right act is not simply certain properties of the act but also that it is carried out by a person with good state of mind. A basic norm in Rich's theory is that social institutions ought to be designed so that they are humane and good for human beings. Christian faith specifies what is humane on the basis of the belief in the coming Kingdom of God and the humanity which is manifested in Jesus Christ. It is a humanity which is characterized by three existentials namely Faith, Hope and Love. The ideal of love motivates in turn certain criteria for what is good for human beings. According to Rich these are (a) critical distance (b) relativity (c) relationality (d) human fellowship (e) participation (f) concern for the rest of creation and (g) participation in the creation. These criteria together with knowledge about social reality provide the motivation for certain maxims for social decision. These are not unchangeable rules of action but recommendations for certain concrete situations which are not of general validity. Rich rejects both a pure rule ethics and a pure act ethics. He rejects utilitarianism and criticizes Rawls' theory of justice. In reference to Max Weber, he claims to embrace an ethics of responsibility also involving considerations pertaining to acting person's state of mind. What makes an act right is not only the consequences of the act but also other qualities both in the act and in the acting subject. The acting subject must be a responsible person characterized by critical distance, human fellowship and concern for the rest of creation.

John Atherton is the only one of the theologians I discuss who embraces a teleological ethics. Like Brakelmann, he puts forward arguments for certain fundamental rights but in contrast to Brakelmann Atherton holds that the reason why these rights ought to be respected is that they promote certain fundamental values. His theory can therefore be characterized as a "teleological ethics". Fundamental to Atherton's theory are two teleological principles. First of all, in our political action, we should try to bring about a society where there exists a community akin to the Christian community which is symbolized by the Body of Christ where all are mutually dependent on one another and where all have a contribution to make. Secondly we ought in our political acts to strive for what is good for all human beings in society i.e. we ought to seek the common good. Among the values which ought to be promoted are *inter alia* community, liberty, equality and solidarity. On the basis of these principles Atherton argues for a Christian social vision which constitutes an image of the common good. One should strive for a "participating and reciprocal society". In a "participating society" everyone participates in the life of the community and in decision making and justice reigns. In a "reciprocal society" there is a balance between rights and duties. In such a society, we respect that each and every one has certain negative and positive rights and at the same time each and every one has an obligation to make a contribution to society.

These different social ethical theories are combined with different views about the relationship between individual ethics and social ethics. Emil Brunner embraces what I have called "the dualistic thesis". His individual ethics is a deontological act ethics which is based upon the Revelation in Christ. The criterion for a right private act is that it agrees with the Will of

God in the actual situation. Brunner's social ethics is on the other hand an ethics of justice based upon a doctrine of natural law. The criterion for a right political act is that it agrees with God's Will regarding the orders of creation.

This dualistic thesis is criticized by Aukrust and Brakelmann. Tor Aukrust maintains that there is no difference between a human being's personal morality and his or her morality associated with office. God's absolute requirements as they come to us in the Sermon on the Mount have a relevance for both individual and social ethics. Günter Brakelmannn maintains that the love which expresses itself in personal concern for others constitutes a unity with the love which expresses itself in concern for other human beings through an alteration of social structures. It is the same ideal of love which is valid for both our private and political acts.

The "amorality thesis" is also criticized by several of the theologians I deal with. Aukrust maintains that this standpoint is contrary to a Christian view of man. Because human beings have been given responsibility for the creation it is also necessary to subject political and economic acts to ethical judgement. Rich also rejects the thesis of the "autonomy" of economics and politics and maintains that ethics is not simply a matter of individual and personal ethics. Brakelmannn holds that the ideal of love which is valid within individual ethics is relevant also to political and economic acts and consequently he rejects the amorality thesis.

What kind of considerations form the basis for the differing social ethical theories to be found in the writings of contemporary Protestant work ethicists? What kind of arguments do these six theologians put forward for their differing views concerning the criteria for a right political act? There are three different types of theories and consideration which form a basis for these theories.

First of all these social ethical theories are combined with differing theories of man. Brunner's view of justice is based upon a view of man according to which there are both fundamental similarities and dissimilarities between human beings. We are equal in the sense that we are all created in the image of God and every human being has the same value. Simultaneously human beings are created as individuals and differ in kind and function and justice must take this into account. Oldham's act ethics is based upon a view of man according to which human beings are free and responsible persons who realize themselves in communion with God. Every human being is responsible before God and his neighbour and is called to respond to God's call in every new situation. To construct more detailed rules of action would contradict the freedom of the individual. At the same time Oldham holds that human beings are social beings who are connected to other persons and achieve fulfilment in relation to them.

Aukrust's social ethical theory is also based upon a view of man. His principle of equality is combined with the view that all men are equal before God by being created in the image of God and by being objects of his love. We are all created equal even if there are also inequalities between human beings. Aukrust's criticism of the amorality thesis is also combined with the view that human beings are responsible for the creation and are given the task of ruling over the earth. Rich's social ethics is also combined with a definite view of man. He holds that social institutions ought to be constructed so that they are good for human beings and that the Revelation in Christ illuminates what is humane. According to Rich a truly human life is characterized by Faith, Hope and Love. He also maintains that human beings bear the responsibility for the ecological environment while at the same time being created in the image of God, they have a special position in relation to the rest of creation.

Günter Brakelmann's deontological theory of rights is also combined with a view of man. His principle of human value is based upon "a Christian personalism" according to which the individual develops as a person only in their encounter with other human beings. Brakelmann rejects both an individualistic view of man which does not do justice to the social character of human beings and a collectivist view of man which does not do justice to the independence of the person. Similarly John Atherton's teleological ethics is also combined with a view of man. His view that all should participate in society is based upon the view that human beings realize themselves through an active and participatory life in the community of which they are part. We are all mutually dependent upon one another like limbs in a body. Atherton's view that all human beings have certain basic rights is based upon the view that every person, being created in the image of God and an object of His love, is a unique individual of great value.

Secondly these social ethical theories are combined with other theoretical views which make up a Christian system of belief. There are however different components in Christian system of belief which form the basis for the ethics of these theologians. Emil Brunner's social ethical theory is based upon a doctrine of creation. He holds that God in the creation has given human beings certain orders which constitute the necessary preconditions for human life. They are the family, the economic order, the state, culture and the Church. The criterion for a right political act is according to Brunner that it is in agreement with God's Will with the orders of creation.

Several other theologians, however, base their social ethics on Christology. This is the case with J H Oldham. According to him, what makes an act right is that it agrees with God's Will and insight about what is God's Will is attained only through the Revelation in Christ. It is only through the guidance which Christ gives that we can decide what is right in the actual situation. In a similar way, Tor Aukrust also holds that the Revelation in Christ is a fundamental source of insight about God's ethical demands. It provides us with the insight that the ultimate goal is the Kingdom of God. The principle of human value is motivated not by some inner property in human beings but by God's infinite love for man in Christ. The principle of liberty is motivated by the freedom which human beings possess in Christ. The principle of equality is motivated by Christ's work of atonement which makes us all equal before God.

Christology also forms the basis of social ethics in the case of Arthur Rich. He holds that the Revelation in Christ makes clear what is humane and good for human beings. Thereby the fundamental social ethical norm according to which we ought to promote what is humane is also clarified. Günter Brakelmann's social ethics is also based upon Christology. The foundation for the Christian ideal of love is according to him to be found in God's concern for the human being in Jesus Christ. In Him, God has revealed His love for humanity and in Him we also perceive how God conceives a truly human life. Brakelmann also provides a Christological motivation for the principle of the equal value of all human beings. Christ's act of atonement implies that all human beings are equal before God. Moreover Brakelmann also gives a Christological basis for certain values. Freedom for example is based upon the freedom that is possible in Christ.

Two of these theologians also base their social ethics on eschatology. For a start, this is so with Tor Aukrust. According to him, a primary criterion is an eschatological principle according to which the fundamental aim is to establish the perfect Kingdom of God where human beings will be made perfect. According to Aukrust, Christian ethics is an eschatological ethics with an absolute demand which presupposes an eschatological reestablishment of God's Kingdom. This is also true of Arthur Rich. According to him, social ethics has an eschatological entry point. It is on the basis of our hope in a future Kingdom of God that it specifies what is humane and what consitutes a desirable design for social institutions. On the basis of this perspective every social order is relative. Since the Kingdom of God cannot be realized here in time it is a question of adopting "critical distance" to every existing social order.

The doctrine of the Church is the part of the Christian system of belief which forms the basis of John Atherton's social ethical theory. He holds that we ought to strive for a society where there exists a community similar to the Christian community which is symbolized by the Body of Christ. The Church as the Body of Christ is a symbol of the kind of unity and community which God envisages for the whole of humanity. Of these six theologians, Atherton is the only one to give an ecclesiological basis to social ethics.

Thirdly the social ethical theories which are encountered in the writings of contemporary Protestant work ethicists are also combined with certain common human experiences and considerations which do not reflect a specific philosophy of life. This is the case with Brunner, Aukrust and Atherton. The orders of creation which Brunner writes about are understood by him as part of the natural law. Every human being can perceive what is God's Will regarding these orders independently of the Revelation in Christ. According to Brunner, it is a common view that it is just to pay attention to both the equality and inequality of human beings. In a corresponding way, Aukrust also holds that certain of the criteria he specifies have a natural law character. Every human being can achieve insight into these through common considerations. This is true in the case of the principle of liberty, the principle of equality and the principle of justice. For these principles common arguments which are not tied to a philosophy of life can be adduced. However Aukrust does not say what these arguments are.

John Atherton also holds that common human considerations can form the basis for social ethics. According to him a fundamental principle is that we ought to try to bring about the common good. These are values like community, solidarity, liberty and equality which are common for human beings with different philosophies of life. For these values, common arguments can be adduced. Atherton also writes that it is part of human nature to promote these values.

There are, however, no such common human considerations serving as a basis for the social ethical theories of Oldham, Rich and Brakelmann. Their ethics are instead strongly based upon Revelation in Christ. Like Aukrust and Atherton, Oldham and Rich hold that in order to be able to formulate what they call middle axioms and maxims for social decision, knowledge is needed about social conditions which can be obtained from the social sciences. However, there are no common human considerations which form the basis of their social ethical criteria.

Thus we find that there are three different kinds of consideration which serve as a basis for social ethical theories within the contemporary Protestant work ethics. These are theories of man, other theoretical views which form part of a Christian system of belief together with common human experiences and considerations which are not tied to a philosophy of life. The convictions in a Christian system of belief which in addition to a view of man can serve as a basis for social ethical theories are the doctrine of creation, Christology, eschatology or the doctrine of the Church. The interrelationships between these different components can be illustrated as follows:

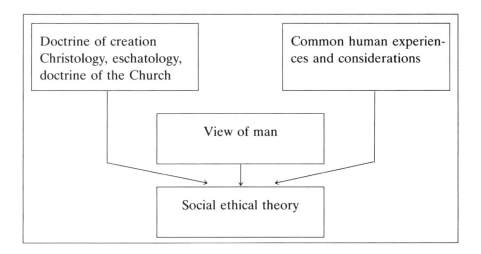

The relationships which are illustrated above are valid for Emil Brunner, Tor Aukrust and John Atherton. However Oldham, Rich and Brakelmann do not employ any common human considerations as a basis for their social ethical theories. Brunner combines his social ethical theory with a doctrine of creation. On the other hand, Oldham and Brakelmann's social ethics are based upon Christology. Aukrust and Rich combine their social ethics both with Christology and eschatology. Atherton's social ethics on the other hand is based upon a doctrine of the Church.

5. Theories of human nature

In the three previous chapters, I have clarified the content of those work ethical theories which are to be encountered within contemporary Protestant theology. At the same time I have investigated what types of consideration form the basis for the three components which make up a work ethical theory. We have seen that differing social ethical theories, differing theories of the meaning of work and different work ethical recommendations are based upon *inter alia* different theories of human nature. Theories of human nature are theories which contain a number of general views about what is common and characteristic for human beings as a species and about what defines a good human life. They also contain views about what prevents human beings from realizing a truly human life and about human possibilities of contributing to the achievement of a good life through their own efforts. A "view of man" of this type forms one of the theoretical components which make up a philosophy of life.

In this chapter I shall give a more detailed presentation of the view of man which is to be found in the writings of contemporary Protestant work ethicists. Its aim is first of all to clarify the content of their differing theories of human nature. In order to do this, I raise four analytical questions regarding my subject matter. These are: (1) What characterizes human beings as a species? This question asks what is common for all human beings and what is it that sets human beings apart from other living beings. (2) What is a good human life? What are the characteristics of a worthwhile human life? (3) What is it that prevents human beings from achieving a truly human life? In other words, the question takes up the reasons for the difference between the good life and the human situation as it actually is. (4) How far have human beings the capacity themselves to contribute to realizing a good human life? This question is concerned with how a truly good human life can be achieved.[1]

The "theories of human nature" which are to be found in the writings of contempary Protestant work ethicists do not consist of views about human beings which arise from empirical research. Within different sciences such as biology, medicine, sociology and psychology, one finds such empirically based theories of human nature. Such theories give us "knowledge about man". In contrast to them I shall deal here with those theories which constitute a "view of man". Such a view of man consists of a number of views which provide an overall image of man and which are based upon other types of commitments and rational arguments than those which rest upon empirical research. They are views which can be said to involve a philosophy of life. A view of man can consist of theories of the most differing type. They can be (a) empirically open theories which in principle but hardly in practice are empirically testable (b) theories of knowledge i.e. theories of the nature and grounds of knowledge (c) metaphysical theories i.e. theories which place human beings in a larger context without completely basing themselves upon empirical science (d) evaluative theories and (e) theories of salvation i.e. theories which assume a divine sphere of reality and specify how man can achieve an extra-empirical goal for his life.[2]

In an analytical survey, Anders Jeffner has identified no less than twenty different types of problem which the theories making up a view of man can be thought to answer. Among them is the question of what is the standard for rationality to be preferred.[3] Among them is also the question of what is the cosmic frame of human beings. A "metaphysical materialism" views man as a distinctive formation in an eternal, material universe while a "theory of creation" holds that the universe and thereby also human beings have come about through the intervention of a divine reality.[4] The question of the ontological status of human beings also belongs to these types of problem. A "strict materialism" is a monistic theory which holds that human mental processes and their products can be reduced to material objects while "an ontological idealism" is a monistic theory which holds that material objects can be reduced to mental processes. "Epiphenomenalism" is a dualistic theory which holds that there is a mental reality in addition to material reality although it exists as a reflection of the processes in the physical world while a "strict dualism" holds that mental reality is a form of existence of the same fundamental character as the material one. A "tripartite theory" assumes that human beings participate in three different fundamental forms of existence e.g. matter, soul and spirit.[5]

Other types of problem to which a view of man can provide an answer, are the question of whether human beings have free will and the question of whether human beings have a special mental standing in the animal kingdom. Is human life distinguished from that of other animals by some special property e.g. reason or self consciousness?[6] There is also the question of whether human beings have a special moral standing i.e. are there norms which ought to be applied only to human beings but not to other living beings.[7]

Two other questions which belong to this complex of problems are what distinguishes specifically human behaviour and the question of how different strategies to improve the human situation ought to be ranked. In the liberal individualistic tradition we encounter theories which give priority to the individual while within Marxist collectivist tradition we find theories which give priority to social structure and which hold that the individual is to be changed by a change in society.[8]

The theologians I deal with, do not provide an answer to all those distinct complexes of problems in their theories of human nature. In a couple of these question they also appear to adopt at least partly the same position. For example they adopt a common view about what is the cosmic frame of human beings. They all embrace a "theory of creation" according to which human beings have come about through an intervention by a divine reality. The view of man they adopt, is combined with a theistic view of reality and a doctrine of creation although this latter doctrine can be formulated in somewhat different ways. They also appear to share in part a common view about the ontological status of human beings. They all reject strict materialism but at the same time they do not seem to align themselves with epiphenomenalism. Their position would seem rather to be that of a strict dualism or a tripartite theory. They hold that human beings are part of a mental reality which is a form of existence of the same character as the material. Human beings are not simply bodies but also souls.

These theologians can also be said to adopt a "personalistic view of man". Ragnar Holte holds that such a view is crucially different from a "reductionist view of man". The latter is an understanding of man based solely upon what is empirically observable. A reductionist view of man involves not only methodological reduction but also an ontological reduction in the sense that it claims to exhaustively describe and explain human beings in terms of what is accessible to us through empirical observation.[9] In contrast to this view-point, the personalistic view of man holds that in every human beings there is an "I" which gives the person their own individual identity and which is not accessible to empirical observation. Human beings are "persons" with individual centres of personality while at the same time they operate within a social context and are influenced by others.[10] As Anders Jeffner maintains, such a personalistic view of man presupposes an idealistic, dualistic or tripartite theory about the ontological status of human beings. A reductionist view of man on the other hand presupposes a materialistic theory or possibly an epiphenomenalistic theory of some kind.[11]

154

The theologians I deal with are thus in agreement about these two questions. In order to elucidate the differences which exist between their theories of human nature, I have therefore chosen to limit myself to four other problem areas. The first concerns the question of what is characteristic of human beings as a species in contrast to other living beings. A common view in Christian tradition is that it is specific for human beings that they are created in God's image. But what then does this imply? One possible view is that it entails that human beings are rational in the sense that they can make conceptual determinations and have the capacity for self-consciousness. Another possible view is that human beings being made in the image of God possess a unique freedom and a unique moral responsibility. A third view is that it is specific for human beings that they have a capacity to achieve communion with God. A fourth view is that human beings as creatures made in the image of God are creative beings with a responsibility for their ecological environment. In this connection it can be of interest to pose the question of whether work is one of those things which are characteristic of human beings as a species.

The second complex of problems deals with the question of what constitutes a good human life. A conceivable answer to this question is that a good human life is one where human beings realize those properties which are specific for them as a species. When human beings realize themselves as rational or free beings or when they achieve communion with God, they are happy. Another possible view is that a good human life is one where human beings satisfy certain basic human needs such as the needs for food and shelter, love and community and the need to foster and develop the special talents of the individual. Theories of what constitutes a good human life can also differ by attaching a different emphasis to the values which are desirable.

The third complex of problems deals with what it is that prevents human beings from achieving a truly human life. A common view in Christian tradition is that every human being is a sinner. But what does this imply? What is the extent of human corruption? A more pessimistic view of man maintains that the true humanity of human beings has been completely lost and that human beings on account of original sin lack the capacity both to achieve insight about God and to perceive what is right. A more optimistic view of man maintains on the other hand that the Fall does not entail that human beings lose their status as creatures made in the image of God and that they therefore continue to be characterized by rationality, freedom and the capacity for moral insight.

The fourth complex of problems deals with the question whether human beings can themselves contribute to the achievement of a good human life. In Christian tradition, it is maintained that the communion of human beings with God is reestablished through the salvation brought about by Jesus Christ. But can human beings themselves in some sense contribute to their salvation? One possible view is that the possibility of salvation depends on human beings' own deeds. Another possible view is that salvation can be brought about by cooperation between God and human beings. A third view is that human beings are completely unable to contribute to salvation through their own acts. In this context, it can also be of interest to raise the question of whether the work of human beings can somehow contribute to the attainment of a good human life.

The aim of this chapter is however not simply to clarify the content of the theories of human nature put forward by these theologians. The aim is secondly also to clarify the types of arguments they adduce for their views of man. What kind of considerations and theories form the basis of their theories of human nature? Are they motivated by those views making up a Christian system of belief? If so, what components in such a system of belief form the basis of their views of man? Or are these theories motivated by common experiences and reflections which are not linked to a philosophy of life? I also set out to answer these questions in this chapter.

Human responsibility and factual differences

Emil Brunner's social ethical theory and theory about the meaning of work is combined with a view of man which exhibits clear similarities with the view of man to be encountered within the so-called I-Thou philosophy whose foremost exponent is the Jewish thinker, Martin Buber. He maintains both that human beings are free and individual persons and that they are social beings who realize themselves in relation to a divine "Thou". Brunner writes that it is characteristic of human beings that they are created in the image of God. This implies that they have been given reason by their Creator. This reason, according to Brunner, only realizes itself in freedom. This freedom is the substance of reason and constitutes an essential characteristic of human beings.[12] At the same time, Brunner emphasizes that human beings are not isolated individuals. They are placed in relation to a divine "Thou" and they realize themselves only through this relationship to God. Human beings achieve a truly human life only when God encounters them as a "Thou".[13]

Brunner writes that human beings as social beings are also responsible beings. Human existence is a responsible existence. The "I" can only develop in relation to a "Thou" and this "Thou" makes certain demands upon me. This makes me a responsible person, a person who has a responsibility for another. The power making the "I" responsible for the "Thou", according to Brunner, is God. It is the encounter with Him which transforms human existence into a responsible existence. Human beings are placed in an I-Thou relation not only to God but also to their fellows. Brunner writes that this implies that the meaning of existence is love. We achieve insight about this through the Creator revealing Himself as one who has created us in love, through love and for love.[14]

Brunner criticizes an exaggeratedly individualistic view of man. Such a view is to be found in certain formulations of liberalism where emphasis is laid upon the freedom of the individual and the state is conceived as a product of a social contract between individuals. At the same time he also criticizes an exaggeratedly collectivist view of man. Such a view is to be encountered within certain formulations of socialism where the collective whole is emphasized to such an extent that the individual becomes a mere subsidiary part of the collective. Contrary to these views, Brunner maintains that indiduals and society belong together. The individual cannot be imagined without community and the community cannot be conceived without the individual.[15] According to the Christian view of man, the individual has a personal value as a being created in the image of God. At the same time human beings are not isolated individuals but are social beings which form part of a community with others. It is through this community that they become individuals and responsible, free personalities.[16]

Because human beings are responsible and social beings, it follows that work belongs to that which is characteristic of human beings. In their work human beings are God's co-workers in his continuous act of creation. Man is to rule over nature through his work. Because they are created in the image of God, human beings have a special standing in relation to other living beings and have a responsibility for the world about them. As we have seen in Chapter 3 this implies that Brunner advocates what I have called the "activity line" according to which work is an activity by means of which human beings can realize those aspects of themselves which are specific to them as a species.

Brunner emphasizes both the similarities and differences which exist between human beings. He writes that on the one hand according to the Christian view of man there is a fundamental equality between human beings. All human beings are created in the image of God and therefore every human being has a value as a person and a human value which is equal to that of every other human being. For this reason one ought to treat all human beings equally and all human beings must enjoy certain rights to an equal extent.[17] On the other hand it is characteristic of Brunner that he emphasizes that human beings differ in kind and function. We belong to social orders and in these orders we have completely different functions and roles. God has created individuals and therefore there are factual differences between human beings. Brunner holds that these inequalities are a necessary presupposition for community between human beings.[18]

This emphasis upon the factual differences which exist between men has obvious consequences for Brunner's social ethical theory. According to him, justice entails having a regard to those differences in social position and function. This is to take place in such a way that the person with a higher social position receives the greater portion of the good. Another implication according to Brunner is that it is God's Will regarding the divine orders of creation that there exist a hierarchical order of superiority and inferiority *inter alia* in economic life. As we have seen in Chapter 2, this social ethical theory is in turn combined with what I have called "the merit line" and a criticism of what I have called "the participation line".

Brunner does not only discuss the question of what characterizes human beings as a species and what it means for man to be created in the image of God. He also touches upon the question of why human beings fail to realize a truly human life. He holds that every human being is a sinner. This implies that they are divorced from God and that their nature is perverted. Sin has created a breach in human life and therefore human beings fail to carry out those acts which are right.[19] The fact all human beings are sinners means that they place a great reliance upon themselves and believe themselves capable of accomplishing that which is good. Human beings rebel against God and have therefore too great a belief in their own powers. They do not perceive their own limitations.[20]

According to Brunner the fact that human beings are sinners does not imply that they completely lack the capacity to perceive what is right and good. In Brunner, we do not encounter as pessimistic view of man as in Barth. To be sure, he holds that human beings independently of the Revelation in Christ, lack the possibility of perceiving what constitutes a right private action. But within social ethics, Brunner holds, human beings have a capacity of their own to achieve insight into what characterizes a right political action.

Human beings as persons and social beings

J H Oldham's work ethical theory also derives its motivation to a large extent from a definite view of man. It forms the basis of both his theory about the meaning of work and of his work ethical recommendations. He himself also explicitly states that the Christian doctrine about the meaning of work must be justified on the basis of a Christian view of man. According to the Christian view of man, human beings are both persons and social beings. Oldham writes that the source of the Christian doctrine of work must be the

Christian view of man as a person and social being, as it is to be found in the Biblical Revelation.[21]

What then is the content of a Christian view of man according to Oldham? In answering this question, he begins by addressing the question of what is characteristic of man in contrast to other beings. According to the Christian view of man, what is specific for human beings is first of all that they are persons. This implies *inter alia* that they realize themselves in communion with God. Human beings are true human beings in relation to God. They are infinite beings. Their lives are in the deepest sense, a conversation with God.[22]

According to Oldham, this also implies that human beings are stewards. They must cooperate with God in his continuous act of creation and thereby use their resources in agreement with the Will of God. In their stewardship, human beings must also use the powers they have obtained from science and technology. But these powers must be employed as a humble and loving response to God's own creative work so that they are useful and not injurious to human beings.[23] Human beings whose lives are a conversation with God, are humble and have a sensitive conscience which continually seeks to ascertain the Will of God. This is also true within political life. To acknowledge life in response to God's call entails that human beings must also try to promote God's purpose with human life through their political acts.[24]

Oldham's view that a true human life is a life in communion with God has clear consequences for his theory about the meaning of work. He holds that human beings consequently achieve a true life not only through work but above all through contemplation. Human beings achieve their supreme definition not in work but in communion and worship. In contrast to Brunner, Oldham adopts what I have called a "contemplation line" according to which human beings realize a truly human life not through work but through communion with God.

Oldham's view of man has also implications for his social ethical theory. Since human being become true human beings in communion with God, a right action constitutes a response to God's call. According to Oldham, human beings are responsible and responsive persons. Like Brunner, Oldham seems to share several of the views to be found in Buber's I-Thou philosophy. He would seem to hold that every human being is formed as a person in the meeting with a divine Thou. Every human being is also responsible before God and called upon to act in response to God's call in each new situation. Human beings have to discharge this responsibility freely. A rule ethic which specifies the type of acts which are right, would according to Oldham deprive human beings of the freedom which is their due.[25]

A Christian view of man maintains secondly according to Oldham that human beings are essentially social beings. They are social beings which do not exist in isolation but are linked to other human beings. The relation to other human beings can be of different kinds. It can be (a) a direct person-to-person relation in total self-devotion e.g. in the love between man and woman (b) a coming together in an association or fellowship when one cooperates to achieve a common purpose or (c) a relationship to fellow human beings in and via collectives and institutions such as the Church, the state, science and the labour movement. In these different ways human beings according to Oldham are persons who are linked to other persons. They are persons who achieve fulfilment in their relations to other human beings. In short they are social beings. Because human beings are social beings who live in relation to other human beings, they are called in their work to serve their neighbour and society.[26]

Thirdly a Christian view of man, according to Oldham, also entails a certain way of looking at the relationship between human beings and nature. He writes that nature is God's creation and that as such it must be accepted and venerated by human beings. Human beings are God's co-workers in the realization of his purpose with the world and ought as such to respect the divine order of creation.[27]

According to Oldham, the Christian view of man does not only contain a view about what defines a truly human life. It also involves a view that human beings have a limited capacity to realize a good life. Oldham claims to have a "realistic view of man". This is a view which contains both an insight into human limitations and a hope in the victory of the good. According to a realistic view of man, it is impossible to establish a perfect society here upon earth. At the same time, Oldham holds that this view must be distinguished from a "pessimistic view of man". For it holds namely that God's acts in the world are directed towards the good and that this therefore will ultimately be achieved.[28]

On the basis of this realistic view of man, Oldham criticizes the American Social Gospel movement. This liberal theological movement according to him, took a far too optimistic view of human nature. This was expressed in the view that the Kingdom of God is a perfect society which could be realized here in time. It was also expressed in the assumption that all human beings of goodwill have a capacity to see what is right. As a result, the content of Christian ethics was reduced to something purely humane.[29] Oldham rejects these views. In fact he can be said to go further than Brunner in his criticism of liberal theology in the sense that even in social ethics he does not reckon upon human beings independently of the Revelation having a capacity of their own to see what is right. In this sense, Oldham takes a more pessimistic view of man than Brunner.

The equality of human beings before God

What is it that characterizes human beings in relation to other living creatures? Like Brunner and Oldham, Tor Aukrust maintains that a fundamental feature of the Christian view of man is that human beings are created in the image of God. But what does this imply? Aukrust writes that human beings by virtue of this dignity share in God's sovereignty over nature. Human beings take charge of the earth and become rulers over nature. Being made in the image of God, they are responsible for their environment both individually and collectively. This responsibility is discharged not least through work.[30] God's work of creation is not a finished chapter but something which continues. Human beings are called upon to be God's co-workers in this continuous act of creation by making use of nature and ruling over their environment.[31]

The theologians I study are agreed that human beings are created in the image of God. What is characteristic of Aukrust is that he emphasizes that this entails that all human beings are also equal before God. The principle of the equal value of all human beings is justified not by some intrinsic human property: it is justified instead by the fact that all human beings are objects of God's unbounded love. But all human beings are the same before God. They are the same because they are created in the image of God. Therefore equality ought to be pursued. Aukrust maintains certainly that all human beings are in fact dissimilar. He writes that each and every one is created as a person. The individual is not simply a mechanical example of the species. Human beings differ with respect to talent, interest and character. As a result, the pursuit of equality does not entail a pursuit of conformity. In contrast to Brunner, however, Aukrust does not hold that justice requires that one should take into account these differences so that the good is distributed according to the results achieved. Instead he holds that it is just to take account of the different needs of human beings. In the wage question, Aukrust therefore rejects the "the merit line" and proposes instead an "equal wages line".[32]

Like Brunner, Aukrust rejects an exaggeratedly individualistic view of man. The individual cannot understand their humanity in isolation from others. The individual always stands in relation to other human beings. They are referred to and depend upon other human beings. The relationship of human beings to other human beings always takes place in terms of certain social orders. Their relationships to others and to themselves is always influenced by the form these social orders take.[33]

For this reason, Aukrust also criticizes the existentialist view of man which he holds is too individualistic. According to existentialism, human beings realize themselves when they on their own and with full personal responsibility make a choice. To live is to choose and the individual person must act completely independently of conventional norms and rules. Contrary to this type of individualism, Aukrust maintains that human beings are not independent in this sense. Individuals do not make an ethical choice on their own. Ethical choices are not simply an individual matter where the community plays no part. On the contrary, human beings are citizens in a society and they are always part of a human community. Aukrust therefore cannot accept the kind of act ethics to be found in J H Oldham.[34]

Simultaneously Aukrust rejects an exaggeratedly collectivist view of man. Human beings cannot be exclusively treated from a social perspective. They always stand in relation to something but they also enjoy a relationship to themselves.[35] For this reason, Aukrust also criticizes a Marxist view of man which he holds, is too collectivist. Despite the humanist perspective associated with this ideology, it would appear to view society as primary in relation to the individual. With the Marxist emphasis upon society, the individual human being risks being forgotten. Nor does Marxism perceive that an end to human alienation presupposes both an alteration of society and an alteration of the individual's attitude to life.[36]

What is it that prevents human beings from achieving a truly human life? According to Aukrust, the impediments are to be found not only in certain social situations but also in a limitation of human beings themselves. While human beings are created in the image of God, they are also according to the Christian view of man, sinners. Human nature is ambivalent; it is characterized by both good and evil. Aukrust even writes that "nature" i.e. the work of creation, became "completely corrupted" with the Fall. This does not imply, however, that the work of creation is completely evil. However God's orders of creation are not identical with existing social orders. These also bear the mark of the Devil and man's rebellion against the Will of God.[37]

Aukrust maintains that evil according to the Christian view of man, is something which not only pertains to social structures but is to be found in human beings themselves. He therefore criticizes a Marxist view of man. He holds that Marxism fails to take the reality of evil with sufficient seriousness. It maintains that class society is permeated by evil but it fails to see that the evil is a constituent of human beings themselves. Marxism does not perceive that human alienation is caused both by certain external social factors and by the individual's personal attitude to life. Aukrust writes that evil does not cease to exist when society has been changed. Therefore both a change of society and of the individual are needed in order for human alienation to be suspended.[38]

Human sin, according to Aukrust, has an influence upon the capacity of human beings to see what is right and good. In contrast to Oldham, he maintains that human beings being created in the image of God, have a capacity independently of the Revelation, to perceive what is right, i.e. what is God's ethical demand. Because of the Fall, however, human insight into natural law is fragmentary and incomplete. Human reason can err and does not give sufficient guidance about what is right. A corrective to natural law is therefore needed. This is provided with the Revelation. It is only through the Revelation, we receive complete insight into the absolute demand.[39]

What possibilities have human beings themselves to contribute to achieving a good human life? According to Aukrust, human beings cannot contribute to achieving a perfect life in communion with God. Such a state is achieved only through Christ's work of atonement. However he holds that human beings through their own efforts can contribute to their own "self realization" in another sense. Aukrust does not discuss the issue concerning the possibilities of realizing those properties which are common for human beings as a species. In contrast to Brunner, he does not put forward a species-realization theory. On the other hand, he discusses how individuals can develop their own individual talents and capacities. Such a development of personality can according to Aukrust take place through work. He puts forward what I have called "a self-actualization line" according to which human beings through their work can develop their individual characters. Work can also contribute to an all-rounded development of personality in the sense that the individual develops all their various capacities. At the same time, Aukrust maintains that this kind of self-realization does not occur only through work. For an all-rounded development of personality, creative leisure activities are also required.[40]

A Christological humanism

Arthur Rich's work ethical theory is also closely related to a view of man. This is the case with respect to his theory of the meaning of work according to which work belongs to a human being's "humanum" i.e. what makes a human being, human. According to Rich, human beings in their work can realize themselves as responsible and creative subjects. It is also true of his social ethical theory according to which social institutions ought to be organized so that they are good for human beings. According to Rich, the nature of humanity is elucidated by the Revelation in Christ where it becomes clear what characterizes a truly human life.

What is it that sets human beings apart from other living beings? Rich holds that what characterizes a truly human existence are faith, hope and love. In an allusion to existential philosophy, he formulates it so that

163

humanity is characterized by three fundamental "existentials" i.e. fundamental structures in human existence. These existentials are faith, hope and love. Rich writes that these expressions denote common human experiences. Faith is an act of trust and confidence, hope is trust in the future and charity is a combination of faith and hope.[41]

According to Rich we all have an experience of the gap between actual human existence and what is truly human. It is an experience of evil which can be of both personal and structural character.[42] But human beings also have an experience of "the completely other". This is the Christian experience of the encounter with Jesus Christ. With Him, God's Kingdom intervenes in existence and thereby the meaning of a true human life is made clear. A specific aspect of Christianity is the belief in the Resurrection which implies that human beings and the world have a future. There exists something which is completely different and as a result there is also a possibility of finally achieving a truly human life.[43]

According to Rich, the specifically Christian interpretation of humanity as faith, hope and love is combined with this belief in resurrection. It leaves its mark upon faith, hope and even love. According to Rich, it is the Revelation in Christ which ultimately illuminates these existentials and thereby shows us what is humane. The experience of faith, hope and love conceived in their most radical sense is specifically Christian. It is an experience of how these existentials are rooted in the completely different which is encountered in Jesus Christ.[44]

According to Rich, work also belongs to that which is characteristic for human beings. Like Brunner, he can, as we have seen in Chapter 3, be said to embrace what I have called "the activity line". Rich holds that it is part of truly human life that human beings are not only objects but also creative and responsible persons. As persons they are related to other persons and placed in an I-Thou relationship to other human beings. As creatures made in the image of God, they have a special status in relation to other living beings while at the same time they have a responsibility for their ecological environment. It is as such creating and responsible persons that human beings can realize themselves in their work. In this latter sphere, they can take responsibility for other human beings and devote themselves to a creative activity whereby they can thus transform nature and bring about things which nature cannot create by itself. For this reason, according to Rich, work can be said to belong to human beings' "humanum" i.e. that which makes human beings, human beings.[45]

What possibilities have human beings to achieve a good human life? Arthur Rich stresses that human beings by themselves cannot finally realize a truly human life here in time. He asserts this in a criticism of the view of man which is associated with Marxism. According to Marx, the capitalist system of production has brought about an alienation i.e. a difference between human beings as they are and the true human being. In a classless society it is possible to overcome this alienation. In that society, a truly human life can be achieved.[46] This Marxist humanism, according to Rich, is an "absolute humanism". It holds that the absolute human being can be created through a change in society. Human beings are ascribed the capacity to realize their true being themselves. Thereby human beings take God's place. They become their own Creator and their own Redeemer.[47]

Rich holds that this Marxist view of man is far too optimistic. In contrast, he holds that a Christian humanism is a "realistic humanism". It is a view of man which is combined with an eschatology which involves a hope in the future Kingdom of God. In the light of this future Kingdom of God, no existing institution or society can be taken to be definitive. All that can be achieved here in time is a relatively superior social order. In this world, it is impossible to achieve a perfect society where the true human being can finally be attained. It is first in the future Kingdom of God that human beings can realize their true being. Rich writes that this viewpoint is not anti-revolutionary. While holding that society must be changed to something which is relatively better, it has a realistic expectation about what can be achieved here in time. By changing society, human beings do not achieve a definitive liberation.[48]

A Christian personalism

Günter Brakelmann's theory of rights is based upon a view of man which he himself calls "a Christian Personalism". It maintains that human beings are unique and independent individuals who have an individual personality centre. At the same time, it maintains that human beings discover their "I" through their relations to other individuals. The individual develops as a person in the encounter with the other's "Thou". Personality manifests itself in social intercourse; the "I" is formed in relation to others. Like Brunner and Oldham, Brakelmann seems to link his views with those within the so called I-Thou philosophy. Like Brunner, Brakelmann also criticizes both an individualistic view of man which does not do justice to the social character of human beings and a collectivist view of man which does not do justice to the independence of the individual. Human beings are persons who are placed in a social relationship to others.[49]

According to Brakelmann, a characteristic feature of human beings is that they are created in the image of God. What does this imply? According to Brakelmann it entails that human beings have a responsibility for the world about them. Human beings are God's co-workers and responsible stewards. Work is therefore, Brakelmann writes, an "anthropological basic datum". It is something which belongs to what is human and something which is characteristic for human beings as creatures made in the image of God. By means of work, human beings can realize themselves as creating and free beings.[50] At the same time, Brakelmann stresses that human beings become persons and realize a truly human existence not through working but through standing in relation to God. It is when God makes demands upon human beings that their humanity is manifested. For this reason, human beings cannot create themselves i.e. become true human beings, through work. A truly human existence presupposes that human beings stand in relation to God.[51]

According to Brakelmann human beings are not simply made in the image of God. They are also sinners. This implies that they are characterized by pride and that they act contrary to the Will of God. For this reason, they cannot by themselves realize a truly human existence. Brakelmann rejects those "self-realization theories" which hold that human beings by their own powers and efforts can bring about a good human life. According to the Lutheran doctrine of justification, human beings cannot realize a true life through their own efforts. It is something which can only be received through faith. Human beings have to make efforts, not in order to be saved but to serve others. As persons, human beings realize themselves through their belief in God and not through their own efforts.[52] Brakelmann can therefore be said to embrace what I have called "the contemplation line" according to which human beings become true human beings not through work but through their relation to God.

The Christian view of man, Brakelmann maintains, is realistic. It does not simply maintain that human beings are created in the image of God but also that human beings are sinners. It does not deny the power of sin but at the same time it maintains God's power to provide a life in freedom. Thereby it rejects both an exaggeratedly optimistic and an exaggeratedly pessimistic view of man. In this sense, according to Brakelmann, there are great similarities between a Christian view of man and the humanistic view of man to be found within democratic socialism. This ideology is not so optimistic that it believes that it is possible to create an ideal society with perfectly good human beings. Instead it is tempered by a realistic view of man which perceives the limitations of politics when it comes to creating a perfect society.[53]

Democratic socialism, writes Brakelmann, believes that it is able to create a more humane society but it does not believe that it can finally remove every form of alienation. It is not characterized by any naive expectation in the future but makes a more realistic judgement of the possibilities of achieving

166

relative progress towards freedom and justice.[54] Democratic socialism is characterized by a realistic view of man which exhibits great similarities with the view of man which is associated with Christian belief. According to the Christian view of man, human beings have a responsibility to act at present even if it is impossible to bring about the Kingdom of God here and now. It is desirable to strive for a more human future even if human beings will never succeed in creating a perfect society here on earth.[55]

When one maintains that socialism has an exaggeratedly "optimistic view of man" which cannot be combined with a Christian anthropology, one expresses according to Brakelmann an unjustified criticism of socialism. It is a criticism which is often combined with a conservative view according to which human sin entails a strong state and strong social orders. In order to keep sin in check, a hierarchical order is required. On the basis of a pessimistic view of man, this conservatism rejects the pursuit of freedom, equality and fraternity. Brakelmann holds that such a conservative theology of order is right inasmuch as we must not have an unlimited faith in human capacity but in his view it is combined with too pesssimistic a view of man. There is no justification for using a Christian view of man to legitimize hierarchically structured social orders.[56]

Human beings as active and participating beings

What kind of theory of human nature is to be found in the writings of John Atherton? This British work ethicist has not given any detailed presentation of his view of man in his writings. At the same time, we have seen that certain anthropological assumptions form the basis of his social ethical theory and his theory of the meaning of work. Above all, there are certain assumptions about what is characteristic for human beings as compared with other living beings.

First of all according to Atherton, a Christian view of man maintains that every individual human being is a free and unique individual. Every person has a unique significance and great worth as a being created in the image of God. It is a value which the individual has independently of their efforts and results. The basis of a person's value is to be found in the fact that they are the object of God's love in His work of creation and atonement. Atherton writes that for this reason, all human beings have an equal value. All human beings are ultimately equal.[57]

Secondly according to Atherton, a Christian view of man also maintains that every human being is part of a community. We are all mutually dependent upon one another like limbs in a body. Atherton writes that the human family forms a fundamental unity in God. Therefore the Christian view of man does not differ only from every form of collectivism: it also differs from every form of individualism. Atherton criticizes both the collectivism of totalitarian ideologies and the neo-liberal view of the person as an atomized individual.[58]

Atherton holds that because human beings are social beings, their lives are essentially active and participatory. According to the Christian view of man, human beings realize themselves through an active and participating life in the community. All human beings must participate in the life of the community and in decision making. Every human being is namely a steward of the divine order of creation. We therefore realize ourselves as human beings by making a contribution to society.[59]

Atherton thus also holds that work is important for human self realization. Work is a kind of activity which contributes to the personal development of the individual. In contrast to Brunner and Rich, Atherton does not embrace a species-realization theory but rather a personal development theory. Like Aukrust, he would seem to hold that individuals in their work can develop their individual capacities and talents. This is the viewpoint I have called "the self-actualization line".

Conclusion

What theories of human nature are to be found in the writings of contemporary Protestant work ethicists? What are their views about what is characteristic for human beings as a species and about what constitutes a good human life? What are their views about what prevents human beings from realizing a truly human life and about human abilities to contribute to the realization of a good human life? In this chapter, we have seen that the theologians I deal with, provide partly differing answers to these questions.

Their theories of human nature exhibit great similarities in certain respects. They have a common view about the human cosmic perspective. All hold that human life is to be understood as a gift of the Divine Creator. They can be also said to embrace a personalistic view of man in the sense that they assume that every human being is a person with an individual personality core. At the same time, they hold that human beings are social beings. This implies that their "I" develops both in its relationship with God and other human beings. Brunner, Oldham and Brakelmann link their views expressly to the so-called I-Thou philosophy. This however, does not prevent certain differences arising between their theories of human nature.

The answer to the question concerning what is common for all human beings and specific to human beings in contrast to other living beings is given in six partly divergent ways. All are agreed that human beings are created in the image of God but they have somewhat different views about what this implies. A first view is that it implies that human beings are free and responsible beings. This view appears in Emil Brunner. He holds that human beings as creatures made in the image of God are rational beings and furthermore that their freedom is something which is characteristic of them. At the same time, according to Brunner, human beings are social beings who realize themselves as true human beings only in relation to a divine Thou. They are also placed in a social community with other human beings and as such are responsible and creative individual beings. Brunner therefore rejects an exaggeratedly individualistic and an exaggeratedly collectivist view of man.

Another view is that human beings are creative and responsible beings with a unique capacity for faith, hope and love. This view is to be found in the writings of Arthur Rich. While allowing that rationality and liberty are specifically human, he places more emphasis upon the fact that human beings, as creatures made in the image of God, have a responsibility for their environment. According to him, a truly human life is defined by faith, hope and love. Rich writes that humanity is characterized by these three "existentials". The unique capacity of human beings for love entails that they are creative and responsible persons. They are related to other persons and have a responsibility for the ecological world about them.

A third view is that human beings are both persons and social beings who are characterized by freedom and a unique capacity for communion with God. This view is to be found in J H Oldham. He lays great emphasis upon human freedom while at the same time emphasizing that it is in the capacity for communion with God that man's status as a being created in the image of God finds expression. A unique feature of human beings is that they are persons who realize themselves in communion with God. Human beings are infinite beings whose lives in the deepest sense are a conversation with God. A right action is therefore also a response to God's call in the particular choice situation. Moreover, according to Oldham, the Christian view of man maintains that human beings are essentially social beings. They are social beings who are linked to other human beings. According to the Christian view of man it is also the case that human beings stand in a relationship to nature and are required to respect it.

A fourth view is that human beings are responsible for the world about them and have a unique capacity for communion with God. We have encountered this view in Günter Brakelmann. Like Oldham, he lays great emphasis upon the fact that the status of human beings as creatures made in the image of God is expressed in their capacity for communion with God. At the same time like Rich, he also relates this status to the responsibility of human beings for their environment. Brakelmann claims to embrace a "Christian person-alism" according to which human beings discover their own "I" through their relationship to other individuals. Brakelmann criticizes an individualistic view of man which does not do justice to the social nature of human beings. At the same time, he rejects a collectivist view of man which does not do justice to personal independence. Like Oldham, he stresses that human beings realize themselves as persons only in their relationship to God.

A fifth view is that human beings by virtue of the fact that they are created in the image of God, are stewards with responsibility for the world about them. This view is to be found in Tor Aukrust. His view of human beings as creatures made in the image of God shows certain similarities to the views of Rich but in contrast to the latter he does not link them to existential philosophy. Aukrust holds that human beings as creatures made in the image of God share in God's sovreignty over nature and have been given the task of ruling over the world about them. Like Brunner, Aukrust rejects an exagger-atedly individualistic view of man which does not take account of the fact that individuals are always placed in certain social orders which they are influen-ced by. He does not stress the freedom of human beings as strongly as Oldham and furthermore criticizes the act ethics of the type which we have met in Oldham. Aukrust also rejects an exaggeratedly collectivist view of man which neglects the significance of the individual.

A sixth view is finally that human beings are active and participating beings who are always part of a social community. This view is to be found in the writings of John Atherton. He links the status of human beings made in the image of God with their capacity for concern for others and he emphasizes more strongly than does Oldham that human beings are social beings. Ather-ton holds that human beings by virtue of the fact that they are created in the image of God, are free and unique individuals of great worth. All human beings because they are objects of God's love, have an equal value. At the same time, Atherton stresses that every human being also is part of a community. We are all dependent upon one another like the limbs in a body. The human family forms a fundamental unity in God with the result that Atherton criticizes exaggeratedly individualistic views of man. Because hu-man beings are social beings, their lives are essentially active and participa-tory. We realize ourselves as human beings by contributing to society.

These differing views are combined with two different views about whether work is a defining feature of human beings as a species. As we have seen, Brunner and Rich embrace what I have called "the activity line" according to which work is a characteristic of human beings. Brunner conceives human beings as responsible and social beings and holds therefore that work belongs to that which is specifically human. Through work, human beings have to rule over the earth and to be God's co-workers in creation. Rich holds that human beings are creative and responsible persons and that as such they realize themselves in work. This activity belongs to that which makes a human being, human.

Oldham and Brakelmann, on the other hand, embrace "the contemplation line" according to which contemplation and communion with God more than work are what uniquely characterize human beings. Oldham holds that it is above all in communion with God that human beings realize themselves. Brakelmann admits that work belongs to that which sets human beings apart but at the same time he stresses that human beings realize themselves as persons first in standing in a relationship to God. A truly human life is therefore something which can only be received in faith.

These differing views are also combined with two different views about the implications of the status of human beings as creatures made in the image of God, for how the good ought to be distributed. One view can be called "the difference line". It proposes that the just distribution of the good ought to take into account the actual differences which exist between human beings. This standpoint is to be found in the writings of Emil Brunner. He holds that there exists a fundamental similarity between human beings since they are all created in the image of God and as such they have the same value. At the same time, Brunner stresses that there exists actual differences between human beings both in kind and function. These differences ought to be noted in distributing power and income and as a result Brunner rejects the participation line and puts forward the merit line.

The second viewpoint we can call "the equality line". It maintains that a just distribution of the good ought preeminently to note that all human beings are equal before God. This viewpoint is put forward by Tor Aukrust. He stresses that all human beings are created in the image of God and have therefore equal value. Certainly all human beings are different in the sense that each and every one is created as a unique person but it is their equality which is critical in the matter of a just distribution.

The question of what it is that prevents human beings from realizing a truly human life is also dealt with in different ways by these Protestant work ethicists. All are agreed that human beings are not only made in the image of God but are also sinners. But they have partly different views about what this implies. Several of them maintain that a Christian view of man is "realistic". This implies, they hold, that this view neither entails too "optimistic" belief in human possibilities for achieving a good human life nor too "pessimistic" a view about the capacities of human beings. J H Oldham maintains that this realistic view of man contains an insight into man's limited capacity to achieve a good human life. At the same time, Oldham also seems to hold, that human beings on account of sin, have a limited capacity, independently of the Revelation, to perceive what is right.

Arthur Rich, like Oldham, criticizes an exaggeratedly optimistic view of man and stresses that a truly human life cannot be realized here in time through social change. A truly human life, according to Rich, can be achieved only in the future Kingdom of God. On the basis of an eschatological perspective, he argues against an absolute humanism for what he calls a "realistic humanism". Similarly Brakelmann also holds that human beings cannot realize a truly human life through their own efforts. A Christian view of man is realistic in the sense that it takes account of the fact that human beings are sinners while at the same time it emphasizes God's power to grant us a life in freedom.

Oldham, Rich and Brakelmann, according to my view, take a relatively "pessimistic" view of human capacity for moral insight. A view which has, in this respect, somewhat greater faith in human beings is to be found in Brunner, Aukrust and Atherton. They hold that human limitations do not imply that human beings lack the capacity independently of the Revelation to perceive what is right. Brunner holds that it is true of all human beings that they are created in the image of God and are sinners. But at the same time, he holds that they have a certain capacity to perceive what is right at least in political life. Aukrust stresses that the evil is to be found not only in social structures but also in human beings themselves. The sinfulness of human beings entails that their capacity to see what is right is limited but all human beings despite their imperfections have a certain capacity in this respect. Atherton also shares this faith in human capacity.

What opportunities have human beings themselves to contribute to the realization of a good human life? The theologians I deal with all hold that their possibilities are extremely limited. This is especially emphasized by Brakelmann. He stresses that human sin entails that human beings cannot realize a truly human life through their own efforts. This is something which can only be received in faith and which is a gift of God. It is only in relation to God that human beings realize themselves as persons. In a similar way, Rich also emphasizes that a good human life cannot be achieved through social changes but only in the Kingdom of God.

Two of the theologians I deal with, however, hold that human beings through their own efforts can contribute to achieving a good human life in another sense. They hold that it is possible through work to develop one's own individual talents and capacities. This is a viewpoint which I have called "the self actualization line". It is to be found in the writings of Aukrust and Atherton. For Aukrust, work can contribute to human self-realization, not in the sense that human beings can thereby realize what is characteristic for themselves as a species but in the sense that they can thereby develop their individual talents. According to Atherton, work is also a means for human self realization in the sense that it can contribute to the personal development of the individual.

What kinds of consideration form the basis for the differing theories of human nature which are to be found in the contemporary Protestant work ethics? What kinds of arguments do these six theologians adduce for their differing views about the implications of the fact that human beings are simultaneously made in the image of God and are sinners? These theories are based upon two different types of theories and considerations.

First of all they are combined with other theoretical views which belong to a Christian system of belief. However, different components in a Christian system of belief form the basis of the views of man adopted by these theologians. Several of them base their view of man upon the doctrine of creation. This is true of Emil Brunner. His view of man is closely related to his theology of the orders of creation. It is God who has created all human beings in His image and has thereby supplied the basis for equality of value. At the same time God has also in the creation produced the fundamental differences which actually exist between human beings. Human beings are created with certain social orders which are part and parcel of their existence. It follows, according to Brunner, that the individual and the community are indissolubly linked to one another.

Oldham's view of man is also closely related to the doctrine of creation. Because the life of human beings is a conversation with God, human beings must cooperate with God in his continuous act of creation. Because nature is created by God, human beings must respect and honour nature. In a similar way, Tor Aukrust's view of man is based upon a doctrine of creation. It is fundamental to Aukrust's standpoint that human beings are created in the image of God. This implies that they are God's co-workers in the continuous act of creation. They have the task of ruling over the earth. Human beings are created equal before God, while simultaneously we are created with different talents and possibilities. Through our work, we can contribute to realizing our individuality.

Brakelmann's view of man is also based upon a doctrine of creation. According to him, the fact that human beings are created in the image of God, means that they are stewards who are responsible for the world around them and their work is a mandate. According to Brakelmann, work is therefore an "anthropological basic datum". Similarly Atherton also combines his view of man with a doctrine of creation. According to him, human beings are stewards of the divine order of creation. They therefore realize an active and participatory life by contributing to the community.

Two of these theologians also base their view of man upon Christology. This holds for Emil Brunner and Günter Brakelmann. According to Brunner, it is through the Revelation in Christ that we receive insight that human beings are individual persons who are at the same time placed in a social community. God reveals himself in Christ as Perfect Love and he shows thereby what a truly human life means. It is through this Revelation that we receive insight into what is a true human being and what it means to be made in the image of God.

Similarly Brakelmann also maintains that we see in Christ how God conceives the true human being. Christ is a norm both for human beings' relationship to God and to other human beings. Christ's work of atonement also entails that all human beings are equal before God and that therefore all human beings have the same value.

A clearly Christologically based view of man is to be found in Arthur Rich. He holds that it is the Revelation in Christ which shows us what is humane by illuminating the three existentials – faith, hope and love. In Christ we encounter the completely different and thereby we also receive insight into what a truly human life means. Rich's view of man can therefore be called a "Christological humanism".

In Rich's particular case, he also bases his view of man upon eschatology. He writes that a truly human life cannot be realized here in time through social change or through other human efforts. It is only in the Kingdom of God that the true human being can finally be attained. According to Rich, eschatology justifies a "realistic humanism" which takes a realistic view about what can be accomplished here in time.

One of the theologians bases his view of man also upon a doctrine of the Church. This is so in the case of John Atherton. He lays great emphasis on the fact that human beings form part of a social community. He writes that we are all mutually dependent upon one another like limbs of the body. Humanity is to form the same community and unity as the Church. Atherton criticizes the individualistic view of man which he holds is to be found in neo-liberalism.

Secondly the theories of human nature which are to found in the writings of contemporary Protestant work ethicists are also combined with certain common human experiences and considerations. This is so in the case of Oldham and Rich. According to Oldham, it is the Creator's intention with human nature that human beings should be both persons and social beings. At the same time, he maintains that this view of man can be also held by human beings who do not share a Christian philosophy of life. The view of beings as a person bound to other persons is shared by many others who are not Christians as an alternative both to individualism and collectivism.[60]

Rich also refers to common human experiences as a basis for his view of man. These do not provide support for his views about what is characteristic for a truly human life. On the other hand they support his view about the limitations of human beings. There is, he seems to hold, a common human experience that there is a gulf between human existence as it actually is and what is truly human. In Brunner, Aukrust and Atherton, however, there is no corresponding explicit reference to common human experiences when they argue on behalf of their theories of human nature.

Thus we find that there are two different types of consideration which form the basis of the theories of human nature to be found in contemporary Protestant work ethical theories, namely other theoretical views which make up a Christian system of belief along with common human experiences and considerations which are not conditioned by the philosophy of life held. The convictions in a Christian system of belief which form possible bases for these theories of human nature are the doctrine of creation, Christology, eschatology and the doctrine of the Church. The relations between these different components can be illustrated as follows:

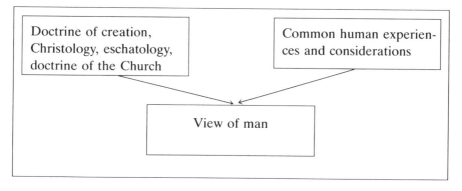

The relationships illustrated above hold in the case of J H Oldham and Arthur Rich. On the other hand, Brunner, Aukrust, Brakelmann and Atherton do not base their theories of human nature upon any common human considerations. Oldham and Aukrust combine their views of man with a doctrine of creation. Brunner and Brakelmann's theories of human nature are based upon a doctrine of creation and Christology while Rich on the other hand bases his view of man both upon Christology and eschatology. Atherton's view of man rests partly upon a doctrine of creation and partly upon a doctrine of the Church.

6. Ethics and a Christian system of belief

In the three previous chapters we have seen that the differing theories of the meaning of work, the differing social ethical theories and theories of human nature to be encountered within the contemporary Protestant work ethics are motivated *inter alia* by the kind of theoretical views which make up a Christian system of belief. At the same time, we have seen that there are different components in a Christian system of belief which form the basis for those views which form part of a work ethical theory. These views can be based upon a doctrine of creation. They can also be based upon a Christology, i.e. a doctrine of the nature and work of Christ. They can also be motivated by an eschatology i.e. a doctrine about the future Kingdom of God.

The fact that ethical views in this way are combined with theoretical convictions which are part of a philosophy of life is not specific to Christian ethics. In ethical argument in general, we can distinguish four different levels. At the first level we encounter the attitudes adopted towards concrete ethical problems. These are clearly demarcated ethical instructions of the kind which I have called work ethical recommendations. At the second level one encounters those common human experiences and considerations which form the basis for such concrete ethical recommendations. These can be empirically based judgements about reality e.g. assertions about the probable consequences of alternative lines of action. At the third level, there are those value judgements or norms which form the basis for more concrete ethical recommendations. They can be those principles and values which form part of a constructive ethical theory. At the fourth level we encounter those considerations which form the basis of the views about what is right and good. These can be considerations which are common in the sense that they do not presuppose some definite philosophy of life. They are often combined with a metaethical theory which specifies how ethical statements can be justified. At this fourth level, we also encounter those theoretical convictions which form part of a philosophy of life e.g. a view of man, a theory of history or a view of reality. These wide-ranging assumptions of a philosophy of life character support and strengthen certain ethical values and norms while at the same time providing motivation for acting in accordance with them. In Christian ethics these assumptions are composed of those theoretical views which form part of a Christian system of belief.[1]

The purpose of this chapter is to clarify what components in a Christian system of belief form the basis for the differing work ethical theories which are to be found within contemporary Protestant theology. In order to achieve this purpose, I shall investigate how the views which form part of work ethical theories are related to the content in the three articles of faith which in general lend structure to presentations of a Christian system of belief. Therefore I raise three analytical questions with respect to the material being discussed: (1) To what extent does the doctrine of creation affect the views which form part of work ethical theory? (2) To what extent are these views based upon Christology? (3) To what extent are these views which make up a work ethical theory combined with eschatology? In this chapter, I shall also investigate how the theories of human nature which are to be found in the writings of contemporary Protestant work ethicists are related to these three other components in a Christian system of belief. My aim is thus to clarify how these three parts of a Christian system of belief influence (a) theories of man (b) theories of the meaning of work and (c) social ethical theories which are to be found in the Protestant work ethicists whom I study.

In order to clarify the answers which the theologians give to these analytical questions, I shall relate them to those views dealing with the relation between ethics and a Christian system of belief which are to be found among other representatives of Christian ethics. Among Christian theologians there are different views about which parts of a Christian system of belief provide a basis for an ethical theory. A first view is that ethics is based upon a doctrine of creation. This viewpoint can be called "a theology of creation ethics". Such a viewpoint is to be found e.g. in the writings of the German Lutheran theologian, Helmut Thielicke. He holds that God as Creator has given certain fundamental ethical commandments. Human beings are created in the image of God and as such have a responsibility for the world about them. As such they are also placed in an I-Thou relationship to their Creator and they must exercise their responsibility according to his commandments.[2] Thielicke proposes a Lutheran theology of order according to which human responsibility is to be exercised within a framework of certain orders such as work, the Church, the State, marriage and culture. According to Thielicke these are not to be understood as orders of creation but rather as orders by means of which God maintains the epoque which we now live in, that is to say, post-Fall but prior to the final realization of the Kingdom of God.[3]

A theology of creation ethics of another kind is to be found in the writings of the Danish ethicist, K E Løgstrup. He bases ethics upon what he calls the conception of life which is implicit in the idea of creation. According to this, there is a structure which is given in creation and which provides a definite framework for human life. We are all dependent upon one another : we all have something of the life of others in our hands. This belief in creation is combined with a definite view of man. According to Løgstrup, there are certain sovereign manifestations of life which reflect the fundamental conditions of life and maintain life. He emphasizes in particular three such manifestations of life, namely trust, sincerity and compassion. According to Løgstrup, the ethical demand corresponds to these sovereign manifestations of life. It is the demand to take take care of the life of another person, to love one's neighbour as oneself. He shows in particular how this radical demand develops from trust. It is part of human life, he holds, that we normally meet one another in a spirit of trust. We expect to become ourselves in our relation to other persons. As a result we demand from others that they should look after our lives. In every meeting between human beings, there exists such a radical and unexpressed demand.[4]

A second view is that ethics is based upon Christology. This viewpoint may be called "a Christological ethics". Such a viewpoint is to be found in the writings of the influential Reformed theologian, Karl Barth. According to him, the criterion of a right action is that it is in agreement with the Will of God. Natural man cannot discover what is the Will of God with the help of his own reason. In his polemic against liberal theology, Barth rejects a natural theology in all its forms. He holds that human beings learn to know God only through the Revelation in Christ. We therefore learn the criterion for a right action only through this Revelation. Barth writes that Jesus Christ is He who shows what God requires of us. He obeys The Will of God and thus shows us what is a truly human life. He is the demand which God places upon all human beings. Christ embodies not only God's Grace, the Gospel, but also the form of Grace, the Law. The criterion that a demand is a divine demand is thus that it claims that Jesus lives, reigns and is victorious. God wills Jesus. In Him, we perceive God's demand, the content in the Law.[5]

A third view is that ethics is based upon eschatology. This viewpoint may be called "an eschatological ethics". Such a view is to be found in the German theologian, Jürgen Moltmann. He holds that the expectation in the coming Kingdom of God forms the core of Christian faith. Eschatology is not only part of a Christian doctrine of belief but the characteristic aspect of the proclamation of Christian belief. All Christian existence is a life in expectation of the future Kingdom of God.[6] This eschatological theology has three consequences for social ethics. First of all, in attacking every form of privatization of Christian faith and ethics, Moltmann emphasizes that one of the tasks of Christians is to help to change society in the direction of the promised Kingdom of God.[7] Secondly Moltmann, argues against every form of Christian conservatism, that the Church's task from an eschatological perspective, is to continually criticize existing social conditions. Thirdly he holds that Christian hope provides guidance for the political action of Christians. We receive insight about what the ideal of the Kingdom of God means through the Revelation in Christ.[8]

A fourth view is that ethics is based both upon a doctrine of creation and upon Christology and eschatology. Of these three components in a Christian system of belief, the doctrine of creation and eschatology are especially of fundamental importance for the formulation of ethics. This viewpoint can be called "a trinitarian ethics". Such a viewpoint has been put forward by the German ethicist, Wolfgang Trillhaas. He holds that the advantage with an ethics that is based upon a belief in the creation is that ethics becomes linked to common human experiences and considerations. The disadvantage with such an ethics is, however, that it tends to be conservative and to defend the status quo. The advantage with an ethics which is based upon Christology and eschatology is that it is open for social change. Such an ethics, however, has the disadvantage that it rejects cooperation with philosophical and humane ethics. Trillhaas wishes to combine the positive aspects in both these views. He wishes to devise an ethics which is humanely based. At the same time he wishes to avoid falling back into the conservatism of the theology of order. The questions which are treated in ethics are common for all human beings and thus every ethical system must make a universal claim. Therefore one must also in Christian ethics seek to use rational arguments and not refer to an exclusively Christian basis of knowledge. At the same time, Trillhaas holds that Christian ethics has also made a special contribution to morality in the form of the ethical views to be found in the Sermon on the Mount which are based upon the hope in a future perfect Kingdom of God.[9]

A trinitarian ethics of another type is to be found in the writings of the Americal social ethicist, J Philip Wogaman. He puts forward a social ethical theory according to which Christian belief motivates certain "moral presumptions" i.e. assumptions about what is good and right which are valid if there are no acceptable counterarguments. The moral presumptions in Christian ethics are based upon certain theological views. Wogaman writes that Christian faith provides certain theological "entry points" which motivate certain basic moral assumptions. Among these, there is the doctrine of creation which entails that the material world is something good and that human life has a high value. Christology is also part of these theological views. In Christ is revealed that Divine Love by virtue of which salvation is something which we receive as a gift despite our own imperfections. Finally eschatology also belongs to these theological views. According to Christian belief, the fulfilment of history is a work of God which however, does not rule out but rather inspires us to political commitment.[10]

In this chapter, I shall thus try to clarify which components in a Christian system of belief form the basis of work ethical theories within contemporary Protestant theology. At the same time, I shall discuss whether the work ethicists I study, can be said to embrace an ethics which is of a theology of creation, Christological or eschatological kind. In this way, I can relate their ethical theories to views which are to be found in other formulations of Christian ethics.

A theology of creation ethics

In Emil Brunner, we encounter a social ethical theory which is very closely related to a doctrine of creation. He formulates a theology of the orders of creation according to which the criterion for a right action is that it is in agreement with the divine orders of creation. There are according to Brunner certain orders which are given to man by God in the creation. These are the family, the economic order, the State, culture and the Church. These orders are necessary for human life and the sign of a right political action is that is in agreement with the Will of God concerning these orders of creation.[11]

Brunner maintains that existing social orders are not only expressions of the Will of God with the creation. They are also expressions of the reality of sin. No existing system therefore, should be treated as sacrosanct and completely identified with the Will of God. At the same time, however, Brunner's theology of the orders of creation has a clearly conservative character. According to him, it is the Will of God concerning the orders that there should exist a hierarchy of superiority and inferiority. Justice is a distribution which takes account of the factual differences which exist between human beings both as regards their characteristics and their social functions.

Brunner's theory of the meaning of work is also closely related to his doctrine of creation. He holds that work belongs to God's orders of creation. It is something which is in agreement with the Will of God in the creation and with the nature of human beings. Human beings in their work are also co-workers of God in His continous act of creation. One of the purposes of work is to be such an instrument of God's creation in the present. The fact that work is such a means for God's continuous act of creation is one of the bases for its value.[12]

180

The view of man in Brunner is also combined with a doctrine of creation. Human beings are created in the image of God and as such, according to Brunner, they are rational creatures intended for freedom. They are independent individuals but at the same time also social individuals. This implies that they are responsible for other human beings and that they are placed in social orders which are necessary for their existence. The fact that there are such orders which are given in creation shows that the individual and community are indissolubly linked to one another. Because every human being is created in the image of God, they have, according to Brunner, an equally high value as every other human being. At the same time, he stresses that human beings are created different. We have different properties and different social functions. In the creation God has created fundamental factual differences between human beings.

Brunner's social ethical theory, his theory of the meaning of work and his view of man are thus firmly based upon the first article of faith. At the same time, Christology also has a certain significance at least for his view of man. Our insight that human beings are individual persons and at the same time social beings is obtained according to Brunner through the Revelation in Christ. God reveals Himself in Christ as Perfect Love and thus shows what a truly human life consists in. When we encounter God's Love in Christ, we understand also that we are responsible persons who are responsible for other human beings.[13]

Christology has also great significance for Brunner's individual ethics. In Christ is revealed a morality which surpasses the idea of justice associated with natural law. Christ reveals Love, the divine agape which is something completely different from justice. This ideal of love is valid, however, only in individual ethics. In social ethics, the idea of justice namely that social orders must correspond to the original order of creation, applies instead. Christology has thus no influence upon social ethics according to Brunner. His social ethics is completely based upon the first article of faith.[14]

Eschatology plays no great part in Brunner's ethics. His social ethics is based upon the doctrine of the orders of creation. It is however important to note that Brunner does not identify existing social orders with the Will of God concerning these orders of creation. Existing social conditions, he holds, are also permeated by human sin. The hope in a future Kingdom of God can also inspire us to work for a change of existing social conditions. In judging that social conditions are desirable, the criterion is not however the vision of the Kingdom of God but the Will of God as expressed in the creation.[15]

A Christological act ethics

In J H Oldham, there is to be found an ethics which in contrast to Brunner's is based upon Christology and not upon the doctrine of creation. This, however, does not prevent the doctrine of creation from having a certain influence upon his work ethical theory. Like Brunner, Oldham embraces a view of man which is closely related to a Christian doctrine of creation. Human beings are partly persons whose lives are a conversation with God and partly social beings who stand in relation to other human beings. The fact that human life is a conversation with God implies *inter alia* that human beings must cooperate with God in his continuous act of creation. The circumstance that human beings must respect and revere nature is linked to the fact that nature is also God's creation.

Oldham's theory of the meaning of work is also based upon a doctrine of creation. He holds that work belongs to God's order of creation. It is an expression of human existence to be created in the image of God. Oldham holds that God's creation is not something which is finished but is something which is continuously going on. The purpose of work is to be God's co-worker in his continuous act of creation. The task of human beings is to rule over all living beings and to cooperate with God in his continued creation.[16]

In contrast to Brunner, however, Oldham does not base his social ethical theory upon a doctrine of creation. Oldham also explicitly criticizes two ethical theories which are based upon the first article of faith. The first is the Thomist formulation of the doctrine of natural law. This is a teleological ethics which assumes that every human being, having been created by God, is capable of seeing what is right and good even if due to sin, they are uncertain about the content of the natural law. According to Oldham, the defect with this doctrine is that it runs the risk of leading to clericalism since it maintains that the content in natural law because of human sin and uncertainty must be clarified by the authority of the Church.[17]

Secondly Oldham criticizes the social ethics to be encountered within Lutheran theology. He holds that on the basis of the doctrine of the two kingdoms, this theology emphasizes the conflict between Church and the world. It is combined with an individualistic view of Christianity according to which the task of the Church is to preach the gospel for individual human beings and according to which Christian ethics is primarily an individual ethics. At the same time, it is combined with the view that the Church does not have a direct political responsibility and that the Christian ideal of love cannot be directly applied in social questions. Social ethics is humane in the sense that Christians and non-Christians have common values and norms. Oldham, however, does not affirm this social ethical theory either.[18]

Instead Oldham puts forward a social ethical theory which is based upon Christology. According to him, the criterion for a right act is that it is in agreement with God's Will and the Will of God is something that we learn only through His Revelation in Christ. This implies that it is only through the Revelation in Christ that we can decide what is right and wrong. The confession that "Christ is Lord" is the source, centre and goal for Christian action. It is in the light of this affirmation that we can decide what characterizes a right action.[19]

In contrast both to a Thomist doctrine of natural law and a Lutheran doctrine of the two kingdoms, J H Oldham puts forward the doctrine of the Lordship of Christ. This is a type of reformed social ethics which is to be encountered primarily within Calvinism. The universal Lordship of Christ in the world is to be interpreted here not in an exclusively eschatological sense as something which only relates to the future. This Lordship also justifies an activism on the part of the Church as regards today's society. The Church has a gift to offer here and now in time.[20]

The doctrine of the Lordship of Christ in Oldham is combined with an eschatological base for social ethics. The doctrine can, however, according to him be formulated in two distinct ways depending upon how the doctrine of the Kingdom of God is formulated. The first is an eschatological view which does not contain an optimistic belief that God's kingdom can be established within human history. According to this view, the Kingdom of God is not something which human beings can create here upon earth but which is a gift which is received from God. According to this view, the Church has also its own specific view about what is good and right. God is a transcendent reality whose ways are hidden from human beings. It is His Will which forms the norm for the life of human beings and it is only through the Revelation that the Church can perceive what is a right action.[21]

The second formulation of the doctrine according to Oldham is combined with a more optimistic view about the world. This view is to be found in the social gospel movement, e.g. in Walter Rauschenbusch. The latter views the Kingdom of God as a perfect society which can be realized here in time. This is combined with an optimistic view of man which reduces the difference between God and human beings while at the same time minimizing the difference between the Church and the world. God's purpose for the world is identified with human purposes and all human beings of good will can according to this view perceive what is a right action.[22]

According to Oldham both these viewpoints contain insights which are worthwhile developing. For his own part, he appears however to prefer the first viewpoint. He puts forward three objections to the social gospel standpoint. It does not do justice to God's sovereignty and transcendence. It reduces the content of Christian ethics to something which is purely humane. It is also combined with an exaggeratedly optimistic view of man. As we have seen in the previous chapter, Oldham claims to have a more realistic view of man. Christian belief entails an insight into human limitations and at the same time a hope in the victory of the good. It does not believe that it is possible to establish a Christian society here on earth. At the same time its view of man is not pessimistic because it knows that God acts in the world to bring about the good.[23]

A natural law and eschatological ethics

In Tor Aukrust, we encounter an ethics which has both a theology of creation and an eschatological basis. Aukrust's view of man is closely related to a Christian doctrine of creation. He holds that human beings are created in the image of God. This implies that there is a basic similarity between human beings while at the same time they are also different in character and have different possibilities. Because they are created in the image of God, all human beings share in God's sovereignty over nature and have the task of ruling over the earth. God's work of creation is not something which is finished but something which continues and human beings are called to be God's co-workers in his continuous act of creation.[24]

Aukrust's theory of the meaning of work is also related to this doctrine of creation. The basis of a Lutheran doctrine of vocation, he writes, is the belief in creation. Work is an order of creation in the sense that God creates through human work. God's work of creation is not something which is finished but which continues: creatio continua. God performs this continuous act of creation by making use of human beings who work. Aukrust writes that working life thus represents acts of creation which God himself performs via human hands. The purpose of work is therefore also to enable human beings to be co-workers in God's continuous act of creation. Work is co-activity in God's continuing creation.[25]

Tor Aukrust's social ethical theory is also related to the first article of faith and the doctrine of creation. Because human beings are created in the image of God they have a capacity to achieve a certain insight about what is right independent of Revelation in Christ. Already in the encounter with his fellow human beings, each and every one can discover the demand for concern for others. Aukrust criticizes Brunner's theology of the orders of creation but he still holds that there is a natural law the content of which can be perceived by all human beings because they are made in the image of God.[26]

At the same time, Aukrust also holds that the Revelation in Christ is a basic source regarding insight about what is good and right. Through the

184

Revelation in Christ, we perceive that the ultimate goal for our efforts ought to be the Kingdom of God. As we have seen in Chapter 4, Aukrust motivates the principle of the equal value of all human beings on the basis of God's infinite love in Christ. In a similar way, the principle of freedom is justified by freedom in Christ and the principle of equality is justified by Christ's work of atonement which makes us all equal before God. In these respects, social ethics is Christologically based.

Aukrust holds that with the Revelation in Christ, social ethics is also given an eschatological basis. The Revelation primarily through the Sermon on the Mount, gives us namely an insight into God's absolute demand. Here the absolute demand is combined with an eschatological proclamation of the Kingdom of God. In the Sermon on the Mount, we encounter an eschatological ethics with a demand which presupposes an eschatological reestablishment of the Kingdom of God. It is within this framework that one must understand natural law. Thus Aukrust can speak of an eschatologically based natural law and a natural law within an eschatological framework.[27]

A basic problem is now how the absolute demand which is encountered in the Sermon on the Mount is to be related to the relative demands which are to be faced here and now. How do these absolute demands relate to life in the world? Differing answers have been given to this question. A first view is that the absolute demand of the Sermon on the Mount applies to all areas of temporal life. Tolstoy, for example, holds this position. According to Aukrust, however, this viewpoint is based upon an unacceptable theological view. Because the absolute demand can only be realized where the Kingdom of God is complete reality, this viewpoint presupposes that the Kingdom of God can be brought about here in time. The Kingdom of God is however an eschatological reality.[28]

Another viewpoint is that the absolute demand is only valid within clearly demarcated zones of existence while other zones are exempt. This demarcation can come about in different ways. One can hold that the absolute demand in the Sermon on the Mount is valid only for a certain epoch or only for certain human beings e.g. for monks and nuns or for only a certain area of human existence. Thus for example the doctrine of the two kingdoms holds that the absolute demand is valid only for the spiritual kingdom while the social life is exempt from this demand.[29] Aukrust rejects this viewpoint and holds that the absolute demand has relevance for all areas of human life.

A third viewpoint is that the absolute demand of the Sermon of the Mount cannot be used as a direct norm for life in the world but at the same time it cannot be limited to a definite sector of human life while others are completely exempt. This is the viewpoint which Aukrust himself adopts. He holds that the morality of the Sermon on the Mount applies to the whole of human life.

It is relevant not only to individual ethics but also to social ethics. At the same time, he holds that the absolute demand must be related to realizable norms which are valid for life here in the world.[30]

Aukrust's standpoint can be said to be based upon a doctrine of two epochs. According to this, human beings live in a kingdom of the Fall, the old epoch. The Sermon on the Mount proclaims a new epoch with a reestablishment of the orders of creation and proclaims God's absolute will. Despite the fact that the new epoch has begun, the old epoch however continues. The Kingdom of God and the Kingdom of sin are contemporaneous and therefore according to Aukrust, we must distinguish between the absolute demand of the Sermon on the Mount and the norms which Christian ethics gives for life in the world.[31]

According to Aukrust, Christian ethics is relative. It contains "approximate" ethical demands i.e. norms which form a compromise between the ideal and the possible. These relative norms which relax the absolute demands are not greatly different from those norms which make up a humane ethics.[32] According to Aukrust we encounter approximate ethical demands of this type already in the Bible. The Sermon on the Mount contains not only an eschatological absolute Revelation ethics but also an ethics which is based upon natural law.[33]

Aukrust gives an interpretation of these approximate ethical demands in terms of salvation history. He holds that in the Kingdom of the Fall, that is to say the intervening period between the Fall and the full reestablishment of the Kingdom of God, Christian ethics is relative. There God's absolute demand is approximate to those relative demands which apply in the world which carries traces of human imperfection. These constitute a compromise in relation to the absolute eschatological demand.[34]

An eschatological social ethics

A more purely eschatological basis for ethics is to be found in Arthur Rich. The doctrine of creation has no very great relevance for Rich's social ethical theory and work ethical theory. On the contrary, he explicitly criticizes the theology of creation ethics which is to be found for example in Paul Althaus and in Brunner. These order of creation theologians hold that human beings are placed in definite social orders, certain basic structures for human society. These orders of creation are made concrete in forms of human community which are based upon creation itself. As a result, the orders of creation illuminate what is the Will of God and what is a right political act.[35] Rich criticizes this social ethics based upon a theology of creation. He holds that Brunner's social ethics takes on a conservative aspect where the static and the given predominate. Existing social structures are erroneously identified with orders of creation which is an expression of the fact the structural evil is not taken seriously.[36]

Rich also criticizes the Christological social ethics to be found in Karl Barth's later work on the social ethical doctrine of analogy. According to Barth, ethics is a doctrine about God and His Will. In social ethics, he formulates analogies which rest upon Christology and which thereby are accessible, not to reason but only to faith. Via this doctrine, Barth builds a bridge between such absolute and unconditional norms which apply to the Kingdom of God and those relative conditional norms which apply to this world. Rich holds however, that it is still doubtful whether Barth takes the relative sufficiently seriously.[37]

Nonetheless Rich's social ethics is in part based upon Christology. Christ is according to him also the fundamental source of ethical insight which specifies what is good and right. This is a consequence of the significance Christology has for Rich's view of man. A fundamental norm within social ethics is to promote what is humane and it is through the Revelation in Christ that we receive insight about what is humane i.e. a truly human life. In Jesus Christ is revealed not only the truly divine but also the truly human. Thus the three existentials, faith, hope and love which are the marks of humanity and a truly human existence are made clear.

According to Rich, eschatology, however, forms the primary theological basis for social ethics. The starting point for his ethics is the doctrine of the coming Kingdom of God which has come in Jesus Christ and which opens a way to a new existence in faith, hope and love. On the basis of this hope in the Kingdom of God, criteria for what is humane can be formulated and social institutions can be designed accordingly. In Rich's view, eschatology is not simply a doctrine about last things. Eschatological existence consists in living in tension between the Kingdom of God which has already come in Christ and the Kingdom of God as it shall come about in the last days. This eschatology forms the basis of Rich's view of man. It provides a motivation for a realistic humanism since a truly human life can be realized only in the future Kingdom of God. As a result, eschatology also forms the basis of Rich's social ethical theory. What it means to promote that which is humane, can be specified on the basis of the hope in the future Kingdom of God.

Rich holds that eschatology can provide a basis for ethics in two different ways. The first he calls a "transcendental-eschatological entry point" for ethics. This view, he holds, is to be found in the early writings of Karl Barth. On the basis of the proclamation of the Kingdom of God, he subjects everything temporal, including both capitalism and socialism as well as religion, to radical criticism. The absolute and unconditional norms which are combined with eschatology mean for Barth a cessation of everything which belongs to this life. Christian ethics becomes a radical eschatological criticism of those moral views which belong to this world. On the other hand, Barth provides no constructive proposals for a relative and conditional ethics and all such relative norms are questioned.[38]

Another way of basing ethics upon eschatology is what Rich calls an "existential-eschatological entry point". This viewpoint is to be found in Heinz-Dietrich Wendland and this is also the view which Arthur Rich himself prefers. He seeks to devise a social ethics which mediates between those absolute norms associated with the Kingdom of God and those relative norms associated with this world. Unlike Barth, Rich does not wish to make a sharp distinction between these while at the same time he does not wish to place as much importance on the *status quo* as Brunner does. It is the task of Christian social ethics to advocate responsibility for the social orders here in time while at the same time doing justice to the demands of the absolute. Thus Christian existence involves both critical distance towards the relative and a responsibility also for what is imperfect here in time. This assumption of responsibility is based upon the striving for humanity and upon the criteria for a truly human life which are given in Jesus Christ.[39]

Humanity as faith, hope and love has according to Rich an eschatological dimension. God is active in this humanity for which the ultimate goal is the future Kingdom of God. This eschatological dimension has in turn an existential character. It involves a definite type of human existence, namely a responsible life where demands are made upon human beings by the Kingdom of God in the midst of the existing world's harsh realities. Thereby human beings must also be ready to work for social change. In this way, Rich holds, social ethics can do justice to both the absolute and the relative.[40]

Working in terms of this eschatological perspective, Rich interprets the view about the Christian attitude to society which Paul expresses in Romans 13:1–7. Christian existence, he holds, is eschatologically determined and permeated by the hope in the future Kingdom of God. This hope in the coming Kingdom of God is founded upon Christ's work of atonement whereby eschatology is combined with Christology. At the same time, Paul maintains in Romans 13 that the Christian lives in this world with its orders and therefore also has a political task. The citizen in the coming Kingdom of God lives simultaneously in Caesar's empire. The Christian must not blindly obey the state but must affirm that he finds himself in a political context here in time.[41]

On the basis of this eschatological perspective, Rich criticizes the type of orders of creation theology which we have encountered in Brunner. While Christians affirm that they belong in a political context, they are also citizens in the future Kingdom of God. Thus Christian acceptance of the state becomes simultaneously critical and revolutionary.[42] Since Christians live in the hope of the coming Kingdom of God, they know that this world is not final. The state does not have a final character but is relative. Therefore Christians loyally accept the existence of the state while at the same time subjecting existing social orders to critical review. According to Rich, this kind of critical distance to the *status quo* is lacking in the conservative orders of creation theology.[43]

Thus it is eschatology which forms the basis both for Rich's view of man and for his social ethical theory. For him, eschatology is also combined with a definite view of the Church. Rich criticizes the Protestant Church of the People idea according to which human beings belong to the Church by birth and according to which there exists an indissoluble link between the people and the Church. This Church of the People idea cannot be defended in a liberal democracy with its insistence upon religious liberty in a secularized society. Instead, Rich holds that the Church must be understood as an eschatological reality. The Church is the body of Christ, a community of believing human beings who wait upon the Kingdom of God but which cannot be identified itself with the Kingdom of God. As a waiting Church it adopts a critical distance towards the state. According to Rich, it adopts a dialectical world relationship i.e. its members are citizens in a society while at the same time they have a critical attitude towards the state and the world.[44]

A Christological theory of rights

What components in a Christian system of belief form the basis for Günter Brakelmann's work ethics? In Chapter 3 we have seen that Brakelmann's theory of the meaning of work is based upon a doctrine of creation. In contrast to Brunner, he does not speak of work as a "divine order of creation". On the other hand, Brakelmann holds that work is a "mandate" i.e. an activity that God has given human beings with the creation. Through work, human beings are to reign over the earth, to be God's co-workers in the work of creation. One purpose of work is to take part in God's creation by assuming responsibility for the world about one.

At the same time Brakelmann criticizes a conservative order of creation theology which views the Will of God concerning the orders of creation as a norm for how society is to be organized. Against such a viewpoint, he maintains that there are no social and economic orders corresponding to the Will of God concerning the creation, which are given once and for all. There is no "Christian social order" and it is not possible to identify definite social orders with the Will of God.[45] Brakelmann writes that the theology of orders has been combined with many mistakes. It has justified the hierarchical state and social inequalities and it has viewed every form of revolution as disobedience. On the basis of the theology of orders, one has opposed enlightenment, democracy, liberalism and socialism. Such a religious legitimization of existing power structures is however mistaken.[46]

Brakelmann relates his theory of the meaning of work to the doctrine of creation. However, he does not base his view of man upon such a doctrine of creation. As we have seen in Chapter 5, his view of man is instead based upon Christology. In Christ, we can see how God conceives the true human being. In Him, we understand what it means to be a person in relation to God. Nor is Brakelmann's social ethical theory based upon a doctrine of creation. His social ethics is instead clearly Christological. It is a social ethics which is based upon a doctrine of Jesus Christ's existence in the present. The doctrine of the Lordship of Christ would seem to be of greater importance for Brakelmann's social ethics than the Lutheran doctrine of the two kingdoms.

According to Brakelmann, Christology forms the basis for our understanding of the Christian ideal of love. The basis of love is God's concern for the human beings in Jesus Christ. In Him, God has revealed his love for mankind. In Him, we also see how God conceives the true human being. Thereby Christ constitutes a measure for human beings' relationship to God and to their fellows. Faith recognises in Christ the true human being and sees it as its task to live in the imitation of Christ.[47]

Brakelmann also argues Christologically for the principle of the equal value of all human beings. Christ's work of atonement implies that all human beings are equal before God. This provides a criterion for how we must behave towards our fellow human beings. All human beings have equal value since they are equal before God. The whole of humanity is saved in Christ and therefore there is no difference between human beings.[48] Since the principle of human value is combined with certain fundamental human rights, these rights are ultimately based upon Christology. Brakelmann also provides a Christological motivation for the view that we ought to seek to promote freedom. The basis for striving after freedom in the world is that human beings become free through their belief in Christ. It is a freedom which expresses itself in a concern for other human beings.[49]

The Christological social ethics which is encountered in Günter Brakelmann, is also combined with an eschatological entry point. Christian faith is a faith in Jesus Christ, he writes, and in Jesus, the Kingdom of God has broken in. Since the Kingdom of God has not yet been completely realized, Brakelmann writes, Christian faith is characterized by a tension between what is already come to pass and that which is still to be achieved. Faith has an eschatological dimension which implies that it lives in the world but is not of it. Belief in Christ has as a consequence that the Christian adopts a critical distance to every social order and system of norms. From an eschatological perspective, the Christian human being adopts a critical distance to such orders as the family and marriage, the economy and the state.[50]

A consequence of this critical distance, according to Brakelmann, is a continual reformism i.e. a striving for a continual change in society. It is fine to have orders but they must be changed so that they promote a life that is more worthy of human beings. No existing social structure can according to Brakelmann be identified with the Will of God. Marriage, the family, the state and the economy must exist but it is an open question what form they are to take.[51] Every form of the orders is provisional. On the basis of an eschatologically based distance to reality, Christians relativize all orders. They adopt a critical distance to the *status quo* . They affirm order but treat existing social structures as relative.[52]

This eschatological distance, Brakelmann holds, also implies a critical relationship to history and tradition. The past contains positive and negative aspects. Both mercy and brutality are part of it.[53] The eschatological perspective creates an awareness that it is impossible to create a world in which freedom and justice are completely realized. A continual change of society will always therfore be necessary.[54]

Brakelmann writes that eschatological distance entails that politics in general is relativized. Christians have the responsibility for promoting a humane life. At the same time, however, they perceive that life does not exclusively consist of politics. Political commitment is necessary but there are other things which are equally urgent. It is also important that politics is not perceived as an end in itself but as a means of creating a more humane existence. All totalitarian claims must therefore be rejected from an eschatological perspective.[55]

An ecclesiological ethics

John Atherton does not discuss in detail how ethics is related to the content in a Christian system of belief. It is obvious, however, that the doctrine of the Church – ecclesiology – has a great influence upon his social ethics. Atherton's view of man is obviously related to a doctrine of creation. He maintains that human beings are valued highly because they are created in the image of God. A person's value is based upon the fact that they are the object of God's love in both the creation and in the salvation and therefore all human beings have equal value.[56] Man's obligation to participate in the life of the community is also related to the doctrine of creation. According to Atherton, every human being is a steward of God's order of creation and as such is a social being.[57]

Atherton's social ethical theory and his theory of the meaning of work do not, however, appear to based to any great extent upon the doctrine of creation. There is, however, a certain linkage in his writings to the orders of creation theology. There are certain fundamental structures, he writes, which belong to life itself and which we ourselves do not choose. These divine structures are the family, the economic order, the political order and culture.[58] On the basis of the doctrine of creation, it also perhaps possible to understand Atherton's view that it is part of human nature to promote certain fundamental values which can be perceived by all human beings independently of their philosophy of life. He himself however, does not provide any specific theological motivation for this view.

It would also seem to be the case that the third article of faith plays a more important role in Atherton's social ethics than the first article of faith. Atherton's social ethical theory would seem to be based upon the view of the Church as the body of Christ. He writes that the Church forms a community where there exists a mutual dependence between all. The parts of the community are mutually dependent upon one another and each and every one has a necessary contribution to give to the whole. The Church as Christ's body provides an image, Atherton holds, of the unity and community which ought to prevail in society. In this way, he bases his social ethical theory upon ecclesiology.[59]

Eschatology has also an influence upon Atherton's social ethical theory. He emphasizes that "the common good" is not the Kingdom of God. Rather it is a question of goals which stand between God's Kingdom and this world. They are necessary but not sufficient conditions for the perfect life which is realized in the future Kingdom of God.[60] In the light of the Kingdom of God the goals which are realizable here in time are relativized. We see that society has a provisional character and that no society can be said to be perfect and absolute.[61]

Conclusion

What components in a Christian system of belief form the basis for those work ethical theories which are to be encountered within contemporary Protestant theology? To what extent, are these work ethical theories combined with a Christian doctrine of creation, Christology or eschatology? How do these different parts of a Christian system of belief influence those theories of man, theories of the meaning of work and social ethical theories which are to be found in contemporary Protestant work ethicists? In this chapter, we have seen that the theologians, I treat, have five distinct views about the relationship between work ethics and the Christian system of belief.

The first view can be called a "theology of creation work ethics". It takes the view that work ethics is primarily based upon the doctrine of creation. This view is to be found in the writings of Emil Brunner. His social ethical theory is closely related to a doctrine of the divine orders of creation. The criterion for a right political action is that it is in agreement with the Will of God in respect of these orders of creation. Brunner's theory of the meaning of work is also closely related to this doctrine of creation. Work belongs to God's order of creation and is thus an activity which agrees with the Will of God regarding human existence.

The view of man in Brunner is also based upon the doctrine of creation. Although every human being as a creature made in the image of God has an equally high value, God has introduced in the creation certain fundamental differences between human beings. At the same time, Christology also has a certain influence upon Brunner's view of man. It is the Revelation in Christ which ultimately shows us what a true human life entails. Christology, on the other hand, has no influence upon Brunner's social ethical theory. He formulates a Christological individual ethics according to which the criterion for a right act is perceived only through the Revelation in Christ. But his social ethics is completely based upon the first article of faith.

The second view can be called a "Christological work ethics". It holds that work ethics is primarily based upon Christology. This viewpoint is put forward in the writings of J H Oldham. His social ethical theory is based upon the second article of faith. The criterion for a right action is that it is in agreement with the Will of God and we learn what is the Will of God in a particular situation through his Revelation in Christ. Oldham combines a deontological act ethics with a doctrine of the Lordship of Christ in the world. At the same time he relates his social ethics to eschatology. He emphasizes that the Kingdom of God cannot be achieved here upon earth through human efforts and that we must therefore adopt a critical distance towards existing orders of society.

In contrast to Brunner, Oldham does not base his social ethics upon a theology of creation. He criticizes both a Thomist doctrine of natural law and the doctrine of the two kingdoms in Lutheran theology. On the other hand, Oldham's view of man is closely related to a Christian doctrine of creation. The fact that human life is a conversation with God implies that human beings must cooperate with God in his continuous act of creation. The doctrine of creation also forms the basis of Oldham's theory of the meaning of work. Work belongs to God's order of creation and its purpose is to allow human beings to be co-workers in God's continuous act of creation. But

Oldham's social ethics is based upon Christology and not upon the first article of faith.

We have also encountered a Christological work ethics in the writings of Günter Brakelmann. His social ethics is not a deontological act ethics of the same kind as Oldham's but rather a deontological theory of rights. However this theory is also based upon Christology. Brakelmann holds that Christology forms the basis of our understanding of the Christian ideal of love. Christology also provides the motivation for the principle that all human beings are equal. All human beings have an equal value for all are objects of God's love in Christ. According to Brakelmann, Christology also provides a motivation for our pursuit of freedom and our defence of certain fundamental rights.

Brakelmann also relates his social ethics to eschatology. Hope in a future Kingdom of God provides critical distance to every now existing social order and thereby justifies the pursuit of unremitting social change. On the other hand, he criticizes a theology of creation ethics of the type which is to be found in Brunner. The orders of creation theology has legitimized lack of equality, he holds, and has tended mistakenly to identify existing social orders with the Will of God.

Brakelmann's view of man is also based upon Christology. He holds that we perceive in Christ God's vision of the true human being. On the other hand, his theory of the meaning of work is based upon a doctrine of creation. He views work as a "mandate" which has been given to human beings by God with the creation and it is therefore also something which is characteristic of human beings.

The third view can be called an "eschatological work ethics". This holds that work ethics is primarily based upon eschatology. This viewpoint is to be found in the writings of Arthur Rich. The basis of his social ethical theory is the expectation in the coming Kingdom of God which has been manifested in Jesus Christ and opens the way to a new existence in faith, hope and love. On the basis of the hope in the future Kingdom of God, it is possible to specify what is humane and thereby to say what constitutes a correct organization of social institutions. Rich claims to prefer an "existential eschatological" rather than a "transcendental eschatological" entry point for social ethics. The eschatological dimension has an existential character in the sense that it involves responsible human existence where the Kingdom of God makes demand upon human beings. It is combined both with a critical distance towards the relative and a responsibility for what is imperfect here in time.

On the basis of an eschatological perspective, Rich criticizes a theology of creation ethics of the type to be found in Brunner. Such an ethics has too conservative a hue in that it tends to view existing social structures as an expression of the Will of God regarding creation. Rich also criticizes Christological social ethics of the type to be found in Karl Barth and J H Oldham. At the same time, his own social ethics is closely related to Christology. According to Rich, a fundamental norm within social ethics is that we should promote what is humane. Insight about what is humane and thereby about a truly human life is received only through the Revelation in Christ.

In this way, Rich's view of man is also based upon Christology. The Revelation in Christ shows us what is humane by clarifying the three existentials – faith, hope and love. At the same time, Rich's view of man is also based upon eschatology. He holds that it is only in the future Kingdom of God that the true human being can finally be attained.

A fourth view can be called a "trinitarian work ethics". It holds that work ethics is both based upon the doctrine of creation and upon Christology and eschatology. This viewpoint is to be found in the writings of Tor Aukrust. His social ethical theory is closely related to the doctrine of creation. Every human being as a creature made in the image of God has the possibility of achieving a certain insight into what is right independently of the Revelation in Christ. Aukrust's view of man is also closely related to the doctrine of creation. Human beings are created in the image of God which implies that all human beings shall reign over the earth and participate in God's sovereignty over the world around them. Aukrust also bases his theory of the meaning of work upon the doctrine of creation. Work is an order of creation in the sense that God continues his act of creation through the work of human beings.

At the same time, Aukrust also holds that the Revelation in Christ gives us an insight into what is good and right. Through this Revelation, we perceive that the ultimate goal of our striving ought to be the Kingdom of God. Social ethics is thereby, according to Aukrust, also based upon eschatology. We receive insight into the content of God's absolute demand only through the Sermon on the Mount. It is within this eschatological framework, Aukrust holds, that human beings are to understand natural law. Eschatology's absolute demand, as it appears in the Sermon on the Mount, is not only valid within individual ethics but also within social ethics. On the other hand, it must be approximated in the Kingdom of the Fall by relative demands which are valid in this world. These views of Aukrust are based upon a doctrine of the two epochs.

A fifth view can be called "an ecclesiological work ethics". It holds that work ethics is primarily based upon the doctrine of the Church. This view is to be found in the writings of John Atherton. His social ethical theory would appear to be based upon a doctrine of the Church as the body of Christ. The Church, he holds, constitutes a community where there exists a mutual dependence between all and such a community also ought to hold in society. Atherton also combines his social ethical theory with eschatology. The common good is not the same as the Kingdom of God. From an eschatological perspective, the goals which are attainable here in time, are relativized.

Atherton's social ethics is not based to any large extent upon a doctrine of creation although he assumes that there are certain basic values which can be perceived by all independently of the Revelation. However, his view of man is combined with a doctrine of creation. He holds that every human being as a creature made in the image of God, has great worth. As stewards of God's orders of creation, human beings have also the task of participating in the life of the community.

Thus we find that there are different views within contemporary Protestant work ethics about the relation between on the one hand the doctrine of creation, Christology, eschatology and the doctrine of the Church and on the other hand theories of human nature, social ethical theories and theories of the meaning of work. In particular, there are different views about what components in the Christian system of belief form the basis for a social ethical theory. A possible view about the relationship between these different components can be illustrated as follows:

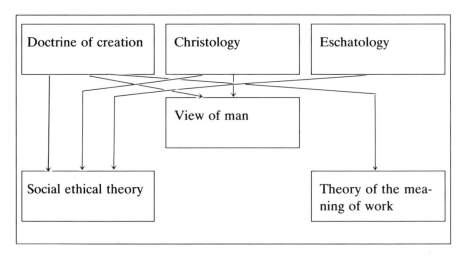

The connections illustrated above are closely linked to the view to be found in Tor Aukrust. Aukrust however does not explicitly base his view of man upon Christology. Emil Brunner holds that the doctrine of creation forms the basis for his social ethical theory, his theory of human nature and theory of the meaning of work while Christology and eschatology have no influence whatsoever upon his social ethical theory. J H Oldham, on the other hand, bases his social ethical theory upon Christology and eschatology while the doctrine of creation has an influence upon his view of man and theory of the meaning of work. A similar view is to be found in Brakelmann who however does not explicitly base his view of man upon the doctrine of creation. In the case of Arthur Rich, eschatology and Christology form the basis for both his social ethical theory and his view of man. John Atherton exceptionally bases his social ethical theory upon the doctrine of the Church while eschatology has an influence upon his social ethical theory and his view of man is based upon the doctrine of creation.

Common to all these six theologians is that their differing theories of human nature and social ethical theories and theories of the meaning of work are to a great degree based upon certain parts of the Christian system of belief. At the same time, we have earlier seen that these theories are also partly motivated by common human experiences and considerations which are not dependent upon a philosophy of life. These common human experiences and considerations, together with theories of human nature, social ethical theories and theories about the meaning of work provide a motivation for differing work ethical recommendations. We have also earlier seen that social ethical theories and theories of the meaning of work are often based upon theories of human nature just as theories of the meaning of work are often based upon social ethical theories. If we now combine the results of my analysis in Chapters 2−6, the possible interconnections between the different components can be illustrated as follows:

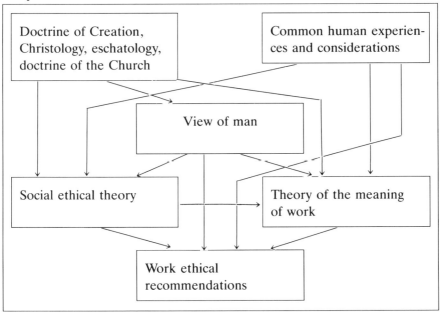

This above diagram illustrates the central importance which a view of man has as a connecting link between the theoretical and ethical philosophy of life components. A view of man also contains both certain theoretical views about man as well as certain views about what is valuable. The connections illustrated above are not valid for any one of the six theologians being studied. On the other hand, all these connections are to be found in the material being studied, considered as a whole. As we have seen, there are highly different views regarding what components form the basis for the content in a work ethical theory.

7. Christian and humane ethics

The five previous chapters have dealt with two fundamental problems. The first is concerned with the type of argument which can be adduced for work ethical recommendations. We have seen that within contemporary Protestant work ethics, such recommendations are based upon differing theories of the meaning of work, differing social ethical theories, differing theories of human nature and upon certain common human experiences and considerations. The second problem is concerned with those considerations forming the basis of the philosophy of life components which make up a work ethical theory. We have seen that the theories of the meaning of work which are to be found in contemporary Protestant theology are motivated by different social ethical theories, different theories of human nature, a Christian doctrine of creation and certain common human experiences and considerations. The social ethical theories of the theologians I deal with are based upon differing theories of human nature, other convictions which form part of a Christian system of belief e.g. a doctrine of creation, a Christology, an eschatology or a doctrine of the church along with certain common human considerations. Finally we have also seen that these theologians' theories of human nature are based partly upon those theoretical views which form part of a Christian philosophy of life and partly upon common human experiences and considerations which do not have a philosophy of life character.

This entails that the work ethical theories which are to be found in contemporary Protestant theology are at least partly based upon those theoretical views which make up a Christian philosophy of life. The social ethical theories and theories of the meaning of work of these theologians are based upon a Christian view of man and other convictions belonging to a Christian system of belief e.g. a doctrine of creation, a Christology or an eschatology. At the same time we have also seen that these work ethical theories are at least partly based upon common human experiences and considerations. These are "common" in the sense that they are not part of some philosophy of life but can be shared by human beings who embrace differing philosophies of life. However these considerations are not common in the sense that they are universally adopted by all human beings.

With this in mind, I shall now pass on to deal with a third problem, namely the question of how Christian work ethics relates to those work ethical theories which are combined with other philosophies of life. Does the Christian philosophy of life provide a specific contribution to the treatment of problems in work ethics? Or is there at least partly certain contentual points of agreement between a Christian and a humane work ethics? The answer to this question depends on how one in general views the relationship between Christian and humane ethics.

The aim of this chapter is to clarify the differing views about the relationship between Christian and humane ethics which are to be found within contemporary Protestant work ethics. By "Christian ethics", I understand a constructive ethical theory which is based upon a Christian philosophy of life. By "humane ethics", on the other hand, I mean a constructive ethical theory which is based upon another philosophy of life. It is an ethical theory which is based upon human experiences and considerations about what is good for human beings but which is not combined with a Christian belief in God. In order to clarify the differing views about the relationship between these, I pose two analytical questions in relation to the material being studied. These are: (1) How is the content in Christian ethics related to the content of a humane ethics associated with some other philosophy of life? This question is concerned with whether the content in a Christian ethics is completely different from the content in humane ethics or whether there is at least some partial contentual agreement between them. (2) What type of arguments can be adduced for the principles and values which make up a contructive ethical theory? This question is concerned with whether we receive insight into what is right and good through common considerations and experiences or whether it is the Revelation in Christ which provides the insight into what characterizes a morally right action.

In order to clarify the answers to these analytical problems given by the theologians, I shall relate them to those views about the relationship between Christian and humane ethics which are to be found in other contemporary theologians. Among Christian theologians, there are differing views about how the content in Christian ethics relates to the content in humane ethics. The first view can be called an "identity theory". This viewpoint asserts that the content in Christian ethics is in no way different from the content of ethical theories which are combined with other philosophies of life. Christian and humane ethics are in complete agreement as regards content. This viewpoint is to be found in K E Løgstrup. He holds that there is no specifically Christian ethics in the sense that Christian ethics does not have a content which cannot also form part of a humane ethics.

Another view can be called a "contrast theory". This viewpoint asserts that the content in Christian ethics is completely different from the content of humane ethics. There is no agreement whatsoever between Christian and humane ethics. This view is to be found in Karl Barth. He holds that the divine demands encountered in Christ are contentually completely different from those ethical theories which belong to other philosophies of life.

A third view can be called a "combination theory". It asserts that the content of Christian ethics in part agrees with the content in humane ethics. At the same time it holds that there are also parts of Christian ethics which are specifically Christian i.e. which are distinct from the content in humane ethics.[1] A viewpoint of this kind is to be found in the writings of the American social ethicist, Reinhold Niebuhr. He maintains that the Christian ideal of love which requires a self-sacrificial concern for others is in agreement with common moral views to be found outside Christianity. At the same time, he holds that its content cannot be completely reduced to common moral views.[2]

The attitude one adopts to these three theories depends upon the type of consideration which one holds forms the basis for the content of a constructive ethical theory. Is ethics based upon common considerations and experiences or is it through the Revelation in Christ that we only receive insight into what constitutes a right action? Among Christian theologians there are also different answers to this question. A first view can be called a "strictly humane ethics". This view asserts that all the arguments which can be adduced for fundamental ethical principles and values are those which are based upon common rational considerations and experiences. Ethics is based not upon the Revelation in Christ but upon rational considerations which can even be accepted by those who do not embrace a Christian faith. A standpoint of this kind is to be found in the writings of K E Løgstrup. Such a strictly humane ethics is in general combined with an identity theory.

A second view can be called a "strictly theological ethics". It maintains that all the arguments which can be adduced for ethics are based upon the special Revelation in Christ. It is only through the Revelation in Christ that we receive insight into what characterizes a right action. This viewpoint is to be found in Karl Barth. He holds that it is only through the Revelation in Christ that we can have knowledge about what constitutes the Will of God and thereby about what is right and good. A strictly theological ethics of this kind is in general combined with a contrast theory. It can however also be combined with a combination theory. In this case, it maintains that all the reasons that can be adduced for fundamental principles and values are based upon the Revelation, even if the content in Christian ethics partially agrees with the content in a humane ethics.

A third view can be called a "partially Revelation based ethics". This viewpoint maintains that Revelation arguments can be adduced for certain parts of ethics, but at the same time common human experiences and considerations can form the basis for the content of ethics. Christian ethics is linked to common human experiences and calculates upon these providing certain insights about what is right while at the same time it holds that the Revelation in Christ has a special authority in questions of morality.[3] A standpoint of this kind is to be found in the writings of the American ethicist, James M Gustafson. He maintains that common human experiences provide us with certain insights about fundamental principles and values while at the same time he holds that the Christian Revelation and the New Testament provide us with more definitive knowledge about what is good and right.[4] A partially Revelation based ethics of this type is in general combined with a combination theory. It can however also be combined with an identity theory. In such a case, it maintains that Christian and humane ethics share a common content while at the same time arguments from Revelation can be adduced for at least certain moral principles and values.

Both a strictly humane ethics and a partially Revelation based ethics assume that ethics is based upon human experiences and considerations about what is good for man which do not presuppose a Christian belief in God. They are two forms of a "humanely based ethics" according to which common human experiences and considerations at least partly form the basis of fundamental principles and values. A partially Revelation based ethics can in turn be formulated in different ways. It can be formulated as (a) a "theological addition ethics" according to which common human experiences and considerations form the basis for certain principles and values while the Revelation in Christ supplies other principles and values which distinguish it from a humane ethics. It can be formulated (b) as a "theological clarificatory ethics" according to which common human experiences and considerations provide us with fragmentary insight into what is right and good while the Revelation in Christ clarifies and gives depth to these insights. It can also be formulated as (c) a "theological motivation ethics" according to which Christian faith provides a specifically overall viewpoint of existence which reinforces our moral commitment and forms the basis for the content of ethics while at the same time this content exhibits certain areas of agreement with an ethics combined with other philosophies of life.

The way in which one understands the relation betweeen Christian and humane ethics is closely related to those parts of the Christian system of belief which are held to provide a basis for Christian ethics. In the previous chapter, I distinguished between four different views about the relationship between ethics and the Christian system of belief. A "theology of creation ethics" maintains that ethics is primarily based upon the doctrine of creation. This viewpoint is in general combined with a humanely based ethics. Thielicke and Løgstrup hold that because ethics is based upon the first article of faith, there is already an ethical insight preceding the encounter with Christ.

A "Christological ethics" maintains on the other hand that ethics is primarily based upon Christology while an "eschatological ethics" holds that ethics is primarily based upon eschatology. These two viewpoints are in general combined with a strictly theological ethics. Barth and Moltmann maintain that it is only the Revelation in Christ which provides us with insight about what is right and good while common human experiences and considerations provide no ethical insight whatsoever.

A "trinitarian ethics" maintains finally that ethics is based both upon the doctrine of creation and upon Christology and eschatology. This viewpoint is in general combined with a partially Revelation based ethics. Trillhaas holds that there are certain points of agreement between Christian and humane ethics while at the same time he maintains that the Revelation in Christ, primarily through the Sermon on the Mount, provides a specific contribution to morality.

In the previous chapter, I explained the differing viewpoints which exist within contemporary Protestant theology regarding the relationship between work ethical theories and the different components in a Christian system of belief. In this chapter, I shall now try to clarify how these views are related to differing views about the relationship between Christian and humane ethics. Is the content of Christian ethics completely different from the content of humane ethics or are there at least some points of agreement between them? Is ethics based upon the Revelation in Christ or upon common human experiences and considerations? These are the questions which I shall deal with in this chapter.

A humanely based social ethics

The social ethics to be found in the writings of Emil Brunner is a deontological and monistic theory of duty. In his view, the criterion for a right political action is that it is in agreement with the Will of God with respect to the orders of creation. According to Brunner, the Will of God respecting these orders is that the good is to be distributed justly so that each and every one obtains their due taking into account both the similarities and dissimilarities which exist between human beings. How then does the content in this Christian social ethics relate to the ethical views to be found in other philosophies of life?

Brunner's view would seem to be that the content in a Christian social ethics agrees with the content in humane ethics. The view that it is just to assign to each and everyone their due (*suum cuique*) is a view which forms part of natural law. This law stands above all human arbitrariness and specifies what is right in itself but its content is accessible to human beings with different philosophies of life. In a Christian doctrine of natural law, "nature" is synonymous with God's order of creation. It is this order which gives every created being its essence and thereby specifies what is good and right. The view that one ought to promote what is in accordance with nature and what is just, is not however specifically Christian.[5]

In the Revelation in Christ, Brunner writes, we encounter a morality which goes beyond natural law and which is in opposition to what we call just. Christ reveals an ideal of love and a righteousness which cannot be applied in temporal matters. The Christian ideal of love to be found in the New Testament is an ideal of love which completely differs from the ideal of love to be found outside Christianity. This ideal is an agape which is not motivated by the value of the person who is loved: on the contrary, it is a love which creates value.[6] This ideal of love according to Brunner is something completely different from the common human ideal of justice. Within individual ethics, he would thus appear to embrace what I have called a contrast theory according to which Christian ethics completely differs contentually from humane ethics.

The specifically Christian ideal of love, however, only applies within individual ethics. It is valid, he writes, on the purely personal plane as a norm for relationships between individuals. On the other hand, it is not valid for social ethics. That sphere is governed by the demand for social justice and the requirement that social institutions must reflect the original divine order of creation. Thus the content of social ethics is and remains completely humane.[7] Although Brunner embraces a contrast theory within individual ethics, in social ethics he would seem to embrace an identity theory according to which the content in Christian social ethics is in no way different from those social ethical views which are combined with other philosophies of life.

What kind of arguments can be adduced to show that certain fundamental ethical judgements are valid? Within individual ethics according to Brunner, ethical judgements are based not upon common rational considerations but upon the Revelation in Christ. Because of the gulf which exists between human beings and God, it is only in the light of the Revelation that we can perceive what is right. The criterion for a right action, according to Brunner, is that it is in agreement with the Will of God. We receive insight into what is the Will of God only through his Revelation. God reveals Himself in His

Word, in Jesus Christ, and clarifies in this way what is good and right. Because of sin, we cannot recognize the Will of God unaided. God, however, reveals himself in Jesus Christ and thereby shows what love is.[8] Thus Brunner within individual ethics would seem to embrace what I have called a strictly theological ethics.

This is true only, however, within individual ethics. Within social ethics, according to Brunner, we can receive insight about what is right independently of the Revelation in Christ. The criterion for a right action in this sphere is that it is in agreement with the divine orders of creation. These orders are an expression of God's original Will and as such constitute necessary conditions for human life and community. With the exception of the Church, these orders exist independently of belief. Since they are given in the creation, it is also possible for every human being to receive knowledge about the Will of God regarding these orders, independently of the Revelation in Christ. Their nature and existence is recognized through reason, not through belief: that is, through the capacity for knowledge which every human being has as a human being. Brunner writes:

> "Sie werden nach ihrem Wesen und Bestand durch die Vernunft erkannt, nicht durch den Glauben, durch das rein natürliche Erkenntnisvermögen, das jedem Menschen, weil und sofern er ein Mensch ist, gegeben ist."[9]

In contrast to Barth, Brunner does not deny the existence of a natural theology and the capacity of every human being with the help of reason to decide whether a political action is right. The true nature of the the orders of creation, can be perceived certainly only through belief but they are given in creation and operate even if God is not recognized as the Creator. Even those who do not believe in Christ can perceive what is right.[10] Brunner's ethics thus has a markedly dualistic character. At the same time as his individual ethics is strictly theological, his social ethics is humanely based. In the latter sphere, it is held that the Revelation in Christ is not a necessary presupposition for receiving insight about what is right and good. Social ethics is also largely based upon common human experiences and considerations.

In Brunner, this humanely based social ethics is combined with a theology of creation ethics. His social ethical theory is primarily combined with a doctrine of creation. At the same time, Brunner's social ethical theory is not only based upon those convictions which make up a Christian system of belief. It is also combined with common considerations which are not of a philosophy of life character.

A strictly theological social ethics

J H Oldham's social ethics is of a completely different kind from the orders of creation theology to be found in Brunner. He claims to embrace an "inspiration ethic" which would seem to imply a deontological act ethics according to which the criterion for a right action is that it is in agreement with the Will of God. This ethic is based upon Christology. Oldham embraces a doctrine of the Lordship of Christ according to which we recognize the Will of God through His Revelation in Christ. But how is the content of this Christian social ethics related to the ethical views within other philosophies of life?

According to Oldham, the content of Christian ethics is completely different from the content of humane ethics. There is a conflict between Christian understanding of life and the values which exist in modern society. This is the case for example with regard to the attitudes towards the significance of power and the understanding of the principle of the equal value of all human beings. According to Oldham, there is a sharp difference between the values which belong to the Kingdom of God and those which operate in the world.[11] He would thus seem to adopt what I have called a contrast theory according to which there is no agreement between Christian and humane ethics.

According to Oldham this is due to the fact that Christian ethics has a special perspective in terms of which it judges what is right and wrong. Its view of what constitutes a right action is dependent upon Christ. Certainly human beings have differing experiences and views for example about how society should be shaped. Christians, however, act on the basis of values which distinguish them from those which exist in society at large.[12] The principal question for Christians is what is the Will of God. They have a special vocation to be instruments of God in pursuing his Kingdom. The aim of society on the other hand is never completely identical with and is often directly opposed to the aims which Christians are called upon to serve. Therefore according to Oldham, there are noticable differences between Christian and humane ethics.[13]

This view is based upon the position adopted by Oldham regarding the question of the type of argument which can be adduced for saying that certain fundamental ethical judgements are valid. He would seem to hold that all the reasons which can be adduced for ethical views are based upon the unique Revelation in Christ. The criterion for a right act is that it is in agreement with the Will of God. This we discover in the light of His Revelation in Christ, in the Bible and in the experience of the Church. It is only through the Revelation in Christ that we can decide what is right and wrong.[14] It is this standpoint which I have labelled a strictly theological ethics.

Oldham adopts a doctrine of the Lordship of Christ. The fact that Christ is Lord, he holds, is both the source and goal for Christian action. It is that which ultimately decides what is Christian and non-Christian. All knowledge which is based upon other sources, must be judged in the light of this unique Revelation. Oldham writes that Christ is the factor which constitutes the ultimate criterion in Christian decision. Christian belief is a belief in the Incarnation, the Cross and Resurrection and this belief in Christ also forms the basis for Christian witness in society.[15]

The ethics to be found in Oldham is very similar to that in Barthian theology. He rejects the doctrine of natural law and would seem instead to adopt a strictly theological ethics. He himself maintains that his approach has points of contact with Reformed ethics as put forward in the Calvinist tradition where it is held that there are obvious differences between Christian and humane ethics. Thus Oldham's ethics has great similarities with Karl Barth's strictly theological ethics according to which (1) the criterion for a right action is that it is in agreement with The Will of God and (2) we have knowledge of the Will of God only through the Revelation in Christ.

In *The Function of the Church in Society*, Oldham discusses the concept of the Church and the forms for the Church's action in society, in part through the individual Christian and in part through the Church as an organized community. At the same time, he proposes a constructive social ethical theory. Oldham maintains in this context that Calvinism in contrast to the Thomist doctrine of natural law emphasizes the difference between Christian and humane ethics. According to Calvinist theology, the Church has its own special message and its own criteria so that it cannot unreservedly accept even the most noble striving after social justice and international peace but first must ask to what extent these will promote the Lordship of Christ.[16]

Oldham also puts forward such a strictly theological ethics. Christian ethics, he writes, is independent of all common human ideals and ideologies and judges what is right and wrong in the light of Christ and from its own special perspective. According to Oldham, this does not imply that there is a specifically Christian social system or a specifically Christian political programme. On the other hand, it implies that Christians hold that an action is right and obligatory only if it is in agreement with the Will of God. The question of whether an action is right can only be decided by responding to God's vocation and guidance in the given situation.[17]

When the Church seeks to decide what is a right action it must thus according to Oldham stand on its own ground and preserve its own independence in relation to other groups. It has to direct criticism against society from a centre which is outside society. The basis of Christian ethics is the belief in a living personal God who has revealed His grace and His will in Jesus Christ.

Thus the gift and promise of God precedes every ethical demand.[18]

Oldham's view of the relationship between Christian and humane ethics as we have seen is combined with a Christological ethics. His social ethical theory is based upon the second article of the creed and upon a doctrine of the Lordship of Christ. Thereby it is also related to eschatology. In contrast to Brunner, Oldham however does not relate social ethics to the doctrine of the creation. Nor in his arguments for basic social ethical views does he refer explicitly to common human experiences and considerations.

A partially Revelation based ethics

As we have seen, Tor Aukrust adopts a pluralistic theory of duty according to which an action is right if it is in agreeement with the Will of God. He holds that there are several criteria for the Will of God which can be formulated as general moral principles. These are an eschatological principle, a principle of human value, the decalogue, a principle of freedom, a principle of equality, a principle of justice and the commandment to love. As we have seen in the previous chapter, these principles are based both upon Christology and upon common human considerations. But how does the content in this Christian ethics relate to those ethical views to be encountered in other philosophies of life?

Aukrust writes that one can speak of a "specifically Christian ethics" in the sense that Christianity organically contains an ethical requirement which it conceives as identical to the Will of God. According to Christian belief, the Will of God is the norm for what is good and right. At the same time, however, Aukrust maintains that there is no "specifically Christian ethics" in the sense that the content in Christian ethics differs completely from the content in humane ethics. Considered purely contentually, the Christian determination of the good does not differ from the ethical insight which can be obtained on a humane basis.[19] Aukrust thus rejects the standpoint which I have called a contrast theory.

This agreement between Christian and humane ethics entails that there is an insight into what is the Will of God which is independent of the Revelation in Christ. God's ethical demands are valid for all human beings. Thereby there is also a universal Revelation of and insight into the content of this demand.[20] According to Aukrust there is a common insight into what is right and good which is independent of the Revelation in Christ. This insight arises from the fact that we are human beings created in the image of God. To be a human being namely implies being referred to others. God's demands reach the individual through their encounter with their fellow human beings.[21] As a result, there are also moral views which are shared by Christianity and other philosophies of life. Instead of a contrast theory, Aukrust seems to adopt what I have called a combination theory.

The view that there are certain moral views which are common to Christians and non-Christians is to be found in the classical doctrine of natural law. Aukrust enters into a detailed discussion of this doctrine. He maintains that it can be formulated in different ways. In the case of such thinkers as Grotius, Pufendorf, Hobbes and Locke, one encounters a "rationalistic theory of natural law". It is an individualistic theory according to which the social orders depend upon a contract between individuals. According to this theory, natural law is valid even if God does not exist.[22] However, according to other theories, natural law requires a "metaphysical corrective". Human nature constitutes a norm for right action. In order to decide what is "human nature", a metaphysical corrective, an outside norm, is required.[23]

The Catholic doctrine of natural law includes such a "metaphysical corrective". This is eternal law (*lex aeterna*) which forms the basis of natural law (*lex naturae*). Eternal law specifies what is the order of creation, the objective order which came into existence with the creation.[24] According to this doctrine, all human beings by virtue of their conscience and moral sense have an ability to perceive the content of the natural law but at the same time human beings on account of sin can also be mistaken. Church dogmatic authority then provides the correct interpretation of natural law and the concrete ethical demands.[25]

Tor Aukrust provides an account of the critique which has been aimed at this Catholic doctrine of natural law within Protestant theology. Objections have been raised because the doctrine has been associated with a tendency towards casuistry and the emphasis upon the Church's role as an ethical interpretative authority.[26] At the same time, Aukrust maintains that one also encounters a doctrine of natural law within Lutheran theology. According to this doctrine, every human being upon the basis of his reason can achieve insight into the content of the law. Because of the Fall however, human reason is uncertain about the content of natural law with the result that it cannot give sufficient guidance. In this situation, God clarifies the content of the law. This is done with the help of the Decalogue which is the clearest expresssion of natural law. The law is later also illuminated by the Revelation in Christ and above all by the commandment to love and the Golden Rule.[27]

Within contemporary Protestant theology, there are differing views about the doctrine of natural law. Some theologians, e.g. Karl Barth, reject this doctrine and hold that the Revelation in Christ is the only source of insight into what is right and good.[28] Others recommend a traditional theory of natural law and hold that what is right can be perceived independently of the Revelation. Such an order of creation theology is to be found for example in

Emil Brunner. Tor Aukrust rejects both these standpoints and wishes personally to adopt an intermediate position. This entails that he rejects both a strictly theological ethics and a strictly humane ethics. On the one hand, like the doctrine of natural law, he holds that there is a common human insight into what is right and also that God makes His Will known independently through the Revelation in Christ. On the other hand he holds that ethics is not only based upon the belief in creation and common human experiences. Although the moral norms can be understood philosophically, it is the Revelation which is the real source concerning what is right and good.[29] Aukrust thus prefers what I have called a partially Revelation based ethics. This is combined in his writings with a combination theory according to which there exists a certain partial agreement between Christian and humane ethics.

Aukrust writes that he presupposes an eschatological framework for natural law. According to him, Lutheran theology cannot recognize a natural law which is independent of the Revelation in Christ. The Sermon on the Mount places natural law and moral reason within a framework for the absolute demand which goes together with the eschatological proclamation of the Kingdom of God. Aukrust holds that within this framework, evangelical theology can however speak of natural law as an expression of God's approximate demands. God's absolute demand which presupposes the reestablishment of the Kingdom of God is illuminated by the Revelation in Christ. Natural law which is accessible to one and all specifies on the other hand God's relative demands which are valid here in time.[30]

In discussing natural law, Aukrust also answers the question of what kind of reasons can be adduced for the validity of fundamental ethical judgements. Aukrust holds that Christianity provides ethics with a foundation which goes beyond humane ethics. Christian and humane ethics provide different answers to the question of what is the basis of the ethical demand. By "humane ethics" Aukrust understands the view that the basis of ethics is not belief in God but human beings themselves.[31] According to this view, ethics is based exclusively upon common rational arguments. A humane ethics of the type to be encountered for example within moral philosophy is based exclusively upon rational arguments and does not depend upon a particular system of belief and philosophy of life.[32] By "Christian ethics", Aukrust on the other hand understands an ethics which is based upon a Christian system of belief. Although according to him such an ethics has rational elements it is primarily based upon a Christian belief in God.[33]

Aukrust writes that there are certain areas of agreement between Christian ethics and humane ethics. They reject for example "moral nihilism" according to which everything is permitted because they both hold that there are certain norms which are obligatory for human beings. Contrary to moral

210

nihilism which according to Aukrust is a consequence of a non-cognitive metaethical theory which maintains that ethical statements have an emotive function, both Christian and humane ethics maintain that there is a rational basis for morality. Although Christian ethics is based upon the Revelation, it also has a content which at least partially agrees with the content in humane ethics.[34]

According to Aukrust, there are therefore certain areas of agreement between Christian and Marxist ethics. Theologically Marxist ethics can be seen as a branch of humane ethics. Like it, Marxist ethics maintains that ethics is independent of a belief in God and Revelation and that it is completely based upon human experiences and considerations about what is good for human beings. In contrast to this standpoint, Christian ethics maintains that we attain insight into what is good and right also through God's Revelation. This however does not rule out certain fundamental aims which are common to Christian and Marxist ethics.[35]

What then are the arguments which can be adduced for the contents of ethics? As we have seen previously, Aukrust combines a partially Revelation based ethics with what I have called a trinitarian ethics. His social ethical theory is based upon the doctrine of creation so that he also holds that every human being has a possibility of attaining a certain insight into what is right. At the same time he holds that the Revelation in Christ is a fundamental source of insight into God's ethical demands. According to Aukrust, Christology motivates the principle of human value, the principle of freedom and the principle of equality. He also holds that eschatology forms the basis of social ethics. We obtain insight into the content of God's absolute demand primarily through the Sermon on the Mount. Thus Aukrust presupposes in his social ethics partly certain primary criteria which are specifically Christian and based upon Christology and eschatology, and partly certain secondary criteria which are humane and have a natural law character. The latter are also based upon certain common human experiences and considerations.[36]

An eschatologically based combination theory

As we have seen, Arthur Rich adopts a subject related and eschatological social ethics. He holds that social institutions ought to be given a humane form and that it is on the basis of the coming Kingdom of God as revealed in Jesus Christ that we can determine what is humane. According to Rich, a truly human existence is characterized by faith, hope and love. These existentials provide a motivation for certain criteria about what is good for human beings e.g. human fellowship, participation, critical distance and relativity. On the basis of these criteria, one can then in turn formulate certain maxims for social decision. But what is the relationship between the content in this Christian social ethics and those ethical views which are to be encountered in other philosophies of life?

Rich holds that the maxims which are formulated within the framework for a Christian social ethics are not specifically Christian. They are humane and can be understood even by those who are not Christian. Nor are the social ethical criteria which motivate these maxims specifically Christian in the sense that they are completely different from those criteria which can be accepted by human beings with another philosophy of life. Rich thus rejects the viewpoint which I have called a contrast theory. At the same time, it is clear that he holds that there is a specifically Christian contribution to social ethics. He criticizes a creation theological entry point for social ethics and holds instead that social ethics is based upon eschatology and Christology. The Kingdom of God is revealed in Christ and with him we obtain the criteria for a truly human life. The Revelation provides us with a specifically Christian understanding of what humanity entails and thereby also special guidelines for social ethics. Rich's view coincides with what I have called a combination theory.

Unlike the contrast theory, Rich holds that the Revelation in Christ does not give us a new morality in the sense that we obtain new values. The morality which is associated with the Revelation contains only one imperative namely the commandment to love. It does not however contain any specifically Christian values. On the other hand, it is associated with a special attitude towards those values which are humane. These values are relativized and conceived as complementary. Thus for example Christian social ethics conceives freedom and obligingness as two values which complement one another.[37]

According to Rich, this specifically Christian contribution to social ethics goes together with the eschatological entry point. For an eschatologically directed humanity, only the Kingdom of God has finality. It therefore adopts a critical distance towards what exists and affirms it relatively. A Christian social ethics also conceives the maxims and criteria which it formulates as relative. These are not absolutes but specify what is relatively good and right. The specifically Christian contribution is therefore not to be found in these maxims which even non-Christians can accept nor is it to be found in the criteria. Instead it is to be found in an understanding of the humanity which belongs with the coming Kingdom of God. This Kingdom of God gives humanity another dimension and thereby relativizes all social ethical criteria and maxims.[38]

What type of arguments then according to Rich can be adduced for fundamental ethical views? Rich is one of the few contemporary Christian work ethicists who explicitly deals with the moral philosophical discussion of metaethical problems. He distinguishes between "non-cognitive theories" according to which it is impossible to verify scientifically or to falsify statements about what is right and good and "cognitive theories" according to which statements about what is right and good give us a form of knowledge and therefore can be verified or falsified.[39] Rich does not clearly specify his own standpoint but there are certain statements in his writings which indicate that he would seem to adopt a form of non-cognitivism which can be called "ethical prescriptivism". According to this standpoint, ethical statements have a prescriptive function i.e. they provide exhortations and recommendations.[40] Rich writes that when social ethics maintains that society ought to be so constructed that it is good for human beings ("Menschengerecht") it is making a prescriptive statement. "Menschengerecht" is namely a prescriptive concept. It is not possible with scientific methods to provide objective knowledge about what is "Menschengerecht" and therefore the statements of social ethics are prescriptive.[41]

Rich does not specify what type of rational arguments can be adduced for and against such prescriptive statements. However it is clear that according to him, the Revelation in Christ is a fundamental source of insight into what is good and right. Rich criticizes the doctrine of natural law according to which there are certain common moral views into which we have a universal insight. According to this viewpoint, there are norms which are based upon human nature. In Rich's view, such a timeless human nature is problematic.[42] Rich also criticizes the Lutheran doctrine of two kingdoms. This draws too sharp a distinction between belief and political decision thus entailing political passivity.[43] Despite the fact that he adopts a combination theory, Rich would seem to reject every form of humanely based social ethics.

Instead Rich prefers a doctrine of the Lordship of Christ of a type which is common within Reformed theology. This doctrine maintains that at the very centre of Christian belief there is to be found the living Christ, the fundamental criterion of what is right.[44] For Christian belief, it is only God's love as it is revealed in Jesus Christ which is the basis and measure of what is good and right. It is a question of examining what is right and wrong on the basis of this love because only Christ who is the centre of the Scriptures is the source of ethical insight.[45] This is a standpoint which I have called a strictly theological ethics. According to Rich, it is in the last analysis the Revelation in Christ which decides if fundamental ethical judgements are valid. There are no common human considerations underpinning his social ethics.

A Christologically based combination theory

I have previously characterized Günter Brakelmann's social ethics as a deontological theory of rights. According to him, the Christian ideal of love is a fundamental ethical criterion. It is associated with a principle of the equal value of all human beings. This principle of human value encourages us to respect certain fundamental human rights such as the right to participate in decision-making and the right to a meaningful and human tolerable work. But what then is the relationship between the content in this Christian ethics and those ethical convictions associated with other philosophies of life?

Brakelmann would seem to hold that there are at least certain points of agreement between the content of Christian ethics and the content of humane ethics. He holds that there are moral principles and values which are shared by Christians and human beings with other philosophies of life. This can be the case as regards the principle of human value and he holds that the view that we ought to defend freedom and justice can be embraced by human beings with different philosophies of life.[46] Like Rich, Brakelmann thus rejects a contrast theory. His viewpoint would rather seem to be what I have called a combination theory.

What then are the types of arguments which can be adduced for fundamental ethical views? Brakelmann holds that those principles which are common to Christian and humane ethics are motivated by different philosophies of life and their bases are different. They can therefore also be given a specifically Christian motivation. As we have seen in the previous chapter, Brakelmann adopts a Christological social ethics. The social ethical criteria he proposes, are primarily based upon Christology. The basis for the Christian ideal of love is given by God's concern for the human being in Jesus Christ which gives us a measure also for a true love between human beings. Christology also provides the basis for the principle of the equal value of all human beings. Christ's work of atonement entails that all human beings are equal before God and therefore that all human beings have an equal value. Moreover Christology motivates our striving for freedom and our defence of certain fundamental human rights. Our pursuit of freedom is based upon the fact that human beings become free through their belief in Christ.[47]

Although Brakelmann holds that there are certain contentual points of agreement between Christian and humane ethics, he would seem to justify those social ethical criteria he specifies, exclusively from a viewpoint of Christian belief. He would seem to hold that principles such as the ideal of love and human value are solely based upon the Revelation in Christ. Brakelmann does not refer to common human experiences and considerations when he motivates these principles. On the other hand, he holds that we should make rational considerations of a humane character when we apply these principles. He writes that we must use our intellect guided by love to reflect over how these principles are to be put into practical politics under given conditions. These criteria however are not based upon any common human rational considerations.[48] Thus Brakelmann like Rich adopts a combination theory with a strictly theological ethics.

An ecclesiologically and humanely based ethics

John Atherton is the only one of the theologians I deal with, who adopts a teleological social ethics. Two moral principles play a fundamental role in his theory. According to the first of these principles, we ought in our political acts to strive for a society where there exists a community similar to the Christian community symbolized by the Body of Christ. According to the second principle, we ought to strive for what is good for all human beings in society i.e. the common good. These two principles entail that we ought to strive for a "participating and reciprocal society".

Atherton holds that the content in this Christian social ethics agrees at least partly with the content in those ethical theories which are to be encountered in other philosophies of life. Since the goal for our political acts ought to be "the common good", this means we ought to promote certain values which are accepted by human beings with different philosophies of life. Although today's society is pluralistic, there are certain fundamental values about which there is a consensus. They are, Atherton writes, such values as community, freedom and equality.[49] In a pluralistic society, different philosophies of life can contribute to the common good. There is a common basis regarding questions of values which permits cooperation between different philosophies of life.[50]

Atherton thus rejects a contrast theory. His view is rather of the kind I have called a combination theory. He writes that the pursuit of the common good provides a basis for a common commitment for human beings with different philosophies of life. "The common good" is made up of values which are supported by Christian belief but they are not exclusively Christian. They can also be motivated on the basis of other philosophies of life.[51] Even the social ideal which Atherton advocates, that of a "participating and reciprocal society", is an ideal which holds for both Christians and non-Christians. It is a common goal which does not have a specifically Christian character.

This also entails that the arguments which can be adduced for fundamental moral principles and values are humane in character. According to Atherton, they can be motivated by arguments which are acceptable to both Christians and non-Christians. Like Brunner and Aukrust, Atherton would thus appear to adopt a humanely based social ethics. He holds that social ethics is at least partly based upon common human experiences and considerations. Such humane reasons can be adduced for those values which are associated with the common good. At the same time, Atherton holds that there are specifically Christian reasons for at least certain parts of the contents of ethics. Thus for example, the principle of the equal value of all human beings can be justified by the fact that God loves all human beings and expresses this love in his work of creation and atonement. In this way, theology provides a motivation for what Atherton referring to J Philip Wogaman, calls certain "moral presumptions."

Certain of the theological arguments which Atherton adduces for fundamental ethical views are also those which presuppose the unique Revelation in Christ. The clearest expression of this is that he holds that there is an ecclesiological basis for social ethics. According to Atherton the Church as the Body of Christ is an image of the society worth pursuing. In our political acts, we ought to strive for a society where there exists a mutual dependence between human beings similar to the community which is symbolized by the Body of Christ. This is an image which can only be accepted by those who accept the Revelation in Christ. Thus Atherton like Aukrust would seem to adopt what I have called a partially Revelation based ethics. Particularly in the case of Atherton, this is combined with a social ethics which is largely based upon ecclesiology.

Conclusion

What views about the relationship between Christian and humane ethics are to be found within contemporary Protestant work ethics? What are the views of the theologians I deal with regarding how the content in a Christian ethics is related to an ethics associated with another philosophy of life? What type of arguments do they hold can be adduced for the principles and values which make up a constructive ethical theory? In this chapter we have seen that the theologians examined provide six different answers to these questions.

Three of these theologians adopt what I have called a humanely based ethics. This is so in the case of Emil Brunner, Tor Aukrust and John Atherton. They hold that common human experiences and considerations at least in part provide a basis for fundamental principles and values. The arguments which can be adduced for ethics are not all based upon the unique Revelation in Christ. Such a humanely based ethics, however, is formulated in three different ways by these theologians.

A first form of humanely based ethics is associated with a theology of creation ethics. This is so in the case of Emil Brunner. His social ethical theory is primarily based upon a doctrine of creation. The criterion for a right political action according to Brunner is that it is in agreement with the Will of God regarding the orders of creation. Because these orders are given in the creation, it is possible for all human beings to know what is the Will of God regarding them. Social ethics is also based upon common human considerations and experiences. Within individual ethics, Brunner assumes that we obtain insight about what is right only through God's Revelation in Jesus Christ. This holds, however, only within individual ethics. Within social ethics, all human beings can perceive what constitutes a right action. Thus Brunner would seem to combine a strictly theological individual ethics with a social ethics which is more or less strictly humane.

As a result Brunner also holds that the content in Christian social ethics agrees with the content in humane social ethics. A fundamental social ethical principle is that one ought to pursue justice and according to Brunner this is humane in character. With the Revelation in Christ, we encounter a radical ideal of love which is completely different in kind from the content of a humane ethics. This specifically Christian ideal, however, holds only within individual ethics. Within social ethics, the common ideal of justice is valid instead. Thus Brunner combines his humanely based social ethics with a contrast theory within individual ethics and an identity theory within social ethics.

A second form of humanely based ethics is combined with a trinitarian ethics. This is so in the case of Tor Aukrust. His social ethical theory is combined with a doctrine of creation and he holds that every human being has a possibility of achieving a certain insight into what is right. At the same time, he maintains that the Revelation in Christ is a fundamental source of insight into God's ethical demands. According to Aukrust, eschatology also forms the basis of social ethics. He claims to accept a natural law within an eschatological framework. According to this standpoint, common human experiences and considerations provide a foundation for certain social ethical principles. At the same time, there are also certain primary criteria which are based upon Christology and eschatology. This is the standpoint I have called a partially Revelation based ethics.

Aukrust holds that there is a certain agreement between the content of a Christian ethics and the content of a humane ethics. In agreement with the doctrine of natural law, he holds that there are certain moral views which are shared by Christian and non-Christians alike. While Aukrust rejects a contrast theory, he holds at the same time also that there are certain primary social ethical criteria which are specifically Christian. He would thus seem to advocate the standpoint which I have called a combination theory.

A third form of humanely based ethics is combined with an ecclesiological ethics. This is true of John Atherton. His social ethical theory is based upon a doctrine of the Church. Atherton holds that the Church as the body of Christ is an image of the society which we ought to strive after in our political acts. According to Atherton there are specifically Christian reasons for at least certain parts of the contents of ethics. Certain arguments for fundamental ethical views would seem to presuppose the unique Revelation in Christ. At the same time, Atherton holds that common considerations can also form the basis for certain fundamental principles and values. Such common human experiences and considerations form the basis of the values which belong to the common good. Atherton would thus seem to adopt what I have called a partially Revelation based ethics.

The content in a Christian ethics according to Atherton agrees at least partially with the content in ethical theories within other philosophies of life. Atherton thus rejects a contrast theory. We ought according to him to strive for "the common good" i.e. those values embraced by human beings with different philosophies of life e.g. community, freedom and equality. At the same time, Atherton holds, that there is a specifically Christian contribution to morality. His standpoint is closest to what I have called a combination theory.

Brunner, Aukrust and Atherton share the view that common human experiences and considerations form the basis of social ethics. On the other hand, they have differing views about which components in a Christian system of belief indfluence social ethical theory. Brunner's social ethics is based upon a doctrine of creation while his social ethics is not at all based upon Christology and eschatology. Christology influences his view of man but eschatology does not form the basis of any component in Brunner's work ethical theory.

According to Aukrust, social ethics however, is based not only upon the doctrine of creation but also upon Christology and eschatology. On the other hand, for Atherton in particular social ethics is based upon a doctrine of the Church and partly also upon eschatology. The doctrine of the Church provides the grounds for his view of man while Atherton in no way bases his work ethical theory upon a doctrine of creation.

Brunner's formulation of a humanely based ethics can be illustrated as follows:

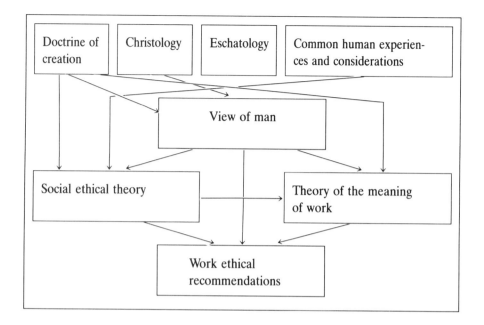

Aukrust's formulation of a humanely based ethics differs from Brunner's in three respects: (1) his social ethical theory is also based upon Christology and eschatology (2) his view of man is not based upon Christology (3) his work ethical recommendations are also based upon certain common human experiences while however they are not explicitly based upon his view of man. Atherton's humanely based ethics distinguishes itself from Brunner's in four respects: (1) his social ethical theory is based not upon a doctrine of creation but upon a doctrine of the Church and eschatology (2) his view of man is also based upon a doctrine of the Church (3) his theory of the meaning of work is not explicitly based upon a doctrine of creation and a view of man (4) his work ethical recommendations are also based upon certain common human experiences.

Three of the theologians I deal with embrace what I have called a strictly theological ethics. This is so in the case of J H Oldham, Arthur Rich and Günter Brakelmann. They hold that all the arguments which can be adduced for ethics are based upon the unique Revelation in Christ. Ethics is not based upon some common human experiences and considerations. This strictly theological ethics is however formulated in three different ways by these theologians.

A first form of strictly theological ethics is combined with a contrast theory. This is so in the case of J H Oldham. He holds that the content in Christian ethics is quite different from that in humane ethics. There is a sharp distinction between the ethical ideals which are part and parcel of Christian belief and those ethical ideals associated with other philosophies of life. This is due to the fact that the criterion for a right action according to Christian ethics is that it agrees with the Will of God.

In Oldham, the contrast theory is combined with a Christological ethics. His social ethical theory is above all based upon Christology. The criterion for a right action is that it agrees with The Will of God and we learn to know the Will of God only through the Revelation in Christ. Oldham adopts a doctrine of the Lordship of Christ. He holds that it is in the light of Christ that we have to judge what constitutes a right political action. This implies that social ethics according to Oldham is completely based upon the Revelation. His social ethical theory is not based upon any common human experiences and considerations.

A second form of strictly theological ethics is combined both with a combination theory and an eschatological ethics. This is so in the case of Arthur Rich. He holds that the maxims and social ethical criteria which are formulated within the framework of Christian social ethics are not specifically Christian. They can be embraced also by human beings with another philosophy of life. Christian belief does not give us new values and principles but rather a special attitude towards those values which in themselves are common. However Christian belief provides a specific contribution to social ethics. It entails namely that common values are relativized and conceived as complementary.

This combination theory is in Rich combined with an eschatological ethics. His social ethical theory is above all based upon eschatology. The hope in the coming Kingdom of God entails a relativization of and critical distance towards all social ethical criteria and maxims. Rich's social ethics is not based upon any common human experiences and considerations. The fundamental source of insight into what is good and right is instead the Revelation in Christ. Rich puts forward a doctrine of the Lordship of Christ according to which the Revelation in Christ decides if a fundamental ethical judgement is valid.

A third form of strictly theological ethics is combined with a combination theory and a Christological ethics. This is so in the case of Günter Brakelmann. He maintains that there are moral principles and values which are common for Christians and human beings with another philosophy of life. Among these principles are the principle of human value and the view that we ought to strive for freeedom and justice. While Brakelmann rejects a contrast theory he also holds that there is a specific Christian contribution to morality. Even common values can be given a specifically Christian motivation.

In Brakelmann, the combination theory is combined with a Christological ethics. His social ethical theory is above all based upon Christology. It is this which forms the basis for the ideal of love, the principle of the value of all human beings and the view that we ought to strive for freedom and we ought to defend fundamental human rights. These principles are not motivated by common human experiences but are according to Brakelmann exclusively based upon the Revelation in Christ. Thus he combines a combination theory with a strictly theological ethics.

Common for Oldham, Rich and Brakelmann is the view that social ethics is not based upon common human experiences and considerations. Social ethics is based solely upon the Revelation in Christ. However Oldham and Rich hold that common human considerations form the basis for a view of man. Rich and Brakelmann also motivate certain work ethical recommendations on the basis of such common human considerations.

Also common to Oldham, Rich and Brakelmann is the view that social ethics is based both upon Christology and eschatology although Oldham and Brakelmann lay greater emphasis upon Christology while Rich adopts an eschatological ethics. None of these three theologians however bases social ethics upon a doctrine of creation. According to Rich the doctrine of creation has no effect upon the view of man and the theory of the meaning of work. Oldham and Brakelmann however base their theories of human nature and the meaning of work upon a doctrine of creation.

Oldham's formulation of a strictly theological ethics can be illustrated as follows:

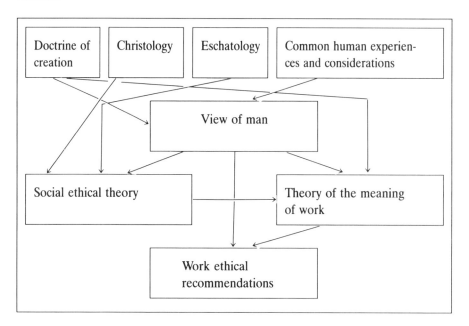

Rich's formulation of a strictly theological ethics differs from Oldham's in three respects: (1) his view of man is not based upon a doctrine of creation but upon Christology and eschatology (2) likewise his theory of the meaning of work is not based upon a doctrine of creation (3) his work ethical recommendations are based also upon a social ethical theory and certain common human considerations. Brakelmann's strictly theological ethics differs also from Oldham's in three respects: (1) his view of man is not based upon any common human considerations (2) his work ethical recommendations are not based upon his view of man (3) his work ethical recommendations are however based upon a social ethical theory and certain common human considerations.

What are the fundamental differences between these three forms of humanely based ethics and these three different forms of strictly theological ethics? First of all these viewpoints are combined with differing views regarding the question of whether common human experiences and considerations form the basis for social ethics. According to a humanely based ethics, ethics has such a common basis but according to a strictly theological ethics it is based purely upon the Revelation in Christ. Secondly, they are combined with different views regarding which components in a Christian system of belief form the basis for ethics. A humanely based ethics is often based upon a doctrine of creation but it can also be formulated so that also Christology and eschatology form the basis of ethics. On the other hand a strictly theological ethics is based upon Christology and eschatology while the doctrine of creation does not form a basis for ethics. Thirdly they are combined with different views about how the content in a Christian ethics is related to the content in a humane ethics. A humanely based ethics is combined with an identity theory or a combination theory. A strictly theological ethics is, however, often combined with a contrast theory but it can also be formulated so that it is combined with a combination theory.

These differing views are closely related to different views about what forms the basis for the content in a Christian system of belief. Some theologians hold that the content in a Christian system of belief is not based upon any natural theology but purely upon those insights and experiences which ultimately are given with God's own Revelation in Christ. We can call this viewpoint a "Revelation positivistic theory". It holds that human beings can receive knowledge about God only through a divine Revelation and through the insights and experiences which it communicates. By themselves, human beings lack the capacity required to attain insight into who God is. Other theologians on the other hand hold that both the Revelation and common human experiences and considerations form the basis of the content in a Christian system of belief. This viewpoint we can call "a connection theory".

It holds that human beings can achieve insight into God and the content in Christian belief even through common human experiences although it can be combined with different views about what these experiences are and about in what sense the Revelation is connected to these.[52]

The theologians I deal with, do not discuss in any great detail the type of argument which forms the basis for the doctrine of creation, Christology and eschatology. It is however probable that a strictly theological ethics is often combined with a Revelation positivistic theory. Theologians with this viewpoint would then maintain that common human considerations neither form the basis for ethics nor the contents in the Christian system of belief. However it is probable that a humanly based ethics often is combined with a Revelation linked theory of some type. Theologians with this viewpoint would then maintain that ethics and a Christian system of belief are based both upon the Revelation and common human experiences.

8. A critique of Protestant work ethics

The first part of this investigation has aimed at analysing those work ethical theories which are to be found in the writings of a number of Protestant theologians. I have tried to clarify the content of their work ethical recommendations, their theories of the meaning of work and their social ethical theories. At the same time I have tried to clarify the types of arguments they provide for their differing types of work ethical theory. We have seen that these are combined with differing theories of human nature, different components in a Christian system of belief and differing views about the relation between Christian and humane ethics.

In the second and final part of the investigation, my aim is to put forward my own constructive proposals for a Christian work ethical theory. I set out to discuss how one can formulate an acceptable Christian social ethical theory and theory of the meaning of work. At the same time, I shall also discuss the question of what constitutes a reasonable view concerning the relationship between Christian and humane social ethics as well as the relationship between a constructive ethical theory and the theoretical components which make up a Christian philosophy of life.

This discussion will be based upon a critical assessment of the six work ethical theories I have analysed. The present chapter sets out to carry out this critique. We have seen that contemporary Protestant work ethicists adopt differing viewpoints in several different questions. In this chapter I shall discuss which of these viewpoints are acceptable and which ought to be rejected.

I shall carry out this critical assessment of contemporary Protestant work ethics on the basis of a view regarding what in general characterizes an acceptable ethical theory. To begin with, I shall therefore formulate a number of criteria for a reasonable ethical theory. These are formal criteria which indicate the type of consideration which forms the basis for such a theory and how the differing components making up such a theory are related to one another and to other views. At the same time, I shall also discus the conditions which have to be fulfilled in order that an ethical theory can be regarded as being a Christian ethic.

As we have seen, the work ethical theories which are to be encountered within contemporary Protestant theology are combined with differing theories of human nature, differing views about the relationship between Christian and humane ethics as well as differing views about how ethics is related to a Christian system of belief. In this chapter, I will therefore secondly give an assessment of these differing viewpoints. I attach particular importance to a critical assessment of the theologians' differing theories of human nature since their view of man is of great significance for how they formulate their social ethical theories.

In the light of this, I shall thirdly in this chapter make an assessment of the social ethical theories, the theories of the meaning of work and the work ethical recommendations which are to be found in the writings of the six theologians I study. This critical assessment of their differing work ethical theories is thus based both upon a number of criteria for what constitutes a reasonable ethical theory and a contentual assessment of their differing theories of human nature.

Criteria for a reasonable ethical theory

On what basis can one decide if an ethical theory is acceptable or not? This question is an essential problem within meta-ethics. Within meta-ethics, one deals with the epistemological question of how one can justify fundamental ethical judgements. This question is concerned with the type of arguments which can be adduced for claiming that an ethical assertion is valid.

In order to answer this question, it is necessary to decide what semantic function ethical judgements have. This semantic problem is concerned with whether the ethical statements express assertions about matters of fact or not. Those propositions which express assertions about matters of fact have an informative function and a theoretical meaning. They are either true or false i.e. they can be verified or falsified. Those propositions which do not express assertions but instead expresss recommendations, feelings or questions have however a practical function and a non-theoretical meaning. These propositions are neither true nor false i.e. they can neither be verified or falsified.

"Cognitive theories" maintain that ethical assertions have an informative function and theoretical meaning. These assertions can therefore be verified or falsified. "Cognitive translatibility theories" maintain that ethical assertions can be translated into non-ethical statements about matters of fact so that they are empirically testable. "Cognitive non translatibility theories" maintain on the other hand that such a translation of ethical assertions is impossible. These theories advocate instead other methods of deciding if ethical statements are true or false. According to "intuitionism", we have a special moral sense – an intuition – by means of which we can decide whether a value property in fact is to be found in an action or experience. According to "moral realism" there exists a moral reality which is independent of our moral views. Through observation of this moral reality, we can decide whether ethical assertions are true or false.[1]

In contrast to these cognitive theories, "non-cognitive theories" maintain that ethical assertions have a practical function and non-theoretical meaning. These assertions are therefore neither true nor false. Representatives of non-cognitive theories have different views about the nature of the practical function of ethical assertions. According to "emotivism" ethical assertions have an emotive function i.e. they express the feelings of those making the judgement. According to "prescriptivism", ethical assertions have a prescriptive function i.e. they express recommendations and orders. Prescriptivism maintains that it is possible to adduce rational arguments for and against fundamental ethical judgements on the basis of certain criteria about what constitutes a reasonable ethical viewpoint. On the other hand, it is not possible to empirically verify or falsify ethical assertions.[2]

There are substantial arguments which speak against cognitive translatibility theories. Ethical judgements cannot be completely reduced to non-ethical assertions which are scientifically testable. Moral disagreement cannot be overcome by empirical investigations. At the same time, there are strong arguments against straightforward emotivism. Even if ethical assertions cannot be empirically verified, it is possible to provide rational arguments for and against fundamental ethical judgements. This shows that they are not simply expressions of feeling.

The fundamental choice therefore seems to me to be between moral realism and prescriptivism. These two theories can be formulated in several different ways. It is however possible to formulate both moral realism and prescriptivism in such a way that they embody the view that one can adduce rational arguments for and against ethical judgements even if these cannot be verified or falsified by empirical investigations. Such rational arguments can be put forward on the basis of certain criteria for what constitutes a reasonable ethical assertion and an acceptable ethical theory. Even if one does not share the moral realist's view that there exists independently of us value properties which we can observe with our usual senses, one can maintain that there are certain conditions which must be fulfilled in order for an ethical theory to be reasonable.

What then are these criteria for a reasonable ethical theory? There are several differing views concerning this question. Here I shall put forward four such criteria of reasonableness on the basis of which I shall test the theories I study. The first of these is what we can call "the criterion of universalizability". It maintains that an ethical judgement which is valid, is universalizable in the sense that it holds for all mankind and for all similar acts. If an act A1 is right for a person in a situation S1 then all acts which are similar in relevant respects to A1 are right for all persons in all situations which are similar in relevant respects to S1. This universalizability criterion holds both for moral principles and general rules of action and for particular ethical norms. Every valid ethical judgement applies to all human beings and to all similar acts.[3]

The universalizability criterion exhibits certain similarities to one of Kant's formulations of the Categorical Imperative. Although, however, universalizability is a necessary criterion, it is not a sufficient criterion for a valid moral principle or rule of action. No rule which cannot be universalized, is acceptable but on the other hand not all rules which are universalizable are reasonable. This criterion is acceptable both to a moral realist and a prescriptivist. Both hold that an ethical theory which is valid, contains judgements which are universalizable so that they apply to all human beings and all similar acts.

A second criterion for a reasonable ethical theory is in my view what we can call "the consistency criterion". It maintains that an ethical theory which is acceptable contains only statements which taken together are logically consistent. Within an acceptable ethical theory, logical contradictions should not exist. If two assertions in the theory are logically incompatible, they are not both acceptable. In testing a work ethical theory, this implies also that there should be agreement between the differing components which make up the theory. Those judgements which form part of an author's social ethical theory must not conflict with the judgements which make up his theory of the meaning of work and these in turn must agree with his work ethical recommendations.

The consistency criterion is also not a sufficient criterion for a valid ethical theory. In order for a theory to be acceptable, it is necessary that the person embracing it has attained a reflexive equilibrium in the sense that there exists an agreement between their particular ethical recommendations and their general moral principles. However the fact that the person has achieved such a reflexive equilibrium is not sufficient to justify his or her ethical judgements. In order to avoid ethical relativism where several ethical theories consistent in themselves but incompatible with each other, are said to be acceptable, further criteria for a reasonable ethical theory are required.[4]

A third criterion can be callled "the integration criterion". It maintains that a reasonable ethical theory is integrated with our other convictions and knowledge about ourselves and the reality around us. An acceptable ethical theory must agree with what we know from the findings of science and research. This does not imply that one should be able to adduce scientific arguments for moral viewpoints. On the other hand, it is conversely valid that a reasonable ethical theory should not contain views which directly conflict with our knowledge of ourselves and the world around us.

The content in an acceptable ethical theory must also be integrated with other kinds of convictions which we in general accept. This implies that the moral viewpoints we adopt must agree with the other components in our philosophy of life. If a person adopts a Christian philosophy of life, their system of belief must be so formulated that it does not conflict with their value system while at the same time their ethical theory must be so formulated that it does not conflict with the content of their system of belief.[5]

A fourth criterion for a reasonable ethical theory can be called "the experience criterion". It maintains that an acceptable ethical theory involves assertions which agree with human observations and experiences. A reasonable ethical theory is based upon one's own and other peoples' experiences of different types. These can be moral experiences i.e. experiences that certain acts are right and that certain states are good. An acceptable ethical theory must systematize and order these moral intuitions and not conflict with them. They can also be experiences of encounters with and relations to other human beings. These experiences can also form the basis for a reasonable ethical theory.

Like the other criteria of reasonableness, the experience criterion can be accepted both by moral realists and prescriptivists. It can be convenient for a moral realist to attach particular importance to this criterion. But even if one does not maintain that there exists special value properties which exist independently of us, one can admit that we have moral experiences which can form the basis of an ethical theory. This criterion too is insufficient for the acceptability of such a theory. In order for this to be the case, all four criteria must be satisfied.

These criteria specify the properties which characterize a reasonable ethical theory. In this sense they are criteria of reasonableness. The theologians I deal with in this investigation do not, however, simply lay claim to formulating an acceptable work ethical theory. They also claim that this ethical theory must be Christian. In order to judge how far they justify their claims, I shall also put forward two authenticity criteria. These specify the properties characteristic of an ethical theory which is authentically Christian.[6]

A first such criterion for an authentic Christian ethical theory is what we can call "the biblical criterion". It maintains that an ethical theory which is authentically Christian is in agreement with the content in the New Testament and also with the content in the Old Testament as it is interpreted in the light of the New. According to a Christian philosophy of life, the Bible is the Word of God in the sense that it is the clearest witness to the nature of God and His wishes regarding human life. The Bible therefore has a special position as a source of insight into the content of both a Christian system of belief and Christian ethics.

This criterion is however difficult to apply since the Bible contains a variety of partly differing views and theological entry-points. There exists a certain tension between the Old and New Testaments, nor does the New Testament form some unitary volume of text. One way of trying to solve this problem is to distinguish between what is central and peripheral in the Bible by trying to pick out its main message. Of central importance in the New Testament would seem to be the Gospel of Jesus Christ. This Gospel states that God reveals Himself in Jesus Christ and that Christ through His death and Resurrection reestablishes the communion between God and human beings. In a Christian philosophy of life, it would also seem natural to interpret the Old Testament in the light of this Gospel.

In a similar way, there are also certain ethical teachings in the Bible which emerge as more central than others. Obviously the Decalogue in the Old Testament and the ethical views proclaimed in the Sermon on the Mount have great significance. A summary of the content of ethics is given in the double commandment of Love according to which we must love God with the whole of our being and our neighbours as ourselves. This commandment emerges as a fundamental norm in Biblical ethics which implies that other ethical Biblical recommendations are subordinate instances and temporally contingent applications of this fundamental ideal of Love.[7]

The Biblical criterion is insufficient to decide what is the content in an authentic Christian ethics. In Christian tradition, the content of a Christian philosophy of life is being continuously developed in the light of new experiences and in confronting new problems. It is also in the light of these new Christian experiences that the content of the Bible must be interpreted anew in every new era. Thus there is a development of tradition which is open for new insights and experiences while at the same time one strives for a continuity with the content in the Biblical writings.

A second criterion for an authentically Christian ethical theory can be called "the tradition criterion". It maintains that an ethical theory which is authentically Christian agrees with the presentation of Christian ethics to be encountered in later Christian tradition. According to the Christian philosophy of life, God's revelation is not completed with the appearance of the New

Testament. It is possible to obtain insight about His Will through human life and through human cultural expressions of different types, new experiences of Christian people and expositions of the Biblical message to be encountered in the writings of the great theologians in the history of the Church. An authentically Christian ethics must therefore have a content which also agrees with the ecclesiastical tradition.

This criterion is also difficult to apply since the Christian tradition contains a multiplicity of differing views concerning theological and ethical questions. Nevertheless tradition is of great help in understanding the content of the Bible and in further developing the content of a Christian philosophy of life. Sometimes however a conflict can arise between tradition and the Bible. In such a conflict, there is reason to give priority to the content in the Bible because this in a Christian philosophy of life is considered to be a fundamental revelatory document. At the same time it is important to allow that contemporary Christian experience can provide new and deepened insights. It is also in the light of such experiences that we continually interpret the content of the Bible anew.

Theories of human nature

On the basis of these six criteria, how can one judge the different work ethical theories which I deal with in this investigation? According to the integration criterion, an acceptable ethical theory must be integrated with the other components in the philosophy of life to which it belongs. This implies not least that it should be based upon an acceptable view of man. As we have seen, the theologians I study, base their differing social ethical theories, theories of the meaning of work and work ethical recommendations upon differing theories of human nature. To be reasonable, their ethical theories should be based upon an acceptable view of man. This "view of man criterion" is a consequence of the integration criterion.

What then is an acceptable view of man? The theologians I study share two views about man. First of all, their view of man is combined with a theistic view of reality. They embrace a theory of creation according to which the universe including the human beings in it, have been created through an intervention from a divine reality. Secondly they accept a personalistic view of man in the sense that they hold that in every human being there is an "I" which gives that human being an individual identity and which is not accessible to empirical observation. This view of man is either dualistic so that it reckons with a mental reality as a form of existence of the same fundamental character as the material one or it is tripartite so that it reckons that human beings participate in three fundamental forms of existence.

230

Both these views would seem to be authentically Christian. In both the Bible and in later Christian tradition, it is assumed that human life is a gift which has come about through God's work of creation. It is also assumed that human beings are not simply material but are also soul and spirit and that the soul cannot be reduced to something purely physical.

The theologians I study, are also agreed that human beings are created in the image of God. It is this which is characteristic for human beings as a species in contrast to other living beings. However, there are somewhat different views about what this status as a creature made in the image of God implies. It can imply (a) that human beings are rational beings with a capacity for self reflection and philosophical thinking as well as a capacity for purposive behaviour and insight into what is good and right (b) that human beings are free with a will which is not predetermined but controlled by their own personalities (c) that human beings have a capacity for communion with God (d) that human beings are creative beings with responsibility for the world around them and (e) that human beings have a capacity for love and concern for other human beings.

There are reasons to maintain that what characterizes human beings according to a Christian view of man is that they have all these five properties. Such a view of man is in agreement with the image of God to be found in the New Testament and in the later Christian tradition. God is conceived there as the Supreme Intellect which in His Holiness is free and sovereign. He is conceived as the Creator of the universe and He is characterized according to the New Testament by a perfect and infinite love. This view of man also agrees with the image of the true human being which is discovered in Jesus Christ. He is described in the New Testament as a conscious and free human being. He is said to be the one through whom everything is created and is ascribed a unique capacity for communion with God. Above all, He is characterized by an infinite and self-sacrificial love for all.

A view of man of this kind can also be based upon common human experiences which are not dependent upon a philosophy of life. We have moral experiences which show that we have both capacity for purposive behaviour and capacity for ethical insight. We have experiences of moral responsibility which suggest that our will is not completely determined. We have experiences of responsibility for the world about us and experiences of feeling concern for our fellow human beings.

Does work then belong to that which is characteristic for human beings as a species? As regards this question, the theologians I study have different views. In Oldham and Brakelmann, one encounters a "contemplation line" according to which contemplation and communion with God are more characteristic of human beings than work. It is above all in communion with God that human beings realize themselves.

Against this viewpoint, it can be argued that it conflicts with the image of human beings to be found in the New Testament and in later Christian tradition. What is characteristic for human beings, is not only their capacity for communion with God but also their capacity for responsibility for the world around them and their capacity for concern for other people. These properties can be realized by human beings through human work. Thereby human beings can recreate their environment and assume responsibility for the world around them. Thereby they can also accomplish something which is valuable for other human beings. As a result, work is a defining feature of human beings.

It follows that the "activity line" which is encountered in Brunner and Rich would appear preferable. According to this viewpoint, work is part of what characterizes human beings. As a being created in the image of God they are co-workers of God in His work of creation with the task of assuming responsibility for the world around them. Through work, human beings can realize themselves as creative and responsible persons. This standpoint is strongly supported by the account of human beings as creatures made in the image of God which is to be found in Genesis 2−3. The fact that human beings are created in the image of God is there associated with their task of cooperating with God in His continuous act of creation.

The theologians I deal with, have also different views as to what extent the fact that humans being are creatures made in the image of God, affect the distribution of the good. In Emil Brunner, there is to be found a "difference line" according to which a just distribution of the good ought to take account of the factual differences which exist between human beings. Certainly all human beings have equal value since they are all created in the image of God but in fact human beings differ in kind and function. A just distribution of power and income ought to take account of these differences.

This standpoint can be criticized on the basis of the consistency criterion. The view that an unequal distribution of power and income is just, seems to me to conflict with the view that all human beings are equally valuable. If all human beings are created in the image of God, it implies that every human being has an equally great value despite the factual differences which may exist between us. Despite differences in sex, race, achievement and nationality, we have all the same value. This principle of respect for human beings implies also a recommendation to strive for equality and the equal treatment of all human beings. The view that we are equally valuable embodies an exhortation to overlook our factual differences and as far as possible to strive for equality.

For this reason, the "equality line" to be found in Tor Aukrust would seem to be preferable. According to this viewpoint, a just distribution of the good above all takes into account the equality of human beings. It is certainly the case that human beings are factually different and unique personalities but at the same time human beings as creatures made in the image of God, are equally valuable. It is this equality which ought to be decisive for how the good is to be distributed. This standpoint would seem to be more consistent than the difference line.

Among contemporary Protestant work ethicists, there is agreeement not only that human beings are created in the image of God but also that all human beings are sinners. As a result, according to them human beings cannot succeed in realizing a truly human life. These theologians have however different views about what this shortcoming in human beings entails. Oldham, Rich and Brakelmann claim to adopt a realistic view of man. This, however, would seem to be relatively "pessimistic" in the sense that they do not seem to place any great hope in human capacity to attain moral insight. They hold not only that human beings on account of sin, have a limited capacity to act rightly and to realize a good human life. They also hold that sin entails that human beings have an utterly limited capacity independently of the Revelation to perceive what is right and good.

Two arguments can be adduced against this pessimistic view of man. The first is that it conflicts with the view of man to be found in the New Testament and in the later Christian tradition. There it is assumed that human beings although sinners, are also still creatures made in the image of God. Therefore despite their shortcomings, they still retain the capacity to perceive what is good and right. Thus Paul in Romans 1 maintains that even non-Christians have a capacity for moral insight. It is just this capacity which allows them to attain insight into their own imperfection. Augustine, Thomas Aquinas, Luther, Calvin and other classical theologians also argue for a doctrine of natural law according to which every human being despite their imperfections has a capacity to perceive what characterizes a right act.

The second argument is that a too pessimistic view of man conflicts with common human experiences. We all have an experience of our limitations as human beings. Often we fail to accomplish the good which we wish to promote. However, we also have moral experiences i.e. views about what in certain situations is good and right. These experiences indicate that we all have a capacity for moral insight despite our limitations.

Similarly compelling objections can also be raised against the "optimistic" view of man to be found for example in older liberal theology. According to this standpoint, human beings as sinners have not lost their status as creatures made in the image of God. They are still rational and free beings with a capacity for moral insight. They have a limited capacity to do what is right but this shortcoming can be overcome so that they can develop into better human beings.

However this optimistic view of man also does not agree with the view to be found in the New Testament and later Christian tradition. Thus Paul in Romans 7 maintains that even human beings who believe, continually fail to act rightly. A too optimistic view of man also conflicts with our own experiences. We all have experiences of acting contrary to our will. Sometimes we perform acts which we consider wrong and thus we feel that despite our efforts we have not become better human beings.

As a result, a view of man of the type to be encountered in Brunner, Aukrust and Atherton would seem to be preferable. They accept a view of man which is "realistic" in the sense that it allows for both the imperfection and limitations of human beings and also their capacities for moral insight and acting rightly. It is a standpoint which takes seriously human beings both as creatures made in the image of God and as sinners. As sinners, we often fail to do what is right while at the same time as creatures made in the image of God, we often achieve those things which are good for others. Every human being has both egoistical and altruistic impulses.

Human sin implies also that human beings have a limited capacity for moral insight. They often fail to perceive what is good and right. At the same time, human beings as creatures made in the image of God have a certain capacity for moral insight even if it is dimmed. This insight is attainable independently of the Revelation through one's own experiences and considerations. This is a realistic view of man which in this respect is considerably less pessimistic than that to be found for example in Oldham.

What possibilities have human beings themselves to contribute to realizing a good human life? This is also a question which is discussed by the theologians I deal with. They are unanimous that human beings do not have a capacity on their own to achieve a perfect human life. Human sin entails that human beings cannot realize a truly human life through their own efforts. Such a truly human life is attainable only in faith as a gift from God.

On the basis of a realistic view of man, there is reason to agree with this viewpoint. This circumstance, however, does not prevent human beings despite sin having a certain capacity to see what is right and good independently of the Revelation. Nor does it prevent work from belonging to that which characterizes a truly human life. It is an activity whereby human beings can express their nature as creative individuals with responsibility for the world around them and other people. But human beings can never realize such a truly human life through their own efforts.

This realistic view of man provides a contentual criterion for a reasonable ethical theory. The integration criterion maintains that an acceptable ethical theory must be integrated with other components in a philosophy of life including a well considered view of man. If we accept a realistic view of man, this implies that a reasonable ethical theory must agree with a theory of human nature which assumes that human beings are creatures made in the image of God and sinners in the above sense. I shall attach great importance to this view of man criterion in my subsequent critical review of the work ethical theories I deal with.

Christian and humane ethics

All the theologians I deal with in this investigation claim to formulate a Christian social ethics and work ethics. How then does the content in such a Christian ethics relate to the content in a humane ethics i.e. to an ethics which is based solely upon human experiences and is not combined with a Christian philosophy of life? J H Oldham adopts what I call a "contrast theory" according to which the content of Christian ethics is completely different from the content of humane ethics. Two persuasive arguments can be raised against this standpoint.

The first is that it conflicts with what we know about human beings' moral views. There are in fact a number of moral views that are common to Christians and non-Christians. This is the case for more concrete ethical recommendations. Oldham's view that one ought to avoid too far ranging a division of work and to strive after need-directed production is not specifically Christian but is shared by human beings with other philosophies of life. This is also true for more general moral principles. Thus for example the view that all human beings have equal value, that we ought to strive for that which is good and that we ought to promote a just distribution, is shared by many Christians and non-Christians.

The second objection is that it conflicts with the standpoint which has been customary in Christian tradition. Already Paul maintains that human beings who are not Christians, have an insight into what is right and that this insight is a necessary precondition for them to accept the Christian gospel. Such theologians as Augustine and Thomas Aquinas have later developed a doctrine of natural law according to which there are certain fundamental principles and values which are common for human beings with different philosophies of life.

Emil Brunner adopts what I call instead an "identity theory" according to which there is no difference at all between Christian and humane social ethics. Within individual ethics, he adopts a contrast theory according to which the Christian ideal of love is completely unique. This ideal, however, has no relevance for Brunner's social ethics. There he puts forward an ideal of justice which would seem to belong completely to the realm of common human experience.

This standpoint can be criticised both on the basis of the consistency criterion and the universalizability criterion. The ethical theory constructed by Brunner is characterized by a striking lack of agreement between individual ethics and social ethics. This arises from the fact that he does not universalize the ideal of love so that it also applies to political acts. There are however in my view sufficiently great similarities between private and political acts to make such a universalization of individual ethical principles both possible and desirable.

The "combination theory" of the type to be found in Aukrust, Rich, Brakelmann and Atherton seems to be more reasonable. According to this standpoint, there is a partial agreement between Christian and humane ethics. There are certain moral principles and values which Christians and non-Christians are agreed about. At the same time, however, there are also principles and values which are specifically Christian in the sense that they are not embraced by human beings with another philosophy of life. Thus there is no complete agreement between Christian and humane ethics.

What type of reason then can be adduced for or against the content of a constructive Christian ethical theory? In Oldham, Rich and Brakelmann we encounter what I have called a "strictly theological ethics" according to which we only through the Revelation in Christ perceive what characterizes a right act. All reasons which can be adduced for an ethical theory are according to this standpoint ultimately based upon the Revelation in Christ. On the other hand ethics is not based upon any common human experiences and considerations.

A fundamental objection to this viewpoint is that it presupposes too pessimistic a view of man. It conflicts in other words with the view of man criterion. According to a realistic view of man, every human being as a creature made in the image of God, has a capacity with the aid of their reason to attain insight into what is right and good. The fact that human beings are sinners does not imply that this capacity has been lost. As rational beings they can independently of the Revelation achieve at least certain moral insights. As a result, common human experiences and considerations also form a basis for ethics.

A second objection to a strictly theological ethics is that it conflicts with the criterion of universalizability. According to this criterion, an ethical theory must have a universal sphere of application so that its contents are valid for all human beings. If an ethical theory is universal in this sense, it ought also to be possible to adduce reasons for its content which can be accepted by all human beings irrespective of their philosophy of life. This is impossible if one accepts a strictly theological ethics. The fundamental reasons for ethics presuppose according to this standpoint that one accepts a Christian belief in God. Thereby a rational discussion of ethical questions which bridges the gap between philosophies of life is ruled out. The content of Christian ethics is also valid for non-Christians but the latter can only accept the reasons for this content provided they accept God's Revelation in Christ.

In Arthur Rich and Günter Brakelmann, we encounter a special form of strictly theological ethics. They combine the view that ethics is solely based upon the Revelation with a combination theory according to which there are moral views which are shared by Christians and non-Christians. On the one hand, they hold that there are moral principles e.g. a principle of human value and a principle of just distribution which are common for human beings with different philosophies of life. On the other hand, they hold that these principles can only be given a specifically Christian motivation, above all on the basis of Christology.

This view can be criticised on the grounds that it conflicts with the consistency criterion. A combination theory allows itself to be more successfully combined with a humanely based ethics than with a strictly theological one. If one supposes that only Revelation forms a basis for ethics, it appears difficult to explain how Christians and non-Christians come to have certain common moral views. One must then assume that human beings who do not share a Christian philosophy of life do not know why the norms and values they hold are valid. One must also assume that the reasons for these moral views which they themselves emphasize, are not tenable. A more reasonable explanation is however that these views can in fact be motivated not only on the basis of Christology but also on the basis of common human experiences.

There are forcible reasons for the view that the content in Christian ethics is not only based upon the Christian Revelation. Christian ethics is also based upon experiences and considerations which are independent of a philosophy of life in the sense that they do not form a part of a philosophy of life or can be shared by human beings with differing philosophies of life. However, there is reason also to reject a "strictly humane ethics" according to which ethics is based solely upon such common experiences and considerations. It is a social ethics of this kind which is to be found in Emil Brunner. He combines a strictly theological individual ethics with a social ethics which is strictly humane.

An objection to this standpoint is that in limiting the specifically Christian contribution to morality to only individual ethics it conflicts with the criterion of universalizability. The Christian ideal of love has relevance also for our political acts. Moreover a strictly humane ethics also conflicts with the view of man criterion. It presupposes too optimistic a view of man. According to a more realistic view of man, human capacity for moral insight is limited. Because of sin, human reason is uncertain about what is right. Thus we require guidance from the Revelation. This also gives us a deeper insight into social ethical questions.

A "partially Revelation based ethics" of the type to be found in Aukrust and Atherton is therefore preferable. According to this view, ethics is based both upon the argument from Revelation and upon common human experiences. This view may be naturally combined with a combination theory according to which there exists a certain agreement between Christian and humane ethics while at the same time certain moral views are specifically Christian.

Aukrust's exposition of such a partially Revelation based ethics is, however, not wholly without problems. He lays comparatively great emphasis upon the specifically Christian contribution to ethics and maintains that according to Christian belief the Will of God is the sole norm for what is good. Aukrust holds that the good is good because God wishes it. This position, however in my view, is unacceptable. It entails that all morality stands or falls with a belief in God and can only with difficulty be combined with the view that every human being can independently of the Revelation have insight into what is good. It also entails that theological statements that God is loving and wishes what is good, become trivial. It is more reasonable to maintain that God wishes the good because it is good i.e. the question of what is good is independent of the existence of God.[8]

Atherton's formulation of a partially Revelation based ethics is also not unproblematic. He combines this standpoint with an ecclesiological ethics while he does not seem to base his social ethics upon a doctrine of creation. For this reason, he does not succeed in giving a satisfactory theological explanation of the common human character of ethics. Because Atherton bases his social ethics upon a doctrine of the Church, it has an exclusively Christian character in spite of his claim that it is humanely based.

Ethics and a Christian system of belief

What components in the Christian system of belief form the basis for the content in a Christian work ethics? Among the theologians I deal with, we have encountered five differing answers to this question. Emil Brunner adopts what I have called, a "theology of creation ethics". An orders of creation theology forms the basis of his social ethical theory as well as his view of man and theory of the meaning of work. Christology is significant for Brunner's individual ethics but not for his social ethics. It is based purely upon the doctrine of the divine orders of creation. The advantage with this viewpoint is that it provides a theological entry point for ethics which can be easily combined with a humanely based ethics according to which common human experience also forms a basis for social ethics. But at the same time there are two objections to this view.

The first is that a theology of creation ethics is often combined with an uncritical acceptance of existing unjust social orders. As Arthur Rich maintains, the theology of orders tends to identify existing orders with the Will of God as expressed in the Creation. This criticism, however, does not apply to Brunner. He explicitly maintains that the Will of God as expressed in the creation is not identical with existing social structures. However it is obvious that Brunner's theology of orders underwrites social inequalities. It is combined with a hierarchical view according to which justice entails that subordinates must obey their superiors. It thus does not do justice to human equality i.e. that all human beings are to an equal degree created in the image of God and have an equal value. Earlier I have argued against the "difference line" which is combined with Brunner's view of man. If one accepts this criticism, it is then difficult to accept his orders of creation theology.

The second objection is that if social ethics is solely based upon the doctrine of creation, it leads to a strictly humane social ethics and an identity theory. There is then no theological basis for a specifically Christian contribution to morality. It seems paradoxical that Brunner accepts this position while at the same time within individual ethics he speaks of an ideal of love which is based upon Christology. His ethics would appear more consistent if this Christologically based ideal was also relevant for social ethics.

In J H Oldham and Günter Brakelmann, we encounter instead what I have called a "Christological ethics". They base their social ethics primarily upon Christology. Oldham holds that a right act is characterized by the fact that it is in agreement with the Will of God which we recognise through the Revelation in Christ. Brakelmann employs Christology as a basis both for a principle of respect for human beings as well as for certain fundamental human rights. The advantage with this entry point is that it leads one to adopt a critical distance to existing social structures and to work for continual social change. It is also combined with the view that social ethics is related to eschatology which motivates the view that no existing society is perfect. At the same time there are strong objections to Christological ethics.

The first objection is that it is combined with a strictly theological ethics according to which it is only when one affirms the Revelation in Christ that one can perceive what characterizes a right act. I have earlier argued that human beings with differing philosophies of life share certain moral views and that every human being has the capacity independently of the Revelation to perceive what is right and good. This common human moral insight can be given a satisfactory theological explanation if ethics is based not simply upon the second but also upon the first article of the creed. It is only a person who believes that human beings already in creation obtain a capacity to perceive what is right, who can accept that ethics is based not only upon Revelation but also upon common human experiences.

A second objection to a Christological ethics is that it conflicts with the criterion of experience. All human beings, even those who do not believe in Christ, have certain moral experiences, certain intutive experiences of what is good and right. These moral experiences would seem to belong to life itself and the social community of which we are part. If one wishes to provide a theological explanation of this state of affairs, it would seem to be reasonable to have as one's entry point the creation concept and not Christology.

A third objection is that a Christological ethics involves a problematic view of the relationship between the Law and the Gospel. In the Biblical scriptures, it is presupposed that the Law is given with the creation. It exists already prior to the Revelation in Christ and in the New Testament it is emphasized that Christ does not put an end to this Law. The kernel of the Gospel is instead the message of forgiveness which would seem to presuppose a common human insight both into what is right and into one's own limitations.

Arthur Rich adopts what I have called an "eschatological ethics". According to this position, eschatology provides a basis both for social ethics and a view of man. The Christian concept of the Kingdom of God indicates what is humane i.e. what constitutes a truly human life and thereby provides criteria for a proper design of social institutions. The advantage with this entry point is that is combined with an openness regarding social criticisms and a critical distance to existing social orders. At the same time, eschatological ethics is exposed to the same objections as Christological ethics.

Above all, it can be maintained that this position fails to take account of the fact that a common human moral insight exists prior to the encounter with Christ. According to Rich, it is the Revelation in Christ which provides a norm for what is truly human and for what constitutes a right action. He thereby fails to note that common human experiences can also provide the basis for social ethical criteria. I have previously argued for a humanely based ethics. Such an ethics can only with difficulty be combined with a purely eschatological social ethics.

In the writings of John Atherton, we encounter what I have called an "ecclesiological ethics" according to which social ethics is based upon a doctrine of the Church. The Church as the Body of Christ forms a model for how society ought to be organized. The Church should be an example for society as a community where human beings despite their individual differences are mutually dependent upon one another. On the other hand, Atherton does not base his social ethics upon the doctrine of creation despite the fact that he accepts that there exist certain fundamental values which can be perceived by all independently of the Revelation.

Two objections can be raised against this ecclesiological ethics. The first is that Atherton's theory would seem to exhibit a lack of consistency. On the one hand, he maintains that all human beings have a capacity to perceive what is right and good. He adopts a humanely based based social ethics according to which we ought to strive for the common good. On the other hand, an ecclesiological social ethics gives the impression of being exclusively Christian. The view that the Church is an example of the ideal society can be accepted by Christians but hardly by those who do not accept Christian belief. Social ethics thereby loses its common human character.

The second objection is that the Church in today's pluralistic society can hardly serve as an example. It is a community of human beings who belongs to the middle and upper classes of society. It exemplifies a hierarchical structure and would seem to be characterized more by dissension than community. It may be countered that it is not the outer visible Church but the spiritual invisible Church which constitutes an example for society. In this case, however, the gap between the invisible Church and the Church as an external organization would seem to be too great. In a situation when the external Church is not conceived as an example, it is difficult to suppose that the Church as a spiritual community can serve as a social ideal.[9]

How then are we to understand the relationship between Christian social ethics and the Christian system of belief? In my opinion, a preferable view is what I have called a "trinitarian ethics". It maintains that ethics is based both upon the doctrine of Creation and upon eschatology and Christology. It therefore is in close agreement with a partially Revelation based ethics. Given that ethics is based upon the doctrine of Creation, it is possible to admit that all human beings independently of the Revelation can perceive what is morallly right. Given that ethics is based also upon Christology and upon eschatology, it can be maintained that the Revelation in Christ provides us with a moral insight which in part goes beyond common human experience. By being based upon eschatology, social ethics also achieves a critical distance to existing social orders and avoids a conservative defence of the status quo.

This position is to be found in the writings of Tor Aukrust. His formulation of a trinitarian ethics is however not devoid of problems. While he accepts natural law, he holds that the Revelation is the primary source of law and morality. Aukrust speaks of a natural law within an eschatological frame according to which we obtain insight into God's absolute demand only through the Revelation while natural law provides relative demands which apply in the Kingdom of the Fall. A problem with this viewpoint is that it lays too much stress upon the role of the Revelation as a source of moral insight and allows too little room for common human experiences as a basis for insight into what is right. If one accepts a humanely based ethics, it seems reasonable to maintain that every human being independently of the Revelation can achieve a deeper moral insight.

Social ethical theories

What is the relationship between social and individual ethics? The theologians I deal with in the present investigation, all reject what I have called the "amorality thesis". They hold that the Christian ideal of love is relevant both to our private and political acts. As Aukrust maintains, there is reason to share this view if one accepts a realistic view of man. Because human beings have responsibility for their environment, they ought to submit their political and economic acts to ethical scrutiny.

On the basis of a realistic view of man, it is also reasonable to reject a purely "monistic thesis". This standpoint would seem to presuppose a too optimistic view of man according to which it is possible to achieve the ideal of love also through political acts. According to a more realistic view of man which takes human limitations seriously, it would seem instead necessary for this ideal to be approximated by more realizable criteria within social ethics.

Persuasive arguments can also be mustered against the "dualistic thesis" to be found in Brunner. He combines a Christologically based act ethics within individual ethics with an order of theology and justice ethics within social ethics. A first objection to this dualistic thesis is that it conflicts with the criterion of universalizability. There are sufficiently great similarities between private and political acts for the principles which apply within individual ethics to be also applicable to social ethics. Through both these types of act, it is possible to cause suffering or to promote human happiness, to promote or take away human life, to abuse or respect human value and therefore there are ethical principles and norms which apply within both these areas of ethics.

A second counterargument to Brunner's dualistic thesis is that the Christian ideal of love also involves the idea of equality. According to this ideal, we ought not only to be concerned for others but we should also strive for the equal treatment of other human beings. Thus this ideal of love constitutes a critical frame of reference for those ideals of justice that are relevant to social ethics. To confine the ideal of love to individual ethics is to draw too sharp a line between love and justice.[10]

What then is the criterion for a right political act? In Oldham we have encountered a deontological act ethics according to which an act is right if and only if it agrees with the Will of God in a concrete choice situation. A first objection to this point of view is that it does not provide sufficient guidance for deciding what is a right political act. It is difficult to decide what is the Will of God in a concrete situation. Oldham certainly assumes that we can receive guidance through the Bible, tradition and the accumulated experience of the Church. He also holds that it is possible to formulate certain "middle axioms" which can be conceived as tentative rules. But he does not specify in more detail what constitutes a basis for these rules. In order to provide better guidance, he would need to formulate more precise ethical principles.

A second objection to a deontological act ethics is that it conflicts with the criterion of universalizability. According to this criterion, particular judgements are implicitly general. If one maintains that a certain action is right in a given situation then one implicitly binds oneself to maintaining that every similar action is right in every similar situation. For this reason, it is reasonable to maintain that there exist certain general rules according to which all acts of a certain type are right and these provide us with guidance in judging particular acts. An argument for a purely act ethics would be that every act and every situation is unique and it is therefore impossible to formulate any general rules. But against this argument, it can be maintained that if every act and situation is unique, nevertheless there are similarities between different acts and situations in respects which are relevant for moral judgement. For this reason, no purely act ethics is acceptable.[11]

A deontological theory of another kind is to be found in Günter Brakelmann. It is a theory of rights according to which the Christian ideal of love is combined with the principle of the equal value of all human beings and this principle of respect for human value is in turn combined with certain fundamental rights. According to Brakelmann, human value is based upon Christ's work of atonement which entails that all human beings are equal before God and therefore ought to be treated equally.

There are two points which are unclear in this theory of rights. One concerns the question of what constitutes human rights. Brakelmann writes that the right to work is deducible from the obligation to work. An individual can however have a right to a certain activity without for that reason being obliged to participate in that activity. Individual rights can be based upon the principle of the equal value of all human beings which in turn is combined with the view that there exist certain properties that are specifically human. To say that an individual has certain rights, moreover implies that society has certain corresponding obligations. However this fact does not presuppose any theory of the obligations which individuals themselves have.

It is also unclear how the principle of human value is to be motivated and how it is related to a Christian view of man. If one accepts humanely based social ethics, it is reasonable to imagine that this principle can be motivated in a way that can be accepted even by those who do not share a Christian philosophy of life. This principle does not need to be based upon the conviction that all human beings are objects of God's love in Christ. A sufficient motivation of the principle is that human beings have certain specific properties such as a capacity for self reflection and purposive action, a free will and a capacity for concern for others.

If one accepts a view of man of this type, it is, however, reasonable to put forward a social ethical theory in which the principle of human value is fundamental. This principle specifies both that all human beings have an equally high value in themselves and that we are obliged to treat every human being not only as a means but also as an end. However, an objection to Brakelmann's theory of rights is that the principle of human value does not suffice to specify what characterizes a right act. It motivates certain human rights but at the same time it also motivates certain other principles which specify which acts we are obliged to carry out. One such principle is the principle of goodness according to which we ought to strive for what is good for all human beings and to seek to avoid what is evil. Another is the principle of justice according to which we ought to strive for a just distribution of the good.

How then are we to judge Emil Brunner's theory of justice? According to this, a political act is right if it is in agreement with the Will of God as it is expressed in the orders of creation. This implies that it promotes justice which in turn entails that each and every one obtains their due. Justice takes into account the fact that human beings differ in kind and function.

An advantage with this social ethical theory is that it attaches great importance in the principle of the just distribution of the good. In my view, this principle is also a consequence of the principle of the equal value of all human beings. Brunner's theory has, however, two shortcomings. First of all the principle of justice is insufficient. The principle of human value also motivates a principle of goodness according to which we ought to strive for what is good and to seek to avoid what is bad. A pluralistic theory of duty is therefore preferable to a monistic theory of duty of the kind to be found in Brunner.

Secondly, Brunner's view about the meaning of justice seems less reasonable. Brunner holds that a just distribution is essentially a distribution according to a principle of merit. In my view, it is difficult to combine this with the principle of the equal value of all human beings. According to this principle, we ought to strive for the equal treatment of all human beings in spite of the factual inequalities they exhibit. The ideal of justice ought therefore also to embody an ideal of equality.[12]

This can be formulated by saying that Brunner's theory of justice conflicts with the view of man criterion. It is combined with what I have called a "difference line" according to which it is just to take account of the inequalities which exist between human beings. If one maintains that all human beings have an equally high value as creatures made in the image of God, one ought in my opinion to prefer an "equality line" according to which it is just to pay heed to the equality of all human beings. Despite their factual inequalities, one ought according to this view of man to seek to treat all human beings equally.

A social ethical theory of a completely different type is to be found in John Atherton. He adopts a teleological ethics consisting of two fundamental principles. According to the first of them, we ought to strive for a society where there exists a community similar to that symbolized by the Body of Christ. According to the second, we ought to strive for the common good i.e. such values as community, freedom, equality and solidarity. These two principles motivate in turn certain human rights.

An advantage of this theory is that it involves a principle of goodness according to which we ought to strive to do what is good and to avoid what is bad for all human beings, including ourselves. This principle is motivated by the principle of the equal value of all human beings. It is also a reasonable interpretation of the commandment to love one's neighbour which in several places in the New Testament features as a fundamental principle in Christian ethics.

However a teleological principle of this kind is also insufficient for deciding what constitutes a right act for it does not specify how the good is to be distributed between human beings. In certain situations, two acts can lead to an equally large surplus of good over evil for all human beings while at the same time one of these acts entails a more just distribution of the good. In such a case, most people would hold that an act which entails justice is right. This, however, conflicts with a purely teleological theory.

Atherton might counter this objection in two ways. First of all, he might maintain that a principle of justice is already embodied in a principle of goodness. However this is not the case. This principle does not specify in any sense how the good is to be distributed. Secondly he might maintain that justice is one of the intrinsic values which ought to be sought but this leads to a vicious circle. The principle of justice is a principle which specifies how intrinsic values ought to be distributed and thus justice cannot itself be such a value. Therefore it is more reasonable to prefer a theory with two principles, namely both a principle of goodness and a principle of justice. Both these principles can be motivated on the basis of the principle of the equal value of all human beings.

There are thus arguments which support a pluralistic theory of duty involving at least three fundamental moral principles, namely (a) a principle of human value (b) a principle of goodness and (c) a principle of justice. A pluralistic theory of this type appears in Aukrust. He holds that an act is right if it agrees with the Will of God while at the same time he specifies seven criteria for what constitutes the Will of God. These are (a) an eschatological principle according to which the primary aim is the Kingdom of God (b) a principle of human value (c) the rules which make up the Decalogue (d) a principle of freedom (e) a principle of equality (f) a principle of justice and finally (g) the commandment to love according to which we ought to display concern for all human beings.

Several objections can be made to this theory. First of all, it seems problematic to conceive the Kingdom of God as a social ethical criterion. According to a Christian system of belief, it is a goal for Divine action, not a goal for human political acts. Secondly Aukrust's motivation for the principle of human value can be discussed. The motivation does not need to lie in the fact that all human beings are objects for God's love in Christ. It can be based upon the common human experience that human beings have certain specific properties and capacities.

Thirdly the rules which make up the Decalogue do not constitute wide-ranging principles which specify the general characteristics of all right acts. They are instead more limited rules which specify certain types of act which are right or wrong. These can in turn be motivated by more general principles such as the commandment to love and the principle of justice. Fourthly Aukrust's principle of equality would seem have the same implications as the principle of human value. It maintains that all human beings have equal value and it is therefore not required as an independent principle.

An advantage with Aukrust's theory is that it involves both a principle of justice and a principle of goodness. Because Aukrust recommends an equality line, he also in my view has a more reasonable view than Brunner about what justice means. He would seem to understand the commandment to love as a principle of goodness according to which one ought to promote that which is good for all human beings. On the other hand, it is doubtful if the meaning of justice can be clarified on the basis of this principle of goodness. It is more reasonable to conceive these as two social ethical principles which are entirely independent of one another and both of which can be motivated on the basis of a principle of human value.

How then are we to judge the subject related theory of Arthur Rich? He rejects both utilitarian and deontological theories and puts forward instead what in reference to Max Weber, he calls an ethics of responsibility with state of mind components. According to this theory, in judging a political act one ought to take into account its consequences. A right political act promotes those social institutions which are good for human beings: that is to say, they are characterized *inter alia* by fellowship, participation and concern for the rest of creation. At the same time, it is also required that the acting subject has a good state of mind and certain desirable properties. Rich would seem to hold that the acting subject must also be characterized by critical distance, concern both for other human beings and themselves, in addition to concern for the rest of creation.

A social ethical theory of this type constitutes an important corrective to more unalloyed ethical theories of duty. The task of constructive social ethics is not only to specify what characterizes a right political act but also to specify what properties are desirable in the persons performing these acts. A social ethical theory of duty requires to be supplemented by a theory of virtue.

This does not imply that I am prepared to accept a subject related theory of duty. In my view, it is problematic to maintain that a good state of mind or good properties in the acting subject are a necessary precondition for a political act to be right. It is conceivably fruitful in using this to distinguish between good and right acts. In order for an action to be good, it is required both for it to be right and that the acting subject has developed certain desirable properties such as fellowship and concern for other living beings. But an act can be right even if the acting subject is not in this sense a good human being. In order for an act to be right, it is sufficient that it agrees with the principle of human value, the principle of goodness and the principle of justice. In contrast to Rich I therefore prefer an act related theory.

Theories of the meaning of work

An important component in a work ethical theory is a theory of the meaning of work. As we have seen, the theologians whom I deal with in this investigation, have different views about the purpose of work. Rich and Atherton adopt a viewpoint which I have called "the human fellowship line". They hold that the purpose of work is to serve fellow human beings. Through work, human beings are required to show concern not simply for themselves but also for other human beings and thus to contribute to the common good. A viewpoint of this type fits in well with the social ethical theory embodying what I have called a principle of goodness. However, Rich and Atherton do not maintain that the purpose of work is also to be an instrument for God's continuous act of creation. They do not base their theory of the meaning of work upon a doctrine of creation.

It can be maintained that this view conflicts with the Bible criterion. The creation stories which are presented in Genesis would seem to be associated with certain views about human work. As we have seen in Chapter 1, according to Genesis 3, due to the Fall work is associated with toil and suffering. At the same time, in Genesis 2, work is conceived as something which characterizes human individuals as beings created in the image of God. It is an activity which is already given with the creation and an activity through which human beings cooperate with their Creator. Therefore it would seem reasonable to base the Christian theory of the meaning of work upon the doctrine of Creation.

What I have called "the creation line" is therefore to be preferred. According to this viewpoint which is encountered in Brunner, Oldham, Aukrust and Brakelmann, the purpose of work is both to serve one's fellow human beings and to be God's co-worker in His continuous act of Creation. A view of this kind agrees well with the view of man criterion. The fact that human beings are created in the image of God can be understood to imply that they are created beings with a responsibility for the world about them. This responsibility is discharged not least through their work.

The theologians I deal with have also different views about whether work is a means to human self-realization. Oldham and Brakelmann adopt what I have called "the contemplation line". According to this position, human beings realize what is specific for the human species, not primarily through work but through other activities. It is not through work but through communion with God and through prayer that human beings achieve their supreme determination and realize themselves as a species.

This viewpoint conflicts with the view of man I have earlier advocated. It seems reasonable to maintain that a contemplative life i.e. a life in relation to God according to a Christian view of man belongs to that which contributes to human self-realization. But work can also contribute to this self-realization. What is specific for human beings is not only rationality and the capacity for communion with God but also the capacity to rule over the world around them and a capacity for concern for their fellows and other living beings. These capacities can be realized not only through contemplation but also to a large extent through action. Human beings can exhibit their concern for others and express their creative capacities not least through their work. Through work, they can also realize themselves as rational beings since work is a purposive activity which presupposes conscious planning.

Brakelmann maintains that a Lutheran doctrine of justification cannot be combined with the Marxist viewpoint that human beings can realize themselves in work. But this doctrine does not need to conflict with the view that work can contribute to a truly human life. According to a Christian view of

248

man, communion with God belongs to what is truly human and this cannot be obtained through work. But the true humanity also, however involves loving one's fellow human beings as Christ loved his fellow human beings and such a concern for others can also be expressed in human work. However, a Lutheran doctrine of justification is not combined with the same optimistic assumptions as a Marxist view of man regarding the possibility of attaining a truly human life here in time. Through their own efforts including efforts to bring about social change, human beings cannot contribute to achieving the love for God and their fellows which constitutes a life which is truly human.

In Aukrust and Atherton we have encountered the position I have called "the self actualization line". This entails that work can contribute to individuals developing their own talents and capacities. Also according to this viewpoint, work can contribute to human self realization but it is not a species realization theory but a personality development theory.

This view can be questioned on the basis of the view of man criterion. According to the view of man I hold, there are certain properties or capacities which are common to all human beings. Self realization does not imply merely realizing what is specific for the individual but also what characterizes the species. Since the capacity for creation and concern for others belongs to these properties, work can also contribute to ensuring that what is specific for the species is realized. If the working conditions are wrongly devised, they constitute an obstacle for human beings in realizing what is specific for the human species, and not simply an obstacle to developing their own specific talents.

What I have called "the activity line" is therefore preferable. According to this standpoint, work is an activity which can to a high degree contribute to human beings realizing what characterizes them as a species. It is a viewpoint of this kind which is to be found in Brunner and Rich. They hold that work belongs to the fundamental conditions of human existence and to what makes human beings human.

Within contemporary Protestant work ethics, we encounter, as we have seen, differing views of the doctrine of vocation. John Atherton adopts a position I have called "the alternative line". This holds that the doctrine of vocation nowadays needs to be replaced by an alternative Christian work ethics. According to Atherton, there are activities other than paid work which contribute to the common good in society and which therefore have an equally high value. Moreover he holds that rights do not constitute a payment for effort which in his opinion the doctrine of vocation maintains.

This standpoint is open to several objections. First of all, Atherton gives a somewhat misleading presentation of the contents of the doctrine of vocation. There must be few formulations of this doctrine which contain the view that peoples' rights depend upon their contribution to society. The doctrine of vocation also allows in general that activities other than paid work provide such a contribution and are therefore valuable.

Secondly it would seem that this standpoint conflicts with the integration criterion. The criticism of the doctrine of vocation is based upon the questionable assumption that unemployment will become a permanent feature. For this reason, job sharing is conceived as a necessary means to solve the employment problem. But the degree of unemployment is not something beyond our influence. There are several countries where unemployment has been considerably lower than in Britain despite a similar technological development. The level of unemployment we choose to have in a society, depends above all upon our choice of economic policy.

Thirdly the alternative line is combined with too low a valuation of work. The reason why Atherton ascribes to work a relatively low value compared to other activities, is because he looks upon the purpose of work as simply serving our fellow human beings. I have however already maintained that work has in addition two other purposes, namely to be an instrument for God's continuous act of creation and to promote human self-realization. If one accepts that work can also be a method of achieving these goals, one ought to be prepared to accord it a higher value.

In the writing of Emil Brunner and J H Oldham, we find instead a standpoint which I have called "the tradition line". It holds that the views which form part of the doctrine of vocation are still largely acceptable. Among these is the view that work belongs to the divine orders of creation and its purpose is to constitute an instrument for God's continuous act of creation and to serve our fellow human beings.

This viewpoint is open to two objections. First, there are reasons for revising the doctrine of vocation in the light of of the view of man criterion. The doctrine is associated with a patriarchal view of society which conflicts with the belief in the equal value of all human beings. If one accepts what I have called "the equality line", one cannot accept that a fundamental purpose of work is for people in subsidiary positions to obey their superiors.

Secondly there is also reason for revising the doctrine of vocation on the basis of the consistency criterion. Previously I have argued for a social ethical theory which contains what I have called a "principle of goodness". According to this, we ought to strive for what is good not simply for others but also for ourselves. A right act also has good consequences for the acting subject. If one accepts this principle, one cannot accept that the purpose of work is merely to bring about in the imitation of Christ what is valuable for others. Work also ought to provide a reward for the person engaged in it.

For these reasons what I have called "the revision line" seems preferable.

According to this standpoint, the doctrine of vocation must be thoroughly revised if it is to be acceptable in our society. The revision of the Lutheran doctrine of vocation which Tor Aukrust advocates is in several respects reasonable. First of all, it seems necessary to reject Luther's patriarchal view of society even if one holds that work is meaningful as an activity through which human beings are instruments in God's continuous act of creation. The requirement of obedience towards one's superiors can no longer be a fundamental tenet in the doctrine of vocation. Secondly Aukrust maintains quite rightly that the purpose of work is not simply to serve one's fellow human beings but also to provide some compensation for the person indulging in the work, through contributing to human self-realization.

Work ethical recommendations

As we have seen, the different work ethical recommendations are based not simply upon certain empirically testable assertions about matters of fact. They are also grounded upon differing theories of the meaning of work, social ethical theories and theories of human nature. In evaluating these theories, it is therefore also possible to evaluate the work ethical recommendations which are to be found in the six theologians I deal with.

Among these work ethicists, we have encountered two different attitudes towards the employment problem. Atherton and Brakelmann adopt a standpoint which I have called "the work sharing line". It holds that in order to reduce unemployment one ought to strive for work sharing and a reduction in working hours. This standpoint is combined with the view that the doctrine of vocation ought to be replaced by an alternative Christian work ethic according to which activities other than work have a high value.

This standpoint can be criticized in two ways. First of all, it is problematic to suppose that the computerization of working life entails permanent unemployment. As has been earlier pointed out, the degree of unemployment is dependent on the economic policy chosen. Therefore methods other than work sharing for reducing unemployment would appear to exist.

Secondly, the work sharing line is combined with too low an evaluation of work. It is combined with a theory of the meaning of work which does not suppose that work is an instrument for God's continuous act of Creation and a means for human self-realization. The same counterarguments which were earlier adduced against the alternative line apply to the work sharing line.

It would therefore seem preferable to accept what I have called "the full employment line". According to this standpoint to be found in Brunner, society ought to pay attention to the importance of full employment. This standpoint can also be based upon the revised formulation of the doctrine of vocation. According to such a doctrine, human beings participate through their work in God's continuous act of creation while at the same time they thereby also can realize that which characterizes them. The goal should therefore be that each and every one who wishes to work is able to obtain work.

In regard to the wage question, we have also encountered two different standpoints. Emil Brunner adopts a "merit line" according to which the merit principle is the most important principle in determining a just wage. According to this principle, it is just that persons should be rewarded in proportion to their merit.

An objection to this standpoint is that it is combined with a view of man which is unacceptable. Brunner adopts a "difference line" which attributes great importance to the fact that human beings as a matter of fact differ in kind and function. As previously maintained, there is reason to prefer "an equality line" which attributes more importance to the conviction that all humans being, as creatures made in the image of God, have equally high value.

Another objection is that the merit line is combined with an unacceptable social ethical theory. Brunner holds that it is right to take into account the fact that human beings differ in kind and function. If one accepts a principle of the equal value of all human beings, it is reasonable to maintain instead that it is just to strive for an equal treatment of all human beings. For an unequal distribution to be just, it ought to be to the advantage of those worst placed.

For these reasons, "the equal wages line" seems preferable. This standpoint which we have encountered in Aukrust maintains that we ought as far as possible to seek to realize an equal wage principle which takes account of each and every one's needs and the equal value of all human beings. At the same time, it maintains that wage differentiation with regard to the different work contributions ought to take place only if it is necessary. This standpoint is combined with a view of man which attaches great importance to the equal value of all human beings. It is also combined with a social ethical theory according to which the principle of just distribution embodies an ideal of equality.

The organization problem is also dealt with in two different ways in the material studied. According to "the human relations line" one ought to avoid an organization of work which involves too far reaching division of labour and rationalization where individuals becomes replaceable and are unable to see the purpose of their work contribution. This viewpoint is adopted by Brunner, Oldham and Aukrust but they provide few details about how an alternative organization of work can be devised.

The human relations line does not seem to me to present a satisfactory solution to the organization problem. It has often been combined with the view that an aim of work should be to satisfy the social needs of the employee. As in the case of Aukrust and Atherton, there are however reasons for maintaining that work also must satisfy the employees' needs for self actualization. In order to achieve this goal, one ought to strive for job enlargement and increased self-determination for employees.

For this reason, "the socio-technical line" in Rich and Brakelmann, seems preferable. According to this standpoint, we ought to devise the organization of work so that it provides scope for job enlargement, job rotation, job enrichment and partially self-determining work groups. This is a view which allows itself to be combined with a theory of the meaning of work according to which the purpose of work is to satisfy the employee's need for self-actualization.

What position are we then to adopt towards "the participation question"? Emil Brunner adopts a "consultation line" according to which the company board is to be solely responsible for making crucial decisions while allowing that decision making ought to be preceded by consultation where the board of directors listens to the views of the employees. According to Brunner, participation in decision-making conflicts with a just distribution of economic power because justice ought to take into account the factual differences which exist between human beings.

A first objection to this standpoint is that it is combined with an unacceptable view of man. The consultation line is based upon a difference line which attaches great importance to the factual differences which exist between human beings with respect to characteristics and social position. I have earlier criticized this view on the basis of the principle of the equal value of all human beings.

Secondly the consultation line is also combined with an unacceptable social ethical theory. According to this theory, it is just to take account of the factual differences which exist between human beings. If one accepts the principle of the equal value of all human beings, it would seem however more reasonable to maintain that it is just to strive for the equal treatment of all human beings. An unequal distribution of power is just only if it is associated with positions which are open to all those concerned.

For these reasons, "the participation line" would seem to be preferable. This viewpoint which is to be encountered in Aukrust, Rich and Brakelmann implies that employees ought to be allowed to participate in decision-making not only at the work place level but also at the company level. A view of this type fits in well both with a view of man which attaches great importance to the equal value of all human beings and a principle for just distribution which involves an ideal of equality.

Finally we have encountered three different views with respect to the system question. Oldham and Aukrust adopt what I have called "the indifference line". They do not adopt any particular position in regard to the question of whether one ought to strive for a capitalist or socialist system. Instead they content themselves with general guidelines about the desirable form of the economic system.

In my opinion, this standpoint is unsatisfactory. A carefully considered social ethical theory ought also to give more guidance regarding what position we should adopt in regard to this question. One reason why Oldham does not succeed in making his position clear, is perhaps because his social ethical theory is insufficiently worked out in detail. It does not contain any general moral principles and is therefore too sketchy to provide guidance about more specific matters.

I have called the second standpoint "the reform line". It is to be found in Emil Brunner and Arthur Rich. They advocate a capitalistic system while at the same time they recommend certain fundamental changes in it. Thus for example, Rich recommends that the private ownership of the means of production should be combined with participation in decision-making and a socio-technical organization of work.

A third standpoint is what I have called "the socialization line". It is adopted by Brakelmann and Atherton and implies that one ought to strive for democratic socialism, i.e. a society with a market economy and with both political and economic democracy.

I shall leave open which of these two latter standpoints is to be preferred. I shall return to this question in Chapter 10. Before that, however, I shall try to clarify the content of the social ethical theory which I consider the most reasonable.

9. A humanely based social ethical theory

In the previous chapter, I have critically reviewed the six different expositions of Protestant work ethics which have been examined in this study. This critique has been based upon a number of criteria for a reasonable ethical theory. I have called these criteria (a) the universalizability criterion (b) the consistency criterion (c) the integration criterion and (d) the experience criterion. Moreover I have reviewed these theories in the light of two criteria for an authentic Christian ethical theory, namely (a) the Bible criterion and (b) the tradition criterion.

On the basis of these criteria, I have adduced a number of arguments against certain of the viewpoints to be encountered within contemporary Protestant work ethics. At the same time, I have also indicated my own view about what ought to be the content of a reasonable Christian work ethical theory. In the two concluding Chapters, I want to develop this viewpoint in more detail. I shall try to outline a work ethical theory which could form an acceptable alternative to the six theories I have examined.

The aim of this Chapter is to formulate my own proposal for a constructive social ethical theory. I shall discuss how one could formulate a social ethical theory which is both authentically Christian and reasonable. This implies that the theory I propose should be acceptable if one accepts the criteria of reasonableness and the authenticity criteria which I suggested in the previous Chapter.

According to the integration criterion, an acceptable ethical theory is integrated with the other components of the philosophy of life of which it is part. As we have seen in the writings of the theologians I deal with, a constructive social ethical theory is based not least upon a view of man. The form which the ethical theory takes is largely determined by the content of a theory of human nature. For this reason, I shall begin this Chapter by discussing the content of an acceptable Christian view of man.

Thereafter I shall discuss the relationship between a Christian and a humane social ethics. I attach particular importance to the question of how far social ethics is based not only upon the Revelation but also upon common human experience. In this connection, I shall also examine which components in a Christian philosophy of life form the basis of Christian social ethics.

On the basis of all this, I shall try to put forward my own answer to the question of what characterizes a right political act. On the basis of an evaluation of alternative moral philosophical theories, I shall formulate three fundamental moral principles in a Christian social ethical theory. In connection with these principles, I shall discuss the question of what is valuable and the question of what constitutes a just distribution of the good.

Finally in this Chapter, I shall develop my own views about the relationship between individual and social ethics. Especially within Lutheran social ethics it has often been maintained that there is a completely different norm system within social ethics than within individual ethics. Contrary to this viewpoint, I shall argue that the same moral principles apply to both our political and private acts.

A realistic view of man

The form taken by a social ethical theory is to a large extent determined by the view of man adopted. Whoever wishes to develop an acceptable Christian social ethics, has therefore first of all to decide what view they will take of the content in a Christian view of man. In order for such a theory to be authentically Christian, it must agree with the view of man encountered in the Bible and in later Christian tradition. In the Old Testament, the stories of how God creates the world are combined with a view of man. On the one hand in Genesis 1:27, it is said that God creates human beings in His own image. On the other hand in Genesis 3, human beings are represented as sinners who offend against the Will of God. In the New Testament, we encounter an image of Christ who according to Christian tradition is the true human being: it is He who shows us what a truly human life implies. He is represented as the true image of God perhaps mainly because He expresses a perfect and self-sacrificial love for God and other human beings.

In order for a Christian view of man to be acceptable, it must satisfy certain criteria of reasonableness. It must not conflict with the knowledge of human beings we obtain from scientific research. It also must be consistent with human experiences of different kinds. Our view of man can for example be based partly upon experience of our freedom and capacity for concern for others and partly upon experiences of our limitations and our capacity to hurt and injure other human beings.

256

What are the views making up a Christian view of man? To begin with, it contains a view about the cosmic framework of human beings. Like the theologians I have studied in this investigation, I hold that a Christian view of man is combined with a theistic view of reality and a theory of creation. According to this theory, the universe and thus human beings have come about by an intervention of a divine reality. Human life is a gift that we obtain from God. Like everything else which exists, the existence of human beings is ultimately contingent upon the fact that God exists. His work of creation is not completed once and for all time. God continues to create also in the present. He still acts today in human history to maintain and preserve life.

A Christian view of man is also personalistic in the sense that it assumes that in every human being there is an "I" which gives the person their own individual and unique identity. This "I" cannot be objectified and is not accessible to empirical observation. This view of man is to be encountered in all six of the theologians I deal with in this investigation. In Christian tradition, one has often expressed it by saying that there is in human beings a mental reality, a soul or spirit of the same character as material reality. It is a view which coincides with contemporary humanistic psychology according to which one must accept that in every human being there is a personality core if one is going to describe and explain human behaviour. It is this internal "I" which is the bearer of personal identity and which ultimately explains a person's acts.

A Christian view of man also contains the view that there are certain properties which are characteristic for human beings – in contradistinction to other living beings – as a species. These properties are simultaneously common for all human beings despite all the individual differences which exist between us. The view that there are such specifically human characteristics is to be found not only among theologians but also among many philosophers within Western humanism. In Christian tradition human beings are said to be made in the image of God. This property of being made in the image of God defines human essence, the ideal human life. It is this image of God which we see in Christ who according to Christian belief is the true human being.

What does it mean that human beings are created in the image of God? A common view within Christian tradition is that it means that human beings are rational. It is characteristic for the human core of personality, the individual "I", that it is a rational soul. God is the Supreme Intellect and in a similar way every human being is equipped with the capacity for rational thought. This implies that human beings have a capacity for self-consciousness and that they can make conceptual determinations and distinctions. It also implies that they have a capacity for moral insight and that they can act consciously and purposively to realize certain aims. Human beings do not allow themselves to be blindly steered by their feelings and instincts but have a capacity to control their will and emotions according to rational considerations.

By being created in the image of God, human beings also have a unique capacity for communion with God. They have a possibility of coming into contact with the divine reality which has created them. In communion with God, they have a unique possibility of achieving an eternal life. The image of Christ in the New Testament shows us what this communion with God implies. Several Early Church theologians held that the capacity for communion with God is associated with the fact that human beings are rational beings. Part of their rational soul consists of contemplative reason and through exercising this, they can achieve communion with God.[1]

As rational beings, humans however also possess an active reason. This implies that they also have a capacity to see what is good and right. It also implies that they can act purposively i.e. they can act so as to bring about certain predetermined values. Moreover human beings have a unique capacity for showing concern for other human beings. They can go beyond themselves and take account of the best interests of fellow human beings. What this implies is to be seen most clearly in Christ who according to Christian faith is the true image of God. He is characterized by a self sacrificial love which extends to all human beings without exception. He loves all human beings, even those who in themselves are imperfect and He is even ready to sacrifice His own life for the sake of other human beings.

According to Christian tradition, the fact that human beings are created in the image of God implies also that they have a special responsibility for their environment. They are stewards with the task of being the instruments of God in his continued work of creation. As such, they are responsible not only for their fellow human beings but also for other living creatures. This view finds support in Genesis 1:28 where the status of human beings as creatures made in the image of God is associated with the task of ruling over animals and plants.[2]

In my view what is characteristically human is that human beings are rational beings with a capacity for communion with God, concern for others and a responsibility for other living beings. As rational beings, they also have a unique freedom. The capacity of concern for others is combined with the fact that human beings have moral responsibility. They can be criticized when they act unjustly and praised when they do what is right. This responsibility presupposes that their wills are free at least in the sense that their moral decisions depend upon factors within their own personality. This freedom of will and the associated responsibility is also something which characterizes human beings in contrast to other animal species.

258

Does work belong to that which is characteristic for human beings as a species? In the previous chapter, I have criticized what I have called "the contemplation line". The capacity for communion with God belongs to that which is characteristic and common for human beings. But human beings do not realize themselves only or primarily through contemplation. As rational beings, they do not only possess a contemplative but also an active reason.

In my view, therefore the arguments in favour of "the activity line" are stronger. According to this viewpoint, work is an activity through which human beings can express what is specifically human. Among human characteristics is the capacity to act purposively and to show concern for other human beings. Moreover, as beings created in the image of God, they have a special responsibility for the world around them. Through human work they can express this capacity and discharge this responsibility. Work gives them the possibility of producing things which are valuable for others and for functioning as an instrument for God's continuous act of creation.

As creatures made in the image of God, all human beings are equal. Despite the factual differences which exist between different individuals with respect to race, sex, nationality and social class, we have all the same capacity for rationality, communion with God and concern for others. Not every human being has developed these properties to an equally high degree but they are potential capacities which can be developed in every one. It is this equality between human beings which motivates the view that all human beings have an equal value independently of race, sex, nationality and social class. For this reason, one ought to strive for an equal treatment of all human beings. The fact that certain human beings have not actualized their potential capacities for rational thinking and concern for others to an equally high degree, does not justify them being treated worse than others.

The viewpoint which I have called "the difference line" emphasizes the factual differences between human beings and holds that it is just to take account of these differences in the distribution of power and income. In my view, a more reasonable viewpoint is "the equality line". This fits in better with the view that all human beings, despite certain factual inequalities, have the same value. It follows from this view that justice involves an ideal of equality. A just distribution of the good must take into account the equality which exists between human beings in characteristics and value.

According to a Christian view of man, human beings are not simply created in the image of God. They are also sinners. This implies that there exists a gap between ideal and reality, between a truly human existence and the life which human beings actually live. Human beings fail to realize completely their potentialities. They fail to develop their capacities for communion with

God and for concern for their fellow creatures and other living beings. This imperfection applies to all human beings.

As we have seen, there are different views about how far reaching this human shortcoming is. Some theologians adopt a pessimistic view of man according to which sin implies that the true humanity of human beings has been completely lost. As sinners, they therefore lack a capacity independently of the Revelation to perceive what is good and right. In my view, this viewpoint conflicts with the Bible criterion and the tradition criterion. It also conflicts with the fact that we all have certain moral experiences which indicates that we have the capacity for moral insight.

At the same time, there is also reason to reject a too optimistic view of man. Such a view maintains that human beings have the capacity to overcome their imperfections and that each and every one can perceive independently of the Revelation what is right. A standpoint of this kind conflicts with the consciousness of personal shortcomings and limitations shared by all human beings.

I would advocate instead the viewpoint I have called a "realistic view of man". This is a view which treats seriously the proposition that every human being is both a being created in the image of God and a sinner. A view of man of this kind forms the basis for the type of social ethics espoused by the American theologians, Reinhold Niebuhr and John C Bennett and which is often called "Christian realism". Two contemporary representatives of Christian realism are J Philip Wogaman and Ronald H Preston. On the one hand, they maintain that human beings as creatures made in the image of God are rational and have the capacity for concern for others. On the other hand, they maintain that human beings are sinners with a tendency to selfishness and to choosing what is evil.[3]

According to a realistic view of man, human beings often fail to do what is right. As free beings, they often choose to act in a way that offends against the value of other human beings, with the purpose of promoting their own best interests. They also often involuntarily injure other human beings. At the same time, human beings often succeed in acting rightly. By being created in the image of God, they have impulses to do not merely what gives them some personal reward but that which promotes the good of others.

According to a realistic view of man, human sin implies that human beings often fail to see what is right. They have a limited capacity for moral insight and therefore require guidance from the Revelation. At the same time, as beings created in the image of God, they have a certain capacity for moral insight even if it is dimmed. This capacity to perceive what is right is to be found in all human beings and is not completely lost on account of sin.

On the other hand as sinners, human beings lack the capacity to attain a truly human life by their own efforts. The Protestant theologians I deal with in this investigation are unanimous in agreeing that we cannot by ourselves contribute to achieving such a perfect life here in time. The gap between ideal and reality will always characterize our existence. Human salvation does not depend upon the activity of human beings nor entirely upon cooperation between God and human beings. This view seems to me to be a reasonable consequence of a realistic view of man. The extent to which we achieve a perfect life is to be conceived as a gift which we receive in faith.

A partially Revelation based ethics

One of the fundamental problems I deal with in this investigation, is how Christian social ethics is related to social ethical theories associated with other philosophies of life. In the material studied, we have encountered basically two differing views regarding this question. We have a strictly theological ethics according to which all the arguments for ethics are based upon the Revelation in Christ. On the other hand, we have a humanely based ethics according to which ethics is partly based upon common human experiences.

The acceptance of the realistic view of man which I have proposed, has marked consequences for the position one adopts with regard to these two views. The view we take of what type of consideration forms the basis for the content in the social ethical theory, depends upon the view of man we adopt. A strictly theological ethics is combined with a considerably more pessimistic view of man than a humanely based ethics. These two views are also combined with two different views about how the content in Christian ethics is related to the content in humane ethics.

In the previous chapter, I have rejected what I have called "a contrast theory". Christian ethics does not have a completely different content from a humane ethics. At the same time, I do not accept "an identity theory". Christian ethics has a content which is not identical with the content of ethical theories associated with other philosophies of life. Rather it is partly different from them and lends depth to them.

The "combination theory" of the type we have encountered in Aukrust and Atherton, seems more reasonable. According to this viewpoint, there are certain fundamental moral principles and values which are common to Christian and humane ethics. Among them, in my view, are to be found the principle of the equal value of all human beings and the view that one ought to strive for a just distribution of the good. At the same time, there are certain parts of the content of Christian ethics which are at least partly different from the content of a humane ethics. The Christian ideal of love, for example, lends depth to a view about what concern for others implies, by requiring a preparedness in certain situations to completely renounce one's own best interests in favour of the interests of others.

In this respect, my view agree with that to be found in several of the social ethicists who claim to adopt a "Christian realism". There are in today's pluralistic society certain common views about what is valuable. These can be called "the common good". At the same time, as Ronald H Preston maintains, Christianity is also combined with an ethics of the Kingdom of God which contains a characteristic ideal of love. This is partly different from the ideal of love to be found in humane ethics.[4]

What type of argument can be adduced for the content of a Christian social ethical theory? A realistic view of man of the type I have proposed, cannot be combined with a strictly theological ethics. In my view, social ethics is also based upon common human considerations and experiences. These experiences and considerations are not "common" in the sense that they are generally conceived and encountered in all human beings. Among human beings who belong to differing traditions and cultural contexts, there are differences both as regards experiences and fundamental moral views. However, these experiences and reflections are "common" in the sense that they are independent of a philosophy of life. This implies that they do not form part of a philosophy of life or that they can be shared by human beings with differing philosophies of life.

Thus ethics is based not only upon a divine Revelation but also upon experiences which are independent of the philosophy of life held. It is this view which I have called a humanely based social ethics. It broadly agrees with the doctrine of natural law to be encountered in classsical Christian theology, e.g. Thomas Aquinas, Luther and Calvin. They hold that there are certain fundamental moral principles which can be motivated by arguments acceptable to human beings who do not hold a Christian philosophy of life.

Three fundamental arguments can be adduced for a humanely based ethics. First of all, it fits in well with a "combination theory". It provides a reasonable explanation of the fact that there is a certain agreement in content between Christian and humane ethics. Secondly, it fits in well with the criterion of universalizability. Because an acceptable ethical theory should have universal application, it ought to be supported by arguments which everyone can accept.

Thirdly, humanely based ethics is the the standpoint which fits in best with a realistic view of man. As beings created in the image of God, all human beings have a certain capacity to perceive what is right. Sin does not imply that this capacity is completely lost. In spite of their defects, human beings have a capacity for moral insight independently of the Revelation, even if it is limited.

This realistic view of man is not compatible with a strictly theological ethics. At the same time, it also conflicts with a strictly humane ethics. The view that social ethics is based only upon common human experiences and considerations, presupposes too optimistic a view of man. According to my view, all human beings as the result of sin have a limited capacity for insight into what is right and good. For this reason, they also require to be guided by Divine Revelation which clarifies and deepens the content of ethics. This is achieved above all through the radical ideal of love which forms the core of the ethical teachings in the New Testament.

The standpoint which agrees with the view of man criterion, is what I have called a "partially Revelation based ethics". According to this standpoint, ethics is based both upon the Revelation and upon common human experiences. The Revelation provides us with guidance in ethical questions but does not yield completely new moral principles and values. Every human being can achieve a certain insight into what is right and good independently of the Revelation. This is a view which can most easily be combined with a combination theory. The strongest argument in favour of this viewpoint is a realistic view of man according to which human beings are simultaneously creatures made in the image of God and sinners.

A partially Revelation based ethics can however be formulated in several different ways. The version adopted by Atherton and Aukrust in my opinion, attaches too much importance to the special ethical guidance provided by the Revelation. In contrast to them, I hold that one ought to attach more importance to the moral experiences and insights which are independent of the Revelation in Christ. It is not the case that the good is good because God wills it.

A partially Revelation based ethics has sometimes been formulated as a "theological addition ethics". According to this standpoint, common human experiences form the basis of certain moral principles and values while the Revelation motivates other principles and values. This way of conceiving the relationship between common human experiences and the Revelation seems to me however too rigid and static. It would rather seem to be the case that fundamental moral principles and values in a Christian social ethical theory can be motivated both by the Revelation and common human experiences.

For this reason, I advocate instead the view I have called a "theological clarificatory ethics". It holds that common human experiences and considerations provide a fragmentary insight into what is right and good. Due to human sin, however, this insight is limited. The Revelation in Christ provides us with a contribution which clarifies and deepens human moral insight. At the same time, there is a constant interaction between Revelation and human experiences in the attempt to attain insight into what is good and right. This interaction also implies that it is on the basis of experiences of different types that human beings try to understand the content of the Revelation.

A reasonable formulation of such a theological clarificatory ethics is to be found in Reinhold Niebuhr. He holds that the Christian ideal of love is linked to common human moral experiences and ethical ideals to be encountered outside Christianity. It is in partial agreement with those ideals of justice which form part of humane social ethics. At the same time, as Niebuhr stresses, this ideal of love cannot be reduced to those views which make up a humane ethics. By urging us to refrain from pursuing what is best for our own selves in our concern for others, it has a content which goes beyond those ideals which are realizable in political life.[5]

What then is the specifically Christian contribution to morality? In my view the Revelation in Christ does not give us any completely new moral principles. The ideal of love which is central to the ethical teachings of the New Testament can be understood as an exhortation to promote the best interests of other human beings just as much as one's own. This is very similar to those ideals of love to be encountered in humane ethics. One also encounters in humane ethics the view that one ought to promote what is good for others and to strive for an equal treatment of all human beings. On the other hand, the Revelation provides us with a deepened insight into what love for others can imply. This arises primarily from the fact that the Perfect Love which Christ expresses in His life emerges as an ethical ideal. He shows that concern for others applies to all human beings even those who have been rejected by society and those who are our enemies. He also shows that concern for others in certain situations is combined with suffering and a readiness to abstain from our own best interests.

The Revelation in Christ does not give any completely new views about what is valuable. In Christian ethics, one has often held that a good human life is one where human beings realize themselves in the sense that they develop properties and capacities which are specific for the human species. It is such self-realization which makes human beings happy. Similar views are also to be found in humane ethics. The view that happiness is the highest good and that human beings achieve happiness when they realize those properties which are characteristic for the human species, is a fundamental thesis in Aristotelian philosophy. On the other hand, the Revelation can provide us with a deeper insight into what self-realization and happiness mean. The truly human life as revealed by Christ, also includes a close communion with God. This relationship to God would seem according to Christian ethics to be a necessary precondition for perfect happiness.

A trinitarian ethics

As we have seen, a Christian view of man forms the basis of a Christian social ethics. At the same time, social ethics is also based upon other theoretical views which form part of a Christian philosophy of life. What then are the components in a Christian system of belief which form the basis of the content of a Christian social ethics? As we have seen, a humanely based social ethics can be combined with different answers to this question. It can be combined with a theology of creation ethics i.e. the view that ethics is based upon the doctrine of creation. It can be combined with an ecclesiological ethics i.e. the view that ethics is based primarily upon the doctrine of the Church. It can also be combined with a trinitarian ethics according to which ethics is based both upon the doctrine of Creation and upon Christology and eschatology.

On the other hand, a humanely based ethics cannot be combined with a Christological ethics according to which ethics is based solely upon Christology. Neither can it be combined with an eschatological ethics according to which ethics is based purely upon eschatology. Both these standpoints entail a strictly theological ethics. They disregard the fact that ethics is also based upon common human experiences and considerations.

Is then a theology of creation ethics acceptable? A social ethics which is based upon the doctrine of creation has often been formulated so that it motivates an uncritical acceptance of existing social structures and a hierarchical social order. A theology of creation ethics also appears to be irreconcilable with a partially Revelation based ethics of the kind which I have proposed. It attaches no importance to the specific contribution to morality which is provided by the Revelation in Christ. It is therefore instead often combined with a strictly humane social ethics.

In my view, the ecclesiological ethics of the type to be found in Atherton is also unacceptable. This viewpoint would seem to be difficult to combine with a humanely based social ethics. If ethics is based primarily upon the doctrine of the Church, it assumes an exclusively Christian character which make it difficult to accept for people with another philosophy of life.

For these reasons, I prefer the standpoint I have called a trinitarian ethics. It is a standpoint which best can be combined with a partially Revelation based ethics. Because ethics is based upon the doctrine of Creation, it can also be based upon common human experiences. Because it is based upon Christology and eschatology, it also allows for the importance of the specific contribution to morality given by the Revelation.

A reasonable formulation of such a trinitarian ethics has been proposed by J Philip Wogaman. He holds that the moral presumptions which make up

Christian ethics are based upon certain theological views which are rooted in Christian tradion and contemporary experience. These views are made up of several components in a Christian philosophy of life. Like Wogaman, I hold that among these is what I call a realistic view of man. Another component is the doctrine of Creation which motivates the view that both human beings and other living creatures have a fundamental value. Yet another component is Christology which shows us what perfect Love implies. Another component is eschatology which provides critical distance to existing social systems.[6]

According to my view, social ethics is thus first of all based upon a doctrine of Creation. This doctrine of creation also forms the basis for a Christian view of man and a theory of the meaning of work. The fact that ethics is based upon the doctrine of creation entails that it is humanely based. Every human being, as a creature made in the image of God, has the capacity to see what is right.

According to the Christian belief of creation, God has a definite purpose with human life. It is to be characterized by peace and justice, and animals and plants are to be given a chance to develop their own specific characteristics. We human beings have also the task of developing in the image of God i.e. of realizing ourselves as free and conscious beings with a capacity of concern for others. A fundamental ethical norm would seem to be that an act is right if it agrees with God's purpose with the creation. All human beings can perceive which acts have this property. It is a capacity which is given with life itself. As creatures made in the image of God, all human beings have this capacity for moral insight.

According to my view, creation can be conceived as an ever continuous act. God continues to create. He acts in history to maintain and preserve life. For this reason, creation also includes continuous changes in social orders. God also makes use of the contributions of human beings in his continuous act of creation. We are God's co-workers in creation, not least through our work. This view differs from the orders of creation theology which was previously common in the Protestant tradition and which was often combined with too static a view of the creation.

Secondly, social ethics is also based upon Christology. The doctrine of the person and work of Christ also forms the basis for both a Christian view of man and a Christian social ethical theory. Thereby social ethics is not merely based upon common human experiences. It is also based upon a divine Revelation.

According to Christian belief, we encounter in Christ an image of the true human being: One who is the true image of God. Thereby He lends depth to those moral principles and values which form part of humane ethics. He shows what a good human life implies and what it means to realize those properties which are specific for human beings. He also embodies the Christian ideal of love. In His concern for the weak and his readiness to suffer for the sake of others, He makes it clear what it means to love other human beings. A fundamental norm in Christian ethics is that we ought to live in the imitation of Christ. This ideal of imitation has relevance not only for individual but also social ethics.

Thirdly I hold that ethics is also based upon eschatology. The ethical teachings to be encountered in the New Testament, particularly in the Sermon on the Mount, are combined with the idea of a Kingdom of God which comes into being with Christ and which some time in the future will be fulfilled. This perfect Kingdom of God is linked to the exhortation to a self-sacrificial love for all human beings. Human beings cannot establish the Kingdom of God here in time through their own efforts. Eschatology therefore inspires one to a critical distance to existing social orders. In the light of the Kingdom of God, no existing social system is perfect.

According to my view, eschatology thus has great significance for social ethics. In this respect, I share the viewpoint which is to be found in several Latin American liberation theologians, among others José Míguez Bonino. As the latter maintains, the Kingdom of God is not a political utopia. Such utopias are created by human beings. Their function is to inspire us to a protest against existing conditions, to give an image of an alternative society and to exhort us to action in the creation of a new social order. Eschatology has however an indirect relationship to such utopias. The image of the Kingdom of God as a place where there exists peace and justice stimulates human beings to create political utopias which in turn can inspire them to political action.[7]

As Bonino emphasizes, an eschatological basis for social ethics is an important corrective to the pragmatic view which often has characterized the Christian realism of Reinhold Niebuhr and John C Bennett. It can provide motivation for a well informed utopianism which to a higher degree is prepared to question and reassess existing conditions. For this reason I hold that social ethics ought to be based not only upon the doctrine of creation but also upon Christology and eschatology.

Three fundamental moral principles

What then is the criterion for a right political act? What properties are common and specific for acts which are right? In my view, an acceptable social ethical theory ought to be based upon a realistic view of man. This contains the view that there are certain properties which are common for all human beings and specific for human beings as a species. Human beings are rational and free beings with a capacity for concern for others and for communion with God.

This view of man motivates a first fundamental moral principle. It is a principle of the equal value of all human beings. In my view, this principle contains three views. It asserts (a) that each human being has a value in her- or himself and therefore, as Kant expresses it, one ought to treat every human being not merely as a means but also as an end.[8] The principle of human value maintains (b) that all human beings have an equally high intrinsic value independently of race, sex, nationality and social class. It is for this reason, in my view, that it is desirable that all human beings achieve a life which is valuable in itself to an equally high degree. This entails that one ought to strive for the equal treatment of all human beings. The principle of human value maintains (c) that human beings have a unique value. Other living beings have an intrinsic value but the value of human beings is greater.

The principle of human value is motivated by the fact that there exist certain properties which are common for all human beings and specific for human beings as a species. We all have a capacity for self-reflection and purposive action. We all have a capacity for communion with God and for love for other human beings. These capacities are not developed to an equally high degree in all human beings but they exist as a potentiality in each and every one. As a result, every human being has an equally high value. The circumstance that human beings actualize these potentialities in different degrees due to handicap and social circumstances, does not justify treating them differently. Because these characteristics are specific for the human species, human beings have also a unique value in relation to other living creatures.

The principle of the equal value of all human beings is not specifically Christian. It is embraced also by people who do not share a Christian philosophy of life. It is a common human experience that we human beings have certain common properties. In contrast to Aukrust and Brakelmann, I hold that this principle is already based upon the doctrine of creation. Human value is based upon the fact that we are all created in the image of God. The principle of human value is not merely based upon Christology.

The principle of human value motivates in turn another fundamental moral principle. It is a principle of goodness, according to which we ought to strive for what is good and seek to avoid what is bad for all human beings. Because all human beings have an equally high value, it is our duty to strive for that which is good not only for ourselves but also for all other human beings. Respect for human value is simultaneously expressed in efforts to avoid what is bad for all human beings.

The principle of goodness is also not specifically Christian. It can be motivated by common human considerations and it is adopted by people who do not share a Christian philosophy of life. At the same time, it agrees very well with the Christian ideal of love. In the New Testament, the content of the law is summed up in a single commandment: "And thou shalt love the Lord thy God with all thy heart, and with all thy soul and with all thy mind and with all thy strength and thy neighbour as thyself".[9] The first part of this double commandment to love deals with our relationship to God and summarizes the three first commandments in the Decalogue. The second part – the commandment to love one's neighbour – deals with our relationship to our fellow human beings and summarizes the seven remaining commandments of the Decalogue. The content in Christian social ethics ought therefore to fit in well with this commandment to love.

The commandment to love one's neighbour can be interpreted so that it contains the principle of goodness. It exhorts us to strive for that which is good and to avoid that which is bad both for ourselves and for our fellow human beings. This principle is teleological in the sense that the consequences of an action are decisive for whether it is right. It is characteristic of a right act that it implies good consequences and avoids bad consequences for all human beings.

The principle of goodness is universalistic in the sense that it exhorts us to strive for what is good for all. The principle of the equal value of all human beings is not compatible with ethical egoism according to which an act is right if it entails maximally good consequences for the acting subject. If all human beings have an equally high value, then we ought to strive for that which is good both for ourselves and for all others. Ethical egoism also conflicts with the criterion of universalizability. A consistent exponent of this theory will probably not affirm that all other human beings also ought to carry out acts which promote only their own best interests. If one does not presuppose a perfect harmony of interest, such a universalization of ethical egoism would seem to conflict with the ethical egoist's own interests.

In contrast to ethical egoism, the principle of goodness exhorts us to promote that which is good for all human beings. It exhorts us both to self love and love of one's neighbour. Positively it implies that we should promote and respect what is good for all. Negatively it implies that we should eliminate and avoid what is bad for ourselves and others. We ought to promote that which is good and avoid that which is bad.[10]

In several situations, however, we have to choose between alternative acts which entail both good and bad consequences. The principle of goodness implies that in such situations we ought to follow the principle of utility. According to this, an act is right if and only if it entails the greatest possible surplus of good over bad consequences for all human beings. This principle implies that there exist situations where two or more acts can be right. However there is never more than one act which is our duty. According to the principle of utility, an act is our duty if and only if it entails a greater surplus of good over evil for all human beings than every other alternative line of action.

A teleological principle of this type, however, does not constitute a sufficient criterion for a right act. It does not specify how the good to be pursued ought to be distributed between human beings. Suppose that we have to choose between two acts which both imply an equally great surplus of good over evil for all human beings. Suppose further that one of these acts entails a more just distribution of the good. It would then seem reasonable to maintain that the act which entails a just distribution of the good is obligatory while the other act is wrong. According to a purely utilitarian view, however, both acts are right which shows that this theory is inadequate.

The principle of utility therefore requires to be supplemented with a principle of justice. It maintains that a characteristic of a right act is that it implies a just distribution of the good. This third fundamental moral principle can also be motivated on the basis of the principle of human value. Because all human beings have an equally high value, the good ought to be distributed justly so that all are treated as equals independently of race, sex, nationality and class.

The principle of justice is also a principle which is common for Christian and humane social ethics. This principle is also at the same time included in the commandment to love our neighbour. The exhortation to love our fellow man as ourselves can be interpreted as an exhortation to treat every human being as our equal. This entails that a right act should entail a just distribution of the good.

What then is just? The principle of the equal value of all human beings motivates in my view that one should strive as far as possible for an equal distribution. Thus for example certain fundamental liberties should be distributed equally among all. In certain cases, however, an unequal distribution can be to the advantage of all. If it also benefits the most disadvantaged, an unequal distribution of welfare can be just.

An ethical theory with these three fundamental moral principles is a deontological theory. Like utilitarianism, it accepts a principle of utility, according to which an act is right if there is no alternative line of action which entails better or less bad consequences for all human beings. In contrast to utilitarianism, it, however, maintains that the criterion for a right act is not simply that it entails good consequences. The theory also contains a principle of justice according to which another characteristic of a right act is that it entails a just distribution of the good. It also embraces a principle of the equal value of all human beings. According to this principle, good conse-quences are not a sufficient condition for an act to be right.

This deontological theory differs in several respects from an act deontology of the type we have encountered in J H Oldham. According to such an act deontology, there are no general moral principles which can give us guidance in a concrete moral choice situation. Act deontology would also seem to conflict with the criterion of universalizability. In my opinion, there are however sufficiently great similarities in relevant respects between different acts and situations for it to be possible to formulate certain general moral rules.

The deontological theory which I have proposed is a pluralistic theory of duty which contains several fundamental moral principles. It therefore differs from Kant's ethics. In contrast to Kant, I hold that there are rules of action which we can consistently will to be universalized but which are still not valid. The categorical imperative therefore does not seem to be a sufficient crite-rion for a right act. All rules of action which cannot be willed to be uni-versalized are wrong but all rules which can be willed to be universalized, need not be right. Nor in my opinion is the principle of human value a sufficient criterion. Although it is fundamental, it requires to be supplement-ed with a principle of goodness and a principle of justice.

Finally this pluralistic theory of duty is to be distinguished from the theory of justice to be found in two highly different writers like Emil Brunner and John Rawls. They both hold that the only thing which characterizes a right act is that it promotes a just distribution of the good even if they have differing views about what justice implies. However in my view, this is not a sufficient criterion. A right political act ought in addition to bring about a maximal surplus of what is good over what is bad for all human beings.

The principle of human value, the principle of utility and the principle of justice specify according to my view what characterizes a right act. At the same time, these principles can also form the basis for a theory of rights. The principle of human value thus motivates certain fundamental human rights. Because all human beings have an equal value they all have the same rights to realize the properties which are specifically human. This implies that all human beings have a right *inter alia* to work, freedom of expression, freee-dom of religion and freedom of conscience. Corresponding to these rights in the individual are certain obligations on the part of society. These duties are also given by the utility principle and the principle of justice.

The principle of human value, the principle of utility and the principle of justice can also provide the foundation for an ethical theory of virtue. They provide motivation for a view about what features of human character are good. A virtue can be conceived as a property which disposes us to perform actions which are right. Because an act is right if it promotes that which is good and just, it follows that properties which make us act in this way, are good. In order for an act to be right, it is not necessary that the human being who carries it out, is good. In this sense, the theory I have proposed, is act related but not subject related. On the other hand, I hold that an act is good if it is both right and carried out by a person with good features of human character.

A pluralistic theory of values

The social ethical theory which I have proposed contains a utility principle according to which a right act is characterized by entailing a maximal surplus of good over bad consequences for all human beings. But what then are good consequences? What is good for ourselves and for our fellow human beings? This question is primarily concerned with intrinsic values i.e. what is good in itself, independently of whether it is a means to achieve something else which is good.

One answer to this question is given by so called preference utilitarianism. This maintains that we ought to strive in our acts for a maximal satisfaction of the individual preferences of the persons affected. This view seems to me somewhat problematic. The wishes of different individuals vary considerably. Sometimes human preferences are not considered and well-founded. Human beings may even wish things which in a longer perspective injure both themselves and others. One has sometimes tried to solve this problem by distinguishing between rational and less rational preferences. It has been maintained that it is only those preferences which are based upon rational considerations and information about relevant matters of fact which ought to be taken into account. But the question arises how one is to decide which preferences are rational. When one tries to answer this question, it is natural to develop one's own theory of intrinsic value.

Another view is combined with the classical formulation of utilitarianism which is to be found for example in Jeremy Bentham. His utilitarianism is combined with ethical hedonism. It is a monistic theory of value according to which there is but one single fundamental intrinsic value. This value is happiness. It is a view which has been common in Western history of ideas. It is already to be encountered in Aristotle who held that happiness is the highest good and the ultimate aim of human beings. In contrast to Aristotle, however, Bentham and ethical hedonism held that happiness was identical with pleasure i.e. physical and psychical well-being. This implies that the only thing that has an intrinsic value is pleasure.[11]

In my view, this standpoint is also unacceptable. Certainly I can agree that pleasure is a form of satisfaction which is good in itself. But like Aristotle, I hold that happiness contains something more profound than a state of well-being. We achieve happiness when we realize a truly human life. Moreover, it would seem that there are forms of satisfaction other than pleasure which have an intrinsic value.

In what sense does happiness go beyond an experience of well-being? Which forms of satisfaction are valuable in themselves? In my view, welfare is one such intrinsic value. By welfare, I mean the satisfaction of fundamental human needs. In contemporary humanistic psychology, one holds in general that there are certain needs which are common for all human beings. These are needs which are based upon human nature in the sense that they must be satisfied if we are to be healthy, creative and happy. When these needs are satisfied, we attain welfare.

What then are these fundamental needs? In my view, an acceptable answer to this question, has been given by Abraham Maslow. He enumerates five types of human need. These are (1) physiological needs such as the need for food, clothes and shelter (2) the need for security i.e. needs related to the safety of the individual (3) the needs for community and love (4) the needs for self-esteem and the esteem of others and finally (5) the need for self-actualization. These are the five kinds of needs which are common for human beings.[12] By "welfare" I mean the satisfaction of all these needs.

Maslow maintains that there exists a hierarchical relation between these five levels of need so that the physiological needs are the strongest while the needs for self-actualization is the weakest. This implies that as long needs at a lower level remain unsatisfied, needs such as the needs for self-esteem and self-actualization must be deferred. It is first when the needs at the lower levels are satisfied that human beings seek to satisfy a need at the next higher level.[13] In this respect, there is reason to adopt another position. Probably the needs for community and self-actualization are still important for human beings whose fundamental physiological needs remain unsatisfied.[14]

Is then welfare the sole intrinsic value? Do we achieve happiness as soon as we satisfy our needs? The answer to this question depends *inter alia* upon what we mean by "self-realization". When Maslow at the fifth level in his hierarchy of needs, speaks of "self-actualization" he means by this, individual self-actualization, in other words that individuals are able to cultivate and develop their individual talents and potentials.

According to my view, however, "self-realization" implies something more than this. The view of man which I have put forward, maintains that there exist certain specific properties which are common for all human beings and specific for human beings as a species which the individual must realize. Among these properties is our capacity for rationality and our capacity of love for other human beings. Human self-realization implies that human beings realize these properties and do not merely cultivate their own individuality.

For these reasons, I am disposed to adopt a pluralistic theory of value according to which there are several fundamental intrinsic values and not merely one. I can certainly agree with the Aristotelian view that happiness is the sole goal of human beings and the highest good; but happiness embodies in my view three intrinsic values. The first is well-being in a broad sense; the second is welfare in the sense of the satisfaction of needs; and the third is self-realization in the sense of the realization of those properties which are specific and common for all human beings.[15]

In our political acts, we ought therefore to strive for a maximum of well-being over suffering for all human beings. We also ought to strive for increased welfare for all human beings. Moreover our task is also to allow human beings to realize themselves in a more fundamental sense. It is necessary to seek to increase welfare so that human needs for security, community and self-esteem are satisfied. But this is not sufficient. Among the political tasks is also that of creating a society which allows human beings to realize themselves as rational, free and responsible beings.

Are there any specifically Christian values? No. Christianity gives us neither completely new moral principles nor completely new values. On the other hand, it gives us a deeper understanding of what such moral principles and values – which also belong to humane ethics – imply. The Christian ideal of love gives us a deeper understanding of what the principle of goodness and the principle of justice imply. In an analogous way, Christology also gives us a deeper understanding of the meaning of happiness. According to Christian belief, perfect happiness is possible only in communion with God. This happiness cannot be achieved through political action. However, through political action we can create a society which does not hinder but rather enables human beings to create the preconditions for a truly human life.

The concept of justice

The social ethical theory I have proposed contains not only a principle of utility. It also contains a principle of justice according to which a right act implies a just distribution of the good. Both these principles are motivated by a principle of human value according to which all human beings have an equal value. All human beings are created by God in His image, that is to say as rational and free beings with a capacity for communion with God and for concern for others. For this reason, all human beings have an equal value independently of sex, race, nationality or achievement. For this reason, we also ought to strive for a just distribution of intrinsic values.

In Christian tradition, one enounters strong arguments for this principle of justice. Already in the Old Testament, the Prophets are strongly committed to the idea of justice. They sharply criticize the privileged and those who hold power, those who oppress the poor and steal from the downtrodden. The same perspective has been developed according to the New Testament in the life and teaching of Jesus. He spends his life among simple human beings and social outcasts and through his suffering, he reveals the God who identifies with those at the bottom of society. Jesus does not emerge as a political leader but He claims to have come to proclaim the doctrine of joy for the poor and to give freedom to the oppressed.

In the light of this, it seems reasonable to ascribe to the principle of justice a special importance in Christian social ethics. If in some situation it were to come into conflict with the principle of utility, then I hold that the principle of justice should be given priority. But what does it mean then to have a just distribution of the good? In regard to this question, there are at least three different answers.

A first view is that justice is distribution according to a "principle of merit". According to this principle, the good should be distributed according to certain deserving properties or merits. One can have different views about what constitutes merits. It can be maintained (a) that the good ought to be distributed according to colour, nationality or sex (b) that the good ought to be distributed according to good properties of character (c) that the good ought to be distributed according to the contributions each and every one has made so that the person who contributes most, receives the largest share of the good or (d) that the good ought to be distributed according to each and everyone's efforts.

Another view is that justice implies a distribution according to a "principle of equality". A just distribution is according to this principle an equal distribution. The principle of equality can be formulated as a "principle of equal distribution". It holds that every human being ought to have the same share of distributable social resources in order in this way to obtain the same possibilities of attaining a life which is good in itself. But it can also be formulated as a "principle of objective equality". According to this, it is not the distribution of social resources which should be equal. However, all human beings after the distribution should attain a life which in all respects is equally valuable.

A third view is that justice entails a distribution according to a "principle of need". According to this principle, the good is to be distributed so that each and every one can realize the life which is maximally good with respect to their own individual personalities. Each and every one should be allowed to maximally actualize their potentialities, allowing for the fact that different people have different potentialities. This principle departs from the principle of equal distribution because it maintains for example that a person who has a disability ought to receive a greater share than someone who does not have such a disability. Nor does it recommend a distribution which entails objective equality because it presupposes that the factual inequalities which exist between human beings, will not permit such a distribution.

Which of these principles of justice is to be preferred? In Emil Brunner we have encountered a viewpoint which more or less coincides with the principle of merit. He holds that a just distribution ought to take account of the differences which exist between different human beings depending upon their different roles in society. According to Brunner, the divine order of creation is differentiated and hierarchical and therefore the unequal distribution of power and welfare is just.

In my view, a principle of merit of this type is unacceptable. There is reason for agreeing with the classical view that justice means that each and every one obtains their due (suum cuique). Such a distribution entails however, not a distribution according to each and every one's distinctive merits. What it really implies, is specified by the principle of the equal value of all human beings. According to the latter principle, all human beings ought to be treated equally despite the fact that we are unequal. The principle of justice embodies therefore an ideal of equality. It is not just contrary to what the principle of merit maintains, that the good should be distributed so that the factual differences which exist should be maintained and reinforced. Because each and every one has an equally high value, it is instead just despite these differences to strive that everyone may share in that which is valuable to an equally high degree.

My view of justice largely agrees with that to be found in Reinhold Niebuhr. He writes about "an ascending scale of moral possibilities" which is topped by the Christian ideal of love. The latter requires a self-sacrificial love which seeks the best interests of all others and not one's own interests. Like Niebuhr, I hold that the principle of justice which most closely approximates the ideal of love, is what I have called the principle of need. It is a justice which takes into account of our fellow human beings' special organic needs e.g. so that special concern is given to handicapped children. Further down the scale is to be found the ideal of equality which is essentially equivalent to the principle of objective equality. As Niebuhr stresses, the principle of merit can also be seen as a relative expression of the idea of love but it ought to be applied only when it is necessary to reward industry as a way of guaranteeing the maintenance of certain social functions.[16]

Justice ideally conceived thus implies distribution according to the principle of need. Welfare ought to be distributed so that everone attains as good a life as possible in respect of their individual characteristics. At the same time, I hold that this principle ought to be combined with a principle of equality. As Niebuhr puts it, equality is always the regulative principle of justice and in the ideal of equality there is to be found an echo of the Christian ideal of love.[17] According to the principle of equality, there is a minimum level of welfare which all human beings ought to achieve. Above this limit, a variation according to different needs can be accepted. According to the principle of equality, one should also aim at an equal distribution of certain fundamental freedoms i.e. those rights which enable human beings to realize themselves.

A reasonable combination of a principle of need and a principle of equality has been proposed by John Rawls. He formulates two principles of justice. The first maintains that every person should have equal right to certain fundamental liberties. Such liberties as political freedom, freedom of conscience and such freedoms as are associated with the right to private property, are to be distributed equally among the citizens. The second principle of justice maintains that social and economic inequalities are to be arranged so that (a) they can be reasonably expected to be to the advantage of everyone and (b) that they they are attached to positions and offices which are open to all. This implies according to Rawls that (a) incomes and welfare should be distributed equally unless an unequal distribution is to the everyone's advantage and (b) that power and responsibility are to be distributed equally but if power is distributed unequally, it should be attached to positions which are open to all.[18]

The second principle of justice, according to Rawls, is ambiguous. It is unclear what it means to say that an unequal distribution of welfare would be to "everyone's advantage" and that power, if it is unequally distributed, should be associated with positions which are "open to all". Rawls proposes that the principle should be interpreted in accordance with what he calls a democratic ideal of equality. This holds that the liberal principle of equal distribution is to be applied in the distribution of power. All are to have real and not merely formal opportunities of obtaining those positions and offices with which power is linked.[19] In the distribution of welfare and income, what Rawls calls "the difference principle" is to be applied. This entails that welfare is to be distributed equally unless an unequal distribution is to the advantage of those worst placed. One ought in other words to choose the distribution alternative which most benefits the worst placed.[20] The second principle of justice can thus be reformulated as follows: "Social and economic inequalities are to be arranged so that they are both (a) to the greatest benefit of the least advantaged and (b) attached to offices and positions open to all under conditions of fair equality of opportunity."[21]

The two principles of justice specify according to Rawls how "primary social values" are to be distributed. It is those values which rational beings wish independently of what they wish in general. The first principle specifies how (a) rights and freedoms ought to be distributed while the second principle specifies how (b) income and welfare and (c) power and opportunities ought to be distributed. In the case of these two principles conflicting with one another, Rawls holds that the first should be given priority.[22]

I am largely in agreement with this view of the meaning of justice. It specifies in a reasonable way how it is possible to combine a principle of equality with a principle of need. In two respects, I cannot share Rawls' view. First of all, I have a partly different view of what has intrinsic value. Secondly I do not accept that the principle of justice is a sufficient criterion for a right political action. According to my view, the principle of justice requires to be combined with a principle of utility. The criterion for a right act is both that it entails maximally good consequences for all and that it entails a just distribution of the good. However, I agree with the view that fundamental freedoms and rights ought to be distributed equally between all persons. This is a necessary precondition for each and everyone obtaining the same opportunities for realizing those properties which are specifically human. This principle of equality is in my view a consequence of the principle of human value. Like Rawls, I hold also that welfare ought to be distributed so that the persons worst placed benefit most from it. A principle of need of this type in my view is very similar to the Christian ideal of love which exhorts us to to be concerned for all human beings independently of their own merits.

A modified monistic thesis

The principle of human value, the principle of utility and the principle of justice constitute according to my view fundamental criteria for a right political act. But how do these principles relate to those which hold within individual ethics? Do the same criteria for a right act apply within both individual and social ethics or are the characteristics of a right political act completely different from those which characterize a right private act?

There are theologians and political philosophers who have presented arguments for the standpoint which I have called "the amorality thesis". It presupposes in general that it is only private acts which ought to be submitted to ethical judgement. Within individual ethics, one can set up certain criteria for a right act. But politics on the other hand is amoral. It is ruled by the power struggle and particular group interests and ought not to be subjected to any moral requirements. The amorality thesis has often been formulated as a thesis of "the autonomy" of economics and politics according to which political and economic acts are subject to special laws which cannot be influenced by ethical arguments. In the Christian tradition, the amorality thesis has quite often been combined with an individualistic view of Christianity according to which Christian belief is only valid for the individual and Christian ethics applies only to the individual's relation to other individuals.

The theologians I study in this investigation, all reject the amorality thesis. In this respect, I share their view. Political action does not lie outside ethical judgement. It is subject to such fundamental moral principles as the principle of human value, the principle of utility and the principle of justice. The Christian ideal of love is not only applicable to our private acts but also to our political ones. A fundamental argument against the amorality thesis, as Aukrust stresses, is that it conflicts with a view of man according to which human beings are creative beings with responsibility for the world around them. As beings created in the image of God, they have responsibility both for fellow human beings and other living beings. This responsibility cannot be discharged without political action and therefore this too must be subject to morality.

But do the same moral principles hold in both individual and social ethics? In Emil Brunner, we have met the standpoint which I have called "the dualistic thesis". It maintains that both political and private acts should be submitted to ethical judgement but the social ethical criteria for a right political act are different from the individual ethical criteria which apply to a right private act. The ideal of love which is valid within individual ethics, does not hold within social ethics.

As we have seen in Chapter 1, the so-called "doctrine of the two kingdoms" in Martin Luther is also combined with such a dualistic thesis. He holds that we cannot apply the radical ethics of love which we enounter in the Sermon on the Mount, in political life. Luther expresses it by saying that there exists a difference between my duties as "a person" i.e. as an individual related to other individuals and my obligations associated with my "office" i.e. when I perform a social role which is of significance for the whole of society. Within individual ethics, I am subject to the norms which are given in the Sermon on the Mount while in social ethics, I am subject to another system of norms.[23]

According to my view, there are strong arguments for rejecting a dualistic thesis of this type. The foremost is that it conflicts with what I have called the "criterion of universalizability". This criterion implies that if I maintain that an act is right for a certain person in a certain situation, I must be prepared to maintain that all acts which are similar in relevant respects are also right for all other people in all similar situations. This implies also that if I judge on the basis of some criterion that a certain private act is right then I ought on the basis of the same criterion to judge that a political act which is similar in relevant respects, is also right. There are at least certain political acts which as far as moral judgement is concerned have the same relevant properties as certain private acts. If it is the case in individual ethics that it is right to strive for what is good for all men to an equally high degree, this is also the case for political acts.

For this reason, I adopt the standpoint I have called "the monistic thesis". It maintains that the criterion for a right act is the same, whether we are dealing with individual or social ethics. The principle of human value, the principle of utility and the principle of justice apply to both our political and private acts.

Within the classical formulation of utilitarianism, we encounter a monistic thesis of this kind. Jeremy Bentham holds that the principle of utility is valid not only for private acts but also for political acts. It holds for "every act of whatever kind" that to be right it must agree with the principle of utility, he writes, and by that he envisages not only every act of some particular individual but also every government measure.[24] In a similar way, I hold that the principle of human value and the principle of justice are also valid for both individual and social ethics.

The monistic thesis is also adopted by many contemporary representatives of Christian social ethics. This is the case not least for those Protestant theologians who have been influenced by Karl Barth. A Barthian doctrine of the Lordship of Christ is often combined with a critique of the dualistic thesis which is very often motivated on the basis of a Lutheran doctrine of the two kingdoms. A view of this kind has been encountered in Arthur Rich and Günter Brakelmann. They both base ethics upon Christology and hold that the same Christological ethics applies within both social and individual ethics.

Even if I have rejected a Christological ethics, I am prepared to share the view that the same ethical criteria apply both to our private and political acts. At the same time, I hold that this monistic thesis requires to be modified. Those moral principles and intrinsic values which are realizable in private life, are not always realizable to the same extent in political life. This is due to the fact that the tendency to selfishness which is to be found in individual human beings seems to be strengthened when they come together in organized collectives. For this reason, it would seem to be difficult for social groups to act in agreement with the idea of love in its full radicality. A realistic view of man allows itself to be best combined with what we can call "a modified monistic thesis".

Even in this respect, my viewpoint coincides largely with that to be found in Reinhold Niebuhr. He holds that the Christian ideal of love ultimately requires a self-sacrificial love which cannot be completely realized within social ethics. On the basis of what I have called "a realistic view of man", he holds that the selfishness of human beings is particularly apparent in social groups and in the power struggle which characterizes political life. For this reason, we must content ourselves in social ethics with striving for ideals which constitute approximations to altruistic love. Social ethics is governed by different principles for a just distribution which are realizable but are imperfect expressions of the Christian ideal of love. The justice which can be attained within political life, however, agrees in large measure with the ideal of love.[25]

A similar line of argument is to be found in John C Bennett. He uses the concept of "middle axiom" which we have previously encountered in J H Oldham, to describe those instrumental values and rules of action which are common for Christian and humane social ethics. These middle axioms, according to Bennett, are simultaneously expressions of the commandment to love which are realizable in political life. One must content oneself with such middle axioms within social ethics because of the imperfection of human beings and the strength of group egoism. This does not however prevent the same norm system being valid in principle both for our private and political acts.[26]

It is a modified monistic thesis of this kind which I advocate. The principle of human value, the principle of goodness and the principle of justice are fundamental criteria for a right act both within individual and social ethics. At the same time, it is more difficult to completely realize these principles in political as opposed to private acts. According to the principle of goodness, we ought to be prepared in certain situations to abstain from what is in our own best interest in order to promote what is good for others. In political life, it is however realistic to presuppose that we cannot completely sacrifice our own interests and that we must choose acts which entail certain bad consequences. There we must be content with approximations to the Christian ideal of love. This does not imply that I accept the dualistic thesis which is associated with Luther's doctrine of the two Kingdoms. In contrast to this doctrine, I hold that in principle the same moral principles apply both within individual and social ethics.

10. A Christian theory of work

In the previous chapter, I have set forth my proposal for a constructive social ethical theory. It is a theory which contains three fundamental moral principles, namely a principle of human value, a principle of goodness and a principle of justice. It is based upon what I have called a realistic view of man which holds that human beings have a certain capacity for moral insight independently of the Revelation. Social ethics is therefore based not merely upon those views which make up a Christian system of belief but also upon common human experiences and considerations.

The aim of the present chapter is to propose a formulation of a Christian theory of the meaning of work. This theory is based upon the social ethical theory which I have put forward in the previous chapter. This entails that the theory of the meaning of work is also based upon a realistic view of man. Moreover it is based upon various other theoretical views which make up a Christian philosophy of life.

In the present chapter, I shall also develop my own view of the doctrine of vocation in Protestant theology. In Chapter 8, I was critical of the uncritical acceptance of this doctrine and also of the view that it ought to be completely replaced by an alternative Christian work ethics. I shall now discuss how it is possible to revise the doctrine of vocation so that it could be acceptable today.

In this connection, I shall also discuss the question of how a Christian theory of work is related to other theories of the meaning of work. Differing theories of the meaning of work do not need to be totally incompatible; they contain views which can be combined with one another. Thus for example it is possible to combine certain views in the doctrine of vocation with certain other views which make up a Marxist or socio-technical theory of work.

The question of the meaning of work is in my view a question which deals in part with the purpose of work and in part with the value that this activity has. In order for work to be valuable, it must in turn constitute a means of attaining a desirable goal. When in Chapter 3, I analysed the different theories of work in Protestant theology, I raised four analytical questions. These are (1) what is the purpose of work? (2) how is work related to human self-realization? (3) what is the value of work as a human activity? (4) what is it that spurs human beings to work? I shall now try to give my own answers to these questions.

Finally I shall also discuss what work ethical recommendations follow from the social ethical theory and the theory of the meaning of work which I propose. These theories are combined with certain views concerning the solution of the employment problem, the wages question, the organization problem, the participation question and the system question. Before one can adopt a stance with respect to these problems, a careful assessment of the statements about the probable consequences of alternative courses of action, is required. Such an assessment falls outside the framework of the present enquiry. On the other hand, it is possible to specify certain views which appear compatible with my proposals for a social ethical theory and theory of the meaning of work.

A revised doctrine of vocation

The theories of the meaning of work to be encountered in Protestant theology have generally been combined with a doctrine of vocation. As we have seen, this doctrine of vocation has been formulated in different ways in Lutheran and Calvinist theology. A common core, however, has been made up of the views that work is an instrument for the divine work of creation and that its aim is to serve our fellow human beings. For this reason, work in the doctrine of vocation has been assigned a relatively high value.

Several contemporary British and German theologians have criticised this doctrine of vocation and have proposed an alternative formulation of Christian work ethics. In Chapter 8, I have rejected this "alternative line". In my view, it is combined with too pessimistic a view of the possibilities for creating employment opportunities for all those able and willing to work. Moreover, it is combined with too low a valuation of work. The view that work has a high value does not entail making those human beings who are unemployed, feel guilty but constitutes instead a reason for society striving to provide full employment.

In contrast to the alternative line, I hold that the doctrine of vocation in Protestant theology contains certain views which are acceptable. First of all, there is the view that work is an activity which is already given in the creation. Work has been ordained by God and belongs to the fundamental conditions of human existence. This does not require us to conceive work, like Brunner, as a divine order of creation. Rather like Brakelmann, we can look upon work as a "mandate", i.e. a task which human beings have been assigned by God in the creation. In this way, a Christian theory of work can be based upon a Christian doctrine of creation.

A second view which forms part of the doctrine of vocation is that human beings through their work, are co-workers of God in His continuous act of creation. God's creation is not complete but still goes on all the time. For this continuous creation, He makes use of human beings as His instruments. When human beings in their work use their intelligence and their initiative to produce food and shelter, to cure illness and to impart knowledge, they constitute instruments for the divine work of creation. One purpose of work is thus to participate in God's continuous act of creation.

A third view in the doctrine of vocation which I also judge acceptable, is that a purpose of work is to serve our fellow human beings. By working, we must serve the best interests of other human beings and thus fulfil the commandment of loving our neighbour. This comes about through our efforts to produce things which satisfy the needs of other human beings. A view of this kind fits in well with the social ethical theory which I proposed in the previous chapter. We ought to act in agreement with the principle of goodness not only in our leisure but also in the course of our work.

Fourthly the doctrine of vocation also includes the view that work is a Cross, an experience of suffering in the imitation of Christ. When in our vocation, we serve human beings, we meet with reverses. As a means of serving others, work also becomes something heavy and painful so that it can be conceived as suffering in the imitation of Christ. It seems to me that this view is also acceptable. It coincides with many people's experiences of the conditions of working life. It also implies that the vocation to imitate Christ is not to be thought of as an exhortation to withdraw from the world. Instead it is an injunction to serve our fellow human beings at the heart of society and in our ordinary working life.

A fifth view in the doctrine of vocation which I am prepared to accept, is that work has a relatively high value as a means of serving our fellow human beings. Inasmuch as work is able to produce goods and services which satisfy the needs of other human beings, it is valuable. This is true not only of intellectual activities but also of manual work. Manual work is also a means of serving our neighbour and as such, it is a valuable activity.

The fact that I share these five views, does not entail that I agree with the viewpoint I have called "the tradition line". Instead I hold that it is necessary to revise the doctrine of vocation in several respects. First of all, the formulation which the doctrine of vocation has been given in Calvinist theology, appears problematic. This is particularly so because the doctrine has been

284

combined with a doctrine of double predestination. Such a doctrine of predestination conflicts with the view of man I have proposed. According to this, every human being as a creature made in the image of God, has a free will. This freedom of will also includes a freedom in relation to God so that our attitude to the salvation which He offers, is determined by ourselves. Therefore we are not predetermined either to salvation or damnation and as a result it is unreasonable to view hard work as a sign that that one belongs to God's Elect.

In my view, a Lutheran doctrine of vocation also requires to be revised. Firstly the doctrine must be divorced from the feudal character which it enjoys in Lutheran theology. In Luther, the doctrine of vocation is combined with a decidedly patriarchal view of society. It is combined with an acceptance of the social stratification which characterized the feudal society in which he lived. Fulfilling the commandment to love our neighbour in our work means according to Luther to act in agreement with the second table of the Decalogue. Chief among these, he holds, is the fourth commandment which he interprets as an exhortation which calls upon children to obey their parents, woman to obey man, the farm hand to obey his master and in general for each and every one to obey their temporal superiors.[1]

This feudal and patriarchal interpretation of the commandment to love one's neighbour is unacceptable. It conflicts with a view of man which attaches great importance to the fact that all human beings as creatures made in the image of God, have equal value. Such a view of man motivates the view that a just distribution of power includes an ideal of equality. Luther's interpretation of the commandment to love, also conflicts with the social ethical theory I have put forward. This theory contains a principle of human value which exhorts us to treat all human beings as equals. It also contains a principle of justice which rejects distribution according to merit. It is therefore impossible to accept the views that the Fourth Commandment should be given priority among those forming the second table of the Decalogue and that in general it should exhort us to obey our superiors. The commandment to love our neighbour exhorts us instead to strive for equality and the removal of the unequal concentration of power.

A Lutheran doctrine of vocation also requires to be revised in another respect. This doctrine has often embodied the views that work ought to be an act of sacrifice for the sake of other human beings from which the workers themselves are not to receive any personal reward. When Luther maintains that work is a Cross, an act of suffering in imitation of Christ, it would seem to imply that work ought to embody self-sacrificial love. Thus the doctrine of vocation has come to be combined with ethical altruism. Human beings have been exhorted to be self-sacrificing in their concern for others. The purpose of work has been deemed to be serving our neighbour; not that those engaging in the work are to receive fair reward and the satisfaction of their own needs.

Such a formulation of the doctrine of vocation is in my opinion unacceptable. One purpose of work is to show concern for other human beings. But its aim is not a self-sacrificing love where the person doing the work must completely abstain from personal reward. The commandment to love our neighbour contains an exhortation to show concern for the best interests of other people and ourselves. It contains a principle of goodness which is combined with ethical universalism, not ethical altruism. Therefore work ought to promote both that which is good for others and for the person engaged in the work. The purpose of work is both to serve our neighbour and to satisfy the worker's own needs for community and self actualization.

In this respect, I wish to revise the doctrine of vocation in the manner previously indicated by the Swedish work ethicist, Ludvig Jönsson. He also holds that the commandment to love our neighbour is not an altruistic principle. It exhorts us to strive for other people's and our own best interests. For that reason, work should also be a way of showing concern for other human beings and for ourselves. It is the service of others which makes work a vocation, not the absence of personal reward. The purpose of work is both to promote what is good for others and our own self-realization.[2]

Even if one maintains that work has this double purpose, it is possible to hold that human beings in their work can fulfil their vocation to live in the imitation of Christ. We do not fulfil the vocation of living in the same spirit of love as Christ, the true human being, by retreating from the world. We can fulfil it to a high degree through our daily work by trying to accomplish what is valuable for other human beings. This, however, does not imply that in our work, we should be prepared to suffer and to sacrifice ourselves in promoting other people's best interests. The love of our neighbour which is shown through our exertions at work must instead be combined with the fact that we achieve something good for ourselves. Inasmuch as love in the imitation of Christ entails a preparedness to sacrifice ourselves for others, it is not something which constitutes a general duty in working life.

A Marxist and socio-technical theory

How does a revised Protestant doctrine of creation relate to those theories of the meaning of work associated with philosophies of life other than the Christian one? Is a Christian theory of the meaning of work specifically Christian or does it contain views which agree with views to be found in other theories?

As we have seen, various theories of the meaning of work are combined with other theories having a philosophy of life character. They are combined with differing theories of human nature which contain views about what constitutes human needs and about what is specific for human beings as a species. They are also combined with differing constructive ethical theories containing views about what is right and valuable. Despite this, differing theories of the meaning of work are not totally logically incompatible with one another. Each can contain views which can be combined with at least certain of the views to be found in other theories.

A revised doctrine of vocation of the type I have proposed is combined with a definite view of reality and a definite view of man. It is based upon a Christian doctrine of creation and a view of man associated with such a theory of creation. A Marxist theory of work is combined with a view of reality of a completely different kind. A socio-technical theory of work is also not combined with any assumption that human life is a gift of God. Despite this, I hold that there are certain views forming part of these theories which can be combined with those views which are acceptable within a Lutheran doctrine of vocation.

Like Christian social ethics, a Christian theory of work can thus be said to be humanely based. It contains certain views which agree with those contained in theories based upon other philosophies of life. A Christian theory of work is based also upon certain common human experiences. It is related and lends depth to views in other theories of the meaning of work. At the same time, there are also theories of work which cannot be combined with a revised doctrine of vocation.

Among the latter is a Platonic theory of work. In my opinion, it ascribes too low a value to work in relation to other activities. A Platonic theory is based upon a view of man according to which the specifically human consists in the capacity for rational thought. The view of man which I have proposed, shares this viewpoint. But in addition, the Platonic theory holds that human beings realize themselves as rational beings not through their work but solely through their philosophising. In contrast to this view, I hold that work also contributes to human self realization and thereby also to human happiness. For this reason, work does not have a lower value than other activities.

Furthermore a revised doctrine of vocation cannot be combined with a Tayloristic theory of work. This theory holds that the purpose of work is merely to obtain resources for the maintenance of life. In addition, it has too low an opinion of the value of work. In my view, the purpose of work is also to produce goods and services which are valuable for other human beings. Moreover it is possible through work itself to satisfy certain needs in the person engaged in the work. As a means of attaining these goals, work has a relatively high value.

However, in my opinion, it is possible to combine the doctrine of vocation with views contained in a Marxist theory. Like this, a Christian theory can maintain that work can contribute to human beings realizing what is characteristic of the human species. In contrast to the instinctive activities of animals, human work is a conscious and purposive activity. As a result, it can contribute to a realization of ourselves as self-conscious beings with a capacity for purposive action. It is not only through philosophical thinking that we realize ourselves. We can also in our work, realize ourselves as beings with a capacity for concern for others.

In several respects, there are important differences between a Christian and Marxist view of man. A Christian view of man is combined with a theistic view of reality and a doctrine of creation according to which human beings receive their lives as a gift of God. A Marxist view of man, on the other hand, embodies an atheistic view of reality and looks upon theistic concepts as the product of particular economic conditions. Marxism also optimistically assumes that human beings can realize a truly human life by changing the economic organization of production. In contrast to this, a Christian view of man holds that human beings are unable by their own efforts to achieve a truly human life. This, however, does not prevent these two theories sharing certain views about what constitutes specifically human qualities and about the purpose of work.

A revised doctrine of vocation can also be combined with certain views in a socio-technical theory of work. This theory maintains that work can and ought to be the source of the satisfaction of needs. It ought not merely to satisfy social needs. One purpose of work is also to satisfy the human need for self actualization. If we conceive the principle of goodness not as an altruistic but as a universalistic principle, this seems reasonable. For then, according to the doctrine of vocation, the purpose of work is to satisfy both the needs of others and of the person engaging in the work.

In contrast to a socio-technical theory, the doctrine of vocation maintains that the purpose of work is not only to satisfy the worker's needs for self actualization. Through work, we must also fulfil the commandment to love our neighbour. As a result, the purpose of work is also to show concern for the best interests of other human beings. By stressing that the person engaged in the work also ought to receive some personal reward, the socio-technical theory, however, constitutes an important complement to the the doctrine of vocation.

In contrast to a socio-technical theory, the doctrine of vocation also maintains that the worker's own reward does not consist in the mere satisfaction of needs. Work can also contribute to the worker's self realization in the sense that they realize those qualities which are common for all human beings. Through working, they realize themselves as beings with a capacity for concern for others. This species realization theory can, however, be combined with the view that work can and ought to contribute to the individual's development of their own particular talents and capacities.

The purpose of work

What then is the purpose of work? What goals can and ought to be realized through work? In Chapter 8, I have criticized "the human fellowship line" according to which the purpose of work is merely to serve our fellow human beings. "The creation line" according to which the purpose of work is also to be an instrument for God's continuous act of creation, is to be preferred. This latter view fits in better with the views of human work to be found in the Scriptures.

A first purpose of work is thus, in my view, to consitute an instrument for God's continuous act of creation. Divine creation is not a completed, once-only event. It is a process which continues. God continues his work of creation by giving human beings the necessities of life. Thus human beings receive food and shelter, illnesses are cured and human knowledge about the world around expands.

This is accomplished through human work. Through work, human beings are co-workers of God in his continuous act of creation. None of us can, by our own efforts alone, satisfy all our needs. In order to have food and shelter, clothing and medical care we are dependent upon the work of others. All who contribute in this way, can be conceived as co-workers of God. By using their intelligence, initiative and creativity, they constitute instruments of the Creator in His continued designing of human society. Their work contributes to creating those conditions which allow human beings and human civilization to exist.[3]

This view entails that I advocate a Christian theory of work which is based upon a Christian doctrine of creation. An orders of creation theology of the type to be encountered in Brunner, seems to me, however, to be problematic. It runs the risk of obscuring the fact that God's creation is an ever continuing process. In their work, human beings are, at this moment, able to participate in this work of creation. The purpose is not to maintain orders but to serve our fellow human beings. A better way of expressing this is to say, like Brakelmann, that work is a "mandate" i.e. a task which human beings have received from God in the creation.

Basing a Christian theory of work upon a doctrine of creation in this way fits in well with the image of work that is presented in Genesis 2—3. As we have seen in Chapter 1, work is conceived there as a determinant of human existence as something created by God. Human beings are creatures made in the image of God, which implies that they are engaged in work and thereby participate in the divine act of creation. Work is co-operation with God in His creative activity.

This implies that work is not a consequence of the Fall. Human imperfection implies that the cultivation of the soil involves travail and that we must produce what we need for our existence by the sweat of our brows. This implies that work in general involves toil and difficulties. Inasmuch as we must work under inhuman working conditions, in an unhealthy environment and subject to a hierarchical organization of work, this can be conceived as an imperfection in existence which has nothing to do with the Divine purpose with creation. God's purpose with existence, however, is that human beings are to engage in work. Work in itself is not a consequence of the Fall. It is already given in the creation as an instrument for God's continuous act of creation.[4]

A second purpose of work is to produce goods and services which satisfy the needs of other human beings. Through our work, we should fulfil the commandment to love our neighbour in the sense that we produce those things which are valuable for others. To be a fellow human being in the full sense is not only a leisure time activity. Even in our daily work we are called upon to produce those things which satisfy the needs of our fellow humans. In this way, we can express our concern for other human beings in our work.

This view is based upon the social ethical theory which I have put forward in the previous chapter. The principle of goodness is also to be applied in work so that by means of this activity we strive for what is good and avoid what is bad for other human beings. Among those things with intrinsic value is welfare so that according to the principle of goodness we have a duty to satisfy the needs of our fellow human beings. Through work, it is possible to satisfy both fundamental physiological and higher psychological needs. At the same time we should try in our work to contribute to creating a society which enables human beings to realize themselves as rational and free human beings.

As we have seen in Chapter 1, there is no direct support in the New Testament for the view that the purpose of work is to fulfil the commandment of loving our neighbour in this sense. The purpose of work is conceived there primarily as a way of providing for the necessities of life. At the same time, in several places in the New Testament, the commandment to love our neighbour is presented as a fundamental norm which summarises our duties to other human beings. A commandment which has this central place in Christian ethics ought surely to be applicable also to work as an important human activity.

In Christian work ethics, we encounter differing views about what it means to fulfil the commandment of loving our neighbour through our work. According to Luther, it means acting in accordance with the last seven commandments in the Decalogue. Foremost among these is the Fourth Commandment which exhorts us to obey our superiors. This view, in my opinion, is not acceptable. It conflicts with the principle of justice which forms part of the social ethical theory I have proposed. In our work we have to strive for justice which as far as possible embodies the equal treatment of all human beings.

Sometimes the task of serving our neighbour through our work has been conceived as increasing material welfare in society. The purpose of work is to increase company efficiency and productivity, thus bringing about an increase in welfare.[5] However this view also cannot be accepted on the basis of the social ethical theory I have put forward. The needs which ought to be satisfied through work, are not only fundamental physiological needs but in addition needs for security, community, self-esteem and self actualization.

To fulfil the commandment to love our neighbour through our work entails instead according to my view, producing those goods and services which satisfy these differing human needs of our fellow human beings. Production ought to be determined by needs in the sense that a criterion for what is to be produced, is that production should aim at satisfying important human needs. The satisfaction of such needs can be achieved both through the provision of services and intellectual work as well as the production of goods and manual work of various kinds.

A third purpose of work is to satisfy certain needs in the person engaged in it. Work itself ought to be a source for the satisfaction of needs. The purpose of work is not only to promote what is good for other human beings. The person who engages in the work, must also derive some reward from it. In this sense, the doctrine of vocation requires to be revised and supplemented with a fundamental thesis from a socio-technical theory of work.

This view is based upon the social ethical theory which I put forward in the previous chapter. According to the principle of goodness, we ought to strive for what is good and avoid what is bad for all other human beings and for ourselves. We therefore also must seek to satisfy our own needs of different kinds. Work can and ought to contribute to this satisfaction of needs.

Work is necessary for providing human beings with life's necessities. It can and ought to give us material resources for the satisfaction of needs in our leisure. Higher psychological needs, however, also require to be satisfied through work itself. Among these are our needs for community and social intercourse. In our work, we act in a community made up of other human beings with whom we share responsibility for accomplishing something of value. Thereby this activity can satisfy our social needs. At the same time, through our work we can satisfy our needs for self actualization. This entails that the individual person can develop and employ their individual talents and capacities in their work.

A fourth purpose of work is to realize those qualities which are characteristic for human beings as a species. This implies that work ought to contribute to our self realization as free and rational beings with a capacity for self consciousness and purposive behaviour. It also implies that work ought to contribute to the realization of our capacity for concern for others. Even in this respect, the purpose of work is to contribute to human self realization.

This is a view shared by a revised doctrine of vocation and a Marxist theory of work. It is motivated by the principle of goodness which exhorts us not only to pursue the satisfaction of the needs of others and of ourselves. Self realization in a deeper sense also is an intrinsic value. Therefore we ought to strive for a society where we can realize ourselves as free and rational beings with a capacity for concern for our fellows and other living beings.

Work and self realization

Is it possible and desirable that work contributes to human self realization? According to a Platonic theory of work, this is not the case. Human beings realize themselves as rational beings through the activity of contemplation i.e. purely philosophical thinking. A similar standpoint has been encountered in Thomas Aquinas. He holds that the contemplative life which is aimed at communion with God takes precedence over the active life which is aimed at love for our fellow human beings.

Several contemporary Protestant theologians have also a view of a similar type. It is a standpoint which I have called "the contemplation line". It assumes human beings realize what is species specific primarily through activities other than work. It is not in work but in communion with God that humans achieve their essential nature. I have criticised this standpoint on the basis of the view of man which I have put forward. What is specific for human beings is that they are creative individuals with a responsibility for others and a capacity for concern for their fellows. These qualities can be realized through work.

In my view, "the activity line" is therefore preferable. This standpoint assumes that work can make a great contribution towards human self realization. Work belongs to the fundamental conditions of human existence and it is one of the activities which is characteristic of human beings. Through work, it is possible to realize what is species specific for human beings.

292

To begin with we can realize ourselves as rational and conscious beings through our work. Characteristic for human beings as a species is our consciousness, our capacity for self consciousness and our capacity to plan our acts on the basis of consciously held values. As rational beings, we can realize ourselves not only through devoting ourselves to cultural activities and philosophical thinking. In contrast to a Platonic theory, I hold that we can cultivate and develop our consciousness also through our daily work.

As Karl Marx maintains, all work is subject to human planning. It is an activity which is carried out in order to achieve certain human purposes. It is intended to result in a product which initially exists in our imagination.[6] Human work is in this sense a conscious activity whereby human beings can realize their capacity for purposive action. One of the purposes which can be attained through work, is also that we realize ourselves as self conscious beings. As a result, working conditions ought to be organized so that work really becomes a purposive activity. Every individual contribution to work ought to be organized so that it includes not only routine manual work but also conscious planning. Each and every one ought to have scope for intelligence, imagination, creativity and initiative in their work. If it is impossible to organize work in this way, human beings become alienated from themselves as a species.

Through work, we can realize the specifically human also in another respect. The fact that human beings are created in the image of God, does not only mean that they are conscious beings. They are also stewards with the task of ruling over the world and of assuming responsibility for other living creatures. Work can also in this sense contribute to human self realization. Through their work, human beings can fulfil their task of ruling over the world.

It is a view of this type which is to be found in John Paul II's encyclical *Laborem exercens*. There it is stated that human beings are made in the image of God, in particular through receiving from the Creator the task of ruling over the earth. By carrying out this task, human beings mirror God Himself in his activities as Creator. This occurs through work. In their work, human beings are required to imitate God by participating in his act of creation. In this way, work also belongs to that which distinguishes human beings from other living beings. Through this activity, as persons cooperating with others, they can also realize their nature as beings made in the image of God.[7]

The activity line is thus a view which is not confined to Protestant theology. A Lutheran doctrine of vocation has in general beeen combined with a critique of the contemplation line which we have encountered in Thomas Aquinas. Today, however, several Protestant theologians criticize the activity line. At the same time several Catholic moral theologians maintain that work is an activity by which we can actualize those properties which are specifically human.[8]

Work can also contribute to our realization of what is specifically human, in a third respect. As creatures made in the image of God, human beings have a capacity to go beyond themselves and show concern for other human beings. This capacity can also be realized by producing in their work things which are valuable for other people. In this way, there is a close connection between the purpose of work as a means of serving fellow human beings and its purpose as a means for self realization.

A clear exposition of this connection has been given by the Catholic economist, E F Schumacher. He holds that work has three purposes. Namely (a) to produce necessary and useful goods and services (b) to enable each and every one to use and develop their talents and skills and (c) to do it in such a way that we assist other human beings and co-operate with others.[9]

These three purposes are closely interrelated. An aim of human existence, Schumacher holds, is that human beings should fulfil themselves as divine beings. In order to attain such fulfilment, human beings require an activity where they employ their gifts in a way supportive of other human beings. This can be through work. It is an activity which ennobles both the product and the producer. When human beings in their work serve their fellow men, the divine element in their nature is active. By accomplishing what is valuable for others by this activity, their personalities are formed and they realize themselves.[10]

Thus work can contribute to realizing human beings' species specific qualities in three respects. Simultaneously work can also contribute to self realization in a completely different sense. Through work, the individual person can use and develop their own individual talents and capacities. This standpoint I have called "the self actualization line". It constitutes, according to my view, an important complement to the activity line.

The self actualization line is a fundamental viewpoint in the socio-technical view of work. It maintains that work in itself ought to contribute to the satisfaction of needs on the part of the person engaging in it. All the five types of needs which Maslow enumerates in his theory of needs ought to be provided for. Work ought to satisfy our needs for security, intercourse and esteem. Moreover its purpose should also be to satisfy our need for self realization in the sense that each and every one ought to be able to develop their individual talents in their work.[11]

We human beings do not simply have certain common qualities and capacities. Each and every one of us also has unique talents and capacities, gifts and resources. We ought to use and develop them in such a way that they benefit other human beings. This can come about through our work. A presupposition for this is, however, that our tasks and working conditions are organized in such a way that it is possible to use and develop our individual talents.

The value of work

What value then has work in relation to other human activities? The answer to this question depends on the aims which are realizable through our work. Human work is not namely an end in itself which is valuable independently of its potential use. In this sense, it does not have an intrinsic value. On the other hand, work is valuable if it promotes a good purpose. The value of this activity is determined by what it accomplishes. If work realizes one or several good purposes, we value it highly. The value we place in work in relation to other human activities is therefore dependent upon the aims which it can attain.

There are theories which ascribe to work a relatively low value in comparison to other activities. This is true for a Platonic theory and a Tayloristic theory of work. They both hold that the purpose of work is merely to provide resources for our maintenance and to pursue other activities in our leisure time. It is through these leisure activities that we attain happiness and satisfaction and therefore such activities are more valuable than work.

In my opinion, this view is unacceptable. Work is a means of obtaining economic resources for the satisfaction of needs in our leisure time. But it also has other purposes. It is also a means of serving our fellow human beings and of developing specifically human qualities. If work also realizes these aims, it is – relatively considered – a highly valuable human activity.

First of all, work is valuable as an instrument for God's continuous act of creation. A Christian theory of work, in my view, is based upon a doctrine of creation and a view of man according to which human life is a gift from God. According to this view, Divine creation is a process which still continues and which is carried on not least with the help of human work. Human work is an activity whereby God provides human beings with the necessities of life, transforms nature and creates human civilization. It therefore has a high value in relation to other activities.

Secondly, work is valuable as a means of serving our fellow human beings. A Christian theory of work is, in my opinion, based upon a social ethical theory according to which we ought to promote justice and strive for what is good for all human beings. It is therefore a further purpose of work to produce things which are valuable for others. If work in this way is a means of expressing our love for other human beings, it is valuable. Inasmuch as it is an activity which allows us to produce things which other people need, it enjoys a high value.

Thirdly, work is also valuable as an activity whereby the persons engaged in the work can satisfy their own needs. According to the principle of goodness, we ought to strive both for what is good for others and for what is good for ourselves. For this reason, work ought to provide a reward for the person engaging in it. Through work, the latter is able to satisfy social needs. Moreover it is an activity whereby we can satisfy our needs for self actualization in the sense that we can develop our individual talents. To the extent that work satisfies these two needs, it is a valuable activity. It is then good as a means for the person engaging in it to satisfy their need for community and self actualization.

Fourthly, work is valuable as an activity which in a deeper sense contributes to human self realization. A Christian theory of work is, in my opinion, based upon a view of man according to which the specifically human consists in a capacity for rationality, a responsibility for other living beings and a capacity for concern for our fellow humans. These specifically human qualities can be realized in work. Because it is an activity through which we can realize that which characterizes human beings as a species, work is something valuable.

Now as Marx maintains, in certain social systems work is a curse which occasions feelings of displeasure in the person engaged in it. The conditions under which work is carried out are then organized in such a way that they prevent human self realization. In other social systems, however, work can contribute to our self realization as conscious beings with a capacity for concern for others. When working conditions take this form, work appears as something valuable.

Work is thus valuable for four reasons. It is good as an activity through which we participate in the divine work of creation, accomplish what is good for others and promote both the satisfaction of our own needs and our self realization as human beings. There are also other human activities which contribute to our achievement of these four goals. Such activities have therefore also a high value. Work, however, is valuable because it is one of the activities which contributes to the attainment of these goals.

This holds for very different types of human work. These goals can be achieved both through intellectual activities and through manual labour of different kinds. There is no reason generally for ascribing a lower value to manual labour than to intellectual labour. A criterion for the value of work is, however, that it really does contribute to the attainment of these four goals. A necessary precondition that work is good, is that it is a means for serving our fellow human beings and of promoting both the satisfaction of needs and the self realization of the person engaging in it.

It seems therefore difficult to provide a general evaluation of all types of work in all types of social structure. The value of different types of work would rather seem to vary in these different respects. It is possible and desirable to realize these four goals through work. In fact, however, work is not carried out under conditions allowing for all these goals to be attained in all these respects. Different types of work realise these goals to varying degrees.

Certain types of work are valuable as a means of providing valuable products although they do not themselves provide any great satisfaction of needs. Others are valuable as a means of satisfying the employees' needs for community and personal development without resulting in products of greater value. Some types of work are valuable as means for us to realize ourselves as rational and responsible beings while others do not promote such self realization. The value of different types of work, therefore, varies in different respects.

Because we seldom succeed in achieving all the goals which we strive for through our work, we do not always value our work more than certain other activities. What can be said generally, however, is that not all types of work are purely means of obtaining life's necessities. For this reason, work is not ascribed in general a lower value than other human activities.

Motivation to work

What motivates human beings to work? What is it that makes us work hard and efficiently? This is a question for psychology. Theology and ethics have no independent contribution to make to the discussion of this problem. Inasmuch as contemporary Christian work ethicists deal with this problem, they in general align themselves with different theories of motivation which have been developed within psychology.

At the same time, there is, however, a connection between these psychological theories of motivation and different views of the purpose of work. Differing theories in industrial psychology involve in general different views about the purpose and value of work. In the writings of Elton Mayo, J A C Brown and other exponents of the human relations school, we encounter not only the view that there are social stimuli which make us work hard and efficiently. They also hold that the purpose of work is to satisfy social needs. In the writings of Fred E Emery, Einar Thorsrud, Bertil Gardell and other representatives of the socio-technical school, we encounter not only the view that it is the drive towards self actualization which provides the motivation to work. They also hold that work ought to be a means of satisfying higher psychological needs.[12]

Different psychological theories of motivation are also combined with different theories of human nature. They contain different views about the nature of human needs. A Tayloristic theory is most interested in the human drive to satisfy certain physiological needs while the theory of the human relations school is mostly interested in human social needs. A socio-technical theory maintain that human beings also strive to satisfy their needs for self-esteem, and self actualization.

Theologians who within the framework of Christian work ethics, try to judge the different theories of motivation, usually do so on the basis of a critical evaluation of these theories' views regarding the purpose of work and theories of human nature. Thus we have seen that Oldham in several respects accepts the theory of the human relations school. It is a viewpoint which is closely related to a view of man which attaches great importance to the fact that human beings are social beings; they do not exist as isolated individuals but form part of a social community. We have also seen that Brakelmann in several respects accepts a socio-technical theory. Like this, he holds that the purpose of work is not to realize certain qualities which are species-specific but to develop individual talents.

In my opinion, the purpose of work is not simply to obtain life's necessities. For this reason, I cannot accept a Tayloristic theory of motivation. What gets us to work hard, is not simply the desire for economic reward so that we can satisfy our physiological needs outside work. Nor is the purpose of work merely to satisfy the social needs of the employee. For this reason, I maintain that the human relations school theory is inadequate. Our motivation to work effectively derives not merely from the expectations of the work group to which we belong.

The social ethical theory I have proposed contains a pluralistic theory of value according to which welfare in the sense of the satisfaction of needs is one of the intrinsic values we ought to promote. Like A H Maslow, I hold that the needs we ought to try to satisfy are (1) physiological needs (2) the need for security (3) the need for community and love (4) the need for self-esteem and the esteem of others and (5) a need for self actualization. Maslow's theory of needs is combined with a theory of motivation which I also find acceptable. According to this, we are motivated to work not merely through the desire to satisfy our physiological needs, our need for security and our social needs but also through the desire to satisfy our needs for self-esteem and self actualization. It is this kind of theory of motivation which is associated with a socio-technical theory of work.[13]

Work ethical recommendations

In the previous chapter, I have proposed a social ethical theory which is based both upon common human experiences and upon those theoretical views which make up a Christian philosophy of life. In this chapter, I have proposed a theory of the meaning of work which is based upon a doctrine of creation, a realistic view of man and a Christian social ethical theory.

These two theories in turn provide a foundation for certain work ethical recommendations. The latter are also based upon certain empirically testable assertions about matters of fact. Within the framework of the present investigation, it is impossible to test the assertions about the probable consequences of different courses of action. However, I shall discuss which more general views about the employment problem, the wages question, the organization problem, the participation question and the system question are compatible with my proposals for a social ethical theory and theory of the meaning of work.

As regards the employment problem, I have in Chapter 8 argued against the work sharing line. This viewpoint is combined with too pessimistic view of the possibility of getting rid of unemployment. It is also combined with too low a valuation of work. As a tool for God's continuous act of creation and as a means of achieving what is valuable for others, work has a high value. It is also valuable as a means for satisfying needs and for self realization on the part of the person engaging in it. For this reason, a reduction in working hours and work sharing do not constitute a satisfactory solution to the employment problem.

In my view, the full employment line is a more reasonable standpoint. This presupposes that society ought to strive for and try to maintain full employment. All who are able and willing to work, should be given work. This viewpoint is based upon the theory of the meaning of work which I have put forward. Through work, human beings participate in God's continuous act of creation and can accomplish those things which are valuable to other human beings. Work is also valuable as a way of satisfying needs and as a means for self realization. For this reason, it is desirable that every person able and willing to work is given the opportunity to do so. Those who become unemployed, are deprived of an opportunity of participating in the divine creation, of serving their fellows and of realizing themselves as human beings.

This view does not imply that human worth is dependent upon the fact that human beings work. Every human being has a unique value already as a creature made in the image of God. They are not deprived of this value when they become unemployed. They have also an opportunity of achieving what is valuable for other human beings through activities other than paid work. A person who is unemployed, however, is deprived of one of the activities which contributes in a major way to the satisfaction of our needs and to our self realization. For this reason, unemployment is something which should be avoided as far as possible.

Since work has great importance for human beings, every human being has the right to work. As a being created in the image of God, every human being has a responsibility for the world around them and a capacity to contribute in common with others to building human society. For this reason, every human being has the right according to their capacity to make such a contribution. Those who hold political and economic power have a responsibility for ensuring that each and everyone who can work, has work that is suited to their capacities. The social community involves complex cooperation to create the necessary conditions for the mutual satisfaction of needs and human civilization. Nobody ought to be involuntarily excluded from this cooperation.

As regards the wage question, I have criticized the merit line in Chapter 8. This standpoint is combined with a view of man which lays too much stress upon the factual differences that exist between human beings and fails to pay sufficient attention to the equal value of all human beings. It is also combined with a view of justice which I cannot accept. According to my view, it is just as far as possible to treat all human beings as equal and thereby to overlook the factual differences which exist between them.

The equal wages line is therefore more reasonable. It presupposes that one ought to strive for a wage policy which takes into account the needs of each and every one and treats all human beings as equal. This viewpoint is based upon a view of man which attaches great importance to the equal value of all human beings. It is also based upon a social ethical theory which stresses the principle of just distribution. According to this principle, it is just that welfare is distributed equally unless an unequal distribution is to the advantage of those worst placed.

This principle of justice is compatible with a wage policy which takes into account the differing qualifications and accomplishments of employees. In order to increase welfare for all human beings, it may be necessary to take into account these factors. At the same time, however, it is desirable to minimize wage differences as far as possible so that welfare does not become too unevenly distributed. In order for differences with respect to merit to be justified, it is required that it entails increased welfare for those worst placed.

As regards the organization problem, I have made a number of criticisms in Chapter 8 of the human relations line. This viewpoint is combined with a justified criticism of Taylorism and its goals of the division of labour and far reaching rationalization. At the same time, however, it does not give sufficient indications of how work should be alternatively organized.

The socio-technical line seems to me to be a more reasonable standpoint. It asserts that work ought to be organized so that it provides scope for job enlargement, job rotation, job enrichment and partly self determining work groups. The employees ought to obtain varying types of task and influence over how their own work ought to be carried out. At the same time, work ought to be skilled which entails, for example, that those who have a manual job, must be allowed to participate in its intellectual planning.

This viewpoint is based upon a theory of the meaning of work according to which an aim of work is to promote the satisfaction of needs and the self-realization of the employees. Through work, the persons engaged in it, ought to be able to satisfy their social needs and their needs of self actualization. It is reasonable to suppose that such a satisfaction of needs through work is promoted by a work organization which allows a high degree of self-determination and tasks involving variety and skill.[14] Moreover those engaging in work ought to be able to realize themselves in their work as rational beings. This presupposes a work organization which allows manual workers to participate in its intellectual planning.

As regards the participation question, I have in Chapter 8 rejected the consultation line. This is associated with a view of man which attaches too great an importance to the factual differences between human beings. The belief in the equal value of all human beings, in my view, is difficult to combine with a defence of a hierarchical order in economic life. The consultation line is also combined with a view of the meaning of justice which I find unacceptable. According to my view, it is just that as far as possible power is distributed equally and that if it is distributed unequally, then it is linked to positions which are open to all.

For this reason, the participation line seems a more reasonable alternative. According to this, employees ought to obtain influence not only over their own work but over more far reaching decisions affecting company activities. The employees ought to particpate in the decisions made at company level, departmental level and work place level. They can exercise this influence both individually and via trades union representatives.

This standpoint is based upon a view of man which attaches great importance to the equal value of all human beings. All human beings as creatures made in the image of God, have a responsibility for the world around them and a capacity for concern for others. For this reason they ought to participate in political and economic power. The participation line is also based upon a social ethical theory which stresses the importance of a principle of just distribution. This principle holds that it is just to strive as far as possible for an equal distribution of power.

The participation line is also based upon a theory of the meaning of work according to which it is part of the purpose of work to promote the satisfaction of needs and self realization of the employees. With increased participation, the satisfaction of the needs for self-esteem and self actualization on the part of the employees, will probably correspondingly increase. There is also a greater probability that work will become a conscious activity through which employees can realize themselves as rational beings if they obtain real influence over more far reaching company decisions.

Finally as regards the system question, I have in Chapter 8 criticized the indifference line. It is also possible to come to a decision about this work ethical problem on the basis of the social ethical theory and the theory of the meaning of work which I have proposed. However, it is doubtful if these two theories by themselves provide sufficient guidance for deciding whether to adopt the reform or the socialization line.

Different economic systems permit different solutions of the question of how scarce resources are to be allocated. They suggest different methods to decide which goods and services are to be produced and how incomes and welfare are to be distributed. Few today would recommend a straightforward planned economy. It is combined with a considerable bureaucracy which threatens both political and economic democracy. Thereby a planned economy also constitutes a threat to those individual rights which are based upon the principle of the equal value of all human beings.

A market economy therefore provides a superior solution to the allocation of resources. It has also been highly effective in protecting the freedom of the individual and in increasing social welfare. At the same time, a purely market economy does not seem to be acceptable. Within so called neo-liberalism, a far reaching limitation of state economic intervention has been advocated in order to permit a completely free and unregulated market. Such a viewpoint is open to two objections.

First of all, it conflicts with the view that we ought to strive for a just distribution of welfare. A pure market economy tends to create inequality between human beings. It contains no mechanisms for reducing social differences. In order to promote the welfare of all human beings and the just distribution of welfare, the state also ought to have an economic responsibility. An overall regulation of the economy is also needed within the framework of a market economy.[15]

Secondly, the goal of a completely free market is linked to a too individualistic view of man. It defends the freedom of the individual and stresses their individual responsibility. But human beings are also social beings who are part of a community. We are all dependent upon one another for the satisfaction of our fundamental needs. Therefore cooperation and combined planning is also required in economic life.[16]

For these reasons, I hold that the market economy requires to be combined with overall state economic planning in order to promote a just distribution of welfare. In order to promote social justice, the social ownership of certain means of production can also be necessary even if the market economy is primarily linked to private ownership. However, before any final decision can be taken with regard to which economic system should be adopted, a more detailed examination of economic problems than that which has been possible in this investigation, is required.

Here I have principally wished to provide examples of work ethical recommendations which seem to be compatible with the social ethical theory and the theory of the meaning of work which I have proposed. They are recommendations which can be motivated on the basis of a principle of human value, a principle of goodness and a principle of justice. At the same time, they can also be motivated on the basis of a view that the purpose of work is both to promote the best interests of others and the self realization and satisfaction of the needs of those engaging in it.

These work ethical recommendations are also compatible with a Christian view of man and other theoretical views making up a Christian philosophy of life. It does not imply that they are specifically Christian. These recommendations are also based upon common human experiences and considerations. The work ethical theory which I have proposed is in this sense humanely based. At the same time, I hold that it is an example of a work ethical theory which is well integrated with a Christian system of belief.

Summary

In the present study of Protestant work ethics, I have dealt with three fundamental problems. The first is concerned with the types of argument which can be adduced for work ethical recommendations i.e. recommendations about how working life should be shaped. The second deals with the kinds of consideration which form a basis for the two philosophy of life components making up a work ethical theory, namely a theory of the meaning of work and a constructive social ethical theory. The third problem is concerned with the relationship between Christian work ethics and work ethics based upon alternative philosophies of life. This problem is closely linked to the question of which parts of a Christian system of belief form the basis of a Christian work ethical theory.

An analysis of work ethical theories

A primary aim of the investigation has been to analyse the work ethical theories to be found in six contemporary Protestant theologians, namely Emil Brunner, J H Oldham, Tor Aukrust, Arthur Rich, Günter Brakelmann and John Atherton. My intention has been to clarify the content of their work ethical recommendations, their theories of the meaning of work and their social ethical theories. Moreover I have tried to clarify the type of reasons they adduce for these work ethical theories. Above all, I am interested in the relationship between their work ethical theories and their views of man and the other theoretical views which form part of a Christian philosophy of life.

In *Chapter 1* I describe the form taken by work ethics in earlier Protestant theology. It is preceded by way of background by a presentation of the views of work to be encountered in the Bible and in Thomas Aquinas. According to Martin Luther's doctrine of vocation, human beings, by virtue of their labour, are co-workers of God in His continuous act of Creation. The aim of

304

work is to serve one's neighbour which entails that we must follow the seven commandments which make up the second table of the Decalogue. Foremost among them is the fourth commandment according to which we ought to obey our superiors. According to Luther, work is suffering in the imitation of Christ and the worker is not expected to derive any personal reward from it. As Max Weber has shown, the doctrine of vocation in Calvinist theology is combined with a doctrine of double predestination. Thereby hard work is conceived as a sign that one belongs to the elect.

Several contemporary Protestant work ethicists have proposed revisions of the doctrine of vocation. They hold that the patriarchal view of society associated with Luther's presentation of the doctrine, is unacceptable. They also hold that the purpose of work is not simply to accomplish something which is valuable for others but also to provide the worker with some personal reward. At the same time, there are also several contemporary theologians who maintain that the doctrine of vocation should be completely replaced by an alternative formulation of Christian work ethics. They hold that this doctrine embodies too high an evaluation of work. In their view, activities other than paid work are also highly valuable and thus they advocate work sharing as a means of solving the employment problem.

In *Chapter 2*, I analyse those work ethical recommendations which are to be found within contemporary Protestant theology. In regard to the employment problem, Emil Brunner adopts a full employment line acccording to which society ought to try to safeguard full employment. Günter Brakelmann and John Atherton adopt instead a work sharing line, according to which unemployment can be reduced through a reduction in working hours and through work sharing. As regards the wage question, Emil Brunner puts forward a merit line according to which it is just that those who achieve more, receive more. Tor Aukrust puts forward an equal wages line according to which wages should be fixed so as to ensure as far as possible that respect is paid to each and every one's needs and the equal value of all human beings.

As regards the organization problem, i.e. the question of what form the organization of work should take, one encounters in Brunner, Oldham and Aukrust a human relations line according to which too far reaching division of labour and rationalization should be avoided. In Rich and Brakelmann, we find instead a socio-technical line according to which one ought to strive for job enlargement, job rotation, job enrichment and partially self determining work groups. With respect to the participation question, Brunner adopts a consultation line according to which the board of the company should make its decisions after consultation with the employees. Aukrust, Rich and Brakelmann adopt on the other hand a participation line according to which the employees should be allowed to participate in the decision-making bodies of the company. As regards the system question i.e. the form to be taken by the economic system, we encounter in Oldham and Aukrust an indifference line which leaves the choice between a capitalist and socialist system open. In Brunner and Rich, there is a reform line according to which a capitalist system with certain fundamental changes is desirable. Brakelmann and Atherton advocate instead a socialization line according to which democratic socialism is the goal to be aimed at.

What kinds of consideration then form the basis for these differing work ethical recommendations? First of all, they are combined with differing theories of the meaning of work. The full employment line for example in Brunner, is combined with the view that work belongs to the divine order of creation whereas the work sharing line in Atherton is combined with the view that activities other than work are highly valuable. Secondly they are combined with differing social ethical theories. The equal wages line in Aukrust is combined with a definite view of what justice implies and the participation line in Rich is combined with the view that participation is a fundamental social ethical criterion.

These work ethical recommendations are thirdly combined with certain empirically testable assertions about matters of fact. Thus for example the socialization line in Brakelmann and the work sharing line in Atherton are combined with assertions about the consequences of socialism and the possibilities for achieving full employment. Fourthly they are also based upon different theories of human nature. In Oldham for example, the human relations line is combined with the view that human beings are persons and members of a community.

In *Chapter 3*, I analyse the theories about the meaning of work which are to be found in the six theologians I study. These take somewhat differing views about the purpose of work. In Brunner, Oldham, Aukrust and Brakelmann, we encounter a creation line according to which the purpose of work is in part to allow human beings to be God's co-workers in His work of creation and in part to serve their fellows. In Rich and Atherton, we encounter instead a fellowship line according to which the purpose of work is solely to serve one's fellow human beings. As regards the relation of work to human self realization, Brunner and Rich adopt an activity line according to which work is an activity whereby human beings can realize what is specific for them as a species. Oldham and Brakelmann adopt on the other hand a contemplation line according to which human beings realize what is specific for them as human beings primarily through activities other than work. Aukrust and Atherton advocate a self actualization line according to which work can contribute to the individual's development of their own individual talents and potentials.

The question of the value of work is answered differently depending upon what one holds to be the purpose of work. The theologians who adopt the activity line ascribe to work a somewhat higher value than those who adopt the contemplation line. In these theologians we also encounter differing attitudes to the doctrine of vocation in the Protestant tradition. In Brunner and Oldham, we find a tradition line according to which the views which make up the doctrine of vocation are still acceptable. In Aukrust and Rich, we have a revision line according to which the doctrine of vocation requires to be thoroughly revised before it can be accepted. Atherton and also to some extent Brakelmann advocate instead an alternative line according to which the doctrine of vocation ascribes to work too high a value and for this reason, must be replaced by an alternative Christian work ethic.

What kinds of consideration form the basis for these differing theories of the meaning of work? First of all, they are combined with different social ethical theories. The creation line in Brunner is combined with the view that an act is right if it is in agreement with God's orders of creation, while the fellowship line in Rich is combined with the view that fellowship is a fundamental social ethical criterion. Secondly, they are combined with different theories of human nature. Oldham combines a contemplation line with the view that human beings realize themselves as true human beings in relation to God while Rich combines an activity line with the view that human beings are creative and responsible persons.

These theories of the meaning of work are thirdly combined with other theoretical views which form part of a Christian system of belief. This is true of Brunner, Oldham, Aukrust and Brakelmann who base their theories of work upon the doctrine of creation. Fourthly, these theories are also combined with certain common human experiences and considerations which are not part of the philosophy of life held. Such considerations for example form the basis of the critique of the doctrine of vocation which is combined both with the tradition line in Aukrust and the alternative line in Atherton.

In *Chapter 4*, I analyse the social ethical theories to be found in contemporary Protestant work ethicists. The theologians I study hold different views about what characterizes a right political act. J H Oldham adopts a deontological act ethics according to which an act is right if it is in agreement with the will of God in the concrete situation. Günter Brakelmann adopts a deontological theory of rights according to which the Christian ideal of love and the principle of the equal value of all human beings give rise to certain fundamental rights. Emil Brunner adopts a monistic theory of duty according to which a right political act is in agreement with the divine order of creation and thereby promotes a just distribution. In Aukrust, we encounter instead a pluralistic theory of duty according to which there are several fundamental moral principles which together specify what is the criterion for a right act. Among these principles are the principle of liberty, a principle of justice and the commandment to love one's neighbour.

Arthur Rich adopts a subject related theory according to which the criterion for a right act is not only certain properties in the act but also the presupposition that it is carried out by a person with good properties of character. He specifies certain criteria for what is good for human beings, namely critical distance, relativity, relationality, fellowship, participation, concern for the rest of creation and participation in the creation. In John Atherton, there is to be found a teleological ethics according to which a right political act ought to promote a mutual dependence and the common good. The majority of the theologians I study, hold that the same criteria are valid both for a right political act and a right private act. Emil Brunner, however, adopts a dualistic thesis according to which the norm system which applies to social ethics differs from that which applies within individual ethics.

What types of consideration form the basis for these differing social ethical theories? First of all they are combined with differing theories of human nature. Oldham's act ethics is based upon the view that human beings are free and responsible persons who realize themselves in communion with God while Atherton's teleological ethics is combined with the view that human beings are social beings who are mutually dependent upon their fellow human beings. Secondly, they are combined with other theoretical views which make up a Christian philosophy of life. However, there are different components in a Christian system of belief which form the basis for these ethical theories. Brunner's social ethical theory is based upon a doctrine of creation while Oldham and Brakelmann base their ethics upon Christology. The ethics of Aukrust and Rich is based upon eschatology while Atherton's social ethics is based upon a doctrine of the Church.

Thirdly these social ethical theories are also in certain cases combined with common human experiences and considerations i.e. those which do not form part of a philosophy of life or which can be common for human beings with differing philosophies of life. This is the case with Brunner, Aukrust and Atherton. Common human considerations of this kind, however, do not form the basis of social ethics in Oldham, Rich and Brakelmann. Their ethics is instead strongly dependent upon the Revelation in Christ.

In *Chapter 5*, I clarify the different theories of human nature which form the basis of the work ethical theories to be found in the writings of the theologians I study. These theologians adopt somewhat different views about what is common and specific for human beings as a species. According to Brunner, human beings are characterized specifically by rationality and freedom while Rich emphasizes that the status of human beings as creatures made in the image of God is linked to their responsibility for the world about them. J H Oldham stresses human freedom and human capacity for communion with God while Brakelmann links the status of human beings made in the image of God with both their capacity for communion with God and their responsibility for the world around them. Aukrust also holds that human beings as creatures made in the image of God are expected to rule over nature while Atherton stresses that human beings are active beings who are placed in a social community.

These differing views are combined with differing views about the question whether work belongs to that which is characteristic for human beings as a species. Brunner and Rich adopt an activity line according to which work helps to define human beings as a species. Oldham and Brakelmann, on the other hand, adopt a contemplation line according to which the capacity for communion with God is more characteristic than work in defining human beings. Views differ too about what consequences the status of human beings as creatures made in the image of God has for how the good ought to be distributed. In Emil Brunner, we encounter a difference line according to which a just distribution ought to take account of the factual inequalities which exist between human beings. In Tor Aukrust, we encounter instead an equality line according to which a just distribution must take account of the fact that all human beings are equal before God.

The theologians I deal with, differ also about what it implies for human beings to be sinners. Oldham, Rich and Brakelmann adopt a relatively pessimistic view of man in the sense that they ascribe to human beings a limited capacity to see what is right and good. Brunner, Aukrust and Atherton have a greater belief in human capacity to attain moral insight independently of the Revelation.

What are the kinds of considerations which form the basis of these differing theories of human nature? First of all, they are combined with other theoretical views which form part of a Christian philosophy of life. Oldham and Aukrust base their view of man upon a doctrine of creation. The view of man in Brunner and Brakelmann is based both upon a doctrine of creation and upon Christology. Rich's view of man is based upon Christology and eschatology while Atherton bases his theory of human nature upon a doctrine of the Church. Secondly the view of man in certain contemporary Protestant work ethicists is also based upon common human experiences and considerations. This is so in the case of Oldham and Rich.

In *Chapter 6*, I examine in more detail which components in a Christian philosophy of life form the basis for theories of human nature, theories of the meaning of work and social ethical theories to be found in the writings of the work ethicists I study. In Brunner, we encounter a theology of creation work ethics according to which work ethics is primarily based upon the doctrine of creation. His social ethical theory and theory of the meaning of work are closely related to a doctrine of what characterizes the divine orders of creation. In Oldham and Brakelmann, we encounter instead a Christological work ethics according to which work ethics is based primarily upon Christology. Oldham holds that it is through the Revelation in Christ that we attain insight into what in a concrete situation of choice is the Will of God. Brakelmann holds that Christology motivates both an ideal of love and a principle of the equal value of all human beings which in turn gives rise to certain human rights.

Rich adopts an eschatological work ethics according to which work ethics is principally based upon eschatology. His social ethical theory is based upon the hope in the coming Kingdom of God which gives rise both to a critical distance to existing social orders and to certain views about what constitute humane forms of social institutions. Aukrust advocates instead a trinitarian work ethics according to which work ethics is based both upon the doctrine of Creation and upon Christology and eschatology. His social ethical theory, his view of man and his theory of the meaning of work are closely related to the doctrine of creation while simultaneously he holds that we achieve moral insight also through the Revelation in Christ and primarily through the Sermon on the Mount. It is within this eschatological framework, Aukrust holds, that we must understand the natural law.

John Atherton holds an ecclesiological work ethics according to which work ethics is primarily based upon a doctrine of the Church. His social ethical theory is based upon the view that the Church as the Body of Christ constitutes a community based upon mutual interdependence. As such, the Church is an example of the community which ought to exist in society. Atherton's view of man is based both upon this doctrine of the Church and upon a doctrine of creation.

Upon the basis of these ideas, in *Chapter 7* I deal with the question of how Christian work ethics is related to humane work ethics i.e. one which is combined with another philosophy of life and common human considerations about what is good for human beings. Three of the theologians I deal with, adopt a humanely based ethics according to which common human experiences form at least a partial basis for social ethical principles and values. One of these is Emil Brunner who combines a humanely based social ethics with a theology of creation ethics. His social ethics is strictly humane in the sense that the Revelation does not provide in any sense guidance for our political acts. Within individual ethics, Brunner adopts a contrast theory according to which Christian ethics has a completely different content from humane ethics. Within social ethics, however, he adopts an identity theory according to which the content of Christian ethics agrees with ethical views which are combined with other philosophies of life.

Tor Aukrust combines a humanely based ethics with a trinitarian ethics. He adopts a partially Revelation based ethics according to which common human experiences provide a certain moral insight but at the same time eschatology and the Revelation in Christ give us a deeper insight into what characterizes a right act. He also adopts a combination theory according to which there are certain moral viewpoints which are shared by Christians and non-Christians while allowing that there are certain primary social ethical criteria which are specifically Christian.

John Atherton, on the other hand, combines a humanely based ethics with an ecclesiological ethics. He also adopts a partially Revelation based ethics according to which common human experiences form the basis for certain fundamental values while at the same time there are certain specifically Christian reasons for certain parts of the contents of social ethics. Like Aukrust, Atherton adopts a combination theory which holds that certain values are common for human beings with differing philosophies of life while at the same time positing a specifically Christian contribution to morality.

Three of the theologians I deal with, adopt a strictly theological ethics according to which ethics is not based upon any common human experiences but is purely based upon the Revelation in Christ. One of these is J H Oldham who combines a strictly theological ethics with a contrast theory according to which the content in Christian ethics is completely different from the content in a humane ethics. This standpoint he combines with a Christological ethics according to which social ethics is chiefly based upon Christology.

Arthur Rich combines a strictly theological ethics with a combination theory and an eschatological ethics. Although Christian belief provides a specific contribution to morality, he holds that the maxims and criteria which are formulated within the framework of a Christian social ethics, can also be adopted by human beings with another philosophy of life. At the same time, he bases his social ethics primarily upon eschatology and common human considerations play no part.

Günter Brakelmann, on the other hand, combines a strictly theological ethics with a combination theory and a Christological ethics. He also holds that there are moral principles and values which are common for Christians and non-Christians. At the same time he holds that the ideal of love, the principle of human value and fundamental rights are based not upon common human experiences but purely upon the Revelation in Christ.

A construction of a work ethical theory

A second purpose of my investigation has been to formulate my own proposal for a Christian work ethical theory. This is based upon my critical examination of six existing work ethical theories. Proceeding from certain criteria for a reasonable ethical theory, I have proposed a constructive social ethical theory and specified what types of consideration in my view ought to form the basis for a Christian social ethics. On the basis of this theory, I have also put forward a formulation of a Christian theory of the meaning of work and I have also discussed the work ethical recommendations this can give rise to.

In *Chapter 8*, I have made a critical examination of the work ethical theories under discussion on the basis of a number of criteria for a reasonable ethical theory. These are (a) the universalizability criterion according to which an ethical judgement which is valid is universalizable (b) the consistency criterion which states that an acceptable ethical theory does not contain any logical contradictions (c) the integration criterion according to which an ethical theory which is reasonable is integrated with our other convictions and knowledge and (d) the experience criterion which asserts that an acceptable ethical theory includes statements which agree with human experiences of various kinds. My examination is also based upon two criteria for an authentically Christian ethical theory, namely a Bible criterion and a tradition criterion.

According to the integration criterion, a reasonable work ethical theory must agree with an acceptable view of man. I hold that the defining property of human beings is that they are rational and free beings with a capacity for communion with God, concern for other human beings and responsibility for the world around them. Such a view entails the rejection of both Oldham and Brakelmann's contemplation line as well as Brunner's difference line. In contrast to Oldham, Rich and Brakelmann's pessimistic view of man, I also hold that every human being has a certain capacity to attain moral insight independently of the Revelation.

A fundamental objection to the strictly theological ethics to be found in Oldham, Rich and Brakelmann, is that it conflicts with a more realistic view of man. In my view, ethics is based not only upon the Revelation but also upon common human experiences and considerations. Unlike a contrast theory, I also maintain that there are moral views which are shared by human beings with different philosophies of life. At the same time, in contrast to the identity theory, I hold that Christianity provides a specific contribution to morality.

In my opinion, a Christological ethics and an eschatological ethics are not acceptable because they are combined with a strictly theological ethics. A theology of creation ethics of the type to be found in Brunner fails to provide scope for Christianity's specific contribution to social ethics. It would appear difficult to combine an ecclesiological ethics of the type to be found in Atherton, with the view that ethics is humanely based.

Both Brunner's dualistic thesis and Oldham's deontological act ethics conflict in my view with the universalizability criterion. In criticizing Brunner's theory of justice, I hold that the criterion for a right political act is not simply that it promotes justice while in my criticism of Atherton's teleological ethics, I hold that the criterion for a right act is not simply that it entails good consequences. In contrast to Rich's subject related theory, I argue that an act can be right even if the acting subject does not have good character properties.

In my examination of these theories of the meaning of work, I criticize the alternative line because it is combined with misleading views about the nature of the doctrine of vocation. In contrast to the fellowship line, I hold that the purpose of work is also to take part in God's continuous act of Creation. In contrast to the contemplation line, there is reason for maintaining that work contributes to human self realization. Finally, I make certain objections to the work sharing line of Atherton and Brakelmann, Brunner's merit line and consultation line, as well as to the human relations line of Brunner, Oldham and Aukrust.

In *Chapter 9*, I put forward a constructive social ethical theory. This is based upon what I call a realistic view of man. According to this, all human beings are created in the image of God which implies that they are rational and free beings with a capacity for moral insight, a capacity for communion with God and a capacity for concern for other human beings and responsibility for other living beings. This view of man is combined with an activity line according to which work belongs to what is specifically human and an equality line which holds that a just distribution is one which takes into account the equal value of all. According to a realistic view of man, every human being is also a sinner which implies that their capacity for moral insight and acting rightly is limited even if it is not entirely lacking.

Such a realistic view of man motivates a humanely based social ethics according to which ethics is partly based upon common human experiences and considerations. Like Aukrust, I advocate a partially Revelation based ethics according to which the Revelation clarifies and lends depth to the moral insights which are based upon common human experiences. This standpoint can be easily accommodated with a combination theory according to which certain moral views are common for Christians and non-Christians while at the same time the content in Christian ethics is partly specific.

My proposal for a partially Revelation based ethics is combined with a trinitarian ethics. To begin with, social ethics is based upon a doctrine of creation which explains why human beings with different philosophies of life, are nonetheless agreed about certain moral principles and values. Moreover social ethics is also based upon eschatology and partly also upon Christology which entails that Christian ethics has a content which differs in part from the ethical theories which make up other philosophies of life.

The social ethical theory I propose is a pluralistic theory of duty with three fundamental moral principles. The first is a principle of the equal value of all human beings which asserts that all human beings have an equally high value in themselves independently of race, sex, nationality and social class. The second is a principle of goodness according to which we ought to strive for what is good and avoid that which is bad for all human beings. The third is a principle of justice which states that we ought to strive for a just distribution of the good.

I combine these principles with a pluralistic theory of value according to which we ought to promote three intrinsic values. These are (a) physical and spiritual well being (b) welfare in the sense of the satisfaction of needs and (c) self-realization in the sense of a realization of those properties which are common and specific for all human beings. A just distribution of the good implies in my view an equal distribution of fundamental liberties and rights. Thereby each and every one can enjoy the same possibilities for realizing specifically human characteristics. It is also just that welfare is distributed equally unless an unequal distribution is to the greatest advantage of those worst placed.

As regards the relationship between individual and social ethics, I argue on behalf of a modified monistic thesis. The universalizability criterion forms a basis for the view that the same system of norms holds both for individual and social ethics. A realistic view of man, however, suggests that these ethical ideals cannot be realized through political action to the same extent as through private acts. Within social ethics, we must content ourselves with striving for realizable approximations of the Christian ideal of love.

In *Chapter 10*, I put forward a proposal for a Christian theory of the meaning of work. On the basis of the view of man and the social ethical theory I have proposed, I argue for a revised formulation of the doctrine of vocation. According to this, work has been divinely ordained and belongs to the fundamental conditions for human existence. Through work, human beings participate in the divine work of creation, and the purpose of work is also to serve our fellow human beings. However on the basis of the principle of human value and the principle of justice, I hold that the doctrine of vocation must be stripped of the patriarchal character it has in Lutheran theology. To fulfil the commandment to love our neighbour, does not primarily mean to obey our superiors. In contrast to the doctrine of vocation in

Luther, I hold also that the task of serving others through work does not imply that the worker must abstain from some personal reward. According to the principle of goodness, we ought to promote that which is good both for others and for ourselves.

A revised doctrine of vocation of this kind can be combined with certain views making up a Marxist theory of work. Like such a theory, it maintains that work can contribute to human beings realizing those properties which characterize the human species. It can also be combined with certain views in the socio-technical theory of work. Like this theory, it maintains that work can and ought to be a source for the satisfaction of needs, even of those who carry it out.

In my view, work has thus four purposes. The first is to constitute an instrument for God's continuous act of creation. The second is to fulfil the commandment to love one's neighbour by producing goods and services which satisfy the needs of other human beings. The third is to satisfy certain needs also in those who do the work. And the fourth is to realize those properties which are common and specific for human beings as a species.

This implies that I advocate an activity line according to which work can contribute to human self realization. Through their work, human beings can realize themselves as rational beings with a capacity for purposive action. Thereby they can also realize themselves as beings with capacities for displaying concern for other human beings and with a task of assuming responsibility for other living beings. This standpoint also allows itself to be combined with a self actualization line which holds that work can contribute to the development of the individual's talents.

In my view, work has a relatively high value. It is valuable as an instrument for God's continuous act of creation and as a means of serving our fellow human beings. It is also valuable as an activity which can contribute to human self realization. In these different respects, different types of work, however, differ in value depending upon the goals they help to achieve.

The social ethical theory and the theory of the meaning of work which I have proposed, form a basis in turn for certain work ethical recommendations. The value which is attached to work provides support, in my opinion, for a full employment line. The principle of human value and the principle of justice form the basis both for an equal wages line and a participation line. As regards the organization problem, the view that work ought to be a source for the satisfaction of needs, motivates a socio-technical line. However, before a more definitive position can be adopted with respect to the various work ethical problems, a more thorough investigation of the probable consequences of alternative lines of action is required.

In putting forward my own proposal for a work ethical theory, I have also answered the three problems which are central to the present investigation. The work ethical recommendations I adopt are based upon (a) a social ethical theory (b) a theory about the meaning of work (c) empirically testable assertions about matters of fact and (d) a view of man. The theory of the meaning of work which I have proposed is based upon (a) a social ethical theory (b) a theory of human nature (c) other theoretical views in a Christian philosophy of life, primarily a doctrine of creation and (d) certain common human experiences and considerations. The social ethical theory I have proposed is based upon (a) a theory of human nature, namely what I have called a realistic view of man (b) other theoretical views in a Christian philosophy of life, namely both a doctrine of creation and Christology and eschatology and (c) certain common human experiences and considerations which are based upon certain proposed criteria for a reasonable ethical theory.

How then does Christian work ethics relate to work ethical theories which are combined with other philosophies of life? The social ethics which I have suggested, is humanely based. It is combined both with a combination theory and a trinitarian ethics. Since social ethics is based upon a doctrine of creation, it is also based upon certain common human experiences and considerations. Because it is based upon Christology and eschatology, it also acknowledges that there is a specifically Christian contribution to social ethics. This implies that I advocate a theological clarificatory ethics according to which the Revelation in Christ clarifies and lends depth to those moral principles and values which are common for human beings with differing philosophies of life.

Notes

Introduction

[1] For a more detailed discussion of the connection between ethics and morals, see Hospers, John: Human Conduct. Problems of Ethics. Second Edition. Harcourt Brace Jovanovich, New York 1982, pp 1 ff.

[2] This is the kind of work ethics which we have dealt with in the project "Arbetslivets etik "(The ethics of working life) at the theological and philosophical institutions of Uppsala University. We have analysed the arguments put forward by the Swedish Trade Union Confederation (LO), the Central Organisation of Salaried Employees (TCO) and the Swedish Employers' Confederation (SAF) for their views about a just wage, participation in decision-making, computerisation and industrial organisation, with the aim of clarifying the ideological basis of their arguments. The result of our research is presented in Collste, Göran: Makten, moralen och människan. En analys av värdekonflikter i debatten om medbestämmande och löntagarstyre. Acta Universitatis Upsaliensis, Uppsala Studies in Social Ethics, Uppsala 1984; Grenholm, Carl-Henric: Arbetets mål och värde. En analys av ideologiska uppfattningar hos LO, TCO och SAF i 1970-talets debatt om arbetsorganisation och datorisering. Acta Universitatis Uppsaliensis, Uppsala Studies in Social Ethics, Uppsala 1987; Strömberg, Bertil: Arbetets pris. Rättvis lön och solidarisk lönepolitik. Uppsala universitet, Uppsala 1989.

[3] Göran Collste, op. cit., pp 69 f, 74 f, 100 f and 102 showed that both LO and TCO made use of the arguments about increased job satisfaction and greater efficiency in advocating participation in decision-making. LO and TCO also made use of similar arguments on behalf of a democratic organization of work. See Grenholm, Carl-Henric, op.cit., pp 117 ff, 124 f 141 f, 142 ff.

[4] For job satisfaction as a fundamental intrinsic value in the LO and TCO material, see Grenholm, Carl-Henric, op. cit., pp 339 ff. Göran Collste, op. cit., pp. 71 ff, 101 f, shows that LO and TCO also put forward a rights argument in favour of participation in decision-making.

[5] In Grenholm, Carl-Henric, op. cit., pp. 290 ff and 305 ff, I show that LO's and TCO's view of the purpose and value of work exemplifies many of the features of what I call a socio-technical theory of work, which develops certain views in contemporary industrial psychology.

[6] Anders Jeffner in Bråkenhielm, Carl Reinhold et al., (ed.): Aktuella livsåskådningar, del 1. Existentialism, marxism. Doxa, Stockholm 1982, p. 13. In an earlier definition, Anders Jeffner places another restriction on the theoretical convictions which make up a philosophy of life. He suggests that they are those which influence the central value system and /or the basic attitude in a way which the person holding the philosophy of life is prepared to accept. See Jeffner, Anders: Livsåskådningsforskning. Department of Theology Uppsala University, Uppsala 1974, pp. 17 f. This definition of philosophy of life is also consistent with that adopted by Ragnar Holte in Människa Livstolkning Gudstro. Teorier och metoder inom tros- och livsåskådningsvetenskapen, Doxa, Lund 1984, p. 27. But as Jeffner maintains in Aktuella livsåskådningar, del 1, there are good reasons for holding that what is characteristic for the

theoretical convictions which make up a philosophy of life is that they give us an overall view of human beings and the world around them.

[7] In Grenholm, Carl-Henric: Arbetets mening. En analys av sex teorier om arbetets syfte och värde. Acta Universitatis Upsaliensis, Uppsala Studies in Social Ethics, Uppsala 1988, pp. 85 ff, 96 ff and 152 ff, I analyse the ethical theories upon which the views of Plato, Aristotle and Luther about the purpose and value of work are based.

[8] In Grenholm, op.cit., pp. 200 ff I analyse the view of man which forms the basis of Marx's view of the purpose and value of work.

[9] I have provided a detailed analysis of Luther's doctrine of vocation in Grenholm, Carl-Henric: Arbetets mening, pp. 166 ff.

[10] Weber, Max: Die protestantische Ethik und der Geist des Kapitalismus. Verlag von JCB Mohr (Paul Siebeck), Tübingen 1934, pp. 163 ff.

[11] A short summary of Thielicke's ethics of work can be found in Kramer, Rolf: Arbeit. Theologische, Wirtschaftliche und soziale Aspekte. Vandenhoeck & Ruprecht, Göttingen 1982, pp. 24 f. For the presentation which follows, see also the short survey of evangelical work ethics in Kramer, Rolf: "Protestantismus". Article in Ethik der Religionen – Lehre und Leben. Herausgeben von Michael Klöcher und Udo Tworuschka. Band 2: Arbeit. Vandenhoeck & Ruprecht, Kösel 1985, pp. 52 ff.

[12] Barth, Karl: Die Kirchliche Dogmatik. Dritter Band: Die Lehre von der Schöpfung. Viertel Teil (III/4). Evangelischer Verlag AG Zollikon, Zürich 1951, pp. 540 and 543 f. A short summary of Barth's ethics of work is to be found in Kramer, Rolf: Arbeit, pp. 25 ff.

[13] A short summary of Bonhoeffer's ethics of work is to be found in Kramer, Rolf: Arbeit, p. 28. Ronald H Preston puts forward his view in Church and Society in the Late Twentieth Century. The Economic and Political Task. The Scott Holland Lectures for 1983. SCM Press Ltd., London 1983, pp. 130 ff and 102 ff. A short survey of evangelical work ethics after the First World War has been given by Martin Honecker in "Arbeit VIII. 18. – 20. Jahrhundert". Article in Theologische Realenzyklopädie. Band III. Walter de Gruyter, Berlin, New York 1978, pp. 650−653.

[14] Another contribution to this discussion has been made by Wolfgang Schröter in Fahlbusch, Wilhelm – Przybylski, Hartmut – Schröter, Wolfgang: Arbeit ist nicht alles. Versuche zu einer Ethik der Zukunft. SWI-Verlag, Bochum 1987. Schröter takes the view that Laborem exercens overestimates the importance of work and defines the concept of work too narrowly. See Fahlbusch – Przybylski – Schröter, op.cit., p 49.

[15] Chenu, MD: Pour une théologie du travail. Éditions du Seuil, Paris 1955, p. 12. Kaiser, Edwin G: Theology of Work. The Newman Press, Westminster, Maryland 1966, pp. 232−249. An interesting discussion of this theology of work is to be found in Francis Schüssler-Fiorenza's article "Religious Beliefs and Praxis: Reflections on Catholic Theological Views of Work", which appears in Baum, Gregory (ed): Work and Religion. Concilium 131. T& T Clark, Edinburgh 1980, pp. 92 ff. A further contribution to this discussion is that of Herbert McCabe in his article "Theology and Work – A Thomist View" in Todd, John M (ed): Work. Christian Thought and Practice. Darton, Longman & Todd, London 1960, pp. 211 ff.

[16] A good insight into these differences is given by James M Gustafson in his book, Protestant and Roman Catholic Ethics. Prospects for Rapprochement. SCM Press Ltd., London 1978. He deals *inter alia* with fundamental philosophical differences, Gustafson op. cit., pp. 60 ff and with fundamental theological differences, Gustafson op. cit., pp. 95 ff.

[17] However Robert Lowry Calhoun proposes a highly interesting revision of the doctrine of vocation in God and the Day's Work. Christian Vocation in an Unchristian World. Association Press, New York 1943, pp. 47 ff.

[18] I intend however to analyse Wogaman's theories in a forthcoming study of contemporary Christian social ethics.

[19] Siegfried Karg has written an excellent introduction to Rich's thought in Christliche Wirtschaftsethik vor neuen Aufgaben. Festgabe für Arthur Rich zum siebzigsten Geburtstag. Herausgegeben von Theodor Strohm. Theologischer Verlag, Zürich 1980, pp. 474 ff. Rich also contributes an interesting article to this volume. See also Karg, Siegfrid: "Arthur Rich.

Wegweisend für den Dialog zwischen Ethik und Wirtschaft". Article in Gegen die Gottvergessenheit. Schweizer Theologen im 19. und 20. Jahrhundert. Herder, Basel 1990.
[20] Brakelmann has also written another two books which are of interest in the present context.
One is Die soziale Frage der 19. Jahrhunderts. Luther-Verlag, Witten (1962) 1971, 4th Edition
in which he examines different socialist movements and the evangelical church's attempt to
deal with the social question at the end of the 19th century. This leads him to look at the social
thinking of Johan Hinrich Wichern, Rudolf Todt, Adolf Stöcker and Friedrich Naumann. The
other book is Protestantismus und Politik. Werk und Wirkung Adolf Stoeckers. Hans Christians Verlag, Hamburg 1982. In this latter work, Brakelmann deals with Stoecker's criticism of
German social democracy as part of the struggle against enlightenment and modern secular-
ism in general.
[21] I intend, however, to devote attention to Preston's social ethical theory in a forthcoming study
of contemporary Christian social ethics.
[22] I am not aware of any earlier comparative analysis of the work ethics of these theologians.
More cursory surveys of contemporary Protestant ethics of work have been given by Rolf
Kramer in Arbeit, wirtschafliche und soziale Aspekte and by Martin Honecker in "Arbeit.
VII. 18−20. Jahrhundert" which appeared in Theologische Realenzyklopädie (TRE). Band
III. A cursory survey also appears in Ballard, Paul H: Towards a Contemporary Theology of
Work. Collegiate Centre of Theology, University College, Cardiff 1982, pp 14 ff. In contrast to
these, the present study provides a deeper analysis of the views which form the basis of
differing work ethical theories.
[23] These theories have been analysed in Grenholm, Carl-Henric: Arbetets mening, pp. 396 ff,
403 ff, 406 ff, 408 ff and 411 ff.
[24] See Grenholm, op.cit., pp. 444 ff.

Chapter 1: The doctrine of vocation in Protestant theology

[1] Parts of the material in this chapter have previously appeared in Grenholm: Carl-Henric:
"Synen på arbetet i kristen tradition". Article in Arbetets värde och mening. Edited by: Per
Sörbom, Riksbankens Jubileumsfond, Liber förlag, Stockholm 1980, pp. 29 – 55.
[2] See e.g. Blumberg, Paul: Företagsdemokrati i sociologisk belysning. Rabén & Sjögren,
Stockholm 1971, pp. 59 f; Zetterberg, Hans L: Arbete, livsstil och motivation. Svenska
arbetsgivareföreningen, Stockholm 1977, pp. 9 f; Fryklindh, Pär Urban – Johansson, Sven
Ove: Arbete och fritid. Den lekande människan – en framtidsdröm som blir verklighet?
Sekretariatet för framtidsstudier, Karlstad 1978, pp. 49 f.
[3] Engnell, Ivan: "Arbete". Article in Svenskt Bibliskt Uppslagsverk, published by Ivan Engnell, volume I, Nordiska uppslagsböcker, Stockholm 1962, pp. 114 ff.
[4] Richardson, Alan: The Biblical Doctrine of Work. SCM Press Ltd., London, 1952, pp. 24 f
and 27 f. Richardson entertains the doubtful belief that there is a religious unity in the Bible,
which explains why he writes about "the Biblical doctrine" of work and takes no notice of the
the differences which exist between the different parts of the Scriptures
[5] Bienert, Walther: Die Arbeit nach der Lehre der Bibel. Eine Grundlegung evangelischer
Sozialethik. Evangelisches Verlagsverk GMBH, Stuttgart 1954, pp. 57 ff and 392. A similar
interpretation of Genesis 3 has also been given by the Catholic theologian Edwin G Kaiser in
Theology of Work, p. 60.
[6] Agrell, Göran: Work, Toil and Sustenance. An Examination of the View of Work in the New
Testament, Taking into Consideration Views Found in the Old Testament, Intertestamental
and Early Rabbinic Writings. Verbum/ Håkan Ohlssons, Lund 1976, pp. 7 ff.
[7] Agrell,op. cit., pp. 16 ff.
[8] Agrell,op. cit., pp. 68 ff.
[9] Agrell,op. cit., pp. 95 ff.
[10] Agrell,op. cit., pp. 116 ff.

[11] Agrell,op. cit., pp. 150 ff.

[12] Bienert, Walther: Die Arbeit nach der Lehre der Bibel, p. 246.

[13] Agrell, Göran: Work, toil and sustenance, pp. 3, 132 ff and 139.

[14] An exposition of the views of the Church Fathers with regard to work will be found in Kaiser, Edwin G: Theology of Work, pp. 81ff. For Clement of Alexandria and Origen, see Kaiser, op. cit., pp. 85 ff and 87 f, respectively.

[15] Kaiser, op. cit. pp. 88 ff.

[16] Kaiser, op. cit., pp. 110 f and 119.

[17] Kaiser, op. cit. pp. 116 and 112 ff.

[18] A Swedish translation of this monastic rule will be found in Gellerstam, Göran – Görman, Ulf: Textsamling till kristendomens historia med allmän idéhistoria. Studentlitteratur, Lund 1977, p. 70.

[19] Thomas Aquinas: Summa theologica II – II q 182 a 1. I have made use of the German edition of Aquinas, Die deutsche Thomas-Ausgabe, Bd 23 and 24, hg von der Albertus-Magnus-Akademie, Walberberg bei Köln, F H Kerle, Heidelberg – München, Anton Pustet, Graz – Wien – Salzburg 1954 and 1952.

[20] Thomas Aquinas, op. cit., II – II q 182 a 2.

[21] The exposition of Thomas' views which Jan Karlsson gives in Arbetets frihet och förnedring. En antologi, AWE/Gebers, Stockholm 1978, p. 77, is therefore particularly misleading.

[22] Thomas Aquinas: Summa theologica II – II q 187 a 3.

[23] My exposition of Luther's doctrine of vocation is based upon the analysis which is given in Grenholm, Carl-Henric: Arbetets mening, pp. 143–187.

[24] Luther, Martin: Kirchenpostille (1522). WA 10:I,1, 308:6 – 309:13. To be found in Luther, Martin: Werke. Kritische Gesamtausgabe (WA). 10. Band, Erste Abteilung, 1. Hälfte. Herman Böhlaus Nachfolger, Weimar 1910. An exposition of the concept of "vocation" in Luther is given in Wingren, Gustaf: "Beruf. II. Historische und ethische Aspekte". Article in Theologische Realenzyklopädie, Band V, Walter de Gruyter, Berlin & New York 1980, and in Wingren, Gustaf: Luthers lära om kallelsen, Gleerups, Lund 1960, 3rd Edition, pp. 15 f.

[25] Luther, Martin: Von den guten Werken (1520), WA 6, 242:19–25; WA 6, 204:13–24; WA 6, 205:14–22; WA 6, 227:19–22. To be found in Luther, Martin: Werke. Kristische Gesamtausgabe (WA). 6. Band, Herman Böhlau, Weimar 1888.

[26] Luther, op. cit., WA 6, 250:22–28.

[27] Luther, Martin: Deutsch Catechismus (Der Grosse Katechismus, 1529), WA 30:I, 158:34 – 159:18; WA 30: I,168:21–28; WA 30:I, 160:25–32. To be found in Luther, Martin: Werke. Kritische Gesamtausgabe (WA). 30. Band, Erste Abteilung, Hermann Böhlaus Nachfolger, Weimar 1910.

[28] Luther, Martin: Ermahnung zum Frieden auf die zwölf Artikel der Bauerschaft in Schwaben (1525), WA 18, 310:19–36. To be found in Luther, Martin: Werke. Kritische Gesamtausgabe (WA). 18. Band, Herman Böhlaus Nachfolger, Weimar 1908.

[29] Luther, Martin: Ob Kriegsleute auch in seligem Stande sein können (1526) WA 19, 692:14 – 630:2. Luther, Martin: Von weltlicher Oberkeit, wie weit man ihr gehorsam schuldig sei (1523), WA 11, 271:11–26. Luther, Martin: In epistolam S Pauli ad Galatas Commentarius (1535), WA 40:I, 207:17 – 208:25. Ob Kriegsleute auch in seligem Stande sein können (1526) can be found in Luther, Martin: Werke, Kritische Gesamtausgabe (WA). 19 Band, Hermann Böhlaus Nachfolger, Weimar 1897. Von weltlicher Oberkeit (1523) is to be found in Luther, Martin: Werke, Kritische Gesamtausgabe (WA). 11 Band, Hermann Böhlaus Nachfolger, Weimar 1900. In epistolam S Pauli ad Galatas is to be found in Luther, Martin: Werke, Kritische Gesamtausgabe (WA). 40 Band, erste Abteilung. Hermann Böhlaus Nachfolger, Weimar 1911.

[30] Luther, Martin: In epistolam S Pauli ad Galatas Commentarius (1535), WA 40:I, 40:16 – 41:26; WA 40:I, 392:19 – 393:29; WA 40:I, 46:19–22, 28–30.

[31] Luther, Martin: Von weltlicher Oberkeit, wie weit man ihr gehorsam schuldig sei (1523), WA 11, 259:7-21; WA 11, 260:16–20. Luther, Martin: Krucigers Sommerpostille, WA 22, 62:12–25. Krucugers Sommerpostille is to be found in Luther, Martin: Werke, Kritische

Gesamtausgabe (WA). 22 Band, Hermann Böhlaus Nachfolger, Weimar 1929.

[32] Luther, Martin: Predigten des Jahres 1529, WA 29, 564:23−34. Appears in Luther, Martin: Werke, Kritische Gesamtausgabe (WA). 29. Band, Hermann Böhlaus Nachfolger, Weimar 1904.

[33] Luther, Martin: Deutsch Catechismus (Der Grosse Katechismus, 1529), WA 30: I,183:30 − 184:33; WA 30:I, 204:10−29; WA 30:I, 136:4−17.

[34] Luther, Martin: In epistolam S Pauli ad Galatas Commentarius (1535), WA 40: I, 174:12 − 175:24. See also Luther, Martin: Der 147. Psalm, Lauda Jerusalem, ausgelegt (1532), WA 31:I, 436:7-19. To be found in Luther, Martin: Werke, Kritische Gesamtausgabe (WA). 31. Band, Erste Abteilung, Hermann Böhlaus Nachfolger, Weimar 1913. Cf. Wingren, Gustaf: Luthers lära om kallelsen, pp. 133 ff and 138 f.

[35] Luther, Martin: Von weltlicher Oberlichkeit, wie weit man ihr gehorsam schuldig sei (1523), WA 11, 258:1-11; WA 11, 260:30 − 261:8. Luther, Martin: Deutsch Catechismus (Der Grosse Katechismus, 1529), WA 30:I, 178:33 − 179:9. Luther, Martin: In epistolam S Pauli ad Galatas Commentarius (1535), WA 40:I, 51:21−31. Luther, Martin: Krucigers Sommerpostille, WA 22, 295:4−26; WA 22, 297:8−20.

[36] Luther, Martin: An die christlichen Adel deutscher Nation von der christlichen Standes besserung (1520), WA 6, 409: 5−10. Appears in Luther, Martin: Werke, Kritische Gesamtausgabe (WA). 6. Band, Hermann Böhlau, Weimar 1888.

[37] Luther, Martin: Von den guten Werken (1520), WA 6, 270:27 − 271:9; WA 6, 271:28 − 272:4.

[38] Luther, Martin: Von den guten Werken (1520), WA 6, 263:5−28. Luther, Martin: Deutsch Catechismus (Der Grosse Katechismus, 1529), WA 30:I, 148:23−27; WA 30:I, 152:19−35; WA 30:I, 153:29−36; WA 30:I, 156:36 − 157:11. Luther, Martin: In epistolam S Pauli ad Galatas Commentarius (1535), WA 40:I, 543:27−34; WA 40:I, 309:27 − 310:17.

[39] Luther, Martin: Tractatus de libertate christiana (1520), WA 7, 65:6 − 66:6; WA 7, 66:6−28. To be found in Luther, Martin: Werke, Kritische Gesamtausgabe (WA). 7. Band, Hermann Böhlaus Nachfolger, Weimar 1897.

[40] Luther, Martin: An die Pfarrhern wider den Wucher zu predigen, Vermahnung (1540), WA 51, 404:20−34, WA 51, 412:23−28. Appears in Luther, Martin: Werke, Kritische Gesamtausgabe (WA). 51. Band, Hermann Böhlaus Nachfolger, Weimar 1914.

[41] Luther, Martin: Hauspostille (1544), WA 52, 415:32 − 416:14. Appears in Luther, Martin: Werke, Kritische Gesamtausgabe (WA). 52. Band, Hermann Böhlaus Nachfolger, Weimar 1915.

[42] Luther, Martin: Tractatus de libertate christiana (1520), WA 7, 65:10 − 66:38.

[43] Seppo Kjellberg gives a short exposition of the Lutheran and Calvinist doctrine of vocation in "Max Webers tolkning av Luthers arbetsetik". Article in Eripainos, Sosiologia 24, 1987:1, pp 15−21.

[44] Here I accept the view of the Calvinist doctrine of vocation which Max Weber presents in Die protestantische Ethik und der Geist des Kapitalismus, pp. 88 ff. R H Tawney has also given an exposition of the doctrine of vocation in Calvinist Theology in Religion and the Rise of Capitalism. A Historical Study, Penguin Books, London (1926) 1980, pp. 111 ff.

[45] Weber, Max: Die protestantische Ethik und der Geist des Kapitalismus, pp. 103 ff.

[46] Weber, op. cit., pp. 30 ff, 202 f.

[47] Weber, op. cit., pp. 82 f, 204 ff.

[48] Weber, op. cit., pp. 169 ff.

[49] Weber, op. cit., pp. 171 ff.

[50] Weber, op. cit., pp. 165 ff.

[51] Weber, op. cit., pp. 176 f, 190 ff.

[52] Weber, op. cit., p 198.

[53] Weber, op. cit., pp. 200 f. Weber's thesis has been the object of lively discussion and has also been sharply criticized. RH Tawney had already in Religion and the Rise of Capitalism, pp. 312 ff, pointed out that Weber gives a simplistic view of both the capitalist spirit and Calvinist theology. In his book, Ekonomi och religion, Kurt Samuelsson challenges Weber in detail. However I cannot accept the arguments which Samuelsson adduces against Weber's thesis.

Samuelsson overlooks the differences betwen Thomas Aquinas' ethics of work and the doctrine of vocation in Protestant theology and he also overlooks the fact that the latter doctrine's Calvinist formulation is special because it is linked to the doctrine of predestination. In his arguments, Samuelsson also overlooks the fact that Weber's thesis does not entail that the Calvinist morality of work was a necessary precondition for the growth of capitalism. It seems probable, as Samulesson maintains, that economic progress and a development of capitalism can take place without the capital-owners being industrious and thrifty. On the other hand, Samuelsson seems to overlook the fact that it is an advantage for the capital-owners if their employees are busy and industrious since they are then productive and are more easily managed. See Samuelsson, Kurt: Ekonomi och religion. Rabén & Sjögren, Stockholm (1957), 1965, pp. 52 f, 92 ff, 102 f, 162 ff.

[54] Aukrust, Tor: Mennesket i samfunnet. En sosialetikk. Bind II. Forlaget Land og Kirke, Oslo 1968, 2nd edition, pp. 129 ff.

[55] Calhoun, Robert Lowry: God and the Day's Work, pp. 24 f, 47 ff. The American ethicist George F Thomas has proposed a similar revision of the doctrine of vocation. He holds that the purpose of work is to serve one's neighbour by producing goods and services which satisfy human needs. At the same time the purpose of work is also to allow those who carry it out to realise themselves and develop their talents through a creative activity. Thomas maintains that according to the doctrine of vocation the aim of serving one's neighbour is primary while the aim of achieving personal fulfilment is secondary. See Thomas, George F: Christian Ethics and Moral Philosophy. Charles Scribner's Sons, New York 1955, pp. 319 f.

[56] Jönsson, Ludvig: Människan, mödan och arbetsglädjen. Rabén & Sjögren, Stockholm 1974, pp. 56 f.

[57] Jönsson, op. cit., pp. 58, 51 f.

[58] Martin Honecker provides an exposition of the different currents in the Protestant ethics of work in "Arbeit VII. 18. – 20. Jahrhundert". This appears as an article in Theologische Realenzyklopädie. Band III., pp 639–657. A corresponding survey has been provided by Rolf Kramer in Arbeit. Theologische, Wirtschaftliche und soziale Aspekte, pp. 24 ff. Rolf Kramer has also given a briefer presentation in "Protestantismus" which appears as an article in Ethik der Religionen – Lehre und Leben. Band 2: Arbeit, pp. 52 ff.

[59] Thielicke, Helmut: Theologische Ethik. Band II, 1. Teil. JCB Mohr (Paul Siebeck), Tübingen 1955, pp. 398 f, 460 f.

[60] Thielicke, op. cit., pp. 449 f. See also the presentation of Thielicke in Kramer, Rolf: Arbeit, pp. 24 f.

[61] Barth, Karl: Die Kirchliche Dogmatik III/4, pp. 540 ff, 544 ff, 547 f, 552 f. See also the exposition of Barth's ethics of work in Kramer, Rolf: Arbeit, pp. 25 ff.

[62] Søe, NH: Kristelig etik. GEC Gads forlag, København 1962, 5th edition, pp. 288 f, 291 f.

[63] Kramer, Rolf: Arbeit, p 28.

[64] Wogaman,, J Philip: Economics and Ethics. A Christian Inquiry, SCM Press Ltd, London 1986, pp. 32 ff, 35 ff. Wogaman, J Philip: Christian perspectives on Politics. SCM Press Ltd, London 1988, pp. 68 f, 114 ff, 117 ff, 120 f.

[65] In Great Britain several clerical reports have made this criticism of the doctrine of vocation. One of these is Work or What? A Christian Examination of the Employment Crisis. Church Information Office, London 1977. Another is Work and the Future. Technology, World Development and Jobs in the Eighties. CIO Publishing, Church House, London 1979. The latter argues for work sharing through a reduced working week or through a reduced working year by extending vacations, while simultaneously criticizing what is called "the Protestant work ethic" i.e. the attitude to work which most closely approximates Baxter's formulation of the doctrine of vocation. See Work and the Future, pp. 26 f, 19 and 28. A similar critical discussion of the Protestant doctrine of vocation has also arisen in West Germany. Also there the criticism of this doctrine has been combined with the view that a reduction in working hours and work sharing is one way of dealing with increased unemployment. See for example Rainer Ledeganck's arguments for work sharing in Wenke, Karl Ernst (hrsg): Ökonomie und Ethik. Die Herausforderung der Arbeitslosigkeit. SWI Studienhefte 4, Haag und Herchen

Verlag, Frankfurt/Main 1984, pp. 121, 107 ff. Best provides an elucidatory sociological investigation of different methods of work sharing in order to reduce unemployment in Best, Fred: Work Sharing. Issues, Policy Options and Prospects. The WE Upjohn Institute for Employment Research. Kalamazoo, Michigan 1981. Best holds (op. cit., pp. 199 f) that certain forms of work sharing complement other job creation measures.

[66] Anthony, PD: The Ideology of Work. Tavistock Publications, London (1977) 1978, pp. 41 f, 44 f, 301 f, 315 f.

[67] Robertson, James: Future Work. Jobs, self-employment and leisure after the industrial age. Gower/Maurice Temple Smith, Aldershot, Hants 1985, pp. 15 f, 24 ff, 64, 87.

[68] Rose, Michael: Re-Working the Work Ethic. Economic Values and Socio-Cultural Politics. Batsford Academic and Educational, London 1985, pp. 41, 75 f, 83 f and 140 ff.

[69] Bleakley, David: In Place of Work... The Sufficient Society. A study of technology from the point of view of people. SCM Press Ltd., London 1981, pp. 41, 52.

[70] Bleakley, op. cit., pp. 72 f.

[71] Bleakley, op. cit., pp. 75 f.

[72] Bleakley, op. cit., pp. 81, 97 f.

[73] Bleakley, David: Work. The Shadow and the Substance. A reappraisal of life and labour. SCM Press Ltd., London 1983, pp. 73 ff, 79 ff.

[74] Bleakley, David: In Place of Work, pp. 92 ff, 96 f. Bleakley, David: Work. The Shadow and the Substance, pp. 63, 82 f. Bleakley, David: "Employment and the Theology of Work" which appears as an article in Davis, Howard – Gosling, David: Will the Future Work? Values for emerging patterns of work and employment. World Council of Churches, Geneva (1985) 1986, 2nd Edition, p 81.

[75] Bleakley, David: Work. The Shadow and the Substance, pp. 76 f. Bleakley, David: In Place of Work, p 54.

[76] Bleakley, David: Work. The Shadow and the Substance, p 40. Bleakley, David: In Place of Work, pp. 94 f.

[77] Clarke, Roger: Work in Crisis. The Dilemma of a Nation. The Saint Andrew Press, Edinburgh 1982, pp. 49, 72.

[78] Clarke, op. cit., pp. 14 ff, 87.

[79] Clarke, op. cit., pp. 109 f, 116 f.

[80] Clarke, op. cit., pp. 121, 125 f, 128 f, 136 f.

[81] Clarke, op. cit., pp. 140 f, 146 f.

[82] Clarke, op. cit., pp. 183, 173 f, 85 f.

[83] Clarke, op. cit., pp. 166 ff, 176 f.

[84] Clarke, op. cit., pp. 151 f, 188 f and XVIII.

[85] Clarke, op. cit., pp. 158 f.

[86] Clarke, op. cit., pp. 22 f, 25 f and 194 f.

[87] Clarke, op. cit., pp. 194 f.

[88] Clarke, op. cit., pp. 197 f.

[89] Clarke, op. cit., pp. 196 f.

Chapter 2: Work ethical recommendations

[1] Göran Collste gives a readable introduction to the employment problem in Arbete och livsmening. Petra Bokförlag, Arlöv 1985. See for example his discussion of different measures against unemployment in Collste, op. cit., pp. 57 ff.

[2] A penetrating treatment of the wage problem has been given by Bertil Strömberg in Arbetets pris. Rättvis lön och solidarisk lönepolitik. In this work, he analyses an argument put forward by the Swedish Trade Union Confederation (LO) for a solidarity-oriented wage policy, namely what he calls the "work difficulty principle". This states that it is just that A has a higher wage than B if and only if A's work is more difficult than B's work. See Strömberg, op. cit., pp. 46 f, 126 f.

[3] In Grenholm, Carl-Henric: Arbetets mål och värde, I have analysed the different ways in which the organization problem has been treated by the Swedish Trade Union Confederation (LO), The Central Organization of Salaried Employees (TCO) and the Swedish Employers' Confederation (SAF). Their different positions are indicated in Grenholm, op.cit., pp. 109 ff, 133 ff and 155 ff.

[4] In Makten, moralen och människan, Göran Collste has presented a detailed analysis of the different views concerning the participation question of the Swedish Trade Union Confederation (LO), The Central Organization of Salaried Employees (TCO) and the Swedish Employers' Confederation (SAF). He clarifies their different standpoints in Collste, op. cit., pp. 63 ff, 97 ff and 113 ff. My terminology is in accordance with that introduced by Collste in Collste, op.cit., pp. 30 f.

[5] Brunner, Emil: Das Gebot und die Ordnungen. Entwurf einer protestantisch-theologischen Ethik. Verlag von JCB Mohr (Paul Siebeck), Tübingen 1932, p 379.

[6] Brakelmann, Günter: Zur Arbeit geboren? Beiträge zu einer christlichen Arbeitsethik. SWI Verlag, Bochum 1988, pp. 104 f, 197 ff.

[7] Brakelmann, op.cit., pp. 201 ff.

[8] Brakelmann, op.cit., pp. 203 f.

[9] Brakelmann, op.cit., pp. 115 f.

[10] Atherton, John: Faith in the Nation. A Christian Vision for Britain. SPCK, London 1988, pp. 90 f.

[11] Atherton, op. cit., pp. 105 f.

[12] Atherton, op. cit., pp. 103 f.

[13] Clarke, Roger: Work in Crisis, pp. 87, 109 f, 121.

[14] Clarke op. cit., pp. 140 f, 146 f.

[15] Bleakley, David: In Place of Work, pp. 75 f, 72 f.

[16] Brunner, Emil: Gerechtigkeit. Eine Lehre von den Grundgesetzen der Gesellschaftsordnung. Zwingli-Verlag, Zürich 1943, pp. 201 f.

[17] Brunner, op. cit., pp. 203 f.

[18] Brunner, Emil: Das Gebot und die Ordnungen, pp. 392 f.

[19] Aukrust, Tor: Mennesket i samfunnet. En sosialetikk. Bind II, pp. 101 f.

[20] Aukrust op. cit., pp. 103 f.

[21] Aukrust op. cit., p 108.

[22] I have dealt with the rationalisation movement and its significance for Swedish social debate in Grenholm, Carl-Henric: Arbetets mål och värde, pp. 82 ff.

[23] Brunner, Emil: Das Gebot und die Ordnungen, p 379.

[24] Oldham, JH: Work in Modern Society. John Knox Press, Richmond, Virginia (1950), 1961, pp. 12 f.

[25] Oldham op. cit., pp. 14 f. Cf. Oldham op. cit., p 40.

[26] Aukrust, Tor: Mennesket i samfunnet, II, pp. 94 f, 110.

[27] Aukrust op. cit., pp. 97 f.

[28] Rich, Arthur: Mitbestimmung in der Industrie. Probleme – Modelle – Kritische Beurteilung. Eine sozialethische Orientierung, Flamberg Verlag, Zürich 1973, p 147.

[29] Rich op. cit., pp. 148 f.

[30] Rich, Arthur: Christliche Existenz in der Industriellen Welt. Eine Einführung in die sozialethischen Grundfragen der industriellen Arbeitswelt. Zwingli Verlag, Zürich (1957) 1964, 2nd edition, pp. 140 f, 238 f.

[31] Brakelmann, Günter: "Humanisierung der industriellen Arbeitswelt". Article in Theologische Realenzyklopädie (TRE), Band III. Walter de Gruyter, Berlin & New York 1978, pp. 658, 668. For Elton Mayo and the human relations school, see Grenholm, Carl-Henric: Arbetets mening, pp 304-341.

[32] Brakelmann, Günter: Zur Arbeit geboren?, pp. 84 f, 171 ff. Brakelmann, Günter: "Humanisierung der industriellen Arbeitswelt". TRE, Band III, pp. 658 f.

[33] Brakelmann, Günter: Zur Arbeit geboren?, pp. 84 f.

[34] Brakelmann, op. cit., pp. 186, 189.

[35] Brakelmann, op. cit., pp. 192 f, 120 f. Arthur Rich also argues that technological development should be aimed at humane purposes in Glaube in politischer Entscheidung. Beiträge zur Ethik des Politischen. Zwingli Verlag, Zürich 1962, pp. 101 ff, 108.

[36] Brunner, Emil: Das Gebot und die Ordnungen, pp. 399 f.

[37] Brunner, Emil: Gerechtigkeit, pp. 229 f.

[38] Brunner, op. cit., p 205.

[39] Brunner, op. cit., pp. 206 f.

[40] Aukrust, Tor: Mennesket i samfunnet, II, pp. 111 f.

[41] Aukrust op. cit., pp. 117 f.

[42] Aukrust op. cit., pp. 118f.

[43] Aukrust op. cit., p 119.

[44] Rich, Arthur: Mitbestimmung in der Industrie, pp. 41 f.

[45] Rich, op. cit., pp. 109 ff.

[46] Rich, op. cit., pp. 130 f.

[47] Rich, op. cit., pp. 147, 151.

[48] Rich, op. cit., pp. 168 f.

[49] Rich, op. cit., pp. 73 f. See also Rich, op. cit., pp. 210, 167 and 171 f.

[50] Rich, Arthur: Christliche Existenz in der industriellen Welt, pp. 258 f.

[51] Rich, Arthur: Mitbestimmung in der Industrie, pp. 109 ff.

[52] Rich, Arthur: Christliche Existenz in der industriellen Welt, pp. 34, 104.

[53] Rich, op. cit., pp. 43, 48, 74 f, 100 ff.

[54] Rich, op. cit., pp. 81, 84 f.

[55] Rich, op. cit., pp. 110 f, 113 f, 125. Rich also rejects two other proposed solutions, namely anti-industrialism (op. cit., pp. 107 f) and the attempt to make work unconscious (op. cit., pp. 127 f).

[56] Rich, op. cit., pp. 132 f, 135.

[57] Rich, op. cit., pp. 142 f, 148. See also Rich, Arthur: Mitbestimmung in der Industrie, pp 30 f.

[58] Rich, Arthur: Christliche Existenz in der industriellen Welt, p 258. Rich, Arthur: Mitbestimmung in der Industrie, p 208.

[59] Brakelmann, Günter: Abschied vom Unverbindlichen. Gedanken eines Christen zum Demokratischen Sozialismus. Gütersloher Verlagshaus Gerd Mohn, Gütersloh, pp. 83 f.

[60] Brakelmann, op. cit., p 90.

[61] Brakelmann, Günter: Zur Arbeit geboren?, pp. 154 f, 205 ff. Brakelmann, Günter: "Mitbestimmung am Ende?" Article in Christliche Wirtschaftsethik vor neuen Aufgaben, p 318 f.

[62] Brakelmann, Günter: Zur Arbeit geboren?, pp. 146 f.

[63] Brakelmann, op. cit., pp. 154 f.

[64] Brakelmann, Günter: Abschied vom Unverbindlichen, pp. 87 f. Brakelmann, Günter: Zur Arbeit geboren?, pp. 208 f.

[65] Brakelmann, Günter: Zur Arbeit geboren?, pp. 208 f, 157.

[66] Oldham, JH: Work in Modern Society, p 51.

[67] Oldham, op. cit., pp. 57 f.

[68] Oldham, op. cit., pp. 58 f.

[69] Oldham, op. cit., pp. 59 f.

[70] Aukrust, Tor: Mennesket i samfunnet, II, pp. 32 f.

[71] Aukrust, op. cit., pp. 33 f.

[72] Aukrust, op. cit., pp. 36 f.

[73] Aukrust, op. cit., pp. 46 f, 50 f.

[74] Aukrust, op. cit., p 55.

[75] Brunner, Emil: Das Gebot und die Ordnungen, pp. 383 f.

[76] Brunner, op. cit., p 387.

[77] Brunner, op. cit., pp. 386 ff, 384.

[78] Brunner, op. cit., pp. 406 f. Cf. the exposition of the injurious ethical effects of capitalism in Brunner, Emil: Der Kapitalismus als Problem der Kirche, Zwingli-Verlag, Zürich 1945, pp. 7 f.

[79] Brunner, Emil: Gerechtigkeit, pp. 208 f. Brunner, Emil: Der Kapitalismus als Problem der Kirche, pp.15 f.
[80] Brunner, Emil: Gerechtigkeit, p 209. Brunner, Emil: Der Kapitalismus als Problem der Kirche, p 10.
[81] Brunner, Emil: Der Kapitalismus als Problem der Kirche, pp. 14 f, 17, 22 f.
[82] Brunner, Emil: Gerechtigkeit, pp. 212 f. Brunner, Emil: Der Kapitalismus als Problem der Kirche, pp. 17 ff.
[83] Brunner, Emil: Gerechtigkeit, pp. 213 ff.
[84] Rich, Arthur: Christliche Existenz in der Industriellen Welt, pp 152, 155 f.
[85] Rich, op. cit., pp. 191 f.
[86] Rich, op. cit., pp 205, 209 ff, 212, 221 f.
[87] Rich, Arthur: Wirtschaftsethik, Band II. Marktwirtschaft, Planwirtschaft, Weltwirtschaft aus sozialethischer Sicht. Gütersloher Verlagshaus Gerd Mohn, Gütersloh 1990, pp. 341 ff.
[88] Rich, Arthur: Mitbestimmung in der Industrie, pp. 30 f.
[89] Rich, Arthur: Christliche Existenz in der Industriellen Welt, pp. 233 ff.
[90] Rich, op. cit., p 237. Rich, Arthur: Mitbestimmung in der Industrie, pp. 171 f.
[91] Brakelmann, Günter: Abschied vom Unverbindlichen, pp. 9 f, 54 f.
[92] Brakelmann, op. cit., pp. 59 ff.
[93] Brakelmann, op. cit., pp. 65 ff.
[94] Brakelmann, op. cit., pp. 78 ff.
[95] Brakelmann, op. cit., p 83.
[96] Brakelmann, op. cit., pp. 43 f, 45 ff.
[97] Brakelmann, op. cit., pp. 47 ff
[98] Brakelmann, op. cit., pp. 94 ff.
[99] Atherton, John: Faith in the Nation, pp. 52 f, 56.
[100] Atherton, op. cit., pp. 58 ff.
[101] Atherton, op. cit., pp. 62 f.
[102] Atherton, op. cit., pp. 64 f.
[103] Atherton, op. cit., pp. 107 ff.
[104] Atherton, op. cit., pp. 114 ff.
[105] Atherton, op. cit., pp 117, 122 ff.

Chapter 3: Theories of the meaning of work

[1] A more detailed formulation and discussion of these analytical questions is given in Grenholm, Carl-Henric: Arbetets mening. En analys av sex teorier om arbetets syfte och värde, pp. 38 ff. I have also suggested in Grenholm, op.cit., p. 36, a definition of the concept of work which is also relevant for the present investigation.
[2] A more detailed analysis of this theory is given in Grenholm, Carl-Henric: Arbetets mening, pp. 77–142 and 396 ff.
[3] A more detailed analysis of this theory is given in Grenholm., op. cit., pp. 188–263 and 403 ff.
[4] A more detailed analysis of this theory is given in Grenholm, op. cit. pp. 264–303 and 406 ff.
[5] A more detailed analysis of this theory is given in Grenholm, op. cit. pp. 304–341 and 408 ff.
[6] A more detailed analysis of this theory is given in Grenholm, op. cit., pp. 342–394 and 411ff.
[7] Brunner, Emil: Das Gebot und die Ordnungen, pp. 371 f.
[8] Brunner, op. cit., p 372.
[9] Brunner, op. cit., pp. 373 f.
[10] Brunner, op. cit., p 374.
[11] Brunner, op. cit., pp. 374 f.
[12] Brunner, op. cit., pp. 376 f.
[13] Brunner, op. cit., pp. 377 f.
[14] Brunner, op. cit., p 371.
[15] Brunner, op. cit., pp. 369 f.

[16] Oldham, J H: Work in Modern Society, pp. 8 f.
[17] Oldham, op.cit., pp. 44 f.
[18] Oldham, op.cit., pp. 49 f.
[19] Oldham, op.cit., p 51.
[20] Oldham, op.cit., pp. 52 f.
[21] Oldham, op.cit., pp. 27 f.
[22] Oldham, op.cit., pp. 55 f.
[23] Oldham, op.cit., pp. 54 ff.
[24] Oldham, op.cit., pp. 18 f.
[25] Oldham, op.cit., p 55.
[26] Oldham, op.cit., pp. 15 f.
[27] Oldham, op.cit., pp. 23 f.
[28] Oldham, op.cit., pp. 50 f and p 52.
[29] Aukrust, Tor: Mennesket i samfunnet, bind II, p 127.
[30] Aukrust, op. cit., pp. 127 f.
[31] Aukrust, op. cit., p 128.
[32] Aukrust, op. cit., p 129.
[33] Aukrust, op. cit., pp. 130 f.
[34] Aukrust, op. cit., p 131.
[35] Aukrust, op. cit., pp. 133 f.
[36] Aukrust, op. cit., p 134.
[37] Aukrust, op. cit., pp. 128 f.
[38] Aukrust, op. cit., pp. 131 f.
[39] Aukrust, op. cit., pp. 138 f.
[40] Aukrust, op. cit., p 125.
[41] Aukrust, op. cit., p 134,
[42] Aukrust, op. cit., p 136.
[43] Aukrust, op. cit., p 127.
[44] Aukrust, op. cit., pp. 127 f.
[45] Aukrust, op. cit., pp. 134 f.
[46] Aukrust, op. cit., p 78.
[47] Aukrust, op. cit., p 187.
[48] Aukrust, op. cit., pp. 137 f.
[49] Aukrust, op. cit., pp. 79 f, 81 f and 187.
[50] Aukrust, op. cit., pp. 187 ff.
[51] Aukrust, op. cit., pp. 79 f.
[52] Aukrust, op. cit., pp. 81 f.
[53] Aukrust, op. cit., pp. 81 f and 84 f.
[54] Aukrust, op. cit., pp. 84 ff, 94 ff and 121 f.
[55] Aukrust, op. cit., pp. 108 f.
[56] Rich Arthur. "Arbeit als Beruf". Article in Rich, Arthur-Ulich, Eberhard (hrsg): Arbeit und Humanität. Athenäum Verlag, Königstein 1978, p 9.
[57] Rich, Arthur: Christliche Existenz in der Industriellen Welt, p 175.
[58] Rich, op. cit., p 176.
[59] Rich, op. cit., p 116.
[60] Rich, op. cit., p 117.
[61] Rich, Arthur: "Arbeit als Beruf", p 8.
[62] Rich, Arthur: Christliche Existenz in der Industriellen Welt, p 176.
[63] Rich, op. cit., p 177. Rich, Arthur: "Arbeit als Beruf", p 9.
[64] Rich, Arthur: "Arbeit als Beruf", pp. 10 f.
[65] Rich, op. cit., p 12.
[66] Rich, op. cit., pp 13 ff and 7 f.
[67] Rich, op. cit., p 16. Rich, Arthur : Christliche Existenz in der Industriellen Welt, pp 91 f.
[68] Rich, Arthur: "Arbeit als Beruf", pp. 16 f.

[69] Rich, Arthur: Christliche Existenz in der Industriellen Welt, pp. 84 f.

[70] Rich, op. cit., p 125.

[71] Rich, op. cit., pp. 191 f.

[72] Rich, op. cit., pp. 205, 209 ff.

[73] Brakelmann, Günter: Zur Arbeit geboren? pp. 9 f, 43 f, 71 and 110 f. Brakelmann, Günter: "Humanisierung der industriellen Arbeitswelt". Article in TRE, III, pp. 660 f.

[74] Brakelmann, Günter: Abschied vom Unverbindlichen, p 40.

[75] Brakelmann, Günter: Zur Arbeit geboren? pp. 13 f, 46 f. Brakelmann, Günter: "Humanisierung der industriellen Arbeitswelt", TRE, III, p 662. Brakelmann, Günter: Abschied vom Unverbindlichen, p 39.

[76] Brakelmann, Günter: Zur Arbeit geboren? pp. 14, 46 f, 110 f. Brakelmann, Günter: "Humanisierung der industriellen Arbeitswelt", TRE, III, p 662.

[77] Brakelmann, Günter: Zur Arbeit geboren?, pp. 49, 205 f.

[78] Brakelmann, op.cit., p 40.

[79] Brakelmann, op.cit., pp. 79, 86 f, 15 f. Brakelmann, Günter: Abschied vom Unverbindlichen, p 40. Brakelmann, Günter : "Humanisierung der industriellen Arbeitswelt", TRE, III, p 663.

[80] Brakelmann, Günter: Zur Arbeit geboren?, pp. 22 f, 46, 74 f. Brakelmann, Günter: "Humanisierung der industriellen Arbeitswelt", TRE, III, pp. 662 f and 667.

[81] Brakelmann, Günter: Zur Arbeit geboren?, pp. 19 f, 72 f. Brakelmann, Günter : "Humanisierung der industriellen Arbeitswelt", TRE, III, pp. 665, 660 f.

[82] Brakelmann, Günter: Zur Arbeit geboren?, pp. 20, 91 f. Brakelmann, Günter : "Humanisierung der industriellen Arbeitswelt", TRE, III, p 666.

[83] Brakelmann, Günter: Zur Arbeit geboren?, pp 28, 32.

[84] Brakelmann, op. cit., pp. 34 f, 36.

[85] Brakelmann, op. cit., pp. 200 f.

[86] Brakelmann, Günter: Abschied vom Unverbindlichen, pp. 41 f.

[87] Brakelmann, Günter: Zur Arbeit geboren?, pp. 122, 127 f, 129 f.

[88] Brakelmann, op. cit., pp. 162, 174. Brakelmann, Günter: "Humanisierung der industriellen Arbeitswelt", TRE, III, pp. 667 f.

[89] Brakelmann, Günter: Zur Arbeit geboren?, pp. 165, 166 f, 177. Brakelmann, Günter: "Humanisierung der industriellen Arbeitswelt", TRE, III, p 668.

[90] Brakelmann, Günter: Zur Arbeit geboren?, pp. 178 f. Brakelmann, Günter: "Humanisierung der industriellen Arbeitswelt", TRE, III, p 657.

[91] Clarke, Roger: Work in Crisis, pp. 85 f, 166 ff, 173 f, 183.

[92] Clarke, op.cit., pp. 151 f, 188 f, 196 ff.

[93] Bleakley, David: Work. The Shadow and the Substance, pp. 63, 76 f, 82 f. Bleakley, David: In Place of Work. The Sufficient Society, pp. 96 f.

[94] Atherton, John: Faith in the Nation, p 95.

[95] Atherton, op. cit., pp. 95 f.

[96] Atherton, op. cit., p 96.

[97] Atherton, op. cit., p 90.

[98] Atherton, op. cit., p 90.

[99] Atherton, op. cit., p 96

[100] Atherton, op. cit., pp. 90 f, 97.

[101] Atherton, op. cit., pp. 97 f.

Chapter 4: Social ethical theories

[1] Bentham, Jeremy: An Introduction to The Principles of Morals and Legislation. Hafner Press, New York (1789) 1948, p 2. Bentham writes that an action is right if it is in agreement with what he calls the principle of utility. The approval or disapproval of an action according to this

principle depends on its tendency to promote or prevent happiness and happiness acccording to Bentham is the same as pleasure.

[2] Moore, G E: Ethics. Oxford University Press, London (1912), 1966, pp 26 ff, 121 ff, 128 f.

[3] Hare, RM: Freedom and Reason. Oxford University Press, Oxford (1963) 1978, pp 112 ff.

[4] Kant, Immanuel: Grundlegung zur Metaphysik der Sitten. Fünfte Auflage. Herausgegeben von Karl Vorländer. Der Philosophischen Bibliothek, Band 41. Verlag von Felix Meiner, Leipzig 1920, pp 44 and 54.

[5] Rawls, John: A Theory of Justice. Oxford University Press, Oxford (1972) 1976, pp 60 f. According to Rawls, these two priciples are a particular case of a more general principle of justice. This asserts that all social values – liberty and opportunity, income and welfare, bases for self-respect – are to be distributed equally unless an unequal distribution of any, or all, of these values is to the advantage of all. Rawls, op.cit., p 62. A later formulation of the second principle is to be found in Rawls, op. cit., p 83.

[6] For a discussion of the concept of right and different views about the justification of rights, see Hospers, John: Human Conduct, 2nd ed, pp 244 ff.

[7] I have discussed these views more thoroughly in Grenholm, Carl-Henric: Christian Social Ethics in a Revolutionary Age. An Analysis of the Social Ethics of John C Bennett, Heinz-Dietrich Wendland and Richard Shaull. Acta Universitatis Upsaliensis, Uppsala Studies in Social Ethics, Uppsala 1973, pp 23f.

[8] Brunner, Emil: Das Gebot und die Ordnungen, p 39.

[9] Brunner, op.cit., pp 41, 97 f, 101 f, 116 f, 172 f.

[10] Brunner, op.cit., pp 106 f, 116 f, 118, 119 f, 275.

[11] Brunner, op.cit., pp 123 f, 275, 316 ff, 320 f.

[12] Brunner, op.cit., p 275. Cf. Brunner, Emil: Gerechtigkeit, pp 54 ff.

[13] Brunner, Emil: Das Gebot und die Ordnungen, pp 112 f, 321 f.

[14] Brunner, op.cit., pp 359 ff.

[15] Brunner, op.cit., pp 452 ff.

[16] Brunner, Emil: Gerechtigkeit, p 20 f.

[17] Brunner, op.cit., pp 29 f.

[18] Brunner, op.cit., pp 30 f, 51.

[19] Brunner, op.cit., pp 21 f, 57 f.

[20] Brunner, op.cit., pp 58 f.

[21] Brunner, op.cit., pp 35, 40 f.

[22] Brunner, op.cit., pp 47 f, 77 ff.

[23] Brunner, op.cit., pp 80 f, 82 f, 86 f.

[24] Oldham, J H: The Function of the Church in Society. This is contained in Church, Community and State. Vol I: The Church and its Function in Society. By WA Visser't Hooft and J H Oldham. George Allen & Unwin Ltd, London 1937, p 119.

[25] Oldham, op. cit., pp 189 ff, 200.

[26] Oldham, op. cit., pp 216 f, 228.

[27] Oldham, op. cit., p 236.

[28] Oldham, op. cit., p 237.

[29] Oldham, op. cit., p 218.

[30] Oldham, op. cit., pp 243, 249.

[31] Oldham, op. cit., p 247.

[32] Oldham, op. cit., p 237.

[33] Oldham, op. cit., p 238.

[34] Oldham, op. cit., p 209.

[35] Oldham, op. cit., p 210.

[36] Oldham. JH: "A Responsible Society". Article in The Church and the Disorder of Society= Man's Disorder and God's Design. The Amsterdam Series, vol. III. SCM Press Ltd, London 1948, p 136.

[37] Oldham, op. cit., p 142.

[38] Oldham, op. cit., p 147.

[39] In Church and Society in the Late Twentieth Century: The Economic and Political Task, pp 147 f, Ronald H Preston questions this interpretation of Oldham's standpoint. Even if Preston personally does not hold that "the responsible society" is a middle axiom, I maintain however that the view that one should strive for such a society is according to Oldham a middle axiom in the sense that it has the form of a provisional rule.

[40] Aukrust, Tor: Mennesket i samfunnet. En sosialetikk. Bind I. Forlaget Land og Kirke, Oslo 1967, 2nd edition, pp 122 f, 126.

[41] Aukrust, op. cit., pp 106, 108 f.

[42] Aukrust, op. cit., pp 126 f.

[43] Aukrust, op. cit., p 127.

[44] Aukrust, op. cit., pp 128 f.

[45] Aukrust, op. cit., pp 129 f.

[46] Aukrust, op. cit., p 130.

[47] Aukrust, op. cit., p 131.

[48] Aukrust, op. cit., pp 132 f.

[49] Aukrust, op. cit., pp 133 f and 138.

[50] Aukrust, op. cit., pp 139 f.

[51] Aukrust, op. cit., pp 141 f.

[52] Aukrust, op. cit., pp 144 and 146.

[53] Aukrust, op. cit., pp 147 f.

[54] Aukrust, op. cit., pp 149 f.

[55] Aukrust, op. cit., p 151.

[56] Aukrust, op. cit., p 152.

[57] Aukrust, op. cit., pp 154, 159, 162, 165 ff.

[58] Aukrust, op. cit., p 173.

[59] Aukrust, op. cit., pp 175 f, 179.

[60] Aukrust, op. cit., p 192.

[61] Aukrust, op. cit., pp 196 f and 198 f.

[62] Aukrust, op. cit., pp 204 f and 211 f.

[63] Aukrust, op. cit., pp 21 f and 23 f.

[64] Aukrust, op. cit., p 63.

[65] Aukrust, op. cit., pp 82 ff.

[66] Aukrust, Tor: Mennesket i samfunnet. En sosialetikk. Bind II, p 11.

[67] Aukrust, op. cit., pp 12 f, 67, 71.

[68] Rich, Arthur: Wirtschaftsethik. Band I. Grundlagen in theologischer Perspektive. Gütersloher Verlagshaus Gerd Mohn, Gütersloh (1984) 1987, 3 ed., pp 41 ff.

[69] Rich, op. cit., pp 58 f, 60 f and 61 f.

[70] Rich, op. cit., pp 49 f, 51, 53 and 55.

[71] Rich, op. cit., pp 58 and 65. Rich, Arthur: Glaube in politischer Entscheidung, pp 115 ff. Rich, Arthur: Mitbestimmung in der Industrie, pp 50 f.

[72] Rich, Arthur: Wirtschaftsethik, I, p 67.

[73] Rich, op. cit., pp 81 f. Rich, Arthur: Glaube in politischer Entscheidung, pp 119 and 120 f.

[74] Rich, Arthur: Wirtschaftsethik, I, pp 72 f.

[75] Rich, Arthur: Christliche Existenz in der Industriellen Welt, pp 162 f and 164.

[76] Rich Arthur: Wirtschaftsethik, I, p 173. Rich, Arthur: "Sozialethische Kriterien und Maximen humanen Gesellschaftsgestaltung". Article in Christliche Witschaftsethik vor neuen Aufgaben. Festgabe für Arthur Rich zum siebzigsten Geburtstag. Herausgegeben von Theodor Strohm. Theologischer Verlag, Zürich 1980, pp 21 f.

[77] Rich, Arthur: Glaube in politischer Entscheidung, pp 124 f. Rich, Arthur: Wirtschaftsethik, pp 102 f. Rich, Arthur: Christliche Existenz in der Industriellen Welt, p 172.

[78] Rich, Arthur: Glaube in politischer Entscheidung, p 125. Rich, Arthur: Christliche Existenz in der Industriellen Welt, pp 165, 166 f.

[79] Rich, Arthur: Wirtschaftsethik, I, pp 103 f. Rich, Arthur: Christliche Existenz in der Industriellen Welt, p 174. Rich, Arthur: Glaube in politischer Entscheidung, p 131.

[80] Rich, Arthur: Wirtschaftsethik, I, pp 170 f.

[81] Rich, Arthur: Wirtschaftsethik, I, pp 179 f. Rich, Arthur: "Sozialethische Kriterien und Maximen humanen Gesellschaftsgestaltung", p 22. Rich, Arthur: Mitbestimmung in der Industrie, p 53.

[82] Rich, Arthur: Wirtschaftsethik, I, pp 181 f, 183 f. Rich, Arthur: "Sozialethische Kriterien und Maximen humanen Gesellschaftsgestaltung", pp 23 f. Rich, Arthur: Mitbestimmung in der Industrie, pp 53 f.

[83] Rich, Arthur: Wirtschaftsethik, I, pp 184 f, 186 ff. Rich, Arthur: "Sozialethische Kriterien und Maximen humanen Gesellschaftsgestaltung", pp 24 ff. Rich, Arthur: Mitbestimmung in der Industrie, pp 55 f.

[84] Rich, Arthur: Wirtschaftsethik, I, pp 192 f. Rich, Arthur: "Sozialethische Kriterien und Maximen humanen Gesellschaftsgestaltung", pp 26 f. Rich, Arthur: Mitbestimmung in der Industrie, pp 57 f.

[85] Rich, Arthur: Wirtschaftsethik, I, pp 196 f. Rich, Arthur: "Sozialethische Kriterien und Maximen humanen Gesellschaftsgestaltung", pp 27 f. Rich, Arthur: Mitbestimmung in der Industrie, pp 58 f.

[86] Rich, Arthur: Wirtschaftsethik, I, pp 194 f.

[87] Rich, op. cit., pp 174 f and 176 f. Rich presents these two latter criteria in his book Wirtschaftsethik from 1984. They are not to be found in his earlier work Mitbestimmung in der Industrie. There two other criteria, namely "radicality "(pp 56 f) and "sachgerecht" (pp 59 f) are given. Rich has omitted these two criteria in his later presentation.

[88] Rich, Arthur: Wirtschaftsethik, I, pp 225, 228 f, 232. Rich, Arthur: Christliche Existenz in der Industriellen Welt, p 228. Rich, Arthur: "Sozialethische Kriterien und Maximen humanen Gesellschaftsgestaltung", pp 28 f and 31.

[89] Rich, Arthur: Wirtschaftsethik, I, pp 222 f. Rich, Arthur: Christliche Existenz in der Industriellen Welt, pp 226 f, 261 ff. According to Rich there are even maxims to be found in the Bible which because they are tentative and related to the specific situation, are of limited validity. See Rich, Arthur: Wirtschaftsethik, I, pp 234 ff and 240.

[90] Rich, Arthur: Christliche Existenz in der Industriellen Welt, pp 229 ff. Rich, Arthur: Glaube in politischer Entscheidung, pp 127 ff. Rich, Arthur: Mitbestimmung in der Industrie, pp 167 ff, 249, 258 f. Rich, Arthur: "Sozialethische Kriterien und Maximen humanen Gesellschaftsgestaltung", pp 32 f, 34 ff.

[91] Rich, Arthur: Christliche Existenz in der Industriellen Welt, pp 182. Rich, Arthur: Wirtschaftsethik, pp 29 ff.

[92] Rich, Arthur: Wirtschaftsethik, I, pp 27 f.

[93] Rich, op.cit., pp 209, 215, 216 f, 218 f.

[94] Rich, op.cit., pp 34 f, 36 f, 227.

[95] Brakelmann, Günter: Abschied vom Unverbindlichen, pp 9 and 17 f.

[96] Brakelmann, op. cit., p 26. Brakelmann, Günter: Zur Arbeit Geboren?, pp 17 f and 88 f.

[97] Brakelmann, Günter: Abschied vom Unverbindlichen, p 27.

[98] Brakelmann, op. cit., pp 37 and 100.

[99] Brakelmann, op. cit., pp 31 f.

[100] Brakelmann, op. cit., pp 33 and 35 f.

[101] Brakelmann, Günter: Zur Arbeit Geboren?, pp 101 f and 17 f.

[102] Brakelmann, Günter: Abschied vom Unverbindlichen, pp 38 f.

[103] Brakelmann, op. cit., pp 42 f.

[104] Atherton, John: Faith in the Nation, pp 26 f.

[105] Atherton, op.cit., pp 31 and 34 f.

[106] Atherton, op.cit., p 36.

[107] Atherton, op.cit., pp 32 f and 37 f.

[108] Atherton, op.cit., pp 168 f.

[109] Atherton, op.cit., p 72 f.

[110] Atherton, op.cit., pp 73 f, 75 and 77 f.

[111] Atherton, op.cit., p 78.

[112] Atherton, op.cit., p 81.
[113] Atherton, op.cit., p 86.
[114] Atherton, op.cit., pp 88 f.
[115] Atherton, op.cit., pp 93 and 95.
[116] Atherton, op.cit., pp 72 f.
[117] Atherton, op.cit., pp 84 f.
[118] Atherton, op.cit., pp 136 f and 139.
[119] Atherton, op.cit., p 14.
[120] Wogaman, J Philip: A Christian Method of Moral Judgment. The Westminster Press, Philadelphia 1976, pp 40 and 43 f.
[121] Wogaman, op. cit., pp 70 ff, 80 ff, 85 ff and 94 ff.
[122] Atherton, John: Faith in the Nation, pp 139 f and 79.
[123] Preston, Ronald H: Church and Society in the Late Twentieth Century. The Economic and Political Task, pp 107, 141 f and 147. Preston, Ronald H: The Future of Christian Ethics. SCM Press Ltd, London 1987, pp 130 f.
[124] Atherton, John: Faith in the Nation, pp 141 f and 135.

Chapter 5: Theories of human nature

[1] These four analytical questions partly overlap with the analytical questions which Leslie Stevenson presents in his book Seven Theories of Human Nature, Oxford University Press, Oxford (1974) 1979, pp 4 f and 7.
[2] This distinction between scientific knowledge about man and a view of man has been made by Anders Jeffner in Att studera människosyn. En översiktlig problemanalys. Tema T Rapport 21, Linköping 1989, pp 4 and 39 f.
[3] Jeffner, op. cit., pp 14 ff. Jeffner distinguishes between (a) empiricism which maintains that knowledge is based upon sensory impressions (b) rationalism which holds that it is partly based upon capacities or structures in human reason and (c) theories of commitment which hold that we receive knowledge about reality from experiences of commitment.
[4] Jeffner, op.cit., pp 26 f.
[5] Jeffner, op.cit., pp 19 ff.
[6] Jeffner, op.cit., pp 25 f.
[7] Jeffner, op.cit., p 28.
[8] Jeffner, op.cit., pp 8 f.
[9] Holte, Ragnar: Människa Livstolkning Gudstro. Teorier och metoder inom tros- och livsåskådningsvetenskapen, pp 44 f.
[10] Holte, op. cit., pp 74 f.
[11] Jeffner, Anders: Att studera människosyn, pp 24 f.
[12] Brunner, Emil: Das Gebot und die Ordnungen, pp 472 f.
[13] Brunner, op. cit., pp 473 f.
[14] Brunner, op. cit., pp 279 f.
[15] Brunner, op. cit., pp 278 f.
[16] Brunner, op. cit., pp 284 f. Brunner, Emil: Gerechtigkeit, pp 98 f.
[17] Brunner, Emil: Gerechtigkeit, pp 35, 40 f.
[18] Brunner, op.cit., pp 47 f, 77 ff.
[19] Brunner, Emil: Das Gebot und die Ordnungen, pp 48 f.
[20] Brunner, op.cit., pp 56 ff, 137 ff.
[21] Oldham J H: Work in Modern Society, p 34.
[22] Oldham, op.cit., pp 34 f.
[23] Oldham, op.cit., p 36.
[24] Oldham, op.cit., pp 37 f.
[25] Oldham, J H: "A Responsible Society". Article in The Church and the Disorder of Society, pp 136 and 147.

[26] Oldham, J H: Work in Modern Society, pp 39 f.

[27] Oldham, op.cit., pp 42 f.

[28] Oldham, J H: The Function of the Church in Society, p 239.

[29] Oldham, op.cit., pp 146 ff.

[30] Aukrust, Tor: Mennesket i samfunnet, Bind II, pp 25 f.

[31] Aukrust, op. cit., pp 27 f.

[32] Aukrust, Tor: Mennesket i samfunnet, Bind I, p 146.

[33] Aukrust, op.cit., pp 21 ff and 29.

[34] Aukrust, op.cit., pp 108 f.

[35] Aukrust, op.cit., p 22.

[36] Aukrust, op.cit., p 274.

[37] Aukrust, op.cit., p 51.

[38] Aukrust, op.cit., pp 274 f.

[39] Aukrust, op.cit., pp 58 and 45.

[40] Aukrust, Tor: Mennesket i samfunnet, II, p 187 f.

[41] Rich, Arthur: Wirtschaftsethik, I, pp 105 and 106 f.

[42] Rich, op.cit., pp 111 ff.

[43] Rich, op.cit., pp 119 f and 121 f.

[44] Rich, op.cit., pp 122 f and 127.

[45] Rich, Arthur: Christliche Existenz in der Industriellen Welt, pp 116 f.

[46] Rich, Arthur: Glaube in politischer Entscheidung, pp 67 f and 81 f.

[47] Rich, op.cit., pp 79 and 85 f.

[48] Rich, op.cit., pp 94 and 96 f.

[49] Brakelmann, Günter: Abschied vom Unverbindlichen, pp 31 f.

[50] Brakelmann, Günter: Zur Arbeit geboren?, pp 71 f.

[51] Brakelmann, op.cit., pp 72 f.

[52] Brakelmann, op. cit., pp 32 ff.

[53] Brakelmann, Günter: Abschied vom Unverbindlichen, pp 71 f.

[54] Brakelmann, op.cit., pp 73 f.

[55] Brakelmann, op.cit., pp 75 ff.

[56] Brakelmann, op.cit., pp 68 f.

[57] Atherton, John: Faith in the Nation, pp 84 f and 14.

[58] Atherton, op. cit., pp 37 f, 14 and 84 f.

[59] Atherton, op. cit., p 72.

[60] Oldham, J H: Work in Modern Society, p 41.

Chapter 6: Ethics and a Christian system of belief

[1] My reflections about different levels in ethical argument are largely inspired by Ragnar Holte and James M Gustafson. See Holte, Ragnar: Etik och jämställdhet. Acta Universitatis Upsaliensis, Uppsala Studies in Social Ethics, Uppsala 1978, pp 7 and 8f; Holte, Ragnar: Människa Livstolkning Gudstro, pp 121 f; Gustafson, James M: "An Analysis of Church and Society Social Ethical Writings". Article in The Ecumenical Review, vol 40, nr 2, April 1988, p 268.

[2] Thielicke, Helmut: Theologische Ethik. Band I. JCB Mohr (Paul Siebeck), Tübingen 1951, pp 244 f. Thielicke, Helmut: Theologische Ethik. Band II, 1 Teil, pp 350 f.

[3] Thielicke, Helmut: Theologische Ethik. Band I, p 701.

[4] Løgstrup, KE: Den etiske fordring. Gyldendal, Köpenhamn 1966, pp 17 f and 27 f. An analytical exposition of KE Løgstrup's view of reality, view of man and ethics has been given by Kristina Nilsson in Etik och verklighetstolkning. Acta Universitatis Upsaliensis, Uppsala Studies in Social Ethics, Uppsala 1980, pp 20 ff and 146 ff.

[5] Barth, Karl: Die Kirchliche Dogmatik. Zweiter Band: Die Lehre von Gott. Zweiter Halbband

(II/2), Evangelischer Verlag AG Zollikon, Zürich 1946, pp 628 and 630 f. See also Barth, op.cit., pp 590 and 598.

[6] Moltmann, Jürgen: Theologie der Hoffnung. Chr Kaiser Verlag, München (1964) 1966, 5 edition, pp 12, 92 f and 197.

[7] Moltmann, op.cit., pp 290 and 303 f.

[8] Moltmann, op.cit., pp 308 f.

[9] Trillhaas, Wolfgang: Ethik. Alfred Töpelmann, Berlin (1959) 1965, 2nd edition, pp 5 f, 6 ff, 15 ff.

[10] Wogaman, J Philip: Christian Perspectives on Politics, pp 118 f, 117 f and 121.

[11] Brunner, Emil: Das Gebot und die Ordnungen, p 275.

[12] Brunner, pp 371 f.

[13] Brunner, Emil: Das Gebot und die Ordnungen, p 280.

[14] Brunner, Emil: Gerechtigkeit, pp 136 ff, 146 f.

[15] Brunner, Emil: Das Gebot und die Ordnungen, pp 112 f, 321 f.

[16] Oldham, J H: Work in Modern Society, pp 49 f.

[17] Oldham, J H: The Function of the Church in Society, pp 128 f, 132.

[18] Oldham, op.cit., pp 135 f, 137.

[19] Oldham, op.cit., pp 236 f, 243 f.

[20] Oldham, op.cit., pp 143 f.

[21] Oldham, op.cit., pp 144 f, 148 f and 151 f.

[22] Oldham, op.cit., pp 146 f, 148 f and 151 f.

[23] Oldham, op.cit., p 239.

[24] Aukrust, Tor: Mennesket i samfunnet, Bind I, pp 25 ff.

[25] Aukrust, Tor: Mennesket i samfunnet, Bind II, pp 127 and 134.

[26] Aukrust, Tor: Mennesket i samfunnet, Bind I, pp 28 f and 66 f.

[27] Aukrust, op.cit., p 96.

[28] Aukrust, op.cit., pp 80 f.

[29] Aukrust, op.cit., pp 82 f.

[30] Aukrust, op.cit., pp 85 f.

[31] Aukrust, op.cit., pp 87 f.

[32] Aukrust, op.cit., pp 89 f.

[33] Aukrust, op.cit., pp 92 f.

[34] Aukrust, op.cit., pp 94 f.

[35] Rich, Arthur: Wirtschaftsethik, I, p 146.

[36] Rich, op.cit., p 148.

[37] Rich, op.cit., pp 151 f, 156.

[38] Rich, op.cit., pp 137 f and 140 f.

[39] Rich, op.cit., pp 163 and 166 f.

[40] Rich, op.cit., pp 129 f and 132 f.

[41] Rich, Arthur: Glaube in politischer Entscheidung, pp 140, 141 f and 144 f.

[42] Rich, op.cit., pp 151 f and 155 f.

[43] Rich, op.cit., pp 161 ff and 179 f.

[44] Rich, op.cit., pp 37 f, 43 and 46 f.

[45] Brakelmann, Günter: Abschied vom Unverbindlichen, p 13.

[46] Brakelmann, op.cit., pp 14 f.

[47] Brakelmann, op.cit., p 26.

[48] Brakelmann, op.cit., p 31.

[49] Brakelmann, Günter: Zur Arbeit geboren?, p 39.

[50] Brakelmann, Günter: Abschied vom Unverbindlichen, pp 19 f.

[51] Brakelmann, op.cit., pp 20 f.

[52] Brakelmann, op.cit., pp 21 f.

[53] Brakelmann, op.cit., pp 23 f.

[54] Brakelmann, op.cit., p 25.

[55] Brakelmann, op.cit., pp 28 f.

[56] Atherton, John: Faith in the Nation, pp 84 f.
[57] Atherton, op.cit., p 72.
[58] Atherton, op.cit., pp 11 f.
[59] Atherton, op.cit., pp 26 f.
[60] Atherton, op.cit., pp 43 f.
[61] Atherton, op.cit., p 42.

Chapter 7: Christian and humane ethics

[1] This terminology largely agrees with that proposed by Ragnar Holte in the article "Humant och kristet inom socialetiken", which is included in Grenholm, Carl-Henric (ed) : Kyrkans samhällsansvar, Verbum, Stockholm 1975. See in particular op. cit., pp 51 f, 53 f, 56 f and 58 f. Here however I do not speak of an "addition theory" as a fourth theory along with a combination theory. I tend rather to conceive such a addition theory as a form of combination theory. It is a theory which asserts that a determinable part of Christian ethics coincides with humane ethics while another determinable part is specifically Christian. There are however other types of combination theory which assert that that the common core of ethics is not something static which is given once and for all time. Thereby the objection that the specifically Christian features in Christian ethics are marginal is avoided.

[2] Niebuhr, Reinhold: An Interpretation of Christian Ethics. The Seabury Press, New York (1935) 1979, pp 63 and 65 ff.

[3] This terminology largely agrees with that introduced in Holte, Ragnar, et al.: Etiska problem. Verbum/Håkan Ohlssons, Lund 1977, pp 85 and 88 f. Instead of a "theological addition and combination ethics" I have however used the term "partially Revelation based ethics". I consider theological addition ethics to be one kind of partially Revelation based ethics.

[4] Gustafson, James M: Can Ethics be Christian? The University of Chicago Press, Chicago 1975, pp 158 f, 162 f, 164 f.

[5] Brunner, Emil: Gerechtigkeit,, pp 101 f, 104 f.

[6] Brunner, op. cit., pp 148 f. Brunner makes the same sharp distinction between the Christian conception of love and the common conception of eros as does the Swedish theologian Anders Nygren in Eros och Agape. Den kristna kärlekstanken genom tiderna. Aldus/ Bonniers, Stockholm 1966, pp 158 ff.

[7] Brunner, Emil: Gerechtigkeit, pp 137 f, 143 f, 146 f and 153 f.

[8] Brunner, Emil: Das Gebot und die Ordnungen, pp 70 f, 99 f, 106 f.

[9] Brunner, op.cit., p 319.

[10] Brunner, op.cit., pp 204 f.

[11] Oldham, J H: The Function of the Church in Society, pp 211 f.

[12] Oldham, J H, op.cit., pp 203 f.

[13] Oldham, J H, op.cit., pp 241 f.

[14] Oldham, J H, op.cit., p 237.

[15] Oldham, J H, op.cit., pp 243 f.

[16] Oldham, J H, op.cit., p 145.

[17] Oldham, J H, op.cit., pp 234 f. Cf. Oldham, J H, op.cit., pp 178 and 237.

[18] Oldham, J H, op.cit., p 235.

[19] Aukrust, Tor: Mennesket i samfunnet, Bind I, pp 25 f.

[20] Aukrust, op.cit., p 27.

[21] Aukrust, op.cit., pp 28 f.

[22] Aukrust, op.cit., pp 35 f.

[23] Aukrust, op.cit., p 43.

[24] Aukrust, op.cit., p 45 f.

[25] Aukrust, op.cit., p 49.

[26] Aukrust, op.cit., p 50 f.

[27] Aukrust, op.cit., p 55 f.

[28] Aukrust, op.cit., p 65.

[29] Aukrust, op.cit., pp 66 ff.

[30] Aukrust, op.cit., p 96.

[31] Aukrust, op.cit., p 218.

[32] Aukrust, op.cit., p 225.

[33] Aukrust, op.cit., pp 232 f.

[34] Aukrust, op.cit., pp 219 f, 231 f and 236 f.

[35] Aukrust, op.cit., pp 276 and 277 f.

[36] Aukrust holds that the ethical material in the Bible contains norms of both these kinds. It includes (a) ethical instructions which are humane and have a natural law character e.g. the Decalogue and (b) statements of God's absolute demand which is specifically Christian e.g. the Sermon on the Mount. It also includes (c) more detailed instructions which are valid only for a given historical situation. The latter shows why the ethical instruction in the Bible cannot in its totality be considered to be binding for all time. See op.cit., pp 72 f and 74 f.

[37] Rich, Arthur: Wirtschaftsethik, I, pp 184 f.

[38] Rich, op. cit., pp 242 f.

[39] Rich, op. cit., pp 23 f.

[40] A detailed presentation of ethical prescriptivism has been given by R M Hare in Freedom and Reason. Oxford University Press, Oxford (1963) 1978, pp 16 ff, 21 ff and in Moral Thinking. Its Levels, Method and Point. Clarendon Press, Oxford 1981, pp 20 ff.

[41] Rich, Arthur: "Sozialethische Kriterien und Maximen humaner Gesellschaftsgestaltung". Article in Christliche Wirtschaftsethik vor neuen Aufgaben, pp 18 ff.

[42] Rich, Arthur: Wirtschaftsethik, I, pp 83 f.

[43] Rich, Arthur: Christliche Existenz in der Industriellen Welt, p 18.

[44] Rich, op. cit., p 17.

[45] Rich, op. cit., pp 20 f.

[46] Brakelmann, Günter: Abschied vom Unverbindlichen, p 63 ff.

[47] Brakelmann, op. cit., pp 26 and 31. Brakelmann, Günter: Zur Arbeit geboren? p 39.

[48] Brakelmann, Günter: Abschied vom Unverbindlichen, p 38.

[49] Atherton, John: Faith in the Nation, pp 34 f.

[50] Atherton, op. cit., pp 39 f.

[51] Atherton, op. cit., pp 32 f.

[52] This terminology is in agreement with that proposed by Ragnar Holte in Människa, Livstolkning, Gudstro, pp 84 ff and 87 ff. The term revelation positivism for the type of theory to be found in Barth was originally put forward by Dietrich Bonhoeffer. Ragnar Holte discusses different types of connection theories in op.cit., pp 93 ff.

Chapter 8: A critique of Protestant work ethics

[1] G E Moore is an influential representative of ethical intutionism. In Principia Ethica, Cambridge University Press, Cambridge (1903) 1980, pp 6 ff, he maintains that the term "good" is a simple and undefinable property which must not be confused with natural properties. David McNaughton puts forward arguments for moral realism in Moral Vision. An Introduction to Ethics, Basil Blackwell, Oxford 1988. In op.cit., pp 39 ff and 55 ff, he holds that there exist objective value properties which we can observe with the help of our ordinary senses. This observation of moral reality is possible without, like Moore, presupposing the existence of a special moral sense.

[2] R M Hare puts forward arguments for a prescriptivism of this type in Freedom and Reason, pp 4 ff and 16 ff. A similar standpoint is adopted by William Frankena in Ethics, 2nd ed., Prentice-Hall, Englewood Cliffs, NJ 1973, pp 110 ff where he combines a non–cognitive theory with the view that a person adopting "the moral point of view" can justify ethical judgements.

[3] This criterion largely coincides with what R H Hare in Freedom and Reason, pp 10 ff and 30 ff calls the universalizability thesis.

[4] This objection to the theory of reflexive equilibrium has been made by R M Hare in Moral Thinking. Its Levels, Method and Point. Clarendon Press, Oxford 1981, p 12 f.

[5] My formulation of this criterion has been largely inspired by the principle of integration put forward by Anders Jeffner in Kriterien christliche Glaubenslehre. Eine prinzipielle Untersuchung heutiger protestantischer Dogmatik im deutschen Sprachbereich. Acta Universitatis Upsaliensis, Studia Doctrinae Upsaliensia, Uppsala 1976, pp 139 ff. A similar integration criterion has been used in Hemberg, Jarl – Holte, Ragnar – Jeffner, Anders: Människan och Gud. En kristen teologi. Liber Förlag, Lund 1982, pp 51 and 53 ff.

[6] The distinction between criteria of authenticity and criteria of reasonableness was introduced by Anders Jeffner in Kriterien christlicher Glaubenslehre, pp 20 and 55 ff.

[7] The significance of the double commandment of love in Matthew and John has been stressed by Birger Gerhardson in "med hela ditt hjärta". Om Bibelns ethos. Liber Läromedel, Lund 1979, pp 46 ff and 95 ff. A discussion of the centre and periphery in the Bible and of the double commandment of love as a fundamental norm in Biblical ethics is to be found in Bexell, Göran: Etiken, bibeln och samlevnaden. Utformingen av en nutida kristen etik, tillämpad på samlevnadsetiska frågor. Verbum, Stockholm 1988, pp 77 ff and 79 ff.

[8] A detailed critique of the standpoint that the good is good because God wills it, is presented by Bruno Schüller in Wholly Human. Essays on the Theory and Language of Morality. Gill and MacMillan, Dublin 1986, pp 45 ff.

[9] A similar objection to an ecclesiological social ethics has been put forward by Ronald H Preston in Explorations in Theology 9, SCM Press Ltd, London 1981, pp 101 f.

[10] This objection has previously been made by Reinhold Niebuhr in Kegley, Charles W (ed): The Theology of Emil Brunner. The Macmillan Company, New York 1962, pp 270 f.

[11] This objection has been made by William Frankena in Ethics, pp 23 ff.

[12] A similar objection has been made by Reinhold Niebuhr in Kegley, Charles W (ed): The Theology of Emil Brunner, p 269.

Chapter 9: A humanely based social ethical theory

[1] A short exposition of how Augustine conceives a human being's nature as a being created in the image of God, has been provided by Ragnar Holte in Guds avbild. Kvinna och man i kristen belysning, Verbum, Stockholm 1990, pp 14 ff.

[2] Ragnar Holte maintains in op. cit., p 13, that the Early Church theologians who interpreted the concept of God's image in the light of human sovereignty over creation, held that this sovereignty was assigned less to women than to men. In contrast to these theologians, I hold of course that the task of assuming responsibility for other living things, is equally given to men and women.

[3] Wogaman, J Philip: A Christian Method of Moral Judgement, pp 106 f and 108 f. Preston, Ronald H: The Future of Christian Ethics, pp 215 and 218 f.

[4] Preston, Ronald H: Church and Society in the Late Twentieth Century, pp 102 and 130 ff.

[5] Niebuhr, Reinhold: An Interpretation of Christian Ethics. The Seabury Press, New York (1935) 1979, pp 63 and 65 ff.

[6] Wogaman, J Philip: A Christian Method of Moral Judgement, pp 60 f and 68 f. Wogaman, J Philip: Christian Perspectives on Politics, pp 114 ff, 117 ff, 120 f.

[7] Bonino, José Míguez: Toward a Christian Political Ethics. SCM Press Ltd, London 1983, pp 90 f and 92 f.

[8] Kant formulates this principle of human value in Grundlegung zur Metaphysik der Sitten, p 54.

[9] Mark 12:28-34. Cf Matthew 22:34-40. Birger Gerhardsson has provided an elucidatory commentary of the ethics in Matthew and the double commandment to love in "med hela ditt hjärta". Om Bibelns ethos, pp 46 ff.

[10] Urban Forell has proposed a similar interpretation of the Christian ideal of love in Kärlekens motivstrukturer. En etisk och begreppsanalytisk studie. Lund University Press, Lund, 1989. See op. cit., pp 7 f and 13 f. Forell however does not discuss the question of what characterizes a right act but rather the question of what characterizes the intentional element in love, particularly the will's motive. He also question whether the commandment to love one's neighbour embodies an exhortation to self love. See Forell, op.cit., pp 11 f and 77 f.

[11] Bentham, Jeremy: An Introduction to the Principles of Morals and Legislation, pp 1 f and 29 ff.

[12] Maslow, Abraham H: Motivation and Personality. Harper & Brothers, New York 1954, pp 80 ff.

[13] Maslow, op.cit., pp 104 f and 146 f.

[14] A valuable critical discussion of Maslow's theory is to be found inter alia in Allardt, Erik: Att ha, att älska, att vara. Om välfärd i Norden. Argos, Lund 1975, pp 37 f.

[15] In this respect, my point of view differs from the ethical theory put forward by Göran Collste in Makten, moralen och människan. He proposes in Collste, op.cit., pp 54 ff, a need oriented utilitarianism, according to which the satisfaction of needs is a fundamental value. According to Collste, the needs which ought to be satisfied are in part physiological and partly psychological, namely the needs for security, community, self respect, understanding and connection, self realization and autonomy. See also Göran Collste's article in Davis, Howard – Gosling, David: Will the Future Work?, pp 96 f. In contrast to Collste, I hold that that there are other intrinsic values besides the satisfaction of needs. In this respect, my proposed ethical theory differs also from the theory formulated by Urban Forell in Kärlekens motivstrukturer. In Forell, op.cit., pp 37 f, he would seem to hold that welfare in the sense of the satisfaction of needs, is the sole intrinsic value. According to Forell, the principle of human value exhorts us to ascribe to the satisfaction of the needs of each human being, a value in itself.

[16] Niebuhr, Reinhold: An Interpretation of Christian Ethics, 1979, pp 65 ff.

[17] Niebuhr, op.cit., p 65.

[18] Rawls, John: A Theory of Justice, pp 60 f.

[19] Rawls, op.cit., pp 83 ff.

[20] Rawls, op.cit., pp 76 ff.

[21] Rawls, op.cit., p 83.

[22] Rawls, op.cit., pp 61 f.

[23] Luther, Martin: Von weltlicher Oberkeit, wie weit man ihr gehorsam schuldig sei (1523), WA 11, 259:7-21; WA 11, 260:16−20. Luther, Martin: Krucigers Sommerpostille, WA 22, 62:12−25.

[24] Bentham, Jeremy: An Introduction to The Principles of Morals and Legislation, pp 2 f.

[25] Niebuhr, Reinhold: Moral Man and Immoral Society. A Study in Ethics and Politics. Charles Scribner's Sons, New York (1932) 1947, pp XI f, XX, 257 ff, 270 ff.

[26] I have provided a more detailed analysis of Bennett's formulation of a modified monistic thesis in Grenholm, Carl-Henric: Christian Social Ethics in a Revolutionary Age, pp 86 ff.

Chapter 10: A Christian theory of work

[1] Luther, Martin : Von den guten Werken (1520), WA 6, 263:5−28. Luther, Martin: Deutsch Catechismus (Der Grosse Katechismus, 1529), WA 30:I, 148:23−27; WA 30:I,152:19−35; WA 30:I, 153:29-36.

[2] Jönsson, Ludvig: Människan, mödan och arbetsglädjen, pp 56 f and 58.

[3] As maintained by e.g. Paul H Ballard in Towards a Contemporary Theology of Work, pp 43 f, there is in this respect an important difference between a Christian and a Marxist theory of work. According to a Marxist theory, human beings create the world about them by their own efforts. According to a Christian theory, human beings are instruments of Divine Creation and work with material already created by God.

[4] Even in contemporary Catholic moral theology, the theory of the meaning of work in this sense, is generally based upon the doctrine of Creation. An example of this is Herbert McCabe's article "Theology and Work – A Thomist View" in Todd, John M (ed): Work. Christian Thought and Practice, pp 215 f and 216 f.

[5] A view of this type is to be found in Jönsson, Ludvig: Människan, mödan och arbetsglädjen, pp 51 ff.

[6] Marx, Karl: Ökonomisch-philosophische Manuskripte. MEGA I/3, p 88. This is to be found in Marx, Karl – Engels, Friedrich: Historisch-Kritische Gesamtausgabe. Werke, Schriften, Briefe. Im Auftrage des Marx-Engels Instituts Moskau herausgegeben von V Adoratskij. Erste Abteilung, Band 3. Verlag Detlev Auvermann KG, Glashütten im Taunus (1932) 1970. Cf. the presentation in Marx, Karl: Das Kapital, I. MEW 23, p 193. Appears in Marx, Karl – Engels, Friedrich: Werke. Dietz Verlag, Berlin 1962.

[7] Johannes Paulus II : Människans arbete. Laborem exercens. Katolska Bokförlaget, Uppsala 1982, pp 27, 34 f, 80 f. Interesting commentaries to Laborem exercens will be found in Heck, Bruno (hrsg): Arbeit. Ihr Wert, Ihre Ordnung. v Hase & Koehler, Mainz 1984. See inter alia op.cit., pp 40 ff and 67 ff. For Laborem exercens, see also Kramer, Rolf: Arbeit, pp 38 f and 42 f, and Wolfgang Schröter's article in Fahlbusch, Wilhelm – Przybylski, Hartmut – Schröter, Wolfgang: Arbeit ist nicht alles. Versuche zu einer Ethik der Zukunft, pp 42 f.

[8] For a Protestant critique of the activity line, see Fahlbusch, Wilhelm – Przybylski, Hartmut – Schröter, Wolfgang: Arbeit ist nicht alles. Versuche zu einer Ethik der Zukunft, pp 125 f and 128 f. A critique of this standpoint is also to be found in Heinz Eduard Tödt, whose standpoint is discussed in Kramer, Rolf: Arbeit, pp 32 ff. One of the Catholic moral theologians who argues for an activity line is Edwin G Kaiser. See his Theology of Work, pp 232 ff.

[9] Schumacher, E F: Det goda arbetet. För en ändamålsenlig teknologi med mänskliga mått. Prisma, Stockholm 1979, pp 15 and 127 f.

[10] Schumacher, op.cit., p 132.

[11] Bertil Gardell is one of the contemporary industrial psychologists who has formulated such a theory. See Gardell, Bertil: Produktionsteknik och arbetsglädje. En socialpsykologisk studie av industriellt arbete. Personaladminstrativa rådet, Malmö 1971, pp 47, 51, 53 ff. See also Gardell, Bertil: Arbetsinnehåll och livskvalitet. En sammanställning och diskussion av samhällsvetenskaplig forskning rörande människan och arbetet. Prisma, Lund 1976, p 14.

[12] I have given a detailed analysis of these theories in Grenholm, Carl-Henric: Arbetets mening, pp 304 ff and 342 ff.

[13] For a discussion of the significance of Abraham Maslow's theory of needs for different theories of motivation, see the article of Curt Yausky and E Lauch Perkes in Dubin (ed): Handbook of Work, Organization and Society. Rand McNally College Publishing Company, Chicago 1976, pp 535 ff. A motivation theory of this kind is to be found e.g. in Douglas McGregor in The Human Side of Enterprise. McGraw-Hill Book Company, Inc, New York–Toronto–London 1960, pp 36 ff and 40.

[14] Bertil Gardell has shown that there exists such a positive correlation between the degree of self determination and level of skill and the degree of need satisfaction in work. See Gardell, Bertil: Arbetsinnehåll och livskvalitet, pp 21, 31 and 39, and Gardell, Bertil: Produktionsteknik och arbetsglädje, pp 122, 295, 136 and 141.

[15] A similar criticism of neo-liberalism has been made by e.g. Ronald H Preston in Church and Society in the Late Twentieth Century, pp 59 ff and 68. Cf. his arguments in Religion and the Persistence of Capitalism. The Maurice Lectures for 1977 and other studies in Christianity and Social Change, SCM Press Ltd, London 1979, pp 28 f and 48 f.

[16] This argument is also adduced by Ronald H Preston in The Future of Christian Ethics, p 144.

339

Bibliography

Agrell, Göran: Work, Toil and Sustenance. An Examination of the View of Work in the New Testament, Taking into Consideration Views Found in Old Testament, Intertestamental and Early Rabbinic Writings. Verbum/Håkan Ohlssons, Lund 1976

Allardt, Erik: Att ha, att älska, att vara. Om välfärd i Norden. Argos, Lund 1975

Anthony, P D: The Ideology of Work. Tavistock Publications, London (1977) 1978

Atherton, John: Faith in the Nation. A Christian Vision for Britain. SPCK, London 1988

Aukrust, Tor: Mennesket i samfunnet. En sosialetikk. Bind I. Forlaget Land og Kirke, Oslo 1967²

Aukrust, Tor: Mennesket i samfunnet. En sosialetikk. Bind II. Forlaget Land og Kirke, Oslo 1968²

Ballard, Paul H: Towards a Contemporary Theology of Work. Collegiate Centre of Theology, University College, Cardiff 1982

Barth, Karl: Die Kirchliche Dogmatik. Zweiter Band: Die Lehre vom Gott. Zweiter Halbband (II/2). Evangelischer Verlag AG Zollikon, Zürich 1946

Barth, Karl: Die Kirchliche Dogmatik. Dritter Band: Die Lehre von der Schöpfung. Vierter Teil (III/4). Evangelischer Verlag AG Zollikon, Zürich 1951

Baum, Gregory (ed): Work and Religion. Concilium 131. T & T Clark, Edinburgh 1980

Bentham, Jeremy: An Introduction to the Principles of Morals and Legislation. Hafner Press, New York (1789) 1948

Best, Fred: Work Sharing. Issues, Policy Options and Prospects. The W E Upjohn Institute for Employment Research. Kalamazoo, Michigan 1981

Bexell, Göran: Etiken, bibeln och samlevnaden. Utformningen av en nutida kristen etik, tillämpad på samlevnadsetiska frågor. Verbum, Stockholm 1988

Bienert, Walther: Die Arbeit nach der Lehre der Bibel. Eine Grundlegung evangelischer Sozialethik. Evangelisches Verlagsverk GMBH, Stuttgart 1954

Bleakley, David: In Place of Work ... The Sufficient Society. A Study of technology from the point of view of people. SCM Press Ltd, London 1981

Bleakley, David: Work. The Shadow and the Substance. A Reappraisal of life and labour. SCM Press Ltd, London 1983

Blumberg, Paul: Företagsdemokrati i sociologisk belysning. Rabén & Sjögren, Stockholm 1971

Bonino, José Míguez: Toward a Christian Political Ethics. SCM Press, London 1983

340

Brakelmann, Günter: Abschied vom Unverbindlichen. Gedanken eines Christen zum Demokratischen Sozialismus. Gütersloher Verlagshaus Gerd Mohn, Gütersloh 1976

Brakelmann, Günter: Die Soziale Frage der 19. Jahrhunderts. Luther-Verlag, Witten (1962) 1971[4]

Brakelmann, Günter: "Humanisierung der industriellen Arbeitswelt". Article in Theologische Realenzyklopädie (TRE), Band III. Walter de Gruyter, Berlin & New York 1978

Brakelmann, Günter: Protestantismus und Politik. Werk und Wirkung Adolf Stoeckers. Hans Christians Verlag, Hamburg 1982

Brakelmann, Günter: Zur Arbeit geboren? Beiträge zu einer christlichen Arbeitsethik. SWI Verlag, Bochum 1988

Brunner, Emil: Das Gebot und die Ordnungen. Entwurf einer protestantisch-theologischen Ethik. Verlag von J C B Mohr (Paul Siebeck), Tübingen 1932

Brunner, Emil: Der Kapitalismus als Problem der Kirche. Zwingli-Verlag, Zürich 1945

Brunner, Emil: Gerechtigkeit. Eine Lehre von den Grundgesetzen der Gesellschaftsordnung. Zwingli-Verlag, Zürich 1943

Bråkenhielm, Carl Reinhold m fl (red): Aktuella livsåskådningar, del 1. Existentialism, marxism. Doxa, Stockholm 1982

Calhoun, Robert Lowry: God and the Day's Work. Christian Vocation in an Unchristian World. Association Press, New York 1943

Chenu, M D: Pour une théologie du travail. Éditions du Seuil, Paris 1955

Christliche Wirtschaftsethik vor neuen Aufgaben. Festgabe für Arthur Rich zum siebzigsten Geburtstag. Herausgegeben von Theodor Strohm. Theologischer Verlag, Zürich 1980

Clarke, Roger: Work in Crisis. The Dilemma of a Nation. The Saint Andrew Press, Edinburgh 1982

Collste, Göran: Arbete och livsmening. Petra Bokförlag, Arlöv 1985

Collste, Göran: Makten, moralen och människan. En analys av värdekonflikter i debatten om medbestämmande och löntagarstyre. Acta Universitatis Upsaliensis, Uppsala Studies in Social Ethics, Uppsala 1984

Davis, Howard – Gosling, David: Will the Future Work. Values for emerging patterns of Work and employment. World Council of Churches, Geneva (1985) 1986[2]

Dubin, Robert (ed): Handbook of Work, Organization and Society. Rand McNally College Publishing Company, Chicago 1976

Engnell, Ivan: "Arbete". Article in Svenskt Bibliskt Uppslagsverk. Utg. av Ivan Engnell. Band I. Nordiska uppslagsböcker, Stockholm 1962

Fahlbusch, Wilhelm – Przybylski, Hartmut – Schröter, Wolfgang: Arbeit ist nicht alles. Versuche zu einer Ethik der Zukunft. SWI-Verlag, Bochum 1987

Forell, Urban: Kärlekens motivstrukturer. En etisk och begreppsanalytisk studie. Lund University Press, Lund 1989

Frankena, William K: Ethics. 2nd ed. Prentice-Hall, Englewood Cliffs, NJ 1973

Fryklindh, Pär Urban – Johansson, Sven Ove: Arbete och fritid. Den lekande människan – en framtidsdröm som blir verklighet? Sekretariatet för framtidsstudier, Karlstad 1978

Gardell, Bertil: Arbetsinnehåll och livskvalitet. En sammanställning och diskussion av samhällsvetenskaplig forskning rörande människan och arbetet. Prisma, Lund 1976

Gardell, Bertil: Produktionsteknik och arbetsglädje. En socialpsykologisk studie av industriellt arbete. Personaladministrativa rådet, Malmö 1971

Gellerstam, Göran – Görman, Ulf: Textsamling till kristendomens historia med allmän idéhistoria. Studentlitteratur, Lund 1977

Gerhardsson, Birger: "med hela ditt hjärta". Om Bibelns ethos. Liber Läromedel, Lund 1979

Grenholm, Carl-Henric: Arbetets mening. En analys av sex teorier om arbetets syfte och värde. Acta Universitatis Upsaliensis, Uppsala Studies in Social Ethics, Uppsala 1988

Grenholm, Carl-Henric: Arbetets mål och värde. En analys av ideologiska uppfattningar hos LO, TCO och SAF i 1970-talets debatt om arbetsorganisation och datorisering. Acta Universitatis Upsaliensis, Uppsala Studies in Social Ethics, Uppsala 1987

Grenholm, Carl-Henric: Christian Social Ethics in a Revolutionary Age. An Analysis of the Social Ethics of John C Bennett, Heinz-Dietrich Wendland and Richard Shaull. Acta Universitatis Upsaliensis, Uppsala Studies in Social Ethics, Uppsala 1973

Grenholm, Carl-Henric (red): Kyrkans samhällsansvar. Verbum, Stockholm 1975

Grenholm, Carl-Henric: "Synen på arbetet i kristen tradition". Article in Arbetets värde och mening. Red: Per Sörbom. Riksbankens Jubileumsfond, Liber Förlag, Stockholm 1980

Gustafson, James M: "An Analysis of Church and Society Social Ethical Writings". Article in The Ecumenical Review, vol 40, nr 2, April 1988

Gustafson, James M: Can Ethics be Christian? The University of Chicago Press, Chicago 1975

Gustafson, James M: Protestant and Catholic Ethics. Prospects for Rapprochement. SCM Press Ltd, London 1978

Hare, R M: Freedom and Reason. Oxford University Press (1963) 1978

Hare, R M: Moral Thinking. Its Levels, Method, and Point. Clarendon Press, Oxford 1981

Heck, Bruno (hrsg): Arbeit. Ihr Wert, Ihre Ordnung. v Hase & Koehler, Mainz 1984

Hemberg, Jarl – Holte, Ragnar – Jeffner, Anders: Människan och Gud. En kristen teologi. Liber Förlag, Lund 1982

Holte, Ragnar: Etik och jämställdhet. Acta Universitatis Upsaliensis, Uppsala Studies in Social Ethics, Uppsala 1978

Holte, Ragnar, m fl: Etiska problem. Verbum/Håkan Ohlssons, Lund 1977

Holte, Ragnar: Guds avbild. Kvinna och man i kristen belysning. Verbum, Stockholm 1990

Holte, Ragnar: Människa Livstolkning Gudstro. Teorier och metoder inom tros- och livsåskådningsvetenskapen. Doxa, Lund 1984

Honecker, Martin: "Arbeit VII. 18.–20. Jahrhundert". Article in Theologische Realenzyklopädie. Band III. Walter de Gruyter, Berlin, New York 1978

Hospers, John: Human Conduct. Problems of Ethics. Second edition. Harcourt Brace Jovanovich, New York 1982

Jeffner, Anders: Att studera människosyn. En översiktlig problemanalys. Tema T Rapport 21, Linköping 1989

Jeffner, Anders: Kriterien christlicher Glaubenslehre. Eine prinzipielle Untersuchung heutiger protestantischer Dogmatik im deutschen Sprachbereich. Acta Universitatis Upsaliensis, Studia Doctrinae Christianae Upsaliensia, Uppsala 1976

Jeffner, Anders: Livsåskådningsforskning. Teologiska institutionen, Uppsala universitet, Uppsala 1974

Johannes Paulus II: Människans arbete. Laborem exercens. Katolska Bokförlaget, Uppsala 1982

Jönsson, Ludvig: Människan, mödan och arbetsglädjen. Rabén & Sjögren, Stockholm 1974

Kaiser, Edwin G: Theology of work. The Newman Press, Westminster, Maryland 1966

Kant, Immanuel: Grundlegung zur Metaphysik der Sitten. Fünfte Auflage. Hgb von Karl Vorländer. Der Philosophischen Bibliothek, Band 41. Verlag von Felix Meiner, Leipzig (1785) 1920

Karg, Siegfried: "Arthur Rich. Wegweisend für den Dialog zwischen Ethik und Wirtschaft". Article in Gegen die Gottvergessenheit. Schweizer Theologen im 19. und 20. Jahrhundert. Herder, Basel 1990

Karlsson, Jan: Arbetets frihet och förnedring. En antologi. AWE/Gebers, Stockholm 1978

Kegley, Charles W (ed): The Theology of Emil Brunner. The Macmillan Company, New York 1962

Kjellberg, Seppo: "Max Webers tolkning av Luthers arbetsetik". Artikel i Eripainos, Sosiologia 24, 1987:1

Kramer, Rolf: Arbeit. Theologische, Wirthschaftliche und soziale Aspekte. Vandenhoeck & Ruprecht, Göttingen 1982

Kramer, Rolf: "Protestantismus". Article in Ethik der Religionen – Lehre und Leben. Herausgegeben von Michael Klöcher und Udo Tworuschka. Band 2: Arbeit. Vandenhoeck & Ruprecht, Kösel 1985

Luther, Martin: An den christlichen Adel deutscher Nation von des christlichen Standes Besserung (1520). To be found in Luther, Martin: Werke. Kritische Gesamtausgabe (WA). 6. Band. Hermann Böhlau, Weimar 1888

Luther, Martin: An die Pfarrherrn wider den Wucher zu predigen, Vermahnung (1540). To be found in Luther, Martin: Werke. Kritische Gesamtausgabe (WA). 51. Band. Hermann Böhlaus Nachfolger, Weimar 1914

Luther, Martin: Der 147. Psalm, Lauda Jerusalem, ausgelegt (1532). To be found in Luther, Martin: Werke. Kritische Gesamtausgabe (WA). 31. Band, Erste Abteilung. Hermann Böhlaus Nachfolger, Weimar 1913

Luther, Martin: Deutsch Catechismus (Der Grosse Katechismus, 1529). To be found in Luther, Martin: Werke. Kritische Gesamtausgabe (WA). 30. Band, Erste Abteilung. Hermann Böhlaus Nachfolger, Weimar 1910

Luther, Martin: Ermahnung zum Frieden auf die zwölf Artikel der Bauerschaft in Schwaben (1525). To be found in Luther, Martin: Werke. Kritische Gesamtausgabe (WA). 18. Band. Hermann Böhlaus Nachfolger, Weimar 1908

Luther, Martin: Hauspostille (1544). To be found in Luther, Martin: Werke. Kritische Gesamtausgabe (WA). 52. Band. Hermann Böhlaus Nachfolger, Weimar 1915

Luther, Martin: In epistolam S Pauli ad Galatas Commentararius (1535). To be found in Luther, Martin: Werke. Kritische Gesamtausgabe (WA). 40. Band, Erste Abteilung. Hermann Böhlaus Nachfolger, Weimar 1911

Luther, Martin: Kirchenpostille (1522). To be found in Luther, Martin: Werke. Kritische Gesamtausgabe (WA). 10. Band, Erste Abteilung, 1. Hälfte. Hermann Böhlaus Nachfolger, Weimar 1910

Luther, Martin: Krucigers Sommerpostille. To be found in Luther, Martin: Werke. Kritische Gesamtausgabe (WA). 22. Band. Hermann Böhlaus Nachfolger, Weimar 1929

Luther, Martin: Ob Kriegsleute auch in seligem Stande sein können (1526). To be found in Luther, Martin: Werke. Kritische Gesamtausgabe (WA). 19. Band. Hermann Böhlaus Nachfolger, Weimar 1897

Luther, Martin: Predigten des Jahres 1529. To be found in Luther, Martin: Werke. Kritische Gesamtausgabe (WA). 29. Band. Hermann Böhlaus Nachfolger, Weimar 1904

Luther, Martin: Tractatus de libertate christiana (1520). To be found in Luther, Martin: Werke. Kritische Gesamtausgabe (WA). 7. Band. Hermann Böhlaus Nachfolger, Weimar 1897

Luther, Martin: Von den guten Werken (1520). To be found in Luther, Martin: Werke. Kritische Gesamtausgabe (WA). 6. Band. Hermann Böhlau, Weimar 1888

Luther, Martin: Von weltlicher Oberkeit, wie weit man ihr gehorsam schuldig sei (1523). To be found in Luther, Martin: Werke. Kritische Gesamtausgabe (WA). 11. Band. Hermann Böhlaus Nachfolger, Weimar 1900

Løgstrup, K E: Den etiske fordring. Gyldendal, Köpenhamn 1966

Marx, Karl: Das Kapital. Kritik der politischen Ökonomie. Erster Band, Buch I: Der Produktionsprozess des Kapitals (1867). To be found in Marx, Karl – Engels, Friedrich: Werke (MEW). Dietz Verlag, Berlin 1962

Marx, Karl: Ökonomisch-philosophische Manuskripte (1844). To be found in Marx, Karl – Engels, Friedrich: Historisch-Kritische Gesamtausgabe. Werke, Schriften, Briefe. Im Auftrage des Marx-Engels Instituts Moskau herausgegeben von V Adoratskij (MEGA). Erste Abteilung, Band 3. Verlag Detlev Auvermann KG, Glashütten im Taunus (1932) 1970

Maslow, Abraham H: Motivation and Personality. Harper & Brothers, New York 1954

McGregor, Douglas: The Human Side of Enterprise. McGraw-Hill Book Company, Inc, New York – Toronto – London 1960

McNaughton, David: Moral Vision. An Introduction to Ethics. Basil Blackwell, Oxford 1988

Moltmann, Jürgen: Theologie der Hoffnung. Chr Kaiser Verlag, München (1964) 1965[5]

Moore, G E: Ethics. Oxford University Press, London (1912) 1966

Moore, G E: Principia Ethica. Cambridge University Press, Cambridge (1903) 1980

Niebuhr, Reinhold: An Interpretation of Christian Ethics. The Seabury Press, New York (1935) 1979

Niebuhr, Reinhold: Moral Man and Immoral Society. A Study in Ethics and Politics. Charles Scribner's Sons, New York (1932) 1947

Nilsson, Kristina: Etik och verklighetstolkning. Acta Universitatis Upsaliensis, Uppsala Studies in Social Ethics, Uppsala 1980

Nygren, Anders: Eros och Agape. Den kristna kärlekstanken genom tiderna. Aldus/Bonniers, Stockholm 1966

Oldham, J H: "A Responsible Society". Article in The Church and the Disorder of Society = Man's Disorder and God's Design. The Amsterdam Series, vol III. SCM Press Ltd, London 1948

Oldham, J H: The Function of the Church in Society. To be found in Church, Community and State. Vol I: The Church and its Function in Society. By W A

Visser't Hooft and J H Oldham. George Allen & Unwin Ltd, London 1937

Oldham, J H: Work in Modern Society. John Knox Press, Richmond, Virginia (1950) 1961

Olsson, Karl-Manfred: Kristendom – demokrati – arbete. LTs förlag, Stockholm 1965

Preston, Ronald H: Church and Society in the Late Twentieth Century. The Economic and Political Task. The Scott Holland Lectures for 1983. SCM Press Ltd, London 1983

Preston, Ronald H: Explorations in Theology 9. SCM Press Ltd, London 1981

Preston, Ronald H: Religion and the Persistence of Capitalism. The Maurice Lectures for 1977 and other studies in Christianity and Social Change. SCM Press Ltd, London 1979

Preston, Ronald H: The Future of Christian Ethics. SCM Press Ltd, London 1987

Rawls, John: A Theory of Justice. Oxford University Press, Oxford (1972) 1976

Rich, Arthur: "Arbeit als Beruf". Article in Rich, Arthur – Ulich, Eberhard (hrsg): Arbeit und Humanität. Athenäum Verlag, Königstein 1978

Rich, Arthur: Christliche Existenz in der Industriellen Welt. Eine Einführung in die sozialethischen Grundfragen der industriellen Arbeitswelt. Zwingli Verlag, Zürich (1957) 1964[2]

Rich, Arthur: Glaube in politischer Entscheidung. Beiträge zur Ethik des Politischen. Zwingli Verlag, Zürich 1962

Rich, Arthur: Mitbestimmung in der Industrie. Probleme – Modelle – Kritische Beurteilung. Eine sozialethische Orientierung, Flamberg Verlag, Zürich 1973

Rich, Arthur: "Sozialethische Kriterien und Maximen humaner Gesellschaftsgestaltung". Article in Christliche Wirtschaftsethik vor neuen Aufgaben. Festgabe für Arthur Rich zum siebzigsten Geburtstag. Herausgegeben von Theodor Strohm. Theologischer Verlag, Zürich 1980

Rich, Arthur: Wirtschaftsethik. Band I. Grundlagen in theologischer Perspektive. Gütersloher Verlagshaus Gerd Mohn, Gütersloh (1984) 1987[3]

Rich, Arthur: Wirtschaftsethik. Band II. Marktwirtschaft, Planwirtschaft, Weltwirtschaft aus sozialethischer Sicht. Gütersloher Verlagshaus Gerd Mohn, Gütersloh 1990

Richardson, Alan: The Biblical Doctrine of Work. SCM Press Ltd, London 1952

Robertson, James: Future Work. Jobs, self-employment and leisure after the industrial age. Gower/Maurice Temple Smith, Aldershot, Hants 1985

Rose, Michael: Re-Working the Work Ethic. Economic Values and Socio-Cultural Politics. Batsford Academic and Educational, London 1985

Samuelsson, Kurt: Ekonomi och religion. Rabén & Sjögren, Stockholm (1957) 1965

Schumacher, EF: Det goda arbetet. För en ändamålsenlig teknologi med mänskliga mått. Prisma, Stockholm 1979

Schüller, Bruno: Wholly Human. Essays on the Theory and Language of Morality. Gill and Macmillan, Dublin 1986

Stevenson, Leslie: Seven Theories of Human Nature. Oxford University Press, Oxford (1974) 1979

Strömberg, Bertil: Arbetets pris. Rättvis lön och solidarisk lönepolitik. Uppsala universitet, Uppsala 1989

Søe, N H: Kristelig etik. G E C Gads forlag, København 1962[5]

Tawney, R H: Religion and the Rise of Capitalism. A Historical Study. Penguin Books, London (1926) 1980

Thielicke, Helmut: Theologische Ethik. Band I. J C B Mohr (Paul Siebeck), Tübingen 1951

Thielicke, Helmut: Theologische Ethik. Band II. 1 Teil. J C B Mohr (Paul Siebeck), Tübingen 1955

Thomas av Aquino: Summa theologica. Die deutsche Thomas-Ausgabe, Bd. 23 and 24. Hg von der Albertus-Magnus-Akademie, Walderberg bei Köln, F H Kerle, Heidelberg−München, Anton Pustet, Graz−Wien−Salzburg, 1954 and 1952

Thomas, George F: Christian Ethics and Moral Philosophy. Charles Scribner's Sons, New York 1955

Todd, John M (ed): Work. Christian Thought and Practice. Darton, Longman & Todd, London 1960

Trillhaas, Wolfgang: Ethik. Alfred Töpelmann, Berlin (1959) 1965, 2 Aufl.

Weber, Max: Die protestantische Ethik und der Geist des Kapitalismus. Verlag von JCB Mohr (Paul Siebeck), Tübingen 1934

Wenke, Karl Ernst (hrsg): Ökonomie und Ethik. Die Herausforderung der Arbeitslosigkeit. SWI Studienhefte 4, Haag und Herchen Verlag, Frankfurt/Main 1984

Wingren, Gustaf: "Beruf II. Historische und ethische Aspekte". Article in Theologische Realenzyklopädie, Band V. Walter de Gruyter, Berlin & New York 1980

Wingren, Gustaf: Luthers lära om kallelsen. Gleerups, Lund 1960³

Wogaman, J Philip: A Christian Method of Moral Judgement. The Westminster Press, Philadelphia 1976

Wogaman, J Philip: Christian Perspectives on Politics. SCM Press Ltd, London 1988

Wogaman, J Philip: Christians and the Great Economic Debate. SCM Press Ltd, London 1977

Wogaman, J Philip: Economics and Ethics. A Christian Inquiry. SCM Press Ltd, London 1986

Work and the Future. Technology, World Development and Jobs in the Eighties. CIO Publishing, Church House, London 1979

Work or What? A Christian Examination of the Employment Crisis. Church Information Office, London 1977

Zetterberg, Hans L: Arbete, livsstil och motivation. Svenska Arbetsgivareföreningen, Stockholm 1977

Index of personal names

Rich, A 27, 29, 53, 67 f, 70 ff, 75 ff,
   80−85, 100 ff, 106 f, 110−115,
   117, 133−138, 145 f, 148−151, 163
   ff, 168−172, 174 f, 186−189, 194 f,
   197, 211−215, 219−222, 232 f, 236
   f, 239 f, 246 f, 249, 253 f, 280,
   304−313, 318, 324−328, 330 f, 333
   f, 336
Richardson, A 34, 319
Robertson, J 55, 323
Rose, M 55, 323

Samuelsson, K 321 f
Schröter, W 318, 339
Schumacher, EF 294, 339
Schüller, B 337
Schüssler-Fiorenza, F 318
Stevenson, L 332
Strohm, T 318, 330
Strömberg, B 317, 323
Stöcker, A 319
Søe, NH 28, 53, 322
Sörbom, P 319

Tawney, RH 27, 321
Taylor, FW 65, 67, 88, 95, 107
Tertullian 37
Thielicke, H 23, 28, 52, 177, 203,
   318, 322, 333

Thomas Aquinas 33, 37−41, 47, 49,
   111, 233, 235, 262, 292 f, 304, 320,
   322
Thomas, GF 322
Thorsrud, E 67, 89, 297
Todd, JM 318, 339
Todt, R 319
Trillhaas, W 179, 203, 334
Tworuschka, U 318
Tödt, HE 339

Ulich, E 327

Vissert Hooft, WA 329

Weber, M 21, 48 ff, 87 137, 146,
   247, 305, 318, 321 f
Wendland, H-D 188
Wenke, KE 322
Wichern, JH 319
Wingren, G 320 f
Wogaman, JP 26, 53 f, 142, 179,
   216, 260, 265 f, 318, 322, 332, 334,
   337

Yausky, C 339

Zetterberg, HL 319
Zwingli, H 27